FROM TAIL——UKER
TO MUDMOVER

An aviation career in the Royal Naval Fleet Air Arm,
United States Navy, and South African Air Force

FROM TAILHOOKER TO MUDMOVER

An aviation career in the Royal Naval Fleet Air Arm,
United States Navy, and South African Air Force

DICK LORD

Corporal

By the same author

Fire, Flood and Ice – Search and Rescue Missions of the South African Air Force
Vlamgat – The story of the Mirage F1 in the South African Air Force

Published by Corporal Publications, 2003
P.O. Box 114, Irene 0062, South Africa

Copyright © R. Lord, 2003

Cover design by Thalita Harvey
Design and origination by HRH Graphics
+27 12 664-6340, email: j.design@mweb.co.za

Printed and bound by United Litho, +27 11 869-3445

ISBN 0-620-30762-5

*This book is dedicated to
the memory of my parents
Kay and Jack,
without whom there would have been no story.*

Author's Note

There is a well-known saying in aviation circles: "Only birds and fools fly, but birds don't fly at night". The wisdom of this adage is understood best by night-qualified carrier pilots—theirs being probably the most demanding scenario in the entire aviation spectrum. While I understand the statement, I do not exactly agree with the word "fools". However, I will readily admit that a lot of amusing people have been attracted to aviation in all its forms and have thus enriched aviation history with entertaining anecdotes.

Any career in aviation is studded with incidents both hazardous and amusing, particularly so in the regime of the military. These incidents highlight the trials and tribulations of the young military aviator, as he progresses from the "sprog", "stud", "shirt-tail", "bicycle", or "2nd lieutenant" stage, to admiral, general, or "This is your captain speaking" maturity.

We all have skeletons in the cupboard. Often they remain there only because we were lucky that the boss, senior pilot, or exec, never got to hear of them. If any skeletons air themselves in this book, it is certainly not meant to embarrass anyone. We have all long since reached the age where we can reflect with laughter at our follies and pay just thanks for getting away with some very close shaves and near-misses.

Compared to other arts, sciences, and professions, aviation is a brash and exciting newcomer. Its history has been extensively recorded in words, photographs, and in some sensational film footage. There is, and always will be, a mystique attached to first flights. The names of the "firsts" have become world-renowned. Orville and his brother Wilbur Wright, Louis Bleriot, Charles Lindberg, Chuck Yeager, and Yuri Gagarin need no introduction or further amplification. Many people, the world over, admire the men who have taken up the challenge and emerged triumphant.

A quick survey of the shelves of reputable stationers, in any country, will reveal scores of hard- and soft-covered books, glossy illustrated magazines, and manuals dealing with aviation. To any aviator, whether he is a pupil pilot on Cessna 150s or a grizzled, grey-haired 747 skipper, these books have a magnetic quality. They also attract aviators' sons—boys brainwashed by the stories told to them by their fathers and their father's usually garrulous friends. You will find wives there too, confident in the knowledge that a good flying book is a treasured present for the old man.

On analysis there seems to be a common denominator in this aviation business. The denominator would appear to be the personality of men, and now women, who make flying their career. It takes all sorts to make a world, and that is as true in aviation as in any other sphere of life. There are some extremely clever pilots, and a few who even by the widest stretch of the imagination could not be described as bright. Some are brilliant pole-handlers, while others are competent plodders. Some are extremely painstaking, while at the other end of the scale are those hairy individuals who inevitably make the headlines.

Within each pilot is a characteristic that he shares with his brother aviators—a "can-do" attitude. Indeed, his life from early youth has been governed by this approach—the very reason he was attracted to flying in the first place. It is particularly strong in those who opt for military flying.

'Ground troops are taking fire, the AAA is heavy. Can the fighters help out?'

'It is 03h00, a force 8 is whipping up the channel, a merchant seaman has suffered 60% burns. Can the chopper come and lift him off?'

Of course, the answer is always affirmative. The reasoning behind the yes, when all normal logic would say no, is this "can-do" attitude. One of the strongest emotions that influence this reflex is pride—pride in his ability as a pilot and pride in his professionalism. Then, in turn, fear. Fear that people might think that he is afraid to tackle the job and fear that his professional reputation might suffer. Then the awful fear that if he did not answer the call, then someday he might be the one in need of assistance and some other pilot might not be willing to take a chance.

So there we have this band of men, and some women, who are bonded together by the same zest for a challenge, and who are always comfortable in each other's company, no matter from where they originate. Aviators from all corners of the globe, Europe, the Americas, Africa, Australasia, and I'm pretty sure Asia, all speak the same type of language, and in the right circumstances, could end up enjoying an evening in each other's company.

By its very nature, flying is a flamboyant activity that has certainly produced more than its fair share of flamboyant characters. Most of these personalities have been brought into prominence during periods of crisis, such as the World Wars, Korea, the Middle East wars, Vietnam, the Falklands, Africa's bush wars, the Gulf, and recently the Balkan Campaign. I suppose, being in the right place at the right time has always helped, but when the great deeds and praises of aviation have been sung, it has usually been the right man, in the right place, at the right time, who has stood out above all others.

Since 1958, when I started my career, tremendous advances in techniques, tactics, and technology have followed, particularly in naval aviation, which the modern media has mostly ignored. This fact was brought home a few years ago when I paid a visit to the excellent Fleet Air Arm Museum at the Royal Naval Air Station Yeovilton, in Somerset. For me it was a sentimental journey, having on many occasions several years before, been a night-fighter pilot stationed there. Imagine my utter disappointment when I discovered my beloved Sea Venom and Sea Vixen were hidden away, as in the archives, with little or nothing to show of the many hours of pleasure, and sheer terror, these aircraft had afforded us. Since that time, I am delighted to add, the museum has been completely revamped, and all the aircraft are now magnificently displayed.

I started writing this book after my first visit to the museum. In a Don Quixote attempt to right the unrightable wrongs, I wanted to record my small portion of those years as a dedication to the many lovely people who "bought the farm" along the way. And those who are no longer here to witness the fruits of their labours—or to see how safe this flying business has become, due in great part, to the sacrifice they made. The magnificent new museum has eroded my reason for writing. However, I had such fun that I decided to complete the story. It is a book in three parts, covering my service in the Royal Naval Fleet Air Arm, United States Navy, and the South African Air Force.

I make no apologies for the autobiographical nature of this book. To chronologically record the stories I have to tell, it seemed the only way. Perhaps "stories" is the wrong word, because all the recounted incidents are as true as I can remember them, with perhaps a little embroidery here and there.

About the author

Dick Lord was born in Johannesburg and completed his schooling at Parktown Boys' High, before travelling to Britain to join the Royal Navy as an Air Cadet in 1958.

He qualified as a fighter pilot flying Sea Venoms and Sea Vixens from the decks of the aircraft carriers *Centaur, Victorious, Hermes* and the famous *Ark Royal* on cruises around the world. In the mid 60s, he was selected for a two-year exchange tour with the US Navy, flying A4 Skyhawks and F4 Phantoms out of San Diego, California. He completed tours of air warfare instruction flying Hunters from the naval air stations at Lossiemouth, Scotland and Brawdy, Wales.

He returned to South Africa in the early 70s and joined the SAAF, flying Impalas, Sabres and Mirage IIIs. During the bush war, he commanded 1 Squadron, flying Mirage F1AZs. His last tour of duty was as commander of the Air Force Command Post. He was mentioned in dispatches for his role in the very successful rescue of all 581 people from the ill-fated liner *Oceanos*.

Dick now lives in Somerset West in the lovely Cape where, between the distractions of two boisterous grandchildren and the magnificent wine route, he writes books on aviation.

Acknowledgements

I wish to acknowledge the true friends I have made along the way, in three first-class organizations, many of whom feature in the pages of this manuscript. The advance in technology over the years may have altered the techniques and strategies of modern military aviation, but the ultimate success of operations depended almost entirely upon the men who served.

Chris Cocks who suggested the idea.

Richard and Michael for their unwavering determination to get the book written.

Most of all, June. This story is as much yours, as mine. I can do no better than to quote verbatim the words of the sign placed outside our house:

"In this house lives a lovely lady and a grumpy old man".

CONTENTS

Book One
Royal Naval Fleet Air Arm

Foreword – Book One

I have known Richard Lord for over 40 years. We first met when, as fellow fighter pilots, we served in the Fleet Air Arm of the Royal Navy together. After Richard returned to South Africa, we kept in touch and I watched with interest his eminent rise through the ranks of the SAAF—and his burgeoning role as an author. I, on the other hand, stayed in the Royal Navy largely through luck, timing, and good people rooting for me. I became the tribal chief of the Fleet Air Arm and finally, the chief of personnel and second sea lord, on the Admiralty Board.

The Fleet Air Arm that Richard and I served in during the 1960s had come a long way since its origins in 1912 and was indeed, the pathfinder of most innovations in Aircraft Carrier Development —the "Angled Deck", the "Steam Catapult", and the "Deck Landing Projector Sight" to name but a few. In some ways, aircraft development had run ahead of the ships and as piston aircraft gave way to ever bigger and faster jet aircraft, we faced huge challenges flying aircraft such as the Sea Vixen, Buccaneer, and F4 Phantom off carriers designed to operate smaller, first generation jets such as the Sea Hawk and Sea Venom. Margins for error were small and we lost a number of friends in the process.

The importance of ship-based aviation, so tellingly illustrated during the Second World War and Korea, was just as evident in the post war years. British Defence Policy demanded a permanent deployment of two Royal Navy Strike Carriers east of Suez, and an Amphibious Carrier. Thus, Richard and I spent much of our flying careers in far-flung, turbulent parts of the world.

In due course, we both became Air Warfare Instructors (we liked to think the crème de la crème of the fast jet set!) and from 1968 to 1970, we served together in the Royal Navy's "Top Gun" School at the Naval Air Station Lossiemouth, in Scotland. During our two years together it became clear to me that Richard was not only an exceptionally talented and natural pilot, but also a brilliant teacher. Urbane, unruffled, and with a delicately light touch, he had a rare talent for transferring his wisdom and skills to his young charges, who admired and adored him. They, in turn, did him proud, for they were the skillful leaders of the Sea Harrier Force, which acquitted itself so gallantly in the Falklands Campaign in 1982.

It was a huge privilege to know and serve with Richard Lord, and I was delighted to accept his invitation to write a foreword to this excellent book—a story about a delightful man and a naval fighter pilot in a million.

Admiral Sir Michael Layard, KCB, CBE.

Michael Layard
ADMIRAL SIR MICHAEL LAYARD, KCB, CBE.

Chapter 1

In the beginning...

Born in 1936 in Johannesburg, in the then Union of South Africa, I did not really know my father until I was ten years old. He enlisted, as a private, in the Imperial Light Horse (ILH) infantry regiment at the outbreak of one of the wars Great Britain habitually seemed to get herself into. He only returned home in 1946, one of 23 000 allied troops captured at Tobruk. He spent the majority of the war as an unhappy guest of the Italian and German governments.

I recollect spending my war years playing soldiers—half the time spent marching around our dining room table to the strains of the regimental band of the ILH's quick and slow marches. My dad must have left us the 78-RPM record, which we played on our gramophone—the type where you had to continually change the old steel needles.

When I wasn't marching, I could be found perched in the upper branches of the large Jacaranda tree in our front garden. In a cockpit, formed by overlapping branches, I emulated the feats of Rockfist Rogan, the RAF ace made famous in the Champion comic. On other days I was Biggles, flying here and there, and always winning.

The trauma of the times rubbed off on all children raised during the war. We were fortunate in South Africa to be so far from the actual battlefields. My father managed to keep the letters I wrote to him, during his forced marches and train journeys to prisoner of war camps throughout Europe. All my letters were adorned with drawings of aircraft, usually the Spitfire, dropping bombs or strafing. As a child I made my share of balsa-wood models. My favourite being a P-47 Thunderbolt, probably because the model, like the real aircraft, was very strong and outlasted most of the others.

The other strong motivator towards flying, in my formative years, was my Uncle Duncan Strange. He was a pilot who flew with both the South African and Royal Air Forces and was decorated with the Distinguished Flying Cross. At one stage he flew the Boulton Paul Defiant and the thought of that rotating rear turret thrilled my boyhood imagination. It was only in later years, when reading about the poor flying characteristics of that aircraft, I realized that just to fly the thing probably deserved the DFC!

During the desert campaign my dad had a spell of leave in Cairo. He knew my uncle was in town at the same time, but not where he would be staying. Having a creative nature, my father briefed all his infantry pals to circulate through Cairo. They were to say: 'That's Strange' within earshot of every air-force man they saw. Needless to say the plan backfired, with catastrophic results. The military police had one of their busiest days of the war. Apparently, air-force men do not enjoy being told they are "strange" by the infantry!

So there it was! Between the influence of the war on the one hand, and my uncle and his DFC on the other, the seed had been sown. Instead of going to work for a living, I was going to fly.

In 1948, South Africa changed governments. After British domination, from the day of union in 1910, the Nationalist or Afrikaans Party was voted into power. The new government's earliest task was to ensure British influence would not remain a dominating factor in South African affairs. When I left school, half way through the 1950s, the chances of an English-speaking South African being accepted for pilot training in the South African Air Force were virtually negligible. Fortunately, the Union was still a member of the British Commonwealth; therefore, as a British subject, I was eligible to enlist in the British services.

I followed a similar path to dozens of other South Africans before me—by lovely mauve-hulled Union Castle ship to Southampton. I acquired digs in Earl's Court, through membership of the Overseas Visitors' Club. To keep the wolf from the door while applying to join the Royal Air Force, I found a temporary job at the Lyon's Tea Shop, in Lower Regent Street, below Piccadilly Circus.

The wheels of government grind slowly in most countries. After a long wait, I was finally invited to RAF Hornchurch for aptitude testing and pilot selection. What a thrill to stay at the famous Battle of Britain Air Station! Walking the perimeter track in the evenings, evoked strong emotions. One could imagine the Spitfires scrambling into battle and almost hear the throaty roar of the Rolls-Royce Merlin engines.

The week of testing was nerve-wracking, because the threat of washout was high. Every day there were fewer candidates left. Faulty eyesight, depth perception and hearing all took its toll. By Friday, the tests were completed and all of us could return to our homes or digs to anxiously await the arrival of our results.

My return to the teashop was greeted with a promotion from cleaner-upper to counter assistant. This meant that I traded in my tray and damp cloth for a better position behind the tea and coffee urn. As long as I kept the machines topped up, cleaned and steaming, the manageress tended to leave me alone. In those short weeks at Lyon's I learnt that a woman is a more demanding boss than any male.

Finally the buff-coloured OHMS envelope arrived from the Air Ministry. With trembling hands I opened it and read—then the sledgehammer hit me—I had not been accepted. To have travelled half way around the world to be rejected was a stunning blow. The Royal Air Force, downsizing to peacetime strengths, had recently disbanded nine squadrons of the 2nd Tactical Air Force in Germany; they were overstocked with pilots. It was devastating at the time, but it turned out to be one of the most fortunate decisions to affect my future career.

A sympathetic RAF officer suggested that I try for an appointment in the Royal Navy. When I told him that I wanted to become a pilot not a sailor, he explained that the Fleet Air Arm also needed aviators. I rushed down to the Admiralty, submitted my application, and once again experienced a long wait, which seems customary with all government departments. Because I had been so confident of being accepted by the RAF, I had resigned my job with the Lyon's teashop. If I am to be really truthful, my resignation came at a very convenient time. The day before I left for the tests at Hornchurch, the manageress caught me with one of her ice creams in my mouth; the arrangement was mutually agreeable.

While awaiting the navy's pleasure I took another job. This time I was issued with a long leather apron and a four-wheeled trolley, and set to work as a "beer-stacker" in the Guinness cellar of Mann, Crossman, and Paulin's Brewery at Putney Bridge. The money was more; ten pounds odd per week, as opposed to the six pound 15 shillings at Lyon's. The difference at the brewery was that we did not receive any meals, or ice creams.

Stacking 3 000 crates a day was hardly a challenge intellectually, but very demanding physically. These were the days before convenient cans, when beer was bottled in pint and quart bottles. These bottles were loaded into wooden crates, which then came trundling down a roller conveyor into the cellar. My job was to load up my trolley with cases lifted off the roller system, push the trolley across the cellar floor, and stack the crates against the wall. Pint boxes were stacked ten high and quarts eight high. The amount of physical effort required can be appreciated when one realizes that an average man can only reach to the bottom of the eighth pint crate. Numbers nine and ten had to be lifted chest height and then thrown onto the top of the stack. My first week at the brewery was endured in an agony of stiff muscles.

I had to take temporary leave, to spend a week with the Royal Navy at Lee on Solent. This was a bad week for me. The Royal Navy is a frightfully proper service and expects all its prospective officers to be frightfully proper as well. In my off-the-peg suit, hurriedly purchased from Burton's, the everyday gentlemen's tailors, I felt uncomfortably like a poor relation.

The navy has style, which I was made all too aware of during my final interview, at the end of the week. I was summoned to enter this huge room. Seated on the far side of an enormous table were four men—three naval officers and a distinguished-looking civilian (the "shrink"). Psychologists, or "headshrinkers", have become indispensable to selection committees, particularly for pilot selection. In all my years in the business I have never discovered why. For my money, a panel made up of senior squadron pilots would probably have better success. The shrinks tend to pick "rocket scientist" types who really shouldn't be allowed anywhere near aircraft!

I was shown to an enormous chair and once seated, I felt like a dwarf. Glaring down at me from the walls were larger than life oil paintings of Drake, Frobisher, and Nelson, all attired in frock coats and resplendent uniforms, adorned with decorations, orders and garters, and brandishing telescopes. My own linguistic inadequacies and differences in pronunciations as a colonial were highlighted by the puckered, plumy speech of the board members. The political nature of the questions, especially directed at a South African youngster, would have done justice to the rabid left-wing tabloid press.

By the end of the week, they had convinced me that I had seriously blundered by ever daring to imagine that this miserable person could ever be good enough to serve in Her Majesty's Royal Navy.

In contrast to the previous correspondence from the Royal Air Force, the arrival of the letter from the navy was a relief; it served to put me out of my misery. Only on the third reread did I finally understand that they had selected me for training as a pilot in the Fleet Air Arm. Thus, the decision by the RAF to turn down my application became one of the best things ever to have happened to me and for which I am eternally grateful. Don't misunderstand me, I have nothing but praise for the Royal Air Force, but for the type of career I wanted, the Royal Navy could not have been better.

Chapter 2

Cadet Training

As I stated earlier on, the Royal Navy has style. I was invited to contact Gieves, the tailors of Old Bond Street, to be measured for my uniforms. The navy would do their utmost to make me at least look like what a Royal Navy officer is supposed to look like. As a young lad from the veld, I didn't know how to answer when the gentleman tailor asked if I dressed right or left! The navy greatcoat is a superb article of clothing, so too are the uniforms. They made my brand new, worn-once, off-the-peg civvy suit look positively shabby. Then the pièce de résistance! As prospective officers and gentlemen, we were issued with a trilby hat and told: 'Officers do not go ashore bareheaded.' For a colonial, that hat really was something!

All Her Majesty's officers were supposed to partake in sport. For that purpose we also received tailor-made blue serge rugby shorts. Never in my whole life, before or since, have I seen such magnificent pants—buttoned fronts (no zips for the Andrew), a yellowish lining inside, thick navy blue serge outside, and pockets on both sides. Certainly the most significant and dramatic aspect of these shorts was the length. Cut just above the knee, with sufficient bagginess to ensure the occupants comfort, they were a picture. When attired in these beauties we looked as if we were back in the 1910s, or starring in *Chariots of Fire*.

I don't suppose we were any different from any other bunch of aviation cadets—gangly, pimply, and in most cases, like puppy dogs, eager to please. We spent January to April of 1958 at HMS *Thunderer*, the Royal Naval Engineering College at Manadon, just outside Plymouth. We learnt how to march, salute, and give all the orders to bring a cruiser to a single buoy! In 1958, cruisers were on their way out of service; HMS *Belfast* being probably the last ship of that type to decommission. The chance of a budding aviator ever having to perform that task was, exceedingly remote. Nevertheless Nelson, no doubt, had to learn it as well, and if it was good enough for Horatio, it was certainly good enough for us.

Another subject in which we had to excel, was that of changing from one set of clothing to another at breakneck speed. During the course of a morning we would be required to change from PT kit to uniform with greatcoats, without greatcoats, fatigues, back to seaman's rig; all the time ensuring that our kit lockers remained neat and tidy. Over the years since then I have benefited from the dexterity I acquired, but it was only much later in my career that I discovered the real reasons for the application of this skill.

They taught us a great deal during those winter months. One of the things I learnt was that a seaman's jersey is insufficient to maintain body heat during a double period of parade drill, when the winter wind is whipping in off the western approaches to the English Channel. The absolute misery of one of those periods was relieved by our Etonian, Willie Hare. Following all the correct traditions of that great school, Willie always told the truth. Whilst we were drilling, someone in the squad passed a remark that caused us to grin. This was anathema to our chief petty officer gunnery instructor and he shouted at Willie to: 'Take that bleeding smile off your face.' To our amusement and the chagrin of the chief, Willie said he couldn't because his face was frozen. I genuinely believe it was.

Apart from the freezing conditions, the weekly divisions parades at Manadon were always impressive, with the Royal Marine band providing the martial music. There is no grander military spectacle than the Royal Navy marching to the glorious music of the Royal Marines. At my request, at Manadon, and on all the carriers I was to serve on later in my career, the bandmaster would play the March Past of the Royal Marine Commandos. Knowing I was a South African, I believe they enjoyed playing *Sarie Marais* for me.

The cold Devonshire weather had a bearing on another incident, which took place during this time. It was customary for each cadet course to produce a bugler to play reveille at the morning flag raising parades. In true military fashion, our Chief Petty Officer Davis needed a volunteer. When no one stepped forward he tossed a bugle at Cadet Alan Harmon and ordered him to be the bugler at the following Monday morning parade. Well Harmon practised and practised, but produced nothing more than a succession of fart-like noises.

At school I had been a solo bugler in our cadet band until, during a rugby match, a misdirected boot had removed my four upper front teeth. When playing a bugle considerable pressure is required on the lips and teeth, particularly when reaching for the high notes. Consequently, I had given up playing the instrument due to the extreme difficulty in keeping my dental plate in the proper place. For this reason I had not volunteered my services.

One evening while Harmon was practising in the warmth of our bungalow, I made a serious error of judgement. I picked up the bugle and proceeded to play. Of course, by 07h00 the next morning, I was being castigated by CPO Davis and despite my protests, was told to play the confounded bugle the following Monday.

Because it was January, Monday dawned late and it was bitterly cold. I had traded in my .303 rifle and bayonet for bugle and cord. From my position alongside the flagpole, I watched with envy as my course mates marched onto parade with bayonets fixed. A naval parade, with its tradition dating back hundreds of years, is always impressive and moving.

'General salute, present arms' was ordered. The cadets presented arms with precision. The captain and commander came to the salute. I pressed the freezing instrument to my cold lips and proceeded to play. The reveille starts on a low note and continues up the scale; the seventh note being the highest required. I increased the pressure to ensure a high clear note. This pressure was just sufficient to loosen my dental plate and, to my horror, my false teeth fell down from my upper jaw, cutting off the air supply to the bugle.

Showing remarkable aplomb for a young cadet, I stopped, removed the bugle, replaced the offending teeth into their appropriate place, and started again, with exactly the same result. By this time my embarrassment was complete. My course mates on parade were rocking with amusement, so much so that Jack Smith, subsequently a training captain with Cathay Pacific Airlines, stuck his bayonet through the shoulder of his seaman's jersey. I had turned the parade into a fiasco. Needless to say, I was well known to the captain and staff for the rest of my stay at Manadon—my naval career had truly started on a bum note!

To some extent the bugle debacle was forgiven when it was discovered that, due to New Year appointments, the Manadon 1st XV rugby team was short of a flyhalf. In those days, being a South African almost automatically guaranteed one a place in the team. The Devon and Cornwall leagues are good robust affairs—tough, hard rugby, followed by even tougher, harder thrashes in pubs in the lovely towns of Truro, Redruth, Falmouth and Torquay. My mouth still waters at the thought of a tasty "oggie" (Cornish Pasty) washed down with a pint of sweet "scrumpy" (rough Cider).

Because I was over 21, completion of the course meant promotion from cadet to acting sub-lieutenant; the youngsters (under 21s) became midshipmen. Our next destination was Nuneaton, where we were kitted-out in flying gear. Flying overalls, helmets, oxygen masks, thermal underwear, long johns, string vests, leather gauntlets with silk inners, flying goggles—the lot. All the gear I had pictured, so long ago, in my Jacaranda tree cockpit.

Chapter 3

No 1 FTS, RAF Linton-on-Ouse

In the summer of June 1958 we started our training at No 1 Flying Training School, RAF Linton-on-Ouse, about ten miles north of York. Although it was a RAF establishment, all the pupils were from the navy with one or two Royal Marines mixed in, just to keep the courses amusing. The strange thing about the marines, in the United Kingdom and in America, is that their first loyalty is to the corps; flying comes second. I admire their loyalty, but I honestly believe that if one becomes an aviator, one's first priority must always be to flying. Nevertheless, the marines I met were all first-class people—if not the best of aviators. In America, when a funny flying story is told, it often starts: 'There were these two marines ...'

After what seemed like an interminable time in ground school, we finally made it to the aircraft. We started our flying on the piston-engined Provost T1—a side-by-side, two-seater, tail-dragger with a 550 horsepower Alvis Leonides engine and fixed undercarriage. My first sortie was under the guidance of an experienced instructor, Master Pilot Goodyear. With over 5 000 instruction hours he understood the nervous tension that almost overwhelmed me as we walked out to the aeroplane. I was prattling my way through the external check when I came to the wheels. I was going on about looking for 'cuts and creep, condition, pressure and freedom of valve,' when my instructor kicked the tyres and passed the comment 'these are very good tyres.' Many years later the penny dropped when it finally dawned on me that his name, Goodyear, was the same as the make of tyres. He was trying to relax me with a little joke, but I missed it completely.

For the students, the initial weeks of flying were probably the most tension-packed. The wash-rate was high. Every few days desperately disappointed aspirant pilots departed. After the remainder had managed to go solo, the failure rate decreased, and we realized that barring unforeseen problems, there was every chance we would qualify for the coveted "wings". We rapidly became another cog in the training machine, grinding our way to graduation.

Sticklers for tradition, the RAF insisted on holding formal mess dinners once a week. Every Thursday night we had to don our best bib and tucker—bum-freezer jackets, waistcoats, stiff-fronted mess shirts, the dreaded separate starched collars, attached with studs, and finally bow ties. No imitation, short cut, elasticised, pre-tied models for the Royal Navy. The one-ended, hand-tied design was deemed proper attire for gentlemen of the navy. It took a while before this colonial could make his tie presentable!

Formal dinners hold a particular place in the building of military traditions, ethical behaviour, and gentlemanly manners. The formal mess dinner, with its strict adherence to procedure, is fundamental in maintaining this code of conduct. However, generations of military officers have realized that, after the loyal or royal toasts have been made, relaxation is allowed and usually condoned.

Aviators are inherently high spirited, so this relaxing of rules has led, over the years, to many oft-recalled famous deeds. The RAF have only themselves to blame for the incident which occurred at Linton-on-Ouse on 5 November 1958—Guy Fawkes Night. Any normal service would have taken the sensible precaution of cancelling that night's formal dinner—not so the sticklers in the RAF!

Linton was established before the Second World War and the officers' mess was a permanent, brick-built structure. The dining room was impressively long and narrow with a high ceiling. Entrance was through double doors and, set in the wall, at the end of the room, there were two 16-foot high windows.

Because it was Guy Fawkes Night, mess rules were breached from the moment the diners sat down. Firecrackers mysteriously started detonating under tablecloths and the air was filled with tension. After one particularly large bang, Group Captain Gill, the base OC, stood up and banged his gavel to gain everybody's attention. Thinking a touch of sarcasm might have an effect on the trainee pilots, he said loudly, 'Ha-ha, very funny, now let's have a big bang.'

Most of us took the hint that the group captain was a little annoyed, but not Captain Terence Murphy, Royal Marines. Terence, seated next to me, was an immaculate marine. Smart and neat as a pin; the archetypal Bootneck! Anticipating the mayhem that would occur later in the evening, he brought along a Royal Marine landmine of enormous proportions. The invitation from the groupie was an opportunity not to be missed, so Terence pulled the pin.

The explosion was horrendous, but it paled in insignificance compared to the shockwave that expanded down the length of the long room. Similar to a tidal wave, it seemed to gather momentum during its passage. The pressure build-up was too much for one of the 16-foot windows; it disappeared out into the darkness, frame and all.

Fortunately, no major injuries occurred. However, for the following week all the diners suffered from a high-pitched ringing in their ears. True to stiff upper lip tradition, prevalent in the British services, the mess dinner continued, albeit with a cold November breeze circulating throughout the room.

Between the Pennines and the Yorkshire Moors lies the Vale of York. Although the word vale suggests a valley, in reality the Vale of York is a large plain of arable land, excellent for farming. During the Second World War, and the massive expansion of the RAF, this flat area was ideal for the establishment of airfields. British railway engineers also benefited from the level terrain. The longest straight stretch of railway line in the whole of Britain bisects the Vale between Scotland and the south of England. Between York and Darlington, the track runs arrow straight for nearly 80 kilometres.

This stretch of track is a magnificent navigation feature for learner aviators. However, having spotted the railway line, the only problem is to decide which way to turn to find one's way to base. RAF Linton-on-Ouse, sited just west of the railway line, was ten miles north of the lovely old city of York. Ten miles further north was RAF Dishforth, a transport command base that housed Beverley, Hastings and Valetta squadrons. Another ten miles north was RAF Leeming. All three airfields were sited just to the west of the railway line.

To a pupil pilot, one airfield looks pretty similar to any other. Just to find an airfield is often a major achievement! Regularly, patient air traffic control officers could be heard on the radio explaining to student pilots, joining to land, that the airfield they were seeking was next but one, heading south!

RAF Leeming, an operational night-fighter base, was equipped with Javelin FAW6 all-weather fighters. These were impressive-looking, large, tandem-seater, delta-winged fighters. Two Armstrong Siddeley Sapphire turbojets powered every fighter. Each turbojet produced 11 000 pounds of thrust. Firestreak infrared guided missiles armed the fighters.

On most nights, the Javelin's distinctive sound could be heard, as the crews departed or returned from training missions. Because most air interceptions were carried out at altitudes above 35 000 feet where fuel consumption is reduced, the sorties were nearly two hours in duration. During taking-off, the arrestor barrier was left in the raised position at the far end of the runway, for any emergency situation.

One night, after nearly two hours aloft, a weary crew returned to Leeming for landing. During the night the wind direction had shifted through 180°, so the crew was told to make their approach onto the reciprocal runway from which they took off. Unfortunately, the ATC (air traffic controller) had forgotten to lower the arrestor barrier, which was now at touchdown point of the duty runway. At night, with the high nose-up attitudes common to most fighters, visibility on approach is never very good and pilots rely on the runway lights for orientation. The arrestor barrier, stretched tautly across the threshold, was virtually invisible.

As the crew touched down, the Javelin flew into the barrier. From a speed close to 180 kilometres per hour the aircraft was stopped in less than two seconds. The normal 6 000 feet of landing run had been reduced to 200 feet as the barrier was pulled out. Both crewmen were uninjured but the Javelin was a total write-off. This story has stayed in my mind throughout my career. In the flying fraternity, particularly among military aviators, stories of frights and scares are two-a-penny. However, I can recall very few occasions where the fright experienced by the Javelin crew has been surpassed.

During the early 1960s, the most eagerly read military flying publication in Britain was the Monthly Accident Summary. This document, compiled by the Military Aviation Safety Board, listed all accidents and incidents, which had occurred in the RAF and the Fleet Air Arm the previous month. It mentioned date, time, aircraft type, location, and full names of the aircrew concerned. It covered the incidents of good airmanship, as well as the follies of some crews, fairly and firmly. I think the eagerness to read it was to ensure that one's name was not included.

I read about the following incident in the Accident Summary, but I did not know the RAF crew personally. The Canberra was a three-seater medium bomber. A number of squadrons operated the aircraft with just a pilot and one navigator. The pilot sat in the left seat of the aircraft. The navigator sat in a separate compartment behind the pilot, reached by a narrow passageway on the right-hand side of the fuselage.

It is customary, in all multi-seat aircraft, for checklists to be read out with all the crew taking and reporting the correct actions. In this case, the pilot and the navigator had been flying together for such a long time as a crew that the need to read out checklists was dispensed with. Both men climbed into the aircraft and performed their individual actions without reference to one another.

The Canberra took off, got airborne, and settled into the long climb to altitude. As the altimeter wound passed 25 000 feet, Joe (the pilot) realized that he had not heard Mac's (the navigator) usual humming over the intercom. He called Mac on the intercom, but he received no reply. Realizing that he was already way above the altitude where oxygen is necessary to sustain life, he imagined that Mac had become anoxic and was unconscious. Joe pushed the yoke forward and dived the aircraft as quickly as he could to get below 10 000 feet where his navigator could again breathe.

Meanwhile, Mac had been quietly setting up all his navigation equipment in the back. He had the habit of humming to himself as he went about his tasks. Suddenly, he felt the climbing aircraft bunt rapidly into a screaming dive. He called Joe on the intercom but received no reply. Glancing at the altimeter, he saw the aircraft was above 25 000 feet and assumed Joe was anoxic. Mac tightened his ejection seat straps, but then he decided he could not leave Joe to his fate; they had been friends for too long. Unstrapping from the safety of his ejection seat, he moved down the passage toward the front cockpit. To do this he had to disconnect his oxygen tube and intercom lead.

As soon as the oxygen tube disconnected an alarm bell started to ring in Joe's headset, convincing him that Mac was indeed suffering from a shortage of oxygen. Therefore, he pushed the stick forward to descend to a safe altitude as fast as possible. Having recognized the emergency, Joe now decided to cancel the alarm bell. He had to bend forward over the stick and use the full stretch of his right arm, thus enabling him to reach the cancel button on the warning panel.

Just then, Mac arrived up front to see his anoxic pilot slumped over the control column. Wasting no time, he grabbed Joe's shoulders and pulled him back into the seat. He grabbed the stick and started pulling the Canberra out of the steep dive. Joe felt the pull on his shoulders and looked round to see his anoxic navigator. As captain of the aircraft, Joe regained control of the stick and once again pushed the plane into a dive. It was only after the third or fourth oscillation, as they both fought for control of the aircraft, that it suddenly dawned on both men that the problem was not the shortage of oxygen. It was a simple intercom failure, which neither man had realized at the time!

The 14 months spent at Linton learning to fly passed in a flash. Hard work, stress, and the pure joy of flying, seemed to accelerate the passage of day and night. During the course, I managed to experience the past and catch a glimpse into the future of aviation.

I played cricket for the Base team and, like the rugby in Devonshire, I enjoyed the opportunity to travel around Yorkshire for matches. During conversation with one of the instructors, who was a batsman in our team, I mentioned that as a boy I found the stories of the Isle of Man Tourist Trophy motorbike races fascinating. It turned out that the instructor was also a motorcycling fan and my interest re-aroused his passion for the sport.

Within a few days of our conversation he had organized a cricket match between our team and RAF Jurby. Although interstation matches were common, this one was slightly different. RAF Jurby was situated on the Isle of Man and the date for the match just happened to coincide with the TT races on the island. He solved the transportation problem by inviting his cricket-mad friend, who just happened to be a Transport Command pilot based at RAF Dishforth!

On the morning of our departure, a huge Blackburn Beverley crossed the hedge and landed at Linton. This double-decker anachronism had space for 96 people on the upper deck, and for vehicles below. After loading three cars there was still ample space upstairs for the cricket XI. The huge aeroplane, with four great piston engines, was limited in speed by the thickness of the wing, frontal area of the fuselage and the fixed undercarriage. Although not very fast, and limited to altitudes within the normal weather patterns, it was ideal for our cricket team.

The weekend on the Isle of Man included swims in the freezing Irish Sea, pub-crawls through Douglas, and many hours watching the exciting races through the towns and hillsides of the island. We also played cricket.

Years later I was entertained by an anecdote told by an American navy Phantom pilot. In the mid-1960s, the F4 Phantom was at the cutting edge of technology. Operating from a carrier in the Mediterranean, the RIO (radar intercept officer), in the back of a Phantom, picked up a huge blip on the radar. Excitedly, he directed the pilot into a pursuit curve to come up astern of the contact. The overtaking speed was incredible and the F4 pilot had to use dive brakes and flaps to avoid flashing past the object. As the range closed and the pilot picked up the contact visually, the RIO asked the pilot to describe what they were intercepting. The pilot's description began, 'You're not going to believe this! We have a double-decker, fixed undercarriage, four-engined …' It was a Beverley. The Royal Air Force was still using them as battlefield transport aircraft. I had experienced the past.

Prior to graduating I underwent a period of instruction in a Vampire. It was winter and the inversion, so common over the plains of Yorkshire, had reduced visibility considerably. Out of the grey murk, we spotted an all-white shape crossing from left to right in front of us. Taking control, my instructor threw the aircraft into a tight right-hander, which allowed us to parallel the track of the white aircraft. It was a pre-production NA39, operating out of Brough on a test flight.

This aircraft entered service a few years later as the Buccaneer. Its white livery was the anti-radiation paint scheme adopted to reduce the effects of nuclear explosions. The Buccaneer was developed as a low-level, tactical nuclear bomber. Fortunately, it was never used in that role, but was to earn an enviable reputation as a superb aircraft, in the Royal Navy, Royal Air Force, and South African Air Force. This chance sighting was a glimpse of the future. In June 1959, I joined an elite band of aviators who proudly wore wings on their sleeve.

Chapter 4

738 Squadron, OCU, RNAS Lossiemouth

On 27 July 1959, after ten days leave, I joined 738 Squadron at RNAS Lossiemouth. It was a pleasure returning to the navy after my sojourn with the RAF. I am eternally grateful for the training, probably the best available in the world. However, my career was to be with the navy and I was desperately keen to progress. The thought of an aircraft carrier was uppermost in my mind. Very few pilots were ever washed from advanced training, so I knew that barring misfortune, I would achieve my goal of flying from a ship.

738 Squadron was an OCU (Operational Conversion Unit) equipped with Sea Venom Mk21 aircraft. The Ghost 104 engine powered this aircraft. It was the task of Lieutenant Commander Derek Monsell and his instructors to prepare us for operational flying in the fleet. Aircraft familiarization flights and introduction to battle formation flying covered the first two weeks.

The aircraft was similar in appearance to the Vampire we had trained on, but it had significantly more thrust. The extended wings were fitted with tip tanks. Halfway down the mainspar, the wings were hinged to cater for the cramped space on board a carrier. This feature made us realize that the career we had chosen was something special. Although the aircraft was fitted with side-by-side ejection seats, the OCU flew solo.

Weaponry training, the reason for our existence, began during the third week. Camera guns filmed each attack during the air-to-air exercises. After landing, the instructors played back the developed films to point out faults and give hints on improving technique. The gyro-gunsight would accurately predict aiming points, provided the inputs from the pilot were correct. However, this required considerable practice and coordination.

The aiming pipper stayed on the aiming point—usually the cockpit of the "enemy" aircraft. The pilot accomplished this by using the stick in his right hand to control the elevator and ailerons. He used his feet to control slip and skid and to maintain the balance of the aircraft. His left hand moved the throttle and operated the dive brakes to achieve the correct rate of closure on the "enemy". At the same time, he twisted the throttle handle, in the same fashion as an accelerator on a motorcycle. This movement opened and closed a set of six diamonds displayed in his reflector sight. The inside tips of these diamonds formed an imaginary circle. The pilot had to adjust the size of this circle to just touch the wingtips of the "enemy aircraft". This would feed in the exact range to the gyro-sight, producing the correct angle ahead of the "enemy" to score a hit.

All these movements had to be coordinated while the target was twisting and turning. The instructors described the result as a gentle "stirring of porridge" motion. In fact, in the student's cockpit there was nothing gentle about it at all, just a wild thrashing of arms, hands, and feet.

During one of these exercises Lieutenant Nick Croad, a fellow student, had an exciting experience. On completion of the filming run, Nick was called on the radio to form up into long-line astern, for a tail-chase on the way back to base. Being slightly higher than his instructor, he pushed his stick forward to start a descent. The bunting manoeuvre applied negative "G" to the Venom. Instead of gravity acting downwards, as in normal flight, it now worked upwards.

Unfortunately, due to a maintenance error, Nick's ejection seat had not been correctly secured to the cockpit floor. The upward acceleration, during the bunt, caused the chair in which Nick was firmly strapped to rise out of its housing, banging Nick's helmeted head against the canopy. As the seat rose, a cable pulled a safety catch, which fired the drogue gun attached to the seat's main parachute.

With a tremendous explosion, the drogue shattered the canopy and extracted the seat-stabilizing chute through the resulting hole. A metal bar divided the Venom canopy down the middle. Therefore, before ejecting, occupants had to jettison the canopy. Nowadays, aircrew can eject directly through the canopies.

Now Nick was sitting in a seat that was wobbling about the cockpit. He could not eject as his parachute was threaded through the canopy. Because he knew that at any minute the seat could fire, he was understandably anxious. As the seat rose, it also disconnected the electrical lead to the radio, so he was unable to inform anyone of his predicament.

Nick's instructor, who thought Nick was behind him, suddenly discovered he was on his own, with no idea where his student had gone. Calling Lossiemouth, he notified air traffic control that he had lost his student. A few moments later, a Sea Venom crossed the threshold with a parachute blowing out behind. Unable to call, Nick sneaked in for an extremely gentle landing.

A few years earlier, a similar incident had occurred from a carrier operating close to Malta in the Mediterranean. Lieutenant Carl Davis was launched by catapult in a Sea Hawk. The rapid acceleration lifted the unsecured seat out of its housing until it was stopped by the canopy. The drogue gun did not fire, but Carl, still attached to his seat, was now stuck 30 centimetres behind and above where he should have been.

Carl was not a tall man; he could not reach the throttle, or the undercarriage and flap levers. Fortunately, during launch the throttle was positioned fully forward, so the engine was at full power. His right arm, at full stretch, just allowed his hand to reach the top of the stick, so he could still control the aircraft.

With a loose ejection seat, Carl could not risk a landing back on board the carrier. The arrested landing would have thrown the chair, and Carl, against the instrument panel. He had no option but to divert to Hal Far Airfield in Malta, and unable to use the radio he made an unannounced arrival. This was not the worst of his troubles. Although his legs could not reach the rudder pedals, he landed the aircraft successfully. After touchdown he was unable to reach the throttle to pull it back to idle position. Fortunately, in those days, a handle situated in front of the stick applied the brakes, similar to applying brakes on a bicycle. Even with maximum breaking, the thrust of the engine at full power dragged the Sea Hawk off the end of the runway where the thick sand in the over-run area finally brought the runaway jet to a stop. By the time emergency crews arrived, the vibrating jet had buried itself in the sand up to the main-planes. Only then, could the canopy open from the outside and the engine shut down.

RNAS Lossiemouth was a superb site for operational flying training. Albeit in the north of Scotland, the airfield, on the shores of the Moray Firth, was well protected from the prevailing westerly weather by the Grampians and Scottish Highlands. Consequently, as the cloud base was seldom lower than 2 000 feet, flying was possible on most days. In the 50s and 60s, air traffic was minimal, and military aircraft could operate almost unrestrictedly north of Aberdeen.

What magnificent country to fly over, particularly at low-level! Lochs, glens, mountains, and brilliant coastal shores gave vistas of unparalleled beauty. Weaponry ranges at Tain, near Dornoch, Cape Wrath on the north-western tip of Scotland and Rosehearty, near Banff, added variety to the training programme. For some, it was a long way from the bright lights of London, but for me it was perfect. During my 12 years in the Fleet Air Arm, I completed three tours of duty at Lossiemouth and loved them all.

The one loch most pilots absolutely avoided was Loch Ness. The temptation to fly down its 22-mile length had proved too great for a few pilots, who subsequently regretted their weakness. A tourist venue, with wealthy estates on the shores, Loch Ness became known as the "Lossie speed trap". If one succumbed to the temptation, it was guaranteed that one's aircraft would be reported before there was time to land. The well known, old film actor, James Robertson Justice, used to complain regularly. His home was situated further north on the banks of the Dornoch Firth. Fortunately, he spent most of his time filming in the south of England.

Because they were miles away from the bright lights, pilots had to manufacture their own entertainment. In this regard, the Wrens were a particularly attractive addition to the compliment of the base. The further the base was from London, the rowdier the formal mess dinners were. Lossiemouth, being at the furthest extremity of Britain, probably hosted a large number of the most memorable dinners.

The airfield had been built during the war and a large number of buildings were temporary; the wardroom being a perfect example. It consisted of a number of wooden Nissan huts placed cheek-by-jowl, giving the necessary sized rooms. It consisted of two wings joined by a long passageway. The east wing was the dining room, and the west wing contained the pub (the scene of most of the action). Entrance to the building was via double-doors in the centre, faced by the Hall-porter's office.

The pub was the centre of Lossie's universe. At one end, a large bar counter catered for the eternally thirsty. In the centre was the pièce de résistance, the fireplace. A thick, brick chimney descended from the ceiling and split into two hearths at 180° to each other. Therefore, it was possible to enjoy the warmth of the fire from either side. In Scotland, nearly 58° north of the equator, this was a most welcome feature. Encircling the chimney, exactly at elbow height, was a ledge on which glasses or elbows could rest. It had been perfectly designed by a drinking man for drinking men. Arranged in a semi-circle in front of each hearth, large easy chairs allowed the less active drinkers to relax in almost horizontal posture.

Two formal mess dinners stand out in my memory as the "jewels in the crown" of innumerable similar occasions. The first was a dinner to welcome three United States Navy admirals. The formal dinner passed with the dignity and decorum associated with the Royal Navy. Afterwards, all the diners retired to the pub. It was winter and bitterly cold outside. During dinner, the hall porter built up the fires, which had been burning all day, to warm the throng.

The dignitaries, entertained by the base high brass, had secured pride of place around the central hearth. The three Americans resplendent in their white mess jackets, contrasted markedly with the more sombre black British uniforms. Shortly after drinks had been served, the first ominous sound occurred. The old building had a corrugated iron roof, and those of us who had served a while at Lossie recognized the indication of approaching chaos.

Fred, who flew the Sea Hawk, Scimitar and Buccaneer, was a long time resident of Lossiemouth. Fleet Air Arm members will require no further amplification, as everybody knew Fred. He was the brother of Sir Michael de Labillierre, of British Army and Gulf War fame. Perhaps Fred's greatest claim to fame was his ability to turn a respectable mess dinner into something of cataclysmic proportions. This night was to be no different!

At the first creak of the metal roof, those in the know started edging towards the exits and windows. I am certain Captain David Kirk, the base commander, recognized the sound of impending doom, but felt he could not ask his distinguished guests to evacuate the pub. After a few more heavy footsteps, a hush descended on the room. Like doomed men, we waited for the axe to fall—we did not have long to wait.

Fred released a fire extinguisher down the chimney. The pressure split into both hearths and two clouds, closely resembling the rolling mushroom shape of nuclear explosions, engulfed the room. Ash from the fires reduced visibility to zero. Those escaping from the room did so in IMC (instrument flying conditions). Those of us strategically positioned near exits escaped the worst of the ordeal—not so the visitors!

It took 20 minutes for the smoke to clear and 40 before people stopped coughing. The three USN admirals, who had withstood the worst of the tidal cloud wave, looked remarkably like actors from the Black and White Minstrel Show. Only their eyes were free of dust. The dust clouds had been so thick that even the inside pocket of one's mess dress was filled with ash. I cannot recall what punishment Fred received, but it probably included stoppage of mess facilities; a penance Fred became accustomed to over the years.

A few years later, Buccaneer aircrew decided that one of the mess dinners needed livening up. During a long and tedious after-dinner speech, Lieutenant Geoff Homan, a Buccaneer observer, formulated his plan when most of the diners had retired to the pub. Geoff scuttled off into the darkness, with a posse of aircrew. We waited anxiously for 20 minutes before the posse returned.

They had gone across to the Pony Club stables and invited three horses to attend the dinner. Simulating cowboys at round-up time, they inveigled the animals to enter the building through the double-doors. Then, with a smack on the rump, they set the four-footed "guests" on a trot through the crowded anti-room. An agent opened the double-doors on the far side of the mess, allowing the excited beasts to make their exit, after amusingly watching all the two-legged guests dive for cover.

One of the stallions had obviously not attended a mess dinner before and, instead of galloping straight through the room, as intended, decided to join the party. It stopped alongside the fireplace. Geoff, realizing that he might be forced to pay for the animal's drinks, smacked the horse's rear end in an attempt to get it moving. The horse, upset by this show of bad manners, turned round and bit Geoff in the middle of his starched shirt, before ambling back to the paddock on his own. I believe the entire rodeo crew was placed under stoppage of mess privilege.

At the squadron, the introduction to air-to-ground weaponry began, an aspect not for the faint-hearted. From a height of 6 000 feet, the nose of the aircraft must be aimed at the target below, while descending at an angle of 30°. During the dive, while airspeed is increasing, the pilot must aim his sight precisely at the centre of the target. He must also keep a close eye on the altimeter, which unwinds very quickly, and release his weapon at precisely the correct altitude. All this is done while the ground rushes closer and features, indistinguishable from entry height, suddenly grow in size and clarity.

Immediately after release, the pilot must haul back on his stick to pull out of the dive to avoid flying through shrapnel from the weapon's explosion and to avoid flying into the ground. Four "G" is the required increase in loading to recover from the dive. Normal gravity, namely one "G", affects everything on planet earth. During a dive recovery, one's body weight effectively increases four times. The head becomes four times heavier, requiring a four-fold increase in muscle power to hold it up. The heart has to pump four times harder to allow heavier blood to reach the brain. The heart organ itself, because of its apparent increase in weight, tends to sink downwards inside the chest cavity. It has a greater distance to cover when pumping blood to the head and eyes.

Of course, the wearing of "G" suits assists aircrew to withstand these increases in gravity. After a few sorties, four "G" is hardly noticed. However, with all activities occurring simultaneously during a steep dive, pilots can forget the important altimeter and release low. To avoid flying into the ground, six, seven, or even eight "G" is required. The adrenaline rush, brought on by the proximity to solid earth, gives the pilot the necessary strength to pull out, but the aircraft is often over-stressed.

Most fighters are capable of withstanding "G" loading, ranging between +7 and -2 "G". When exceeded these limits place stress on the airframe, therefore clearance for further flights can only follow stringent tests and adjustments to the aircraft. The authorities look unfavourably upon pupil pilots who overstress aircraft. "G" meters in the cockpit record all "G" applications and are checked between each flight.

Weaponry is an interesting subject involving a great many variable parameters. A Bisley shottist could explain how gravity affects a bullet fired from a rifle. The bullet's flight path would curve downwards as range increases. Crosswinds, causing deflection to the right or left, also affect it. As the bullet moves, friction with the surrounding air causes drag, which decreases its velocity, and so allows gravity and wind deflection to have a greater effect on it.

All these variables compound when the weaponry performs from a moving platform such as an aircraft. Practice is required to achieve accurate results and pilots must have a good theoretical knowledge of ballistics. It also becomes apparent early on in the training cycle that some pilots thrive on the challenges of weapon delivery. However, others do not enjoy the frenetic activities. These men usually graduate to become excellent flying instructors, preferring the more sedate man-management problems to the hurly-burly of air fighting.

An additional hazard for the naval aviator is that of height judgement when operating over the sea, particularly a calm glassy sea. Over land, houses, buildings, and railway lines have definite shapes, which provide perspective to the pilot. Over the sea, unless a ship is within sight, this perspective is lacking and pilots become dependent on altimeters to indicate their height. When delivering weapons during steep dives, this is particularly dangerous.

Rosehearty weapon's range was established for this particular reason. Just off the Banff coast, a circle of buoys anchored to the seabed provided the target. Pilots diving towards the sea had to learn the vital necessity of carefully monitoring the altimeter to achieve safe, weapon-release heights. Years later, whilst giving weaponry instruction over the St Brides Bay range, off the Pembrokeshire coast in Wales, this lesson saved my skin.

I was giving instruction to Lt George Wrigley in a dual-seat Hunter. George was an experienced Hunter pilot, having flown the aircraft while serving in the Rhodesian Air Force. He had never flown over the sea before, because Rhodesia was a landlocked country. He was accustomed to diving at targets on the ground, which grow rapidly bigger the lower the aircraft dives. At the right moment, he would fire his rocket and pull out. Over the sea, however, things do not grow any bigger and the pilot must rely on his rapidly unwinding altimeter to fire at the correct height. George, unaccustomed to watching the altimeter, passed his release height and continued down in his dive. Taking over control, I pulled back on the stick and we managed to avoid hitting the sea, by the narrowest of margins.

Navigation sorties were flown periodically, and the selected routes became progressively more difficult. One of these was a night land-away sortie to RAF Valley, in Wales. The route called for a high-level leg across the Irish Sea, between the Mull of Galloway and Anglesey. The Mk21 Sea Venom had no, as in zero, navigation aids. However, VHF radio could deliver assistance in the form of bearings and steers to allow the pilot to plot his position on his chart. As space within the crowded cockpit was limited, this venerable mark of aircraft had only one radio set.

Checking my position as I crossed the Scottish coastline, I headed out to sea. When I judged my position to be abeam of the Isle of Man, I called on the radio for a confirmatory bearing. Unfortunately, I received no answer and discovered my radio had failed. Late in October, the vast majority of the British Isles lies under a blanket of cloud. Descent was inadvisable and my predicament was serious.

I decided my best option would be to continue on heading and fly out my flight plan. As the second hand of the cockpit clock reached the calculated time, I lowered the aircraft's left wing to see below me. Miraculously, through a hole in the cloud I saw a red aeronautical beacon, flashing the identification of RAF Valley. Without hesitation, I throttled back, put out the dive brakes, and spiralled down through the tiny hole in the cloud. My surname may be coincidental, but that night I felt like the boxer Rocky Marciano who stated, 'Somebody up there likes me!'

After graduation in early December, we were posted to RNAS Yeovilton, in Somerset.

Chapter 5

766 Squadron, AWFS, RNAS Yeovilton

———

I arrived at RNAS Yeovilton, in Somerset, at the beginning of January 1960 with a total of 348 hours' experience. Willie Hare, Nick Croad, and I joined 766 Squadron to complete the All-Weather Fighter course. We paired up with observers completing their qualification phase. Upon successful completion of the course, we would be appointed as a crew to a front-line squadron; the aircraft-carrier dream was coming ever closer.

I crewed up with Nick Child, an ex-merchant navy officer, in what developed into a long-standing partnership. He was extremely clever, an excellent observer, and a man with a sharp wit. Flying with him was a pleasure. I can well recall navigation flights from Yeovilton to Lossiemouth, when we traversed the entire length of Britain. Crossing each county border, he would adapt his voice to the appropriate accent, causing chaos among radar controllers in the Air Traffic Control Centres.

We completed the course on 17 March, after 61 days and 28 night hours of the most demanding flying. The task of an all-weather crew was to protect the fleet from enemy air attacks during the night, or in bad weather. For training purposes, the Fleet Air Arm could not have chosen a better time period for the course. January, February, and March are traditionally the worst weather months of the year in Britain, and 1960 was no exception.

We flew through warm fronts, cold fronts, thunderstorms and snow showers. Only when the cloud base descended below 200 feet were the aircraft grounded. Four miles east of Yeovilton lay a low range of hills called Corton Ridge. The top of the ridge was 200 feet above airfield height and, as it was underneath the main approach path, it had a string of red lights positioned along the spine to denote high ground. The instructors used these lights as their weather guide. If they could see the lights from the airfield, we flew! On many dark, dank, scary nights Nick and I would spend ages completing our pre-flight external check of the aircraft, hoping for the ridge lights to disappear so we could cancel our sortie.

We practised air-interceptions (AI) until they came out of our ears. Initially, under radar control, the fighter directors would give us vectors and heights to fly to position the Sea Venom within aircraft radar range of the target, usually less than 12 miles. Then the observer, using indications from the aircraft's radar, would take over final phase control. To successfully complete an intercept the required flying was without doubt the most exacting form of flying I have ever experienced.

The observer had to control the height, speed, rate of turn, and rate of closing of the Venom all by indications from his radar set. He managed this by issuing a stream of orders over the intercom, sounding much like a horse racing commentary. The pilot was obliged to react to every command in order to fly the aircraft into the correct position astern of the enemy aircraft to visually identify it before destroying it with cannon-fire—this being the era before the advent of missiles.

To achieve this at night, or in cloud, required intense concentration and teamwork. The observer's task was to bring the Venom in directly astern of the enemy, but at a slightly lower height, to avoid collision. Then he had to synchronize speeds to allow the Venom to creep closer, until the pilot caught sight of the enemy aircraft. At night, without navigation lights, the pilot would look for a tiny, half-moon of flame inside the enemy jet-pipe. Usually, this crescent of flame became visual at approximately 200 feet. Up until this time flying would be performed with reference to the aircraft's flying instruments. After acquiring the jet-pipe visually, the pilot would not dare to blink, in case he lost sight of the target. The observer's job then changed to monitoring the aircraft's instruments and keeping the pilot informed of the aircraft's attitude. Vertigo was a real problem, particularly when the target aircraft was manoeuvring.

The basic turn in an interception was a 45° bank, applied rapidly in reaction to the observer's order 'Come starboard' or 'Port'. The rate of turn varied by the orders 'Harder' (add 15°) or 'Ease', when bank would be decreased by the same amount. Height differentials between fighter and target were removed by the orders 'Up gently' (1 000 feet per minute rate of climb), or 'Go up', when the pilot had to use 2 000 feet per minute. Speed increments were ordered in steps of 20 knots. During an intercept's final phase, both crewmembers worked like one-armed paperhangers and the cockpit was a very busy place as the pilot tried to keep up with his observer's rapid-fire commentary.

On our course, Willie Hare teamed up with Midshipman Robin Soar, a young, eager observer. On more than one occasion during the tense final approach phase of an intercept, just before Willie could expect to get a visual sighting on the target, Robin's commentary ceased. Robin's excitement was so great and his commentary so rapid, he would hyperventilate. At the *moment-critique* he would run out of oxygen and be unable to continue speaking. With training he overcame this problem and became an excellent observer.

Another odd feature of the all-weather world was the use of clock-code. In normal aviation a clock face is imagined lying horizontally around the aircraft, with 12 o'clock being directly ahead and six o'clock being behind. Reference to this clock face indicates approaching traffic (e.g., 'Two aircraft, three o'clock high' means directly abeam on your right-hand side above the horizon). The ideal place for a fighter to be in combat is 'locked onto the enemies six' (i.e. directly behind the target in a shooting position).

However, during all-weather interceptions the observers use a vertical clock, positioned ahead of the fighter's nose, as if looking at Big Ben. Twelve o'clock indicates directly above the nose and six o'clock below the nose. Two o'clock would be on an imaginary line extending forwards on a spoke 30° above the horizon on the right-hand side. When edging in close to the target for the pilot to get a visual sighting, the observer ideally places the target at '12 o'clock, five, 200' (i.e. the pilot should look directly ahead, and 5° above the horizon, to spot the jet-pipe. The observer's final commentary would include the range in feet between the two aircraft, in this case 200 feet). Fortunately, the radar, although primitive by today's standards, was extremely accurate at close range.

Initial interceptions were flown during daylight hours. The crews then progressed to night-time intercepts, but with both aircraft displaying navigation lights. Night intercepts, flown "lights out", had to be successfully completed to graduate from the course.

This demanding course had the additional benefit of improving the pilot's instrument flying skills immeasurably, as illustrated by an incident that took place years later. Central Flying School, at RAF Little Rissington, was the "Temple of Learning" as far as flying instruction was concerned. Only the top instructors were appointed to the staff, and for this reason they considered themselves very close to God.

Willie Hare, a good navy all-weather pilot, was under the hood flying a session of instrument training, during his instructor's course. The weather had deteriorated during the sortie and approach conditions were difficult. Therefore, Willie's instructor decided to take control and fly the final approach himself. Under the hood, Willie could not see how bad the conditions had become. However, he did notice that the instructor was having difficulty flying accurately and presumed he was simulating a student pilot. To the chagrin of his instructor, who had been flying his best, Willie assumed control and completed the approach.

On occasions, the winter weather really socked in and flying was cancelled. The training programme was rescheduled and we ended up in ground school, catching up on theory. However, after a long spell of bad weather the odd period of relaxation was allowed. Invariably, the word would spread around the base, 'Nigel is in the coffee bar.' Within minutes, everyone who had free time also ended up there.

Lieutenant Commander Nigel Anderdon, senior pilot of 766 Squadron, was unequalled as a raconteur. His inventory of flying stories was legendary and he became known as "Hans Christian Anderdon" to the younger aircrew. He had developed a typically British "understatement" style of storytelling, which emphasized the punch-line of each tale he told. I suspect quite a number of his stories were suitably embellished, but he kept everyone enthralled. It was an art form that has unfortunately been allowed to decay in these more modern times.

One day at Yeovilton, when poor weather stopped student crews from flying, his stature as a storyteller and pilot increased dramatically. The runways were icy and snowploughs had to be used to clear drift snow from the tarmac surfaces. I don't imagine the instructors relished flying, but I suppose they felt they had to uphold their pose to impress us.

Amongst the snow showers, we watched Nigel land his Sea Venom. It was apparent that keeping direction on the icy runway was causing him problems, because his aircraft yawed with the nose turning more and more to the left. As his aircraft approached a 90° skid, we suddenly heard a burst of power from the engine. To our amazement the Sea Venom shot forward, leaving the main runway precisely at the intersection of a taxiway, and came to a neat standstill on the hardstanding. With Nigel, one could never tell whether it was luck or superb judgement, I suspect a little bit of both, but it certainly impressed the onlookers.

Despite the fact I had qualified for my wings, Nick Child and I were still sprogs! *JACKSPEAK*, the delightful *Pusser's Guide to Royal Navy & Royal Marine Slang*, defines sprog as 'General description of any novice, either to the Navy or some branch of the Senior Service, e.g. a "sprog pilot". Said to be derived from the word for a baby gannet.'

Nick, my tall, slim, intelligent, and newly married observer took to the aircraft's radar set like a duck to water. The last required flight on the course was to complete a landing-away—a night navigation sortie. After dark on 16 March 1960, all three crews on the course took off individually for a cross-country flight from Yeovilton, in the south of England, to Lossiemouth, in the north of Scotland. Nick and I flew in Sea Venom XG 630. After 75 uneventful minutes, we landed off a Ground Controlled Approach (GCA). The night-flying meal laid on by the wardroom staff turned into a mini-celebration on completion of the course—attended by Willie Hare, Robin Soar, Nick Croad, Pat Pinches, and other aircrew. After a good night's rest all that was required was to fly back to Yeovilton to complete our training.

Winter can be very severe in the "frozen" north of Scotland. To protect its aircrew the navy insists they wear immersion suits on all flights during the winter months—a wise precaution that has saved many lives over the years. However, the "Goon suit", is not the easiest piece of clothing to put on or take off.

The suit is made of rubberized, waterproof material and consists of two sections. The trousers and boots are an all-in-one combination—bracers support the weight. The blouse has tight rubber seals around the neck and wrists, which require a liberal sprinkling of "foo-foo" powder to ease its passage over the neck and arms. Once these two sections are in place, rubber seals around the top of the trousers and the bottom of the blouse are rolled together to form a watertight seal around the midriff.

The suit keeps the wearer dry if he falls into the sea, but additional protection is required against cold-water temperatures. Suitable cellular, thermal underwear is worn, which includes long johns, fisherman's socks, and aircrew jerseys. Getting dressed in the morning is similar to a military operation, which requires proper planning and minute attention to detail. This detail includes ensuring that one's necessary bodily functions are completely attended to *before* the final layers of suit are applied. The manufacturers, in a gesture of kindness to the occupants, modified the suits with the addition of a "pee-tube". It was always a wise precaution to check, before flight, that the attached waxed cord securely bound this opening at the crotch.

It was difficult enough for us in those days to keep ourselves comfortable, and we only had male aircrew. The mind boggles when one thinks of the difficulties facing the lady aircrew flying today!

By 8am we were fully attired and had eaten a traditional Scottish breakfast of porridge and kippers. We reported to the weather office to receive our "met" briefing for the flight back to Yeovilton. Wearing his undertaker's expression, the met officer explained dolefully that although the weather was fine in Scotland, advection fog covered the entire southern half of England. Our take-off would be delayed.

Peeling off our Mae Wests, we retreated into the crewroom set-aside for visiting aircrew. Here, ever-friendly Wrens helped us to cups of steaming coffee. Around mid-morning the met officer rang to say that the fog had lifted and we could take off. Thanking the girls for the coffee, we donned our life jackets and hurried out to the three waiting Venoms. All three aircraft started up and were given taxi clearance. The other two aircraft taxied out and took off but I had to cut my engine, because hydraulic fluid was leaking from our aircraft.

Whilst the mechanics started work on our aircraft, Nick and I returned to the Wrens, who consoled us with more coffee. Just before noon, one of the girls came dashing in to say that the Venom was once again ready to fly. Anxious to complete the course, Nick and I hurried out to the aircraft. After a quick external check, to ensure that all the maintenance panels were secure, we started up. This time we taxied and took off without any problems—they had done a sterling job repairing the aeroplane.

Saying cheerio to the Lossiemouth controller, we turned south and started the long climb up to 41 000 feet. This took 21 minutes in the old Venom, and during the climb, physical science took effect. As the aircraft ascended, the outside air temperature dropped by 2° Centigrade for every 1 000 foot increase in height. However, inside the cockpit, the heating system maintained a comfortable temperature.

A more noticeable scientific phenomenon became increasingly apparent as we climbed. As our height increased, the outside air pressure decreased. As this outside pressure decreases, the effect on the human body is similar to an inside pressure increase. Now, I had consumed many cups of coffee during the morning and the higher we climbed the greater became the pressure differential. As we levelled off at the top of climb, I spoke to Nick on the intercom and told him to look at his charts and find a place to land. In answer to his very surprised 'Why?' I told him I needed to pee.

We were sprogs eager to complete our training so, after a discussion, he convinced me that we could not land just anywhere to have a pee. This decision did nothing to relieve my ever-worsening situation. I could not cross my legs because of the offending control column; things were becoming critical.

Looking around the cramped cockpit for some form of salvation, my eyes settled on Nick's helmet. My request was flatly refused. Next I looked at the Cape leather flying gloves we were wearing. Mine was an older pair and the stitching at the end of the fingers was coming adrift. Nick's, however, were brand new and he grudgingly removed one when I convinced him how real the emergency had become. With this glove I held the solution to my problems, but nothing in life is easy!

I was wearing a "Goon suit" with all the required underclothes. I was strapped into my parachute with lap, shoulder, and waist straps. I was also strapped into the ejection seat with a further set of lap, shoulder, and waist straps. Just below my knees, leg garters attached to the seat pan, and across my chest hung my main and emergency oxygen hoses. A radio lead attached my helmeted head to the aircraft. Between my legs was the control column, which protruded from the cockpit floor, and my feet extended below the instrument panel on the rudder pedals.

An additional complication was that the Sea Venom did not have an automatic pilot. This meant that Nick would have to lean his left arm across me, while I endeavoured to unstrap and ease the internal pressure. Having never flown an aircraft before, he would then have to fly the jet left-handed, at 41 000 ft and at 420 nautical miles per hour!

This was the plan, and in accordance with the principles of war, we maintained the aim. While I unstrapped, Nick proceeded with his first flying lesson. We wandered all over Scotland until at last I managed to get the glove, and everything else, into the right position. My intention was to relieve the pressure just a wee bit, if you will pardon the pun, but once you start these things you can't stop.

A warm sense of well-being replaced the excruciating anxiety suffered during the previous 15 minutes. At last I started to see the amusing side of the whole affair. Not so Nick! On completion of the task I had filled the glove to the brim. Feeling relieved, I told Nick he would have to hold it because I needed both hands to fly the aeroplane. Once again, Nick refused, but he agreed we had to do something. The novelty of his first flying lesson was quickly wearing thin.

With a spark of genius he said, 'Throw it out of the window.' After discussing the ramifications, I agreed. The Venom has a triangular window on the left-hand side of the windscreen, which is locked with a large knurled knob before take-off. We remembered to depressurize the cockpit before I opened the window. As soon as I had it open I raised the brimming glove and pushed it out. Right then we learned a very important lesson! Never, ever, try and push a full glove into a 420 nautical mile per hour headwind! There was an immediate blow-back into the cockpit, but fortunately, with the temperature now a frigid -63° Centigrade, it froze on contact. I even had to scratch a little hole in the ice on the windscreen to see where we were going.

Being sprogs, we never dared to try to claim a world record; our future was too precious to give away our secret. In retrospect, if it was not the world's highest un-pressurized pee, it was almost certainly the highest free-fall drop of a frozen glove on record. If any reader happens to spot a single glove when passing through the border town of Carlisle, it belongs to Nick.

After landing, we were congratulated on passing the course and appointed to 891 Squadron. Only after we had received our certificates of qualification did we dare reveal our secret, which has subsequently followed me throughout my entire career.

Chapter 6

891 Squadron, HMS *Centaur*

891 Squadron, equipped with Sea Venom FAW 22 aircraft, appointed Nick and I, as a crew. The squadron, under Lieutenant Commander Johnny Robotham, had just returned to RNAS Yeovilton from a cruise to the Far East on HMS *Centaur*. We spent a couple of months training before the squadron rejoined the ship in mid-June for a cruise to Scandinavia and a visit to Stockholm.

Training concentrated on preparing the new crews for carrier operation. We spent many periods flying MADDLS (Mirror Assisted Dummy Deck Landings). Deck-landing mirrors were mounted on the left-hand side of the runways at Yeovilton and the satellite airfield Merryfield, to cater specifically for this training. Alongside the mirror, the runway was painted to simulate the deck of a ship. Pilots flew circuits and bumps to get accustomed to the mirror and the cramped space on a ship. Experienced squadron pilots, positioned at the mirror, would watch each landing and provide helpful commentary whenever necessary.

The mirror, a marvellous British invention, eliminated the requirement for a "batsman" to assist pilots during deck-landings. It was positioned to the left of the runway, opposite touchdown point. A searchlight, also sited on the left-hand side, was aimed at the mirror. The mirror was tilted at 3° to reflect this light beam back up the aircraft's approach path. On either side of the mirror's centre was a set of green datum lights.

On approach, the pilot would look into the mirror and see a bright yellow ball of light reflected from the searchlight, known as the "meatball". By adjusting the descent path of his aircraft, he would position the meatball directly between the green datum lights. His aircraft would then be on the perfect 3° glide path. If the meatball moved above the datum it meant that the aircraft was high on approach, and the pilot would adjust as necessary to remain exactly on the correct glide path.

Another major difference in landing technique had to be learnt. It is normal procedure, when landing at airfields, for the pilot to cushion the touchdown. By applying gentle backpressure on the stick, rate of descent is decreased to allow the wheels to "kiss" the runway on landing. At the same time, the pilot pulls the throttle back to idle to allow the aircraft to decelerate. Both these tendencies are absolutely taboo when landing on a ship.

Navy pilots fly the aircraft into the deck by staying exactly on the glide path all the way down. If he rounds-out, his arrestor hook will miss the arrestor wires positioned across the deck. A glance at the hefty undercarriage of aircraft like the Buccaneer shows these aircraft were built to withstand heavy landings.

If the pilot reduces power and misses the arrestor wire he will glide off the front end of the deck into the sea. In the Royal Navy, power is kept on until the aircraft is stopped. In the United States Navy, pilots learn to apply full power on touchdown, to allow the aircraft to go round for another approach if the wire is missed. During training, old habits have to be broken and new ones learnt, before pilots are allowed anywhere near the flight-deck of a ship.

HMS *Centaur* sailed from the Rosyth Dockyard on 14 June and the squadron re-embarked after the ship had cleared the Firth of Forth Railway Bridge. In 1960, the newer road bridge was still a dream. After a train journey to Edinburgh, the three new crews boarded the ship before she sailed. We watched with awe the experienced members of the squadron arrive on board.

The following day belonged to us. In near perfect weather the ship cruised gently off the Scottish coast; the three crews arrived for a briefing for their first flight from a ship. Nick and I arrived fully dressed in flying kit only to be met by the senior pilot who, disconcertingly, sent Nick away, saying, 'First flights are solo flights.' Pretending to be disappointed, Nick nipped away quickly, in case he changed his mind! I was a little perplexed at the logic of the decision. Maybe, just maybe, the senior pilot knew what could happen on a first flight!

A long, thorough briefing covered the catapult launch and the landing. The launch is critical and the aircraft has to be properly trimmed to fly off the catapult in the correct attitude. When the steam catapult fires, acceleration forces are so great that precautions are necessary inside the cockpit.

Before launch the throttle has to be fully open and the engine at full power. The pilot places his left elbow firmly in his side, and the outstretched fingers of his left hand prevent the throttle from closing during launch. He must not grip the throttle because the acceleration would force his hand backwards, bringing the throttle to idle, and gliding the aircraft into the sea.

For the same reason, his right hand must not grip the stick. Instead, he jams his right elbow into his right side, opens his fingers, and rests the vee between his thumb and forefinger against the control column. On launch, this prevents the control column from flying backwards and placing the aircraft in an unflyable attitude off the catapult.

Then, the pilot must remember to rest his head against the headrest of his ejection seat, or it will jerk backwards as the catapult fires.

Eventually, the three of us walked out onto the flight-deck to find our aircraft. Performing an external check on an aircraft is difficult, because most of the tail section sticks out over the side of the ship. Six stout cables secure the aeroplane to the deck. Once the engines have started and brake pressures have built up the cables are removed. Before then unsecured aircraft could roll off the deck over the side, particularly as the ship heels over when turning into wind.

After all the checks were completed, we were strapped firmly into the cockpit by the maintenance crew. We had to wait for a minute or two before an announcement over the loudspeaker system ordered, 'Start the jets.' This short interlude gave me time to survey the scene on deck. I was amazed to notice that onlookers jam-packed the ship's superstructure, known as "vulture's roost", with hardly a space for latecomers. First solos from carriers are traditionally worth watching!

The loudspeaker brought my attention back to the job in hand and I started my engine. When we were ready to go, we were marshalled up the deck and told to spread our folded wings. I did this, but glanced many times to ensure the levers were correctly in the locked position.

I was to launch second, behind Neddy Bateman, and I watched wide-eyed as they positioned his aircraft on the port catapult. Finally, with a roar, his engine reached full power and he launched. To my absolute horror, his aircraft disappeared from view as it dived off the front end of the ship. The flight-deck is only 60 feet above the water, so I feared the worst. However, after a long few seconds, I spotted his aircraft climbing away. Neddy is very tall with extremely long forearms, which extended the vee in his right hand, placing the Venom into a dive immediately off the catapult. After landing, he received this explanation. Nevertheless, it sure frightened the hell out of me, watching from behind.

With quaking heart, I moved onto the catapult. A number of events occur very quickly as the aircraft is prepared for launch. A team of men, all wearing different coloured jerseys, scurry around underneath as the main-wheels are stopped by automatic chocks, ahead of the Caley Gear. The catapult shuttle slides under the nose-wheel, jolting the whole aircraft. The Caley Gear is a clever system of rollers on which the main-wheels rest. Both sets of rollers rotate continually inwards towards the centre of the catapult. If the aircraft arrives off centre, these rollers rapidly adjust the aircraft's main-wheels to centre the aircraft.

The automatic chocks are lowered and the shuttle is moved forward to tension the aircraft prior to launch. After completing all the cockpit checks, I turned my head to watch the flight deck officer (FDO). When he was happy that everything was in order he raised a green flag in his right hand and started rotating it. At this signal I went to full engine power. When the RPM and jet-pipe temperatures (JPT) stabilized, I raised my right hand in acknowledgement. The FDO then lowered his flag slowly and deliberately until the tip of the flag touched the deck. From that second on nothing could stop me from flying!

The catapult officer pressed the "Fire" button as the FDO's flag touched the deck. A pause of two seconds occurred as steam pressure was released and the next instant my Sea Venom and I were careering down the deck. The tremendous jolt forces one's entire body backwards as the aircraft accelerates. Two seconds later the aircraft had left the deck and was climbing gently away from the sea. What a sensation and what a rush! It took me considerably longer than normal before I managed to raise the undercarriage and flaps.

I had been excited when I flew my first-ever solo flight, but this was momentous. In those few moments, I felt a freedom and exhilaration unsurpassed by any other event in my entire aviation career.

Shortly thereafter, a disquieting thought returned me to my senses. The long, detailed briefing had covered both launch and land-on, but ignored the 30 minutes between the two main events. Suddenly, I realized that I was out of sight of land, with only the carrier as reference. Afraid to venture out of sight of "mother", the name aptly used to describe the carrier, I spent the next 30 minutes flying circles at 20 000 feet above the ship.

At "Charlie time", the time briefed for return to the ship, I entered the "slot". Carrier circuits are flown differently from airfield circuits. Pilots join by flying down the starboard side of the ship at 400 feet, announcing their position by calling, 'In the slot,' over the radio. One flies ahead of the ship before "breaking" (turning) left onto the downwind leg. This leg is exactly opposite to the ship's heading. Rolling out downwind, the pilot reduces speed, completes his landing vital actions and, when abeam the ship's superstructure, calls 'Downwind, four greens.' Three green lights indicate that the undercarriage is down and locked. The fourth light indicates that the arrestor hook has been lowered.

On an airfield circuit, pilots allow the airspeed to decrease gently until they have rolled out on final approach; adjusting the power holds the selected touchdown speed. As this is an extremely dangerous method of attempting to land on a ship, deck-landings require a different technique. Downwind, the pilot sets his aircraft up by selecting wheels, hook and flaps, and flies at his touchdown speed. This places the aircraft in a nose-up, high drag attitude, which requires high engine power to maintain.

On land, a pilot flies downwind until the aircraft reaches a position where the runway threshold is 45° behind the wingtip, before commencing his turn onto final approach. When downwind at sea, the landing strip is moving in the opposite direction at nearly 30 knots, so the final turn is started abeam of the ship. By completion of the turn, the carrier will have moved forward sufficiently for the pilot to complete his approach safely.

During this turn the pilot maintains 400 feet until he crosses the ship's wake. The landing heading differs from the ship's heading by approximately 10° of the angled deck. After crossing the wake, the pilot rolls out on the extended centreline of the deck. At this time, he looks into the mirror and calls, 'On the meat-ball,' as soon as he picks up the yellow circle of light. After small adjustments to engine power and aircraft attitude, he flies his aircraft down the final approach path.

Stretched across the deck at ten metre intervals are four arrestor wires. These wires, labelled No 1 to 4, are positioned opposite the mirror in the aircraft touchdown zone. They rise about five centimetres above the deck to allow the aircraft's deck hook to "grab" the cable easily. Number three wire is the target wire, positioned as it is above the fulcrum of the ship. This is the centre point about which the ship pitches and rolls, and is therefore the steadiest position onboard.

Catching number one wire, the one closest to the stern of the ship, is seriously frowned upon. It brings the touchdown point closer to the round-down, the curved edge of the deck above the stern. At the extreme end of the ship's pitching arm, the round-down moves 12 feet either side of the level datum, even on a calm day. This 24 feet of deck movement can damage a pilot's ego and aircraft undercarriage oleos (legs). In later years, I flew Sea Vixens from HMS *Ark Royal* and the maintenance personnel referred to one of our pilots as 'The minister without port oleo.' He had developed a tendency to land short and had damaged quite a few aircraft.

So there I was, 400 feet above the sea, 350 knots in the "slot", ready for my first deck-landing attempt. It was a beautiful day, the sea was calm, and HMS *Centaur* was steaming into 15 knots of natural wind. Ahead of the ship, I broke, turned downwind, and completed all my checks. However, on this occasion I did not lower my hook. I knew to fly three or four dummy deck landings before the authorities would order me to lower my arrestor hook. They wanted to watch my approaches and touchdowns, to ensure I could competently arrive onboard. (Naval aircraft do not land—they arrive!)

Apart from my nerves, I found the circuit and approach easier to fly than on an airfield. Over the sea there is no turbulence, as experienced when landing at an airfield. Therefore, exact landing speeds can be accurately maintained. The ship, heading directly into the prevailing wind, eliminated crosswinds. The entire circuit and approach was flown in silky, smooth conditions. My touchdowns must have been satisfactory; I had been quick to reapply power to bounce back into the air. The authorities condescended to allow me to land.

Flying downwind after my third dummy landing, I received orders to lower my hook. I selected the hook and felt the adrenaline shoot through my body as I called, for the first time, 'Four greens.' My approach was good, the speed was correct, and I was on centreline as my Venom crossed the round-down. The impact with the deck was solid, as on the previous dummy landings, but my aircraft did not stop. Forgetting the lessons that had been drummed into me, I had flared very slightly for the touchdown. My hook passed inches above the wires and I had "bolted" (the ignominious term used to describe a missed landing). What a start to my chosen career! Back into the air, another circuit, and finally I arrived safely onboard, courtesy of three wire.

In today's parlance, an arrested landing is "something else". Everybody warns you beforehand, to "strap in tightly" before you launch. I had done so before my flight, or so I thought! As the hook catches the wire, the aircraft arrives at a sudden stop, decelerating from 120 knots to zero in two seconds. Everything in the cockpit, not adequately strapped down, continues forward until the aircraft stops. I discovered my hand, holding the throttle, had moved forward into the full power position. My aircraft, successfully stopped by the arrestor wire, was straining to break free under maximum engine power. My legs had left the rudder pedals and were finally located up under the instrument panel. My right hand, the one holding the stick, had shot forward to the full extremity of the control column movement. Fortunately, this opened up a space for my head, which had ended up almost in my lap.

After a deep breath I reassembled all that belonged to me, reduced power, raised the deck-hook, and started to taxi out of the landing area. This is also a test of coordination. Once the deck-hook rises, applied power starts the aircraft rolling forward. One must select flaps up and, once housed, move the wing-locking lever. The wings are folded by moving another lever.

In the Sea Venom, designed many years before the invention of the word ergonomics, two extremely stiff and hard to move levers were positioned behind the pilot on the rear wall of the cockpit. Moving them, while firmly strapped into the ejection seat, required the strength of Tarzan and the deformity of Quasimodo. Venom pilots were easily identifiable by the permanent bruising and swelling of their left hands.

On subsequent flights, crew cooperation relieved the problem. On touchdown, as the hook caught the wire, Nick would release my right-hand shoulder buckles, allowing my body to twist so that I could more easily reach and operate the offending levers. This procedure was necessary, because after that first arrested landing, I made certain I was firmly strapped in before each flight. Fortunately, the ship's cycle permitted jet flights of only one hour and 20 minutes. Any longer and gangrene would have set in—so tightly were my straps pulled up!

We soon settled down to life on a carrier and in an operational squadron. We practised interceptions at high, medium, and low level.

We fired rockets and 20mm cannons at weapon ranges ashore, and at the "splash target" towed behind the carrier. A 600-metre cable was towed astern with a wooden latticework sled attached to it; underneath this were two metal scoops. Any speed above ten knots caused water to rush through the scoops and throw up a well-defined splash. This splash was the aiming point for aircraft weaponry practice.

Flying took place in a rectangular circuit around the splash and the carrier. Aircraft would attack from "Red 45". The ship's starboard, or right-hand side, was designated green, while the port side was red. "Red 45" indicated that aircraft would attack from 45° left of the ship's heading. A smaller ship, or helicopter, would position itself exactly on the splash target's left-hand side. As the released weapon hit the sea, it too would throw up a splash. Bearings taken from the carrier, and the accompanying ship/helicopter, would then be plotted on a chart to measure the miss-distance of the weapon from the splash target and this information would be passed by radio to the pilot. Good results were usually the order of the day. Pilots realized that their efforts were in full view of the ship's company and therefore their concentration was excellent.

Flying ceased early in July when the ship commenced passage through the Skagerrak (between Norway and Denmark), through the narrow Kattegat (separating Denmark from Sweden), and then into the Baltic Sea. This narrow and congested sea was unsuitable for flying, so aircrews now had time to mentally prepare themselves for the visit to Stockholm.

These were the days of the cold war between Western and Eastern ideologies. Rounding the southern coast of Sweden, a Russian destroyer was waiting for us to pass. It had slipped in under the round-down to watch *Centaur* as she ploughed her way northwards. Ten miles further on, a West German Navy FPB (Fast Patrol Boat) was waiting and she slipped in close astern of the Russian vessel. From line astern, the Russians watched the British, and the Germans watched the Russians. Thank goodness those silly, dangerous days have disappeared along with the Berlin Wall.

Jolly Jack, the British sailor, is by nature a jovial cove and, as we were not flying, almost the entire ship's company visited the round-down to have a gander at their Ruskie counterparts. The difference in political systems was immediately apparent. Jack waved and shouted ribald greetings at the Russian sailors manning the destroyer's forecastle. Jackski never moved a muscle. No return waves, no shouts, and no gestures of any kind—the political commissar must have been amongst them. However, I did notice one of their sailors, standing alone half way back along the superstructure. He would look casually backwards and forwards and when certain none of his shipmates could see him, he would wave quickly. I am sure their men were no different from ours, but it was a sorry indictment of the Communist system.

Entrance to Stockholm was via a narrow, twisting fjord, which must have been a nightmare for the ship's navigator. An aircraft carrier is an enormous vessel to manoeuvre in restricted waterways. As onlookers, we found it to be a terrific passage. It was summer and Scandinavians, enjoying their vacation, occupied each of the hundreds of little islands. In the 1960s, the Nordic countries, especially Sweden, were world leaders in the sexual revolution. From dozens of islands, sun worshippers waved at the ship as we passed. It was almost impossible to get a turn looking through the ship's powerful binoculars, but it was worth waiting for. Swedes sunbathe in the nude—what an appetizer for what turned out to be a good run ashore!

By the end of July, we had disembarked to our home base at Yeovilton and flying continued at the rate of nearly 40 hours per month. When appointed to our frontline squadrons earlier in the year, I had hoped to go to the brand new Sea Vixen training unit. This derivative of the DH-110, which had disintegrated during a high-speed flypast at Farnborough a few years before, was now entering service. Instead of the newest squadron, I was posted to 891 Squadron, the last Sea Venom unit in the navy. To this day I am grateful to their Lordships for their decision. While we were rapidly building operational flying experience, the Sea Vixen crews were struggling along at seven or eight hours per month. Teething troubles always accompany the introduction of new aircraft to service, as I was to experience nearly 20 years later.

The badge of 891 Squadron aptly depicted our status quo. During his famous Kontiki expedition, Thor Heyderdhal tried to conquer the Pacific Ocean sailing on a raft made of straw. His renowned Kontiki mask, above a symbolized sea, was the central theme of 891's crest. The analogy was self-evident. In this modern era of supersonic jets, 891 was still bumbling along in an aircraft with a cockpit built out of balsa wood!

Late in September, 891 Squadron flew across the North Sea to Stavanger in Norway to refuel, before continuing northwards to Bodö.

This Norwegian Air Force Base, situated inside the Arctic Circle, had been Gary Powers' destination during his ill-fated U-2 reconnaissance flight. As a result of negative publicity during his subsequent trial in Russia, the Americans had been expelled from Norway. The town's citizens, therefore, welcomed our arrival, which livened up their existence.

Nick and I arrived a day after the rest of the squadron. Our route from Yeovilton had taken us over The Wash, between Norfolk and Lincolnshire, before starting us on the long leg over the North Sea. An interesting physiological phenomenon affects one's ears whenever the coastline is crossed in a single-engined aircraft. We had taken-off in pairs, with the briefing that the aircraft must stick together for safety reasons. Our leader, one of the experienced crews, suddenly developed engine problems as we crossed The Wash. Obeying the briefing, we landed together at RAF Acklington. He told us his engine was 'making funny noises' so he would continue in our aircraft—and he did!

In the epilogue to his book *Who won the Battle of Britain*, Wing Commander HR "Dizzy" Allen writes at length about Gremlins. He explains that these creatures only make their appearance when pilots are in a tight position and leave the aircraft when the dangerous period is over. He included the following poem, perfectly describing the situation as experienced by Spitfire pilots flying photo-reconnaissance sorties. These highly dangerous missions were flown alone, in unarmed, single-engined aircraft, over hundreds of miles of sea, or German territory, by pilots from photo-reconnaissance units (P.R.U).

When you're seven miles up in the heavens
And that's a hell of a lonely spot,
And it's 50 degrees below zero,
Which isn't exactly hot,
When you're frozen blue like your Spitfire,
And you're scared a Mosquito pink,
When you're thousands of miles from nowhere,
And there's nothing below you but the drink-
It's then that you'll see the gremlins,
Green and gamboge and gold,
Male and female and neuter,
Gremlins both young and old.

White ones'll wiggle your wing-tips,
Male ones'll muddle your maps,
Green ones'll guzzle your glycol,
Females will flutter your flaps,
Pink ones will perch on your perspex,
And dance pirouettes on your prop.
There's one spherical middle-aged gremlin
Who spins on your stick like a top
This is the song on the gremlins
As sung by the P.R.U.
Pretty ruddy unlikely to many,
But fact none the less to the few.

The following morning a test pilot arrived from Yeovilton. He pushed a broom handle up the jet-pipe and rotated the engine. After listening intently, he announced that he could not hear any "funny noises", so we could continue if we chose to. Of course we wanted to so without further ado, Nick and I climbed into the aircraft and headed out over the sea. Perhaps, being "sprogs" our ears were not finely tuned and our flight to Sola, the airfield at Stavanger, was uneventful. The Gremlins had obviously left the aircraft.

While in the tower, filing our flight plan to Bodö, we met a Canadian Air Force crew flying a CF-100 Mk5, the Canadian built all-weather Interceptor. They were happy to show us their brand new, twin-engined aircraft, then politely deigned to have a reciprocal look at our much older, much smaller, Sea Venom. The CF-100 had aircraft controls and instrumentation neatly separated from the radar and navigation equipment, arranged in the rear cockpit. In our aeroplane, the same amount of equipment was crammed into one small cockpit. The Canadian pilot, slightly insensitively, I thought, exclaimed 'Holy mackerel, it looks as if someone has taken two handfuls of instruments, thrown them into the cockpit and screwed them into position where they landed!'

Shortly after take-off sunset occurred, and we were soon flying in darkness towards the Arctic Circle. However, the Norwegians had good ground control radar to keep track of us and an hour later they fed us into a radar guided GCA (Ground Controlled Approach). I was a little perturbed when I received a 25° heading change halfway down the approach, but I relaxed on rolling-out on the new heading when I saw runway lights ahead.

The following day, in daylight I understood the necessity for the large heading change on approach. Bodö Airfield is on the edge of a steep-sided, 7 000-foot high fjord. The only approach is from the sea and the controllers have to "thread the needle" and steer aircraft around the high granite fjord walls.

The job of 891 and the Norwegian F86 Sabre-D squadrons was to act as Russian aggressors and carry out attacks on a large NATO fleet operating in the Norwegian Sea, outside the Lofoten Islands. Day flying was fun; beautiful, snow covered mountains, dramatic fjords, and generally, the late autumn weather was pleasant. Flying low-level, we would dash through the Lofoten archipelago and strike the fleet or engage fleet fighters, before returning to land.

However, night flying was a challenge. Our aircraft were not equipped to carry out night strikes, so we were tasked to simulate Russian TU-16 Badgers and TU-95 Bears. We would approach at medium or high altitude and overfly the fleet, before turning back towards Bodö. For safety reasons we had to fly in pairs. The second aircraft would raise the alarm to one of the pair in case of an emergency. We knew that inside the Arctic Circle ejection over the sea at night would be fatal, so flights had their fair share of tension. We would fly the entire sortie in close formation, including take-off and landings. Having completed the all-weather course, this was not a problem. However, geographical position and climatic conditions resulted in a phenomenon that caused us much anxiety.

At nearly 70° north, the *Aurora Borealis*, better known as the Northern Lights, were incredible, particularly when seen from high altitude. Pastel-shaded, spectral beams would illuminate the entire night sky. The greens, blues, and yellows mingled as the beams moved eerily, creating a truly beautiful, spectacular sight—provided your feet were anchored firmly on the ground. In the air, the sensation was appalling. Flying in formation requires total concentration. When the entire sky appears to move around your aircraft, vertigo, the pilot's enemy, is easily induced. Coupled with this continual movement is the false horizon, which appears 20° above the earth's horizon. Disorientation was so severe that a number of aircrew were physically ill when they climbed out of their cockpits.

On completion of the exercise, one of the NATO submarines failed to make contact with Fleet Headquarters. A sea and air search began, with Nick and I flying wingmen to another Sea Venom tasked to search the Vest fjorden. This 100-kilometre long fjord, on the southern side of the

Lofoten archipelago, extends north-eastwards to the town of Narvik. It was a beautiful, bright, sunny day as we flew slowly either side of this majestic fjord. I suppose we did look for the submarine, but what I vividly remember is the grandeur of the scenery. The submarine had suffered radio problems, but she was otherwise safe and sound.

Technology was fast replacing "seat-of-the-pants" flying. One of the new inventions was fitted, for trial purposes, into two of our Venoms. All pilots had the opportunity to try the new "kit". A consolidated report arose based on our responses. The new instrument was an AOA (angle-of-attack) indicator. The briefing explained that the instrument could accurately indicate the correct aircraft attitude for landing, perform maximum rate turns, and show the pilot how close he was to stalling the aircraft.

Unfortunately, the report received from us was not terribly complimentary. We found that during the tight turn onto finals of a deck landing the indicator showed we were close to the stall. Therefore, we tended to ignore the indication and continue flying in the fashion we had become accustomed to. There are none so blind as those who do not want to see! This instrument, fitted in the heavier, faster and newer fighters, became indispensable.

I was delighted to see my name in the end-of-year appointment list—an initial posting to Lossiemouth for "Swept-wing" conversion course, and then back to 766 Squadron at Yeovilton, this time for the Sea Vixen conversion course. I had flown and learnt a great deal on 891, while serving under Lieutenant Commander Mickey Brown, the best commander of my entire military career.

Unfortunately, Mickey did not progress to Flag rank. His own misdemeanours as a junior pilot had seen to that. Flying Sea Hawks from a carrier, sailing through the Red Sea, Mickey and his wingman performed a beat-up down the main street of a city in the desert. Mickey should have guessed, by the number of minarets and mosques, that Mecca was not the place to buzz! The Royal Navy tends to hold things like that against one.

During my tour on 891 Squadron, we followed orders to exercise with the fleet in the Western Approaches to the channel, for a period of ten days. On completion of the exercise, HMS *Belfast*, the cruiser now anchored in the River Thames, returned to Portsmouth Harbour. As flagship, she presented a splendid sight; her decks lined with sailors and officers in their No1 uniforms. A sight to make the citizens of the British Isles proud.

Mickey, leading eight Sea Venoms, decided to add to the spectacle. Calling us into close formation, he let down in a wide, descending arc and approached Belfast from astern to pass directly over the ship at 200 feet. We all knew that his "oppo" (big friend in naval slang) was an officer on the ship and we thought this was a nice gesture. However, as we approached the ship's stern Mickey's voice came over the radio: 'Standby to jettison.'

The Sea Venom was equipped with wing-tip fuel tanks, each one containing 75 gallons of aviation paraffin. One hundred yards before the ship he ordered 'Jettison, Go' and all eight aircraft dumped their fuel. It must have looked impressive from the shore as the *Belfast* disappeared into a mist of paraffin. However, from the ship it must have been quite the opposite of impressive. We gathered this from the signal of protest, which was waiting for Mickey when we landed back at Yeovilton. These flashes of inspiration presumably cost Mickey his brass hat.

As a commander, he was magnificent. Young pilots are always in trouble of one sort or another. Breaking flying regulations, usually by illegal low flying, was common practice if we thought that we could get away with it. If reported, we would end up in front of Mickey. No shouting or tantrums. He would look at you and in a gentle voice explain how, by your childish actions, you had disappointed him. This was enough punishment, as we all idolized the man. From that point onwards he would fight your battles for you. He would not allow commanders, captains, or even admirals to penalize us further. A number of our careers progressed purely because of his timely intervention.

By his example, Mickey taught us how to extract every ounce of enjoyment out of our chosen career. He made 891 Squadron the unit all of us wanted to serve in. A military flying career calls for innumerable sacrifices, and it can be a tough way of earning a living. Mickey Brown showed us how to enjoy it all. We would have followed him anywhere. What more could you ask of a leader?

Chapter 7

Hunter/Sea Vixen Conversion

January is not the ideal month to spend in the north of Scotland, but the two weeks I spent at RNAS Lossiemouth in January 1961 were wonderful. In the first ten days I flew 16 sorties, completing the Hunter Swept-wing Conversion Course and obtaining my instrument flying rating.

In those days, pilots needed to learn the difference between flying straight and swept-winged aircraft. By sweeping a wing, the chord length increases, decreasing drag and allowing higher performance. The Hunter, while not a fully supersonic aircraft, could penetrate the sound barrier in the transonic zone, usually between Mach 0.9 to 1.1. Through this speed belt, fundamental changes to the airflow around the aircraft occur, and on a swept wing the centre of pressure or lift can move rapidly backwards or forwards. This movement of lift causes handling variations, which the pilot must understand if he is to extract maximum performance while not overstressing the aircraft.

Ernest Hemingway wrote:

You love a lot of things if you live around them. But there isn't any woman and there isn't any horse, not any before nor any after, that is as lovely as a great airplane. Any men who love them are faithful to them even though they leave them for others. Man has one virginity to lose in fighters, and if it is a lovely airplane he loses it to, there is where his heart will forever be.

That cold January in Scotland, I lost my heart to the Hunter.

I consider myself very fortunate to have completed two further tours giving weaponry instruction on the Hunter. Of the 34 different marks of aircraft I have flown, the Hunter is the one I know I could still get in and fly. The navy Hunters were all fitted with cartridge starters. After strapping in, the pilot checked: LP Cock-ON, Gangbar-UP (pulls on all necessary switches), HP Cock-ON, Press starter button. With a roar the engine would spin into life. As hydraulic pressures built up, two switches under the cockpit combing on the port side were raised, turning the ailerons and elevators into hydraulically power-assisted controls. A quick TAFFIOHHH check while taxiing out and the pilot was ready to fly.

After a slight tail-wag while accelerating on the runway, the aircraft became the perfect flying machine in the air. Balance between the servo-assisted controls was ideal; the automatic feel device allowed just the right stick pressures. The rate of roll, although not as high as today's fighters, was still quick. Perhaps the best feature in the cockpit was the nifty little flap lever, positioned just ahead of the throttle. The flap quadrant had six or seven little notches, allowing variations in flap settings to be selected. One notch of flap selected during aerobatics removed buffet and increased lift, giving the pilot perfect control. The superb flying displays put on in the 50s and 60s by RAF Hunter squadrons were striking evidence of this controllability. Who can forget the sight of 111 Squadron flying multi-aircraft loops during the Farnborough Air Show?

But it was during air combat that the flap selection system was superb. When both pilots were flying using maximum turning capabilities it was usually extremely difficult to hold the sighting pipper on the target. By "milking" the flap (lowering or raising a notch at a time), extra lift and increased turn could be achieved, often resulting in a "kill".

Another brilliant feature of the aircraft was the soundproofing of the cockpit, especially in the two-seater version. It was so quiet that all communications, the key to successful fighting, could be perfectly heard. Another favourite aircraft of mine, the McDonnell F4 Phantom, was a notable comparison. The noise in the Phantom "office" was almost unbearable, pushing the aircraft down my favourite list.

Having a few days to spare before trekking southwards again, I decided to try my luck at 736 Squadron, the Sea Hawk training unit. Squadron Commander Jock Mansais, a truly professional aviator, raised me from my knees as I begged a chance to fly, tossed me the Sea Hawk handbook and said that if I could pass the technical quiz I could fly the aeroplane. Two days later I flew three wonderful sorties. The aircraft was so forgiving that after landing from the third flight, I felt that I had performed all that could be achieved in a general flying sortie. Unfortunately, the following day I had to drive back to Yeovilton. I am convinced that a few more sorties would have moved the Sea Hawk almost to the top of my favourite list.

Returning to RNAS Yeovilton, I joined up with Nick Child for our second course on 766 Squadron. It was a time of transformation in the Fleet Air Arm with the introduction of large, twin-engined fighters. The Scimitar replaced the Sea Hawk at RNAS Lossiemouth, while the Sea Vixen took over the all-weather role from the Sea Venom at RNAS Yeovilton. New generation technology substantially increased operational capabilities as the aircraft were supersonic and had a greater range and weapon carrying ability. This provided exciting prospects for the aircrew, because these bigger and faster aircraft would still have to operate off the same size aircraft carriers!

The Vixen was a novel aircraft. Perhaps its most distinguishing feature was the typical De Havilland double-boom tail. The designers had cleverly incorporated the crew accommodation within a combined wing and fuselage shape, which became one large lift-producing surface. This, coupled with the 23 000 pounds static thrust of the two Rolls-Royce Avon engines, produced an aircraft that could *really* fly.

Most of our air interception sorties were flown at 40 000 feet and above, where most other contemporary fighters needed full afterburner just to stay in the air. The only aircraft that out turned me at 45 000 feet was, strangely enough, a bomber. Nick had picked up a blip on his radar and sent me on a course to intercept whatever it was. "It", turned out to be an Avro Vulcan test-bed, flying out of Filton Airfield near Bristol. This particular aircraft was powered by four 16 000 lbst Olympus engines embedded in the fuselage and just like the Vixen the entire shape was a lift-producing body.

I called 'Tallyho' to Nick, indicating I had the target in sight and he could cease his commentary. Nick had placed us nicely at the Vulcan's four o'clock position, two miles away, turning in astern for a "kill". Because it was a "test-bed", the Vulcan pilot, under radar control, knew of our approach. Probably an old fighter pilot himself he threw the huge bomber into a steep bank and turned in towards us. 'Not a problem,' I thought, knowing the Vixen flew well in the rarefied air at that altitude. I tightened my turn to follow the bomber.

To my amazement the Vulcan's turn became tighter and tighter and the bomber started to climb. I could not hold the tight turn or climb, and overshot badly, with my Vixen starting to buffet at the onset of a stall. I watched dumbfounded as the Vulcan continued spiralling upwards too embarrassed to tell Nick a bomber had out-flown us. Only when the Vulcan levelled its wings did I discover the answer. Slung underneath the fuselage was a fifth engine, one of the 50 000 lbst motors, which were eventually fitted into the supersonic Concorde. I can still imagine the test pilot chuckling over my missed intercept.

Another novel feature of the Vixen was the arrangement for the crew. The pilot was displaced off-centre to the left. This was the conventional arrangement in most aircraft; however, the De Havilland designers did not stop there. To conform to the overall streamlining of the aircraft the left-hand cockpit rail was lower than the right-hand rail, producing an illusory feeling of vertigo—most pilots are happiest when their aircraft feels level!

Most cockpit windscreens have clear glass directly in front of the pilot—not so the Vixen. To reduce drag, the Vixen cockpit had two glass screens meeting in a vee directly ahead of the pilot's eyes. The theory was that the optical qualities of the glass would give unhindered vision directly ahead, and someone in Admiralty, who did not have to fly the aircraft, accepted this theory! The sole reason for having fighters is to be able to deliver weapons. Weapon aiming is done through a sight positioned immediately in front of the pilot's eyes. In the Vixen, this sight was directly behind a three centimetre structural beam holding the front glass screens together—far from ideal.

The instrument flying panel was markedly different from earlier aircraft. Replacing the old wind-driven instruments was a MRG (Master Reference Gyro). This all-singing, all-dancing, gyro-stabilized, magic black box fed the entire instrument panel. Lovely when it worked, but a sheer nightmare when it failed, as it did from time to time.

One of its advantages was that the AH (artificial horizon) was "untoppleable". Provided it was daytime, complete looping manoeuvres could be flown by referring only to this instrument. At night, this type of manoeuvre, used during LABS (Low Altitude Bombing System) deliveries, was positively dangerous. The upper half of the AH was painted a light colour to simulate the sky. At night, under cockpit lighting, this colour appeared white. The instrument became progressively whiter as the aircraft nose rose. In the vertical position the entire instrument face became white, and all references to the horizon vanished. This vertigo-inducer was the probable cause of a number of unexplained night accidents.

Another interesting feature of the Vixen "office" was the vertical switch panel, under the combing on the pilot's right-hand side. This difficult-to-see panel, contained 40 switches; all, except one, were selected up for ON and down for OFF.

Cruising on autopilot at 40 000 feet, on a lovely day over Somerset, Mike McCookweir glanced into his cockpit. Sure enough, all the switches were in the up position, except one, which was in neutral—neither up nor down. Thinking this was odd, he put the switch in the up position, like all the rest. To his horror, he felt a thud and glimpsed his Firestreak guided missile falling away from the aircraft's wing. Realizing he had made a blunder, he pushed the switch into the down position to turn it off. A double thud emanated as both his underwing drop tanks went plummeting down to earth. This odd switch happened to be the pylon eject switch.

Another innovation peculiar to the Sea Vixen was the housing for the observer. He did not have a cockpit as in normal aircraft; he was "housed" within the fuselage, in what came to be known as the "coalhole". A hatch on the upper fuselage allowed him to enter his domain and sink down into the very bowels of the fighter. Closing the hatch effectively sealed those poor unfortunate men from the rest of the world. The designers, in a moment of rare consideration, did fit a small side window to the coalhole. However, when firmly strapped in for carrier operations, the observer could not take advantage of this innovation, because he could not crane his neck far enough forward.

There was an opening in the bulkhead separating the crewmembers. Looking down from my perch in the cockpit, I could see Nick's left hand and leg. He, being lower, could see on his left the instrument panel and my hands and legs. All communications were by means of an intercom system. I have read about the Spanish inquisition and the activities of the infamous KGB but, in my estimation, nothing comes close to the horrors of the coalhole.

A fighter spends a large portion of each sortie in unusual attitudes brought on by high "G" forces, inverted flight, and rapid rates of role. In the coalhole, without reference to the horizon, vertigo and spatial disorientation were constant companions. Commentary by the pilot, explaining what he was doing, helped a little, but it was still uncomfortable in the extreme and that was the good part of the flight!

The ultimate experience was the deck landing. The observer relied completely on the skill of the pilot to arrive on board safely. Being blind to the outside world, he could only imagine what was happening, until the force of deceleration relieved him when the deck-hook caught the arrestor wire. Sea Vixen observers were brave men who experienced more moments of sheer terror than any other group of men, past or present. An indication of how they felt can be gauged by the poems written in 890 Squadron's lines book, one of which I've repeated below.

The Observer's Lament
Under a darkened metal hatch,
The poor Observer sits
Dreaming of such wondrous things,
As soft and downy pits:
But not for him, this peace and bliss
Of sleeping in the dark.
'Get airborne, climb to angels',
In the night so grim and stark.

Sweating in his "coal-hole" there
What's that frantic noise?
It's the pilot checking out,
And trying to keep his poise.
The green wands down, it's too late now,
He prays with all his might,
That oneday, say, in ten years time,
He'll see the bloody light.

But wait, what's this, we're airborne,
And splitting for the run.
All signs of stress have vanished,
The sortie's just begun:
His steely eyes sort out the blips,
Contact! … Judy, he calls,
The tension mounts, they're closing in,
Oh! Hell! He's made a balls.

An hours' gone by, his fears return,
He waits that voice in dread,

'Your marshal time is minutes five,
Position … Overhead'.
It's Jim, it's George, he tries to think,
They're famous for their deeds,
You're high, you're low, you're on the sight,
Just watch those falling speeds.

One thirty-five, one thirty-three,
The needles dropping fast,
The "Blue" warns off, the "RAT" goes out,
The round-down flashes past;
All smiles, all grins, he smokes a fag,
He takes the pilot's ribbing
And with this thought he ends the day
'What a way to earn a living'.

The last verse refers to the air speed. The job of the observer on finals was to keep calling the speed, so the pilot could keep an eye on the fast approaching deck. The datum, or touchdown speed, was worked out for each landing, by calculating the aircraft's weight and the wind speed expected over the deck. Experienced pilots landed by the tone of the repeated calls, not necessarily the exact call. If the pitch of the observer's voice started climbing the vocal scale, it was obvious that speed was falling fast and calling for an addition of power to stop the falling needle.

To cater for redundancy, the Vixen had four hydraulic systems, known as the red, green, blue and yellow. The first two were the main and emergency systems operating the undercarriage, flaps, and deck-hook. The blue and yellow did the same for the flying control surfaces. On approach, some pilots tended to "stir the pot" so rapidly, pressure in the blue system would decrease until the low pressure warning light illuminated and the alarm bells started to ring. The observer, sitting with his hand clasping the RAT (Ram Air Turbine) handle, would react by pulling the lever upwards. This action would open a panel between the engines on the upper rear fuselage surface, from which an arm would spring. Attached to this arm was a propeller, which, when rotated by the wind flow, generated additional hydraulic pressure to supplement that being used by the pilots stirring of the controls.

I must mention one other idiosyncrasy built into the Vixen. In most aircraft, an audio warning indicated emergencies. The illumination of the warning panel followed to indicate the nature of the problem. Not wanting the aircrew to miss any oddity, the Vixen designers added a system of "attention-getters". Either side of the gunsight, directly in the pilot's line of vision, were large, pillar-box red flashing lights. Illumination was accompanied by an audio warning, resembling the clanging of a fire-brigade bell in tone and decibel value. Believe me, these "attention-getters" worked as intended. The only problem was that they produced an adrenaline "high", which normally took a fortnight to dissipate and nearer a month if it had been a night emergency!

Perhaps the pièce de résistance of all Vixen design abnormalities was the fitting of the in-flight refuelling probe. All air-to-air refuelling requires practise and expertise. Most fighters are fitted with refuelling probes somewhere on the nose of the aircraft, allowing the pilot to see the probe as he tries to insert it into the refuelling basket. Not the Vixen designers! Some bright engineer fitted the probe halfway down the leading edge of the port wing. Being a swept-wing, this placed the point of the probe 90° to the left of the pilot. Having to formate very closely with the tanker aircraft directly ahead, made things extraordinarily difficult.

Our squadron's Sea Vixens were fitted with the new system for service trials. Because it was new the squadron boss and senior pilot flew the first refuelling sortie; the rest of us waited eagerly for their feedback. We did not have long to wait; the boss exploded out of his cockpit and shuntered his way back to the crew room. 'Bloody impossible,' and 'The buggers must be mad,' were comments that flowed back and forth between him and the senior pilot. We gathered that neither man had successfully plugged.

The temperature was so heated it became obvious that they would not try again. In fact they inferred that we could attempt it if we liked, but it was certain to be another wasted sortie. I jumped at the opportunity and went out to fly, but not before adding some reference marks on the tanker aircraft. I had listened intently to the debrief of the problems experienced by the senior pilots, one of which was how to line-up the offset probe with the basket. After measuring the distance from probe tip to the beam in the centre of the cockpit windscreen, I then marked the same distance from the tanker hose, along the trailing edge of the tanker wing. If I now kept the centre of my windscreen lined up with the mark on the tanker's wing, I must be the correct distance out.

The boss had indicated that by keeping the trailing edge of the tanker's wing exactly equidistant between the upper and lower wing surfaces, then the probe tip would be level with the centre of the basket. Armed with this knowledge, I trailed the tanker up to 10 000 feet. He streamed the hose and I took up position behind his aircraft. Keeping my two visual aids centred, I allowed the Vixen to move towards the tanker. I felt a bump as the probe contacted the basket, and then I pushed the hose until it rewound into its housing. Once stabilized behind the tanker, I glanced out to the left and there, as advertised, was the probe nicely inserted into the basket. I withdrew gently and tried twice more, each time with the same satisfying result.

After the third "plug" the tanker pilot asked me if I would like to try again at 20 000 feet. Feeling cocky, as only young pilots can, I agreed and we climbed. Once stabilized, I repeated the procedure. I felt the now customary bump, pushed the hose in the required distance, and took time to think vainly, 'Not bad, Dicky!'

While in formation, I developed an uneasy sensation, brought about by the fact that the hose seemed to be hanging at a much lower angle than before. Twisting my head, I followed the line of the hose down to the basket. To my horror I saw the probe tip sitting loud and clear above the hose. I had come in slightly high. The basket had knocked the glass nose completely off the Firestreak guided missile, and now hung under the port wing filling the missile with fuel. It was with tail between my legs that I had to account for the damaged missile after landing. The upshot was that the practice missile was carried under the starboard wing from then onwards.

The last major difference between the Venom and the Vixen was its size. With a wingspan of 50 feet and a maximum all-up weight of 35 000 lb, it was two and a half times heavier than the Venom. Similarly, the Vickers Supermarine Scimitar dwarfed the Sea Hawk. Their Lordships had introduced these much larger fighters while neglecting to increase the size of the flight-decks from which we had to operate. This was to be a major factor in the years that lay ahead. This problem was exacerbated a few years later, when the Westland Wessex replaced the Sikorsky Whirlwind helicopters.

The flight-deck and hangar of an aircraft carrier are busy, crowded areas. The advent of these large aircraft significantly increased the difficulties of operating them in the limited space available. The nose of the Vixen was hinged to allow the aircraft to fit onto the aircraft lift between hangar and deck. The critical radar wave-guide, which fed information from the scanner to the observer's scope, was therefore disturbed on every opening of the nose, downgrading radar performance.

The Scimitar had an even greater problem. To launch successfully from the steam catapults, this aircraft had to mechanically rotate to achieve a suitable flying attitude, before the launch commenced. While being loaded onto the catapult, a short stanchion, known as the "donkey's plonk", was lowered from beneath the aircraft's tail. When the catapult shuttle moved forward to tension the aircraft, the nose wheel lifted off the deck until the donkey's plonk rested firmly on the deck. At this angle of incidence the Scimitar could be safely launched.

Fortunately, the Fleet Air Arm training system produced magnificent aircraft handlers. These men, mostly petty officers, trained to drive specialized tractors, were responsible for arranging aircraft on the deck and parking those in need of servicing in the hangar. This task required tremendous skill, particularly when the ship was rolling. The aircraft rolled easily as their tyres, pumped to 400 pounds per square inch pressure to absorb the shock of deck-landings, were so hard that very little rubber touched the deck. The tractors had to be as heavy as the aircraft to prevent a "tail-wagging-the-dog" situation from occurring.

Despite belabouring its peculiarities, I loved the Vixen. It was all wing, powerful, and a superb flying machine. Off the catapult, perhaps the most vulnerable stage of any flight, the Vixen was a beauty. Unlike the slow acceleration of the Venom, which required delicate handling of the elevator, the Vixen screamed off the front end of the ship. At night, you could haul back on the stick and know you would climb safely away from the sea. The Rolls-Royce Avon engines, strong and reliable, were a great comfort particularly as most of our flying was performed way out over the sea.

By mid-May 1961, we had flown 70 hours and completed the Vixen conversion course. Unfortunately, it brought my partnership with Nick Child to an end. I joined 892 Squadron on HMS *Victorious* as a replacement pilot. The first four and a half months of 1961 had been a wonderful period for me. My logbook records that I had flown the Sea Vixen 1, Hunter T8, Sea Venom 21, Sea Vampire 22, Sea Hawk FGA6, and a Chipmunk T10. When people mention the "good old days" in aviation, I know exactly what they mean!

Chapter 8

892 Squadron, HMS *Victorious*

I flew out from England aboard a Bristol Britannia 310, 93-seat passenger aircraft, chartered from British Eagle to fly service men and families to Singapore. It was a long flight with two refuelling stops and this fact, sealed the Britannia's fate as a viable passenger aircraft. Boeing 707s, rolling off the Seattle production lines, provided a much quicker and therefore, a more desirable alternative. Nevertheless, the Britannia provided passenger space and comfort unrivalled by the faster jets.

The first stop, Istanbul, was pleasant and provided good views of both sides of the Bosphorous Strait during take-off and landing. However, the second stop provided interest of a different kind. We landed at Karachi International Airport in mid-afternoon. The heat, as we left the air-conditioned aircraft, was appalling. Before entering the air terminal, we had to have our passports stamped. Everyone on board had British passports, except me. I produced an anathema—my green, Union of South Africa passport.

This was too much for the official. Throwing his hands in the air, he started shouting 'No, No, Bloody No' and went off to call the Sahib. This illustrious gentleman reacted in the same demonstrative manner before making his decision. The rest of the passengers could enter the terminal building, but I had to stand outside on the hot tarmac until we re-boarded the aircraft. In those 45 minutes I saw enough of Karachi to last me a lifetime and I was very glad when at last we took-off on the final leg to Singapore.

We landed after dark so I could not see the island, but as the aircraft door opened, we could smell it. In those days, Singapore was a vastly different city from the modern, antiseptic metropolis that now graces the island. It was old-world, gracious, charming, humid, bustling, unhygienic, odorous, and beautiful. For me it was a case of love at first smell. I believe that long-time residents could recognize exactly where they were in the town even when blindfolded. Each area had a distinctive smell, some good and others more suspect, but all of them creating allure and a mystery that epitomized the city.

HMS *Victorious* was alongside in the Naval Dockyard, but 892 Squadron had disembarked to RAF Tengah, on the north-western side of the 17-mile wide, diamond-shaped island. Alighting from the vehicle at the officer's mess, I experienced the unmistakable scent of Frangipani blossoms and the sight of the lovely Southern Cross constellation in the dark sky. Both sensations vividly reminded me of my life in South Africa, hence my immediate attraction to Singapore.

The following morning I was welcomed into the squadron by Lieutenant Commander Gus Gray. I replaced Captain Don K Hanna, USMC, whose two-year exchange posting had come to an end, and he had returned to America. Unlikely as it may seem, I had grown up with Don. Although American, his family had lived in Johannesburg and we had attended Rosebank Primary and Parktown Boy's High schools together. At age 16, his family moved back to America where Don later joined the Marine Corp as a pilot.

As his replacement, I naturally inherited his observer Wally Selwyn. He was an experienced, capable radar operator, who was leaving the Fleet Air Arm after 16 years service when *Victorious* returned to England in December. In the squadron, he was known as "Old Wal", in deference to his age and seniority. Our partnership ended on a high note, after a very shaky beginning.

As a sprog, I was still full of the joys of youth and my zest for flying was perhaps at its peak. After five flights, which included 39 MADDLS (Mirror Assisted Dummy Deck Landings) on the Tengah runway, we embarked on HMS *Victorious* as she left the dockyard. After four touch and go landings, I could lower the hook for an arrested landing. This time I flew the meatball onto the deck and avoided the embarrassment of another first time "bolter".

Heading out into the South China Sea, the squadron settled quickly back into operational routine. Early one morning, Wally and I were tasked for a session of radar interception exercises. Sitting on the catapult as the ship turned into wind, I realized that our climb-out vector was the reciprocal of the ship's heading. After launch, I accelerated straight ahead until the airspeed reached 450 knots, which happens very rapidly at sea level, then I hauled back on the stick to complete a half loop. Rolling wings level at the top, we were precisely on our briefed climb-out heading, which I thought was "pretty cool".

Not Old Wal—I had forgotten to inform him of my intentions! Expecting a gentle climbing turn, he was busy writing on his plotting chart with a chinagraph pencil, when I suddenly applied four "G". His hand shot across the chart leaving a long, dark trail as the pencil point was pressed into the paper. For the next two weeks he vetted my every move.

Once our strained relationship had healed, my flying returned to normal until one morning when we were pitted against Simon Idiens, the squadron air warfare instructor, in a series of low-level intercepts. The crew of an 849 Squadron Fairey Gannet AEW 3, whose on-board early warning radar was ideal for detecting low-level intruders, controlled these interceptions. We took turns at flying the laborious task of target, while the other aircraft was the attacker.

Simon, an excellent pilot, enjoyed dog-fighting, and could not resist the temptation to convert each intercept into a fight. As the attacker, Simon would flash past buffeting our aircraft with his turbulent wake. Watching him turn in for his fourth attack was the final straw. Forgetting all the promises I had made to Old Wal, I cranked the Vixen into a maximum rate turn towards Simon, surprising him and forcing him to overshoot. My advantage was short-lived when I became aware of moaning noises emanating from the intercom. Looking down into the coalhole, I saw Wally's hands and feet jerking spasmodically in time with his groans. The sudden application of "G" had caught Old Wal unawares and he had blacked out as blood had drained from his head. Releasing the "G" and assuming straight and level flight, enabled Wal to recover. His unrepeatable commentary convinced me he was going to live; although I felt my longevity would be in jeopardy once we were safely back on board. To add insult to injury, Simon barrel-rolled exuberantly around our once again straight and level aircraft.

Victorious headed for a rest and recuperation (R&R) visit to Hong Kong. Waking early on the morning of our expected arrival, I climbed the ladders to "Vulture's Roost", high up in the superstructure, to catch my first glimpse of the famous city. It was nowhere to be seen. We were in the open ocean, leaving an arrow-straight, wide wake, indicating that the ship was at full steam and we were heading south-westwards, away from Hong Kong. The news soon spread through the ship that owing to a crisis between Kuwait and Iraq we were speeding towards the Persian Gulf.

What an anti-climax for the ship's company who had been anticipating the delights of the island Colony! However, the disappointment was replaced by a sense of urgency. Iraq, traditional bullyboy of the Middle East, had threatened Kuwait. As Britain supported Kuwait, we were dispatched to the Gulf as a military deterrent. Traditionally unpredictable, the Iraq government posed a number of threats, one of which included a full-scale invasion of Kuwait. Training suddenly assumed vital importance as we exercised all our roles. Weaponry, dog-fighting, interceptions, and photo-reconnaissance became the order of the day. When not flying, we attended intelligence briefings on the Iraq ORBAT (Order of Battle). Long sessions of aircraft recognition training ensued, to enable us to recognize our potential enemies.

The ship was placed on Readiness State 1 as we sailed through the narrow Strait of Hormuz, separating the Saudi peninsula from Iran, to enter the Persian Gulf. Old salts referred to the Gulf as "the arsehole of the world" and I had often wondered why? Now I knew. In an atlas, the Gulf is reminiscent of the medical posters one sees in doctors' rooms around the world. The Gulf aptly fits the sailor's description. In a matter of minutes, the ambient temperature increased from hot to bloody hot; it was similar to entering a furnace. The flat, steel deck of the carrier absorbed the sun's rays, making life unbearable for all on board. In those days, not all the accommodation or office spaces were air-conditioned. The aircraft hangar, directly beneath the flight-deck, became like an enormous oven.

Although the Gulf averages 150 nautical miles in width, it is very shallow, making only the centre 70-mile wide strip navigable to a carrier-sized ship. When the wind blows, it always comes off the desert and increases the oppressive temperatures. A greater hazard for aircrew was the fine dust that rose into the atmosphere. This dust, often swirling up to 20 000 feet, made flying extremely dangerous. The entire sky assumed the colour of the desert. Despite the absence of clouds, visibility in the dust was severely decreased and the horizon was no longer visible. Flight had to be conducted by reference to instruments, and making a landfall for navigational purposes rivalled night deck landings for excitement. The Royal Air Force lost a Hunter during this period under those exact conditions.

As a junior pilot, I received a cabin in the 6R section of the ship. A large carrier, without portholes, can be a confusing place. Unlike a passenger liner, which has long passageways on every deck, a warship is compartmentalized. Each section of the ship can be sealed off to maintain watertight compartments, which could keep the ship afloat, after sustaining war damage. A nice safety feature to be sure, although it limits free passage inside the ship.

To alleviate the problem, numbers were allocated to all the decks, with the flight-deck being number one. Each deck below was numbered in sequence. Number six deck, below the waterline, was the last deck to house sleeping compartments. Seven deck down to 14 deck housed offices, workshops, and storage facilities. The decks in the island (the superstructure on the starboard side of the flight-deck) were numbered from +1 to +7. Only when the carrier was in dry dock could the true height and size of the ship be appreciated. The 21 decks were the equivalent of a 21-storied building, on top of which were arranged wireless masts, radar aerials, and funnels.

Each watertight compartment was labelled alphabetically, starting at the bow and working back towards the stern. My cabin, in the 6R compartment, was six decks below the flight-deck, and very close to the back of the ship; R being close to the end of the alphabet. The more senior aircrew had cabins on two deck which, unlike mine, were air-conditioned.

During the cruise, an air-conditioned cabin became available, but to the squadron's amazement, I turned it down. My next-door neighbour, a ship's engineer, had tapped the cool air supply from the nuclear weapon store and led it into his cabin. The vent to his cabin passed through mine and I had tapped his tapped supply. In addition to being pleasantly cool, my cabin was far away from that of the senior pilot's. He would pass his gash jobs to aircrew nearer at hand while I was left in peace.

HMS *Centaur* took over duties in the Gulf, allowing us to head for Mombasa for a well-earned break. In those days, before the political upheavals of Uhuru, Kenya was a delightful place—clean, safe, and charming. A special treat was a trip on the night train from Mombasa to Nairobi. With a speed probably never higher than 30mph, it chugged its way up the escarpment during the night. For two hours after sunrise it meandered through the Nairobi National Park, presenting the passengers with marvellous views of the rolling plains and animals; a complete contrast to the Persian Gulf.

After a wonderful ten days it was back to sea and the long delayed visit to Hong Kong. HMS *Hermes* had visited Hong Kong the previous year and 804 Squadron had disembarked a number of their Scimitars to the airfield at Kai Tak. On landing, their aircraft were accommodated by the resident RAF Venom squadron. However, the Colony authorities refused us permission to operate our aircraft from there.

Two of my colleagues from flying school, Sub Lieutenants Jack Smith and Maurice Hynett, had been among the Scimitar pilots from 804 Squadron. Proud of their aircraft and its performance, they must have been insufferable in the RAF officers' mess. The usual inter-service banter was liberally interspersed by comparison of the Scimitar's supersonic capability and the balsa-wood construction of the venerable Venom.

Verbal exchanges reached a climax when the RAF pilots challenged Jack and Maurice to demonstrate this much bragged about capability. Never known to refuse a dare, our two lads donned their flying suits and took to the skies. At 50 000 feet and full power, the two pilots rolled into a steep dive, aiming at the easily distinguishable runway at Kai Tak. At 10 000 feet and Mach 1.3, they started the pullout, bottoming out just above 5 000 feet.

An excited and enthusiastic audience greeted them after landing. The RAF pilots applauded and said that it had been terrific, explaining how all the windows and teacups had rattled as the distinctive double-bang swept across the airfield. All smiles, everyone headed off to the pub. However, before the first pint had been poured, the telephones started ringing.

Apparently, only the edge of the shockwave had affected Kai Tak. The epicentre had struck Victoria Island with catastrophic effects. In those days, the 20-story, glass-fronted, Shell-Mex House was the architectural pride of Hong Kong. This was no longer the case! From top to bottom, the magnificent frontage was destroyed—the glass lying in a heap in front of the entrance. Refugees from Red China had erected flimsy squatter shacks above Victoria on the sides of the well-known peak. These had been flattened by the blast. Residents of the island stood in long queues outside psychiatrists' consulting rooms seeking counselling to help overcome the trauma.

The *Hong Kong Gazette* brought out a special edition of their newspaper. Banner headlines, of a size reserved for the outbreak of a world war, declared: "Devastation". The entire front page listed details of the disaster, and this in a Colony that was accustomed to the ravages of seasonal typhoons. The main photograph on the front page was a neat head and shoulders portrait of Jack and Maurice, in uniform, with enigmatic half smiles that suggested, 'Look what we did.' In later years, after suitable retribution had been extracted, Maurice qualified as a test pilot and Jack became a training captain flying Boeing 747s with Cathay Pacific, ironically out of Kai Tak, the scene of his "crime".

Leaving Hong Kong, we headed for the Philippines to cross-operate with an American fleet. Our Scimitars, Sea Vixens, and Gannets landed on the USS *Ticonderoga*, while Douglas A4D Skyhawks, McDonnell Douglas F3A Demons, and Grumman S2F Trackers landed aboard *Victorious*.

American nomenclature is an interesting subject, especially their colourful adaptation of aircraft names. The British tend to clip names so the famous Spitfire became the "Spit", the Hurricane the "Hurri", and the Sea Vixen just the "Vixen". The Americans are far more innovative and creative. Their very nippy, delta-winged F4D Skyray, quite naturally became a "Ford". The A4 Skyhawk became the "Tinkertoy", because it was so small. The S2F Tracker, in an American drawl, became the "Stoof". Later versions of this propeller-driven aircraft were adapted to carry early-warning radar in huge radomes mounted above the fuselage. In a clever bit of tongue-twisting these aircraft became the "Stoof-with-a-roof". The Demon, probably alluding to its rather average flying performance, became the "Lead Sled".

The excellent A7 Corsair ground-attack fighter had unfortunately lost the elegance of its predecessor, the lovely F8 Crusader, so it became the "SLUF", standing for Short Little Ugly Fellow, or versions thereof. For similar reasons, the massive B52 bombers were called "Buffs". This North American trait moved across the border where Canadian fighter pilots lovingly referred to their F86 Sabres as "Swords".

The American system of aircraft designation is designed to indicate the role of the aircraft. Fighters are designated F, Attack aircraft A, and Surveillance aircraft S. The F3A is therefore a fighter. The number 3 indicates the sequence of aircraft entering service. Subsequent aircraft were the F4 Phantom, A6 Intruder, A7 Corsair, up to the more modern F15s, F16s, and F18 Hornet. The A after F3 indicates the Mark of Demon. As aircraft are improved during the production cycle, the Mark is altered to indicate the changes. The long-serving Phantom started life as an F4A, but the final Marks produced were Ks and Ms. The later Marks usually differed significantly in performance and on-board equipment from the original Mark A.

The cross-operation went well, so too the visit to the huge USN Naval Base at Subic Bay and the adjoining "City of Sin", Olongapo.

Returning to sea, the ship had an unfortunate incident. The squadron received old Etonian Ollie Sutton, as another new replacement pilot. While still inexperienced, his aircraft was marshalled up the deck onto the starboard catapult. He was flying Vixen 219, the oldest and most weather-worn aircraft on the squadron. As the previous junior pilot, I was allotted the aircraft and my name adorned the fuselage directly beneath the cockpit. Because I was not on the programme, I went up to "Goofers" to watch.

Ollie, using a good handful of power, trundled onto the catapult self-centering Caley Gear and into the automatic chocks. Distracted by the order to spread and lock his wings, he forgot to return his engines to idle. Consequently, when the chocks were lowered to tension his aircraft prior to launch, the Vixen jerked forward under its own power, with sufficient momentum to break the hold-back. This fragile locking system normally holds aircraft in place until the force of the steam catapult is great enough to free the aircraft for launch.

At the moment of crisis, Ollie was completing his take-off checklist inside the cockpit. Out of the corner of his eye, he noticed the flight-deck officer disappearing down his right-hand side and realized his aircraft was moving. Being new to the business, his first thought was that they had fired the catapult before he was ready. Slamming both throttles fully forward, he taxied off the front edge of the deck at a rate just faster than walking pace.

Watching from high up in the superstructure, I could not believe my eyes. In slow motion, my beloved 219 dropped out of sight into the path of the carrier. Fortunately, the ever-vigilant bridge staff turned the ship's head to starboard and then to port, to allow the huge vessel to curve around the point of impact. I noticed the canopy and coalhole hatch cover fly off when the crew realized they were about to ditch.

Whenever the ship was at "flying stations", the SAR (search and rescue) Whirlwind helicopter was airborne. During catapult launching it hovered alongside the port catapult for precisely this type of

738 Squadron, RNAS Brawdy, 1964. Left to right: "Dinger" Bell RAF; Colin "Boots" Walkinshaw; Bob Jones, AEO; the author; John Beard; Alan Hickling (driving); Mike Darlington; John Manley; Dia Vaughan, AEO. This 1926 Rolls-Royce was the car Al Hickling drove through the Nissan hut at RAF Linton-on-Ouse.

RNAS Brawdy Hunter Aerobatic Team, 1964.

Sea Vixen Mk1 anchored to the deck. Only the Brits could position an in-flight refuelling probe behind and below the pilot's left shoulder!

Prior to take-off from HMS *Victorious* in March 1962. The author was tasked to fly Rear-Admiral Frank Hopkins to Gibraltar. Note the admiral could wear a flying suit while the lieutenant had to wear the full immersion suit, RHIP!

Sea Vixen Mk1 flies over HMS *Victorious*. The weather was not always this perfect! (Photo courtesy of *Flight*)

766 Squadron Sea Vixens pose for the Christmas card photograph.

Close up of the underside of a Sea Vixen carrying three-inch rockets. Like all British aeroplanes, cars and motorbikes, it oozed fluid from every orifice! (Photo courtesy of *Flight*)

Balliol Term of Air Cadets. *Back row*: NA Thomson, AJ Poirrier, JGL Smith, WF Taylor, WS Hare. *Front row*: AG Harmon, NM Munro, RS Lord, IF Wilson.

Sir Charles Lambe presenting the Flying Trophy to the author at his Wings Parade.
(Photo courtesy of *The Yorkshire Post*)

As HMS *Victorious* turns into wind, the angled deck is clearly visible.

Sea Vixen FAW1 showing off the in-flight refuelling probe and the Firestreak infrared missile.

A dramatic photograph of a condensation cloud obscuring most of a low-level Sea Vixen as it flashes at high speed over the carrier.

HMS *Ark Royal* at "Flying Stations" in the notorious Bay of Biscay, famous for its rough seas!

A Supermarine Scimitar landing on HMS *Ark Royal*.

The **DIRTY OLD MAN** of Cerne Abbas, Dorset. A convenient rendezvous point for jets returning to RNAS Yeovilton. The size of the figure can be gauged by comparing the figure to the size of the two hikers in the foreground.

The admiral takes the salute as HMS *Ark Royal* and her air group arrive in Singapore.

Sea Vixen FAW1 carrying a "full-house" of underwing stores. Outboard pylons house a drop tank and a buddy-buddy refuelling pod, 2" rocket pods and Firestreak missiles.

A Sea Vixen landing-on with tail-hook extended ready to trap the arrestor wires stretched across the deck.

Accelerating down the catapult, the aircraft's offset canopy can be clearly seen. The observer's "coal-hole" is immediately to the canopies right. From wingtip to wingtip, the Sea Vixen had an almost perfect lift-producing aero-dynamic body.

emergency. It seemed to take forever for the carrier to clear the impact zone, until with relief, we could see two little heads bobbing in the wake and the chopper manoeuvring overhead to commence the pick-up.

However, the drama was not yet over. With a piercing yell, Simon Idiens who had also been in the "Goofers", dived down the ladder leading to the bridge. Simon had noticed that the ship was trailing a splash target and as the ship curved around the two in the water, the 600-metre wire was slicing ever closer to their unsuspecting heads. Always alert for every contingency, a Royal Marine was standing by on the aft end of the carrier as the "wire guard". With one hefty swing of his axe, he severed the cable, avoiding possible decapitation of the Vixen crew.

Within a few minutes, Ollie and his observer Darroch Robertson were deposited back on deck, dripping seawater but apparently unaffected by their experience. However, on closer inspection, this perception was invalid. Darroch had two of the blackest eyes imaginable. He looked as if he had spent 15 rounds in the ring with Muhammad Ali. As the Vixen sank, seawater gushed with great speed into the coalhole. Striking the cockpit floor, it had spouted upwards underneath Darroch's helmet visor and given his eyes a tremendous pummelling. Within a few days, both men were declared fit and returned to flying.

Darroch's experience, however, did have repercussions a few years later. Waking one morning at RNAS Yeovilton, after a particularly hectic weekend in London, Darroch felt listless and hung-over. Lying in bed waiting for the effects to dissipate, he noticed with shock that as he breathed only one side of his chest moved up and down. Despite his longer than normal lie in, his chest movement remained the same. He decided he required medical assistance. Rising gingerly from his bed, he stepped across his cabin and opened the door.

By coincidence, the cabin door across the passage opened at the same moment. Peter Sheppard occupied this cabin, a Fleet Air Arm character (who later became well known as the Swordfish pilot of the exhibition flight at airshows around Britain). Peter was also feeling unwell, another common Monday morning experience.

Pete had spent Sunday in the local pub speaking to Harvey, his pet seal. When in his cups, he would frequently imagine the seal seated on the barstool alongside and would hold lengthy, noisy conversations with the mammal. Unfortunately, the denizen of the deep could not speak English, so Peter, being a diplomatic naval officer, always spoke in Seal.

His conversation involved a vast amount of hand movement. By raising his elbows, Pete could slap the upper sides of his hands together and emulate a seal clapping its fins, whenever he wanted to emphasize a point during the conversation. Each clap of Pete's fins accompanied an audible sucking in of breath and emission of seal-like noises—unintelligible to humans, but music to Harvey's ears. That Sunday they had discussed the woes of the world and by morning, Pete's hoarse throat was one of them.

Darroch, whose one lung had collapsed, opened the conversation with a whispered plea to Peter to go and get help. Peter, whose chest was better than Darroch's, but whose throat was decidedly worse, suggested in a whisper that Darroch could go and get knotted. Thankfully, both men recovered after receiving the correct treatment. Harvey still accompanies Pete, but he speaks less frequently these days.

The all-important "wind over the deck" affects carrier flying greatly. Even in calm conditions, the ship, at full steam, can create up to 25 knots of wind down the deck. Heading into a prevailing wind can effectively increase the wind felt over the deck. The higher the wind speed the easier it becomes to operate aircraft. Wind of 30 knots over the deck, effectively reduces the relative ground speed of an aircraft approaching to land at 130 knots, to a very manageable 100 knots. Similarly, aircraft can launch with higher all-up-weights into a strong wind.

Temperature also greatly affects the power output of jet engines. The colder the temperature, the denser the air becomes, and the greater the power output. Conversely, under hot tropical temperatures, power output reduces and must always be calculated to determine, in combination with the strength of the wind blowing over the deck, safe take-off weights.

One morning, with no natural wind and an extremely high temperature, calculations showed that the Scimitars, configured with underwing drop tanks, could not get airborne with a full load of fuel. However, the graphs indicated that with drop tanks only half full, the launch would be safe.

Jim Purvis settled in the cockpit for the first launch of the morning; he rose in the air as his Scimitar tilted back onto the "donkey's plonk". The catapult fired and the aircraft was flung into the air. Without hesitation, the Scimitar's nose rotated higher and higher until the aircraft stalled, at which point Jim pulled his ejection handle. The

Martin-Baker seat hurled him into a high parabola; his parachute opened and deposited him into the sea. His flight had lasted all of seven seconds, including the parachute descent. The ever-alert SAR chopper was immediately overhead; it picked Jim out of the water, and deposited him back on deck within two minutes of his launch. He was wet, but uninjured.

What no one had considered when the launch problem was discussed, was that at the exaggerated angle on the catapult, the fuel in the half-filled drop tanks all flowed to the back of the tanks. The aircraft's centre-of-gravity had moved backwards outside the set limits, causing the uncontrollable nose high rotation after launch—a costly mistake!

Before setting heading for Britain, the ship docked in Singapore and we flew ashore to continue flying out of RAF Tengah. This was a welcomed break after weeks cooped up on the carrier with only seawater and men to look at. Every morning, we would jump into a Combi to drive around to the hangar. This short journey included a stretch of 500 metres on the main road circling the airfield.

Invariably, we would meet a Chinese chap driving a motorcycle with an unusual sidecar. The sidecar had been modified so that a large pig could stand up, facing into the wind, on a platform surrounded by rails. This pig would be snorting as he stared expectantly into the wind that brought streams of tears down the side of his piggy face.

Often, if our timing was good, we would meet them again as the Combi and motorcycle wended their ways homeward. By the afternoon, however, the pig was no longer snorting or staring into the wind. Instead, he would be lying flat-out on his side. His head would loll over the edge of the platform and his tongue would be flapping in the breeze. The next morning there he would be, legs akimbo, snorting and staring expectantly. He was a stud boar who obviously enjoyed his job and gave it all he had. We all enjoyed flying, but after months on board a ship, there was a certain amount of envy for the Tengah pig.

Finally, HMS *Victorious* headed for home. Despite wanting to make the most of the sun before arriving for Christmas in the UK, the powers that be kept the ship operational all the way back. We even flew over the Red Sea, heading for the Suez Canal. This was an unusual occurrence, because the waterway was narrow and crowded. HMS *Plymouth*, a Royal Navy frigate, was on passage out of the canal and seemed like a good target for a dummy airstrike.

Old Wal, on his fifth last flight in the navy, and I were tasked to fly northwards almost to Sinai before returning to attack *Plymouth* as a surprise from the north. As we entered the turn, 196 miles from the carrier, the audio alarm bells started ringing accompanied by the flashing of the bright red attention-getter lights. Looking down at the warning panel, I saw that we had a starboard engine fire. Immediately I went through the drills and shut down the engine. But the warning light remained on. At this juncture, Old Wal decided we should eject. I could not swim 196 miles and the sharks in the Red Sea are monsters, so I vetoed his suggestion.

I went into a hard turn to look for signs of smoke in our slipstream. I could not see anything, but the light burnt brightly. Old Wal lowered his seat and started tightening his straps prior to ejecting. I slipped my hand through the gap into the coalhole and nudged his shoulder, telling him that as I could detect no other signs, the fire warning was probably spurious. He decided to stay and I flew the Vixen back on one engine. It was such a good aircraft that even landing on board with asymmetric power posed no problem.

Old Wal was delighted to get back and our association, which had started precariously, ended on a high note. Every time we bumped into each other during those final days on board, he would pat me on the back or grip my arm in gestures of relief. When I eventually left the navy on completion of my 12-year commission, I understood the anxiety that had obsessed Old Wal. I had lost so many good friends during my 12 years that the pressure also got to me in the end. I was serving at RNAS Lossiemouth, married with a baby boy, and living in married quarters in Elgin. There were two roads I could use to drive to the base. The shorter route, through the town, lacked charm, so I normally used the longer, scenic route, which wound through the beautiful Lossie woods. However, during my final three months in the navy, I could not bring myself to drive on that road. In the woods, just outside Lossiemouth village, was the cemetery where many of my friends were lined up and I did not want to join them.

After passage through the Suez, we flew off from the Mediterranean, on a 2h15m flight across Europe to RNAS Yeovilton. By the end of a long cruise, everyone looks forward to returning home. My home was in South Africa, but I too enjoyed the prospect of being back in England, albeit the middle of winter. A change is like a holiday! The aircraft needed maintenance attention from facilities only available at home base. There was always a certain feeling of "get-home-itis" and if the engines started, pilots would ignore any other deficiencies to get home. The old salts used to say that even if your navigation instruments had failed, all you had to do was point the nose in the direction of the thickest, dirtiest cloud and England would be underneath.

On this flight, although our navigation system worked, the old salts proved correct. The southern half of England, including Somerset where Yeovilton was situated, was under thick, heavy rain clouds. Descent in bad weather was no major problem to any of us used to more trying conditions out at sea. However, landing provided a different form of excitement.

To absorb the tremendous impact of deck landings, Sea Vixen tyres were pumped to a pressure of 400 psi (pounds per square inch). They were so hard that they did not bulge as normal car tyres do; they were virtually solid. As a result, very little rubber touched the runway. Pilots land with caution on dry runways, but on the waterlogged runways that greeted us at Yeovilton, it was almost impossible to stop normally. The hard tyres would simply plane on the water, rather like a skate skims over ice.

Yeovilton had two runways that crossed in the middle like a large X. An arrestor wire was suspended inches high across each runway end as an emergency stopping device. If a pilot felt he could not stop in time, he would lower his deck-hook and engage an arrestor wire, which would bring his aircraft safely to a standstill. This was exactly what happened at Yeovilton. The first four pilots to land, the most senior crews who knew about these things, engaged the wires at each of the four runway ends.

The remaining eight pilots had to cope without the benefit of wires. The remaining fuel after the long flight did not allow for diversions. Eventually, as aircraft came to a skidding stop, the airborne pilots asked those on the ground to fold their wings to allow them to skid through the gaps. All 12 landed safely, but only after an exciting few minutes.

In early February 1962, the squadron re-embarked and *Victorious* sailed down the English Channel, to participate in a NATO exercise in the Atlantic. The exercise wash-up was held in Gibraltar, where all the ships gathered for eight days. Not wanting to have idle aircrew disrupting the ship's routine, the squadrons disembarked to North Front for the duration of the visit.

The massive Rock of Gibraltar lies in a north/south direction. A narrow causeway at the northern end of the Rock links Gibraltar with Spain. Traditionally, relations between the two communities have always been strained; therefore, Gibraltar needed its own airstrip to prevent isolation. The prevailing wind at the western end of the Mediterranean blows from west to east. To cater for this wind, North Front Airfield was built on the causeway, with the runway lying east/west. Both ends of the runway were built on land reclaimed from the sea—extending the runway length to 6 000 feet.

Traffic lights, controlled by the air traffic control officer in North Front tower, allowed vehicular and pedestrian traffic to pass over the runway when the circuit was free of aircraft. However, it was common to see elderly Spanish men pushing bicycles laden with onions across the runway while aircraft were landing. Traffic lights held little significance for these men of the soil.

The approach to either end of the runway was over the sea. This should not have been a problem to carrier pilots where every approach is over the water. However, the combination of prevailing wind, the sheer size of the Rock, and the 400-psi tyre pressures of navy jets, created problems of their own. The prevailing westerly wind usually blew from the southwest. Approaching the Rock, this airflow would divide into three distinct streams. One stream would curl around the northern end of the rock, while another would curl around the southern rock face. It was common for the windsocks at either end of the runway to be 180° out of phase with each other. The approach to land in either case would be downwind. Without getting too technical, a downwind approach could raise the aircraft's relative ground speed by 40 or 50 knots. In those conditions, accurate touchdowns are impossible, because aircraft tend to float down the runway while the pilot struggles to get the wheels safely on the ground. Floating reduces the remaining stopping distance, which, on the near solid tyres of a navy jet, increases the drama.

The third stream of air accelerates over the top of the Rock venturi fashion, and then decelerates as it swirls back to sea level. The turbulence can be felt up to five miles from the Rock and can be seen as an alarming cat's paw pattern on the surface of the sea. Under these conditions, the recommended approach to North Front is parallel to the Spanish coast, with a sharp right-hand turn just before touchdown.

I can remember approaching in a Vixen holding 130 knots. Over the threshold I pulled both engines to idle power, which in normal conditions would have caused an immediate sink and speed loss. This time the Vixen floated upwards and the speed increased to 150 knots; I had no option but to abort the landing and try again.

Aborted landings brought an additional factor into the North Front equation. Because of the unstable political situation, aircraft landing at North Front were forbidden from crossing into Spanish airspace. As the runway was within a few hundred metres of the international border, all circuits had to be flown to the south, around the Rock. This huge circuit was 24 miles in length—wasting time in the case of an airliner and valuable fuel in the case of jet fighters.

Our eight days at North Front were most interesting. When I was not on the flying programme, I would resist the temptations of the nearby town and spend my time in the control tower, particularly if the wind was brisk. Entertainment was continuous and free. British European Airways flew Vickers Vanguard passenger turboprop liners (big brother to the successful Viscount) on the Gibraltar route. On two successive days I watched as pilots burst all the main-wheel tyres bringing their aircraft to a stop.

However, Royal Air Force planners provided the main attraction. These August gentlemen decided that, to protect the maritime approaches to the Mediterranean, a Shackelton squadron needed to be based at North Front. In their wisdom, they deployed the older Mk2s with tail-wheels, and not the Shackelton Mk3 with a nose-wheel. These huge, four-engined, eight-propellered, tail-draggers required deft, delicate handling at the best of times. In a wind, at Gibraltar, they required one to have nerves of steel. Fortunately, these aircraft carried large fuel reserves to allow for the myriad of missed approaches and 24-mile circuits. The officer's mess at North Front seemed to accommodate a higher than average number of prematurely grey-haired officers, all of them Shackelton pilots.

Chapter 9

892 Squadron, HMS *Hermes*

The Royal Navy planners now had a turn to outdo those in the Royal Air Force! Early in April 1962, after we returned to Yeovilton, HMS *Victorious* entered the dockyard for a well-earned maintenance period—HMS *Hermes* replaced her in the fleet. Making a quick, easy decision, and with one swift stroke of a pen, Admiralty planners transferred the entire *Victorious* air group to *Hermes*. One subtle change was made to the inventory of the helicopter squadron. Their old Whirlwind helicopters were traded in for the new Westland Wessex, substantially increasing their anti-submarine capability. On 28 May, the squadrons flew aboard and the carrier headed to the Mediterranean for a four-month work-up cruise.

The implications of the Admiralty's quick decision only then began to manifest. *Victorious* was a ship in the 30 000 ton class. *Hermes* was a little over 20 000 tons. Aircraft numbers remained constant, while substantial reductions to deck and hangar space jeopardized the efficient and safe operation of aircraft. The arrival of the Wessex helicopters compounded the problem. Whirlwind helicopters stood on four wheels positioned below the cabin. Their long tailbooms could project over the side of the carrier, halving the deck space required. The Wessex stood on two main-wheels at the front and a tail-wheel under the boom. These helicopters required double the space of their predecessors.

Aircraft handlers worked all night to arrange aircraft on the deck for the start of the first day's flying programme. A carrier usually worked a rigid flying cycle. Every 1h20m aircraft were launched, and those airborne were recovered. The time in between was spent refuelling, rearming, and respotting the aircraft on the deck, ready for the next cycle. Respotting entailed moving unserviceable aircraft to the hangar for repair, and positioning serviceable aircraft in the range for the next sortie.

Every time an aircraft repositioned, cables had to secure it to the deck to prevent losing it overboard as the ship rolled. Bomb trolleys, refuelling hoses, electrical power supply cables, and oxygen trolleys constantly moved between aircraft. One hitch could have seriously interfered with the commencement of the next cycle. Airborne pilots, returning to the ship low on fuel, could not accept any unplanned for delays. To an outsider, it probably looked haphazard, but in reality, all movements were conducted as if under a maestro's baton.

On that first flying day in the Mediterranean, *Hermes* only completed one cycle. Space problems were so acute that the deck could not be readied for the second launch and it was cancelled. Getting the airborne aircraft back on board turned into a nightmare. Space was so limited that landing aircraft were taxied to any available space out of the landing area. When the last jet was safely aboard, the deck looked like an American Midwest town after a tornado—aircraft everywhere with no semblance of order. To extricate aircraft from the huddle required the expertise of experienced aircraft handlers and tractor drivers.

The carrier staff held serious contingency planning sessions before a workable alternative system evolved. Gannet and Wessex flying were separated from jet operations. This decreased the operational capability of the ship, but at least it maintained the required high safety standard.

Hermes' recent refurbishment included accommodation that was more modern. This time I had an air-conditioned cabin on two deck. Although small, it had all that I required. I was quite comfortable and slept remarkably well. However, I did have problems waking up and only discovered the reason halfway through the cruise. The air-conditioning inlet had been positioned just aft of the funnel. Instead of fresh air, pure funnel gas was pumped through the system. When my alarm clock rang, I would awake and sit on my bunk. I could not open my eyes. Feeling for my towel, I would wrap it around me, push my feet into the previously positioned sandals, and feel my way to the showers like a blind man. Only after the water had been running into my eyes could I force the lids apart!

Each ship had idiosyncrasies, usually incorporated with the compliments of the dockyard workers who had built them. I suspect that *Victorious* had a twist in her hull, making lining up for landing difficult as she corkscrewed her way through the water. Even in harbour, she seemed to gyrate.

Sitting on her quarterdeck one day, I took an interest in a pipe fixed to the deckhead above. Wondering what its purpose was, I followed its circuitous route over support beams and round corners. Completing my search, I found that both ends of the pipe had stoppers in them, so it was doing precisely nothing. One of the ship's engineers explained that this was quite common, especially on ships built in Irish shipyards. When their job was completed, dockyard workers were invariably paid off. To delay the inevitable, workers used to keep occupied for as long as possible, hence my pipe to nowhere.

HMS *Ark Royal*, which I served on in the mid-1960s, had a built in trick herself. Navigation over the sea is never easy, particularly when out of range of any coastline. In the Fleet Air Arm, we relied heavily on TACAN (Tactical Air Navigation). Each of the ships was equipped with a beacon positioned on top of the highest mast. All our aircraft could tune into this beacon, and when within 150 nautical miles at altitude, they could read off a range and bearing to reach the ship—very simple to operate, easy to interpret, and a great comfort to aircrew.

Throughout our year-long cruise on the *Ark*, her TACAN was totally unreliable. For the majority of each flying cycle, the beacon would give accurate information, but during the last 20 minutes, the crucial time when pilots were returning to "mother", the beacon's signal would vanish. Only at the end of our year-long frustration, was the cause of this failure established. A bright dockyard electrician, conscious of all captains' desires to keep their ships looking "tiddly", had routed the TACAN electrical cable from the generator to the beacon up through the inside of the ship's funnel.

At the end of each cycle, the ship would put on power to accelerate, increasing the windspeed over the deck for the following launch and landings. The increased heat exhausting through the funnel raised the temperature, causing the electrical power supply in the TACAN cable to cut out. After launch, the ship would reduce speed, the funnel temperature would decrease, and the TACAN would come back online as if nothing had happened.

During that wonderful summer, HMS *Hermes* docked in Palma, the main port on the island of Majorca. This visit turned out to be one of the highlights of a four-month cruise in the Mediterranean. The simple reason, girls! The island was full of them. More than enough for the crew of the carrier. They had arrived for their summer vacation from all over Europe.

Girls are far more adventurous than young men are when planning summer holidays. Most young lads think no further than the sun and vino of Spain's Costa de Sol. Girls venture further afield, hence the surfeit on the island. The arrival of the huge ship and the men in blue provided the girls with the excitement they had been seeking. It was a most fortunate visit.

An aviator earns his keep by flying. Because this can only be done while the ship is at sea, aircrew are forced to idle away time by going ashore during visits. This is to the chagrin of the ship's officers who have to carry on normal routines even when the ship is in harbour. In an effort to even the workload, flying officers are rostered for duties such as officer of the Shore Patrol or second officer of the Watch. The aircrew compliment aboard a fleet carrier is so large that these duties come round infrequently. On the other hand, they can provide splendid entertainment.

One night I was positioned at the after brow as second officer of the Watch. The after brow is the point from which sailors depart and return to the ship when going ashore. My duty was to ensure that they were properly dressed when leaving and sober when returning aboard. The Royal Navy has had centuries worth of experience of sailors going ashore. They understand that men cooped up together, living an unnatural existence for weeks, are going to relax at the first opportunity. Part of this ritual is to sample foreign beverages, some of which turn out to be extremely potent.

Arriving on the brow, they had to salute the officer and ask permission to go ashore. The officer would return the salute and grant permission after ensuring the man's appearance was satisfactory. This part of the drill was unnecessary, because no man would jeopardize his chance of getting ashore by being improperly dressed.

The return, however, was another matter entirely. Jolly Jack arrived back on the quayside by taxi, horse cart, or even slumped in the back of a rickshaw. In the early hours of the morning, those who had spent all their money arrived by foot. The vast majority of men's wives or mothers would have considered them drunk, but the Royal Navy was a little more pragmatic. The brow, or ladder, which had to be negotiated to get back on board, was purposefully steep and narrow. If the man could negotiate that ladder and salute, he was sober and allowed to proceed to his bunk.

Because my watch covered these early morning hours, no men left the ship but others arrived back in a steady trickle. By 03h00 even this trickled had dried up and the duty had started to drag. Suddenly, after a flurry of activity on the jetty, a sailor arrived at the top of the brow. He was minus his cap and his tropical white uniform was absolutely soaked. It was my duty to unravel the reason for his dishevelled appearance.

He was a young man, probably still in his teens. He had rushed ashore earlier that evening with his shipmates, eager to sample the delights of Palma. Unfortunately, large harbours cover a huge area and *Hermes* was tied up against the jetty furthest from the town. Nobody noticed the distance on the way into town, but it certainly became a factor on the way back to the ship. He had spent all his money, become separated from his mates, and so he had to walk back to the ship. After a long and tiring ramble, he found himself no more than 25 metres from the carrier. Unfortunately, he had forgotten about the dry-dock they had to go around on the way into town. Water now filled this dock and it meant a further trudge around the dock to get back to *Hermes*.

At this juncture he had had quite enough. He was tired and felt he could walk no further. He elected to dive into the water and swim the few remaining metres to the ship. Up to that point I had become engrossed in the youngster's tale and eagerly asked him to continue. He then said that it was only after he surfaced from his dive that he remembered he was a non-swimmer!

Members of the shore patrol had fished him out at the end of a long boat hook and escorted him to the brow. I decided the man was sober and sent him to his bunk.

In Valetta Harbour, Malta, a month later, I was again on the brow, but this time during the mid-afternoon. The shore patrol pulled up at the bottom of the brow in their Land-Rover, and escorted a sailor up the ladder. This time the man was in no state to return to his bunk; he was obviously drunk, and dishevelled. His white uniform had turned brown and he was covered in sand.

In a fit of homesickness, brought on by gallons of Maltese plonk, he decided to return to the United Kingdom. He walked out to Luqa Airfield where the authorities found him leopard crawling through the sand. He was trying to slide under the airfield fence so that he could board an aircraft, because he did not have the money to buy an air ticket. We let him sleep it off—his monumental hangover being penance enough for the disturbance he had caused.

Malta was always an enjoyable visit. In those days the Royal Navy still had a considerable presence on the island and most locals enjoyed the money that the sailors spent in the town. The Fleet Air Arm had a permanent airfield at Hal Far so we always felt very much at home on the island. In earlier days, when aircraft were much smaller, cranes offloaded unserviceable aeroplanes from the carriers onto flat-topped barge-like vessels. This no longer occurred, but the barge, known as a lighter, was still there. It carried no navigation lights; therefore, its use was restricted to daylight hours.

Navy pilots, never short on ingenuity, and versed in strategic arts, realized that this lighter presented fantastic possibilities. A *banyan* (navy picnic) was organized. After work, food, drink, barbecue stoves, and record players were piled on board. Once the invited guests had arrived (Wrens from Hal Far), the bowline cast off and the happy party chugged around the coast to anchor in a beautiful, secluded cove.

After swimming in the crystal clear waters and with glasses in our hands, we watched the sun setting in the west. Without navigation lights, the lighter was stuck there for the night. What a stroke of genius! Forced to spend all night with a boatload of girls!

The fires were soon lit, food was prepared, and the glasses were kept topped up. Once the record player had electrical power, the dancing began. The flat top on the lighter made a perfect dance floor. A plaintive cry heralded the first problem: 'Who brought the records?' A frantic search produced just one disc, which had been on the turntable of the record player. Aptly enough it was *Stranger on the shore* by Acker Bilk. It is a lovely tune, well played on his clarinet, but after 12 hours the novelty wore off.

However, the repetitive music provided many opportunities to explore other avenues of available entertainment. Just as the night's prospects seemed to be brightening, uninvited guests gatecrashed the party. Local residents had detected our presence and the word had spread like wildfire through the community. They came in swarms and took full advantage of the ample delicacies that were freely available. Hundreds and thousands of man-hungry mosquitoes sank their probloscises into exposed flesh. What a bloody night! All the best laid plans of mice and men!

In Gibraltar one night, I had to don the black leather gaiters that go with the duty officer of the Shore Patrol. Apart from the gaiters, you are issued with five large Royal Marines and the ship's Land-Rover. You position your team at the local police headquarters and you are on call if trouble erupts in the town and sailors from your ship are involved.

I would not have missed this evening for all the money in the world. When trouble did erupt, sailors from *Hermes* were always involved. That night the police, my team and I, visited every house of ill repute in Gibraltar. The arguments and disagreements were all settled amicably enough. The local police are very experienced in the comings and goings of navy men and the ladies of the night. Usually the problems occurred over payment for services rendered, if the ladies were to be believed, or non-rendered, if the matelots account was considered. I can still recall plaintive Peter Sellers-type cries of 'But Sir, I neva got me moneys worff!'

Another port of call, during that wonderful Mediterranean cruise, was Beirut, in Lebanon. This was old Beirut, before terrorist bombings reduced the town and economy to rubble. It was the playground of the rich and famous, and the gambling centre of the Mediterranean. The climate was idyllic for swimming in the sea, while 40 miles away in the mountains people were snow skiing. An ideal run ashore for members of the ship's crew.

The first night in harbour was perhaps the most important night of the ship's visit. The ship always threw a cocktail party to which the town mayor, other dignitaries, and officials were invited. In order to balance the gender ratio, the local nurses' home and teachers' training colleges were also invited, hence the importance of the first night "cockers". Invitations stipulate that the party would commence at 18h00 and end at 20h00.

The ship was suitably "dressed" (decorated). Half of the hangar was cleared of aircraft as the venue for the party. Greenery, flowers, and water features softened the stark interior. The Marine Band provided a string orchestra to set the tone of the evening. Officers would be detailed off to play host to arriving guests. Extraneous officers circulated amongst the guests, to ensure they were adequately catered for as far as drinks were concerned and were not left unattended.

The Royal Navy had practised this ritual for centuries and had perfected the art of playing host to members of the port. If you played your cards correctly, it would also benefit the ship's officers. Here was how the game "Baron Strangling" worked. You surveyed the long line of guests as they came aboard, then you decided which guests you would attach yourself to. Some officers, usually the older ones, tended to choose the wealthier looking guests. Aircrew officers usually chose the guests with the prettiest daughters, but the choice was your own preference. This initial process was known as "selecting a Baron".

As the evening progressed, you ensured that your chosen "Barons" were well fed, watered, and unattended to, while engaging them in conversation. Usually they asked questions about the ship and you replied by enquiring about their hometown. Most civilian cocktail parties became laborious, as guests never seem to want to go home. The navy cocktail party catered for that eventuality. At ten minutes before eight, smartly dressed sailors entered the hangar and unwound two long ropes. They effectively divided the hangar into two halves, clearing the centre and gently persuading all the guests to move back to the sides of the hangar. As soon as there was a clear space, the hangar lift descended from the flight-deck with the Royal Marine Band. As the lift stopped level with the hangar deck, the band marched into the cleared space while beating the retreat. The brass and percussion instruments resounded inside the metal confines of the hangar. The guests were always overawed by the military pageantry.

While everyone watched the ceremony, stewards rove through the crowds and removed all drinking glasses. At precisely 20h00, the ceremony ended with the band rising up on the lift, back to the flight-deck. People looked around for their drinks, which had mysteriously disappeared. They then had no option but to take their leave. This became the crucial few minutes for the officers who had spent the evening entertaining. If you had performed your job well, it was only good manners for your selected guests to ask you if you were allowed to accompany them ashore. The good operators had a set of civilian clothes arranged on their bunks; so, in the wink of an eye, they could change their attire and be at their guest's side, as they stepped ashore. You had "selected your Baron" and now you proceeded to step two of the game, "How to strangle your Baron".

Provided you had been a good host, most people were only too willing to reciprocate by showing you the sights of their hometown. It was not unusual for officers to spend the entire visit being looked after by their "Barons". It was for these reasons that I was disappointed to have to stand duty on the sailor's brow, while everyone else attended the "first-night cockers" in Beirut.

The ship was tied up alongside the quay and I had a good view of all the guests as they passed by heading towards the party. My disappointment and envy rose enormously as I gaped at 16 sensational young women tripping their way genteelly to the officer's brow. Coming off watch at 20h00, I ambled despondently to the wardroom to have my supper. At table, I enquired if anyone had managed to arrange dates with the lovely girls. The answer was no one had, because the girls worked at the casino just outside Beirut. The ball was set in motion and after supper five of us shared a taxi to the casino.

Never before had we seen such opulence. Swarthy, Mediterranean-type gentlemen pushed our yearly salaries backwards and forwards across the tables, without batting an eyelid. At 23h00 all patrons were invited to enter the theatre; the Casino Spectacular was about to begin. Imagine our surprise, and delight, when the curtain opened to reveal our beautiful 16, with three feathers and a string of pearls between the lot of them. A most refreshing sight after nearly two months at sea, but unfortunately, way above our price bracket. We ended up visiting the Roman ruins at Baalbek, which, although fascinating, didn't hold a candle to the sights we had already seen.

One of the roles of a carrier air group was to support army operations ashore. During a cruise, every available opportunity was utilized to train with the "Brown jobs". Scimitars of 803 Squadron and Sea Vixens of 892 Squadron made up the strike element of the *Hermes* air group. While operating in the eastern Mediterranean, the air group participated in a ground support exercise with the "Pongos" stationed in Cyprus.

Every hour of the day, pairs of aircraft catapulted off the carrier to take up station over predetermined holding points. Arriving at low level over these points, pilots would be briefed via the radio by their army counterpart. He would describe the target to be attacked, and supply headings and times for the run-in until the aircraft pitched-up for the attack. These necessary exercises were enjoyable, particularly if the army forward air controller was a skilled operator.

Maintaining this strict schedule required absolute adherence to timetables by both the ship's compliment and the aircrew. Every hour, the ship had to change heading to point into wind. Catapult launches and landings had to be accomplished in minimum time—tardiness was inexcusable. Like an orchestra, if one instrument was out of tune, the whole symphony was ruined.

With this thought in his mind, Lieutenant Mike Tristram, leader of a pair of Scimitars, called off his last attack and set course for the ship. A glance at his watch made him realize that unless he hurried he would arrive late for "Charlie", the time his formation was required to land. Informing his wingman, he climbed to 3 000 feet and accelerated to well over 500 knots.

At this speed he did not even see the large eagle that smashed through the armoured glass of his front windscreen. One moment he was speeding happily back to the ship, and then there was chaos. Flying glass, feathers, decompression, and a 500-knot gale hitting him in the face instantly followed the huge impact. Slivers of glass blew into his eyes and he was temporarily confused.

He told his wingman he was going to eject. However, his wingman had other ideas. He took control of the situation and told Mike to slow down. He followed this with a running commentary telling the unseeing Mike what to do to control his aircraft. 'Back on the stick to keep your nose up; lift your right wing; hold that attitude ...'

The ship prepared for the emergency and the deck was cleared of all unnecessary equipment. The wingman positioned Mike on final approach to the carrier, but at half a mile from the ship he had to break away. The mirror control officer then continued the commentary. At the last instant Mike's aircraft dropped dangerously low and he was ordered to "wave off". At this compulsory order the pilot must apply power and climb away for another circuit.

Mike reacted immediately and applied full power. Just then, he had a partial clearing of his vision and he noticed the ship's wake below and the flight-deck ahead. Disregarding all he learnt about deck landing, he pulled back the power and pushed the control column forward. Fortunately, his deck-hook caught an arrestor wire and the aircraft was brought to a safe halt. The entire cockpit looked as if it had been spray-painted with blood.

Mike was removed and taken to the sickbay where the doctor was waiting. Fortunately, all the shards of glass were extracted from his eyes and no permanent damage was suffered. After a week, the dressings were removed and Mike's sight was unimpaired. All's well that ends well, or so he thought!

Mike was married to a highly-strung girl who did not enjoy him going away to sea for long periods. She also abhorred the fact that Mike was dedicated to the dangerous profession of flying from carrier decks. In view of these circumstances, Mike decided, rightly or wrongly, not to tell his wife what had happened.

Nevertheless, it was such a good story, that in a letter home, one of the pilots related the complete incident to his wife. Navy wives, being no different from civilian wives, could not keep the story to themselves and the news spread like wildfire through the married quarters at RNAS Lossiemouth.

Important messages to the Ships Company were "piped" over the loudspeaker system. The shrill whistle announced the message that followed. The most eagerly awaited "pipe" was always the one that announced the mail's arrival aboard. The men rushed away to collect letters from their loved ones.

After one of these "pipes", I was sitting in the wardroom reading letters, when I noticed an officer slip from the settee onto the carpeted floor. I went over immediately and was concerned at the tears that were coursing down Mike Tristram's cheeks. Only after offering assistance did I notice that his tears were from laughter.

He had received a letter from his wife and she was furious. She had picked up a story circulating the Lossiemouth married patch that Mike had been having fun with a bird in Cyprus. In the telling, the story had altered completely, hence her anger and Mike's uncontrollable laughter.

Mike received a Queen's Commendation for his outstanding deed.

The variety of tasks and areas we flew in increased the fun of flying that summer. We bombed on the weaponry ranges near El Adam in Libya and flew inland following the road, in case we had to eject. It was not that we might not be found in the desert, but only the road had been cleared of landmines laid during the Second World War.

We fought the French Navy and the Etendard fighters from *Clememseau* attacked us. We searched for Russian destroyers, carried out dummy strikes against targets in Sicily, flew CAPS (Combat Air Patrols) against US Navy fighters from the 6th Fleet, and fired rockets and cannon at targets on the Filfla Range in Malta.

Occasionally military guests would stay on board for a few days to watch the flying. A carrier deck is always spectacular during flying operations, so those lucky enough to be invited greatly appreciated these visits. I was greatly amused during one sortie briefing. Some guests, seated behind us, glanced at the crew names on the briefing board. I stifled a chuckle when I heard one distinguished guest note very appreciatively that a member of the aristocracy was on the flying programme. My observer for the mission was a chap with a hyphenated surname. There boldly written on the board was Lord Dorman-Jackson. This sort of thing always impresses the Brits!

Our final task at the end of that super summer was to carry out an army support exercise near Thessaloniki in Northern Greece, close to the Albanian and Bulgarian borders. The ship positioned herself in the Aegean and we flew in over the stunning coastline north of Athos. Tiny coves, beautiful small beaches, and craggy headlands with impressive churches on most of them, adorned the coastline.

The exercise included dummy strikes on selected targets, and the exercise was not without an element of tension. Territory north of the close Greek border was under Communist control during the height of the cold war. What those buggers did, whenever NATO exercises were held close to their borders, was to position exceptionally strong navigation beacons inside their territory. The beacon in this case was emitting the same signal as that at Thessaloniki; only the Communist beacon was more powerful. The idea was at best to inveigle our aircraft across their borders to create an international incident. At worst they were not averse to taking you out with SAMs (Surface to Air Missiles), AAA (Anti-Aircraft Artillery), or MiG fighters.

Interestingly, this type of subterfuge raised its ugly head in Southern Africa in 1986. Samora Machel, President of Moçambique, was onboard a Russian TU-134, which crashed into the mountains on the South African side of the international border. The Moçambicans, Russians, and all Liberation Movement officials, immediately claimed that the dastardly South Africans had placed a beacon there to lure the aircraft over the border. I was a senior officer in the South African Air Force at the time and I knew nothing about our involvement. Anyway, that type of dirty trick was not necessary in our inventory. The findings of the professional accident border concurred. I found the claim by the Communists significant; the only group who, in my experience, ever utilized such tactics.

With the army exercise completed, *Hermes* headed for home. Everyone on board looked forward to a few days relaxation on the deck, soaking up the sun, before returning to the early winter in Britain. As we discovered in Malta, all the best laid plans of mice and men can easily be altered. Commander (Air) Neddy Perrett decided that he needed a suitable photograph to adorn the ship's Christmas card.

His plan was to fly off the entire air group. The Wessex choppers and Gannet AEW aircraft would form one formation and approach the ship from astern at 110 knots. The Sea Vixens and Scimitars would form another formation and approach from astern at 350 knots. *If* the timing was correct, the jet formation would overtake the slower, lower formation, as they passed overhead the ship. The SAR helicopter would position overhead so the photographer could take the Christmas shot.

The Gannets and choppers formed up as briefed. The leader of the jets used a cruise ship as a rendezvous point for the jet Balbo. Circling the liner was fun and all the passengers were soon waving happily from their position around the swimming pool. However, to join up 24 jets takes quite a long time and the aircraft burn off huge amounts of fuel at low level.

Finally, with all aircraft in position, the great air armada set course for the ship. Against all odds, Neddy's plan worked and we overflew the ship precisely as required and the photograph was taken. Unfortunately, the moment of self-congratulation was short lived.

To make space for the entire air group on the tiny *Hermes* flight-deck required planning. Every piece of equipment that could be moved had been taken down into the hangar. This included all the aircraft towing tractors. These specialized machines, although small, were extremely heavy to counteract the considerable weight of the large fighters they moved. Because of their size, seven of them fitted on the after lift for transport to the hangar. However, the lift motors, designed to take the weight of one aeroplane, could not cope with the equivalent load of seven aircraft. With puffs of blue smoke, the motors ground to a halt and the lift stuck in the down position. The lift aperture left a gaping hole in the deck at touchdown point.

As we flashed overhead, Ned's voice over the common radio frequency gave the order dreaded by all carrier aviators, 'Conserve.' In layman's terms, this meant there had been a cockup on the ship and landing time would be delayed. With alternate airfields available for diversion purposes being few and far between, this call immediately raised adrenaline levels. Cynical comments in the crewroom had inferred that the navy had introduced two-engined aircraft so we could, 'Conserve fuel on one engine and burn off fuel on the other.'

The previously ordered formation broke up as pilots climbed to altitude to extract the maximum loiter time from the remaining fuel. The order, 'Conserve' was soon followed by the command, 'All jets divert to Gibraltar, heading 275°, range 176 nautical miles.' Loiter configurations were altered to range configurations and all the jets started to climb. The Gannets, designed to spend long hours on task, had plenty of fuel for the flight. Landing vertically, the helicopters could be received back onboard the ship. The jets were the problem.

The Vixens had two distinct advantages over the Scimitar. First, the observers could make the necessary fuel calculations, leaving the pilots to worry about the flying. Second, the Vixen had a lower wing loading than the Scimitar and therefore burnt less fuel, particularly at low-level where we had all been orbiting around the now forgotten cruise ship. By climbing to 42 000 feet and then cruise climbing, we could make it with a few pounds of fuel to spare.

However, 803 Squadron's Scimitars were in a very tight spot. Pilots began debating whether it was best to climb to 32 000 feet and fly on two engines, or level off at 16 000 feet and fly on one engine. The answers were critical, because the entire squadron would arrive at the infamous North Front well below safe landing fuel levels. The perverse wind around the Rock could complicate matters.

However, they all landed safely at Gibraltar. Our Sea Vixens were recalled, because the lift had been repaired—so all's well that ends well. I have always thought that it would have been an interesting board of inquiry if the gods had decided to be unkind.

There was one more throw of the dice before that memorable cruise ended. 892 Sea Vixen squadron flew home to Britain from the Mediterranean, apart from one aircraft that needed a spare part from Gibraltar. As a bachelor, I was unanimously elected to remain behind with the broken aircraft. 803 Scimitar Squadron, with their shorter range, were to fly off when the ship reached the Bay of Biscay and I was to follow them.

Unlike the Mediterranean, the Bay is famous for developing huge sea swells, and on launch day it lived up to its reputation. *Hermes* was pitching way outside of the limits set for normal operations. Because none of the aircraft were to be recovered, the decision was made to launch. All the Scimitars were arranged down the port side of the deck. My aircraft, the last to be launched, was tied down on the stern.

While waiting for the order to start engines, I had an intriguing view of the ship. Positioned on the round-down, I had a grandstand view of the entire deck, as it pitched and bucked in the huge waves. After engine start the launch process began. John Middelton's Scimitar was tensioned on the port catapult to raise it onto the "donkey's plonk". A sudden roll caused the aircraft to swing sideways and fall back onto the deck. Two or three reloads were necessary before his aircraft positioned correctly. With the launch being a very critical portion of the flight, John's, and everyone else's nerves, were on edge.

Finally the launch began. John ran his engines up to full power and was ready to go. The FDO (flight deck officer) touched his green flag to the deck, the signal for the operator to fire the catapult. Unfortunately, flustered by the drama of the re-loads, the FDO initiated the catapult shot when the bow was pointing upwards, instead of downwards. In the two seconds it takes to fire the catapult, the nose of the carrier plunged downwards. John's Scimitar accelerated down towards the sea and a wall of spray that covered the ship's bow engulfed it. Realizing the error, John screamed an expletive as he disappeared into the wall of water. The Collin's dictionary defines an expletive as "an oath or sound expressing emotion rather than meaning". John expressed extreme emotion.

From where I sat, I was convinced John had died. However, at the next plunge of *Hermes'* bow, John's Scimitar could be seen standing on its tail. Leaving a huge plume of spray, he ruddered his aircraft to stay in the dip between swells, while he tried to pick up flying speed. Two hours later, after we had all landed at Yeovilton, John's face was still as white as a sheet. He left the Fleet Air Arm for BOAC shortly after the incident.

Chapter 10

764/738 Squadrons

Air Warfare Instruction

In November 1962, Tim Bolt, Nick Kerr, and I were selected to attend No 31 Air Warfare Instructors' Course. HMS *Excellent*, the Royal Navy Gunnery School in Portsmouth, held the theory portion of the course. This hallowed establishment, traditionally responsible for the maintenance of standards and traditions in the fleet, provided the lecture facilities where we learnt about ballistics, gravity drop, sight settings, and weapons.

On 10 January 1963, we found ourselves back at RNAS Lossiemouth in the north of Scotland in mid-winter. I love Scotland with a passion, but I have to admit that January is not a good month in the "frozen north". The three of us joined 764 Squadron, home of the Naval Air Strike School. We had been selected, because of our flying abilities and penchant for weapon delivery and aerial combat, to undergo intensive training to qualify as AWIs (Air Warfare Instructors).

In his introductory address, the school's commanding officer, Lieutenant Commander Nigel "Hans Christian" Anderdon told us that we would not be on the course if our flying ability was in doubt. Here we would be taught leadership and how to instruct. With those few words we were set to work.

Within three flying days we had completed a QFI (Qualified Flying Instructors) check flight, IRT (Instrument Rating Test) on the twin-seater Hunter T8, and four solo familiarization flights on the

Hunter GA11. By the end of January, we had flown 41 sorties, completing all the aerial gunnery missions, 20° rocketing, and eight low-level tactical navigation exercises. In the short, 28-day month of February, we flew 58 sorties. An extract from my flying logbook confirms this intensity. For example:

Feb 19 4 day and 2 night flights.
Feb 20 2 day and 2 night flights.
Feb 21 4 day and 2 night flights.

If weather permitted, we flew and enjoyed it.

We carried out dive bombing, low-level bombing, and night bombing. We flew and led formations of four aircraft carrying out divisional bombing as a formation. We high dived, pitched-up, and fanned—practising all possible variations of attack profiles. When the cloud base inland was too low to permit safe flying, we would attack targets at Tain Range from the sea, using a teardrop or looping profile. We learnt to adjust our sight-aiming picture to cater for variations in dive angle forced on us by inclement weather.

We learnt LABS (Low Altitude Bombing System); the technique used to deliver tactical nuclear bombs from the navy's inventory. Running in low-level on precise headings at precise speeds, we would initiate a timer as we passed an IP (Initial Point). At the end of the timer run, a horizontal needle would drop in the LABS indicator mounted in the cockpit. Applying four "G" within two seconds raised the needle. Keeping the needle centralized placed the aircraft in a perfect upward looping manoeuvre. As the aircraft nose passed through 45°, the bomb would release and catapult almost five miles towards the target.

At a position overhead the target, the nuclear weapon would detonate. In practice, we tossed a 25 lb bomb. On impact, this bomb detonated a smoke and flash charge, which could be plotted by the range staff. The miss distance would then be passed by radio to the pilots in the cockpit. Anything within 300 metres of the target was a good bomb, particularly as in the real event the explosion would be of similar size to that which destroyed Hiroshima.

If we messed up the run in and missed the IP, we were taught to continue the run to the target. Directly overhead, we would perform a pull-up into a perfect four "G" loop. At 110°, just passed vertical, the bomb would release and be tossed upwards. While the bomb travelled skywards, we would roll out of the loop, dive earth or seawards, and escape at low-level. The bomb, after reaching its apex, would fall directly down onto the target below. Somehow I never really fancied having to perform this alternate attack under real conditions. The only target worthy of attack by a nuclear weapon was bound to be heavily defended. Performing neat aerobatics, after awakening the defences by screaming in low-level over their heads, had an awful kamikaze feel about it.

By March, we combined all aspects of aerial combat by flying dummy strikes against selected targets over the north of Scotland. The strike would involve four aircraft flying in battle formation, escorted by two other Hunters. Two or three of the school's instructors with route and target knowledge would position themselves along the flight path to "bounce" the strike. Positioned to simulate firing Sidewinder missiles or cannons, they could attack at anytime. The fitted gunsight cameras recorded all attacks.

These strikes required professional planning and briefing. The flying involved navigation at medium- and low-level, and getting back on track and time after engaging in combat was never an easy task in a single-seat aircraft. All simulated weapon forms required correct attack profiles. Analysis of camera gun film would determine the success of the dummy attack. Each sortie included a number of dogfights, as the "enemy" instructors attempted to disrupt the strike's progress.

Heated debriefs were held after each mission when claims and counter claims were argued. Afterwards screening of all the camera gun films validated "kills" and "target destroyed" claims. These hectic, involved flights were carried out with strict adherence to safety— breaches carried heavy penalties.

One morning I flew as No3 (deputy leader) on one of these strike sorties. Uncharacteristically, the weather was near perfect as we climbed up to 20 000 feet heading south from Lossiemouth. The bogeys ("enemy" instructors) could not get near us. We could see them approaching from miles away in the perfect visibility, and we could manoeuvre the formation to negate their attacks. We turned eastwards and headed out over the North Sea. Eventually, turning northwards, we started our descent over the sea. The plan was to get to low-level, make a landfall, and fly up a Scottish valley to attack a target inland from Aberdeen.

Descending at 420 knots, I glanced ahead and noticed a small covering of cloud at low-level. Thinking it would be a thin layer on this perfect day, I ensured that I was in good battle formation before entering the cloud. However, the cloud was much thicker than I had expected. Losing sight of my leader, I transferred my gaze to the instrument flying panel. Watching the altimeter unwind rapidly, I realized that the needle was rushing through 600, 500, then 400 feet above the sea. Using strength induced by fright, I hauled back as hard as I could on the control column. Nigel Anderdon, flying as No 2, screamed over the radio to 'Pull out'—so helping to increase my strength.

We broke out the bottom of the cloud as the willing Hunter began to respond. The cloud base was almost at sea level and the bottom of my aircraft missed the waves by a few feet. Bursting back out of the top of the cloud, once again into clear conditions, I noticed that I had pulled eight "G" and overstressed my aircraft. In line with squadron safety policy, I announced my "sin" over the radio, broke out of the formation, and returned to Lossiemouth to land. In truth, I had lost my appetite for the remainder of that sortie; I was glad to fly back straight and level.

At debrief I was duly admonished by the flight leader. He emphasized that my actions had jeopardized the results of the strike. He quite correctly pointed out that in a real war, another formation might be needed to re-attack the same target with all the inherent dangers that involved.... I accepted the chastisement—he was right. In my heart, however, I knew and they knew that I was not the only one to overstress his aircraft. When we reappeared out of the top of the cloud, we were all pointing nose-high in perfect formation, indicating that they must have pulled the same "G" as I. If we had all flown into the sea on that perfect day, another "Bermuda triangle" legend would have been borne.

Live ammunition accompanied graduation sorties. The target was a monolithic rock in the sea off Cape Wrath, on the extreme northwest tip of the British Isles. Flying and fighting while carrying live rockets and bombs over a countryside at peace, requires exemplary discipline. The pilots shoulder huge responsibilities.

The Naval Strike School taught these skills to all its graduates. It was on solid foundations such as these that the much-vaunted "Top Gun" programmes and "Red Flag" exercises were based.

Finally, as a well deserved "jolly" on completion of the course, we flew across the North Sea to the Norwegian airfield, Sola, outside Stavanger. The plan was to make a landfall after a sea crossing, fly a

20-minute low-level leg, and then land to refuel. After lunch and another low-level leg around the fjords, we would fly back to Scotland. Unfortunately, after our crossing the weather closed in with severe snowstorms. Hanging onto Tom Skead's wing, we negotiated the thick snow clouds and landed safely, after the snowplough had cleared the runway. Tom, an instructor at the school, was also a South African. Over lunch we reminisced about the superb weather we had left behind in the land of our birth. Choosing a suitable interval between snow flurries, we dashed outside, boarded our aircraft and high-tailed it for Lossiemouth.

I spent 1964 stationed in Wales. RNAS Brawdy was, following the unwritten rules of naval airfield design policy, as far away from London and civilization as possible. The thought that naval aviators might overstay their welcome in "The Smoke", prompted the powers that be to position RNAS Culdrose almost at Land's End; RNAS Lossiemouth at the far northern extremity of Scotland; and RNAS Brawdy as far west as one could get in Pembrokeshire, Wales. Now while I would be the first to agree that the countryside around all three bases is as good as anywhere in Britain, nightlife and girls, so necessary to a naval aviator, tended to be few and far between.

In the case of Brawdy, the overriding desire to reach the extremities of the United Kingdom seemed to carry more weight than consideration about the prevailing weather conditions. After all, they were only building an airfield! British weather tends to come in from the west. The air masses saturate because of the long sea passage from the American coastline. The first stop-off point for this weather is Brawdy. At 300 feet above sea level, the weather positions above the cliffs overlooking St Brides Bay. Unfortunately, science has an effect on moist maritime air masses. When the air is forced to rise orographically over these cliffs the temperature decreases. When an air mass is saturated, this drop in temperature is sufficient to cause condensation as sea fog. This is Brawdy!

During the summer, RNAS Brawdy became one of the host air stations for the annual "silly season"—the air displays held every Saturday at military airfields around Britain. Display Saturday dawned unsurprisingly foggy. The fog lifted by mid-morning and became a solid cloud base of 200 feet above ground level. An unpromising start to an air display day! Any opportunity for visiting pilots to practise and pick out their required turning points disappeared—or so we thought. Suddenly, the noise of a jet filled the air as it flew at high speed around the airfield. Looking out of the window, one caught glimpses of a bright yellow Gnat twisting and turning around the tower and between the hangars. It was Flight Lieutenant Al Pollock from RAF Valley, practising his horizontal display.

It was quite the best flying display I have ever seen in those restricted conditions, but then I was only a junior pilot! Our commander air, in charge of all flying at the airfield, nearly had a heart attack while rushing to the tower to tell the pilot to land. His need for flying safety was obviously greater than my need for exhilaration!

As often happened at Brawdy, the weather cleared miraculously just after midday, allowing the airshow to take place. Al Pollock put on a marvellous display again, this time using his vertical sequence. His bright yellow Gnat was part of the newly formed "Yellow Jacks" team, which eventually changed aircraft colour and team name to the world famous "Red Arrows". On the completion of his aerobatic sequence, he flew a tight circuit before rolling out of the turn to land. Just before touchdown, he streamed the aircraft's braking parachute. This parachute deployed behind the Gnat. Unluckily, the edge of the chute caught one of the raised, centreline, lead-in lights. This had the immediate effect of changing the aircraft's nose-up landing attitude to one of sharply nose-down.

The aircraft landed heavily on its nose-wheel followed by the main-wheels, as the nose wheel oleo expanded and tossed the little jet back into the air. After a succession of kangaroo-like hops, Al finally managed to bring the sad-looking Gnat to a halt, with fuel and hydraulic fluid running out from countless damaged pipes. Being professionally embarrassed, Al gave the evening's get-together a miss.

Al Pollock had earned the nickname Mad Al. He was a brilliant pilot with fantastic aircraft handling ability and as such, his future in the military aviation world seemed secure. He also had an over-abundance of flair that tended to get him into trouble. He had been posted to Little Rissington, the RAF's Central Flying School, to become an instructor. At the culmination to each course, all the student instructors took part in an individual aerobatic competition. Each pilot got time to practise a display sequence prior to competition day. The Flying School staff took up their positions at the judge's table on the airfield. The student instructors were called in one after the other to perform their display. Each aircraft commenced its sequence from either the left or right of the judges, along the length of the runway.

The pilots then performed for five minutes before breaking into the circuit to land.

Everything was going according to plan until Al Pollock was called in to commence his display. After a suitable pause, the judges started craning their necks to the left and right to pick up Al's approaching aircraft, without any success. Suddenly, from behind the judge's table, and from the direction of the little town of Burton on the Water, down in the valley, the noise of an approaching aircraft was heard. The judges turned round to see Al arrive at low level, over the hedgerow, closely following the uphill terrain from out of the valley. In the judges' eyes, this was not on, particularly as he came over the hedge inverted! He never even had time to roll his aircraft the right way up before the judges called him up on the radio to tell him he was disqualified. From that day on, when people spoke of him, always in terms of reverence I might add, he was referred to as "Mad Al Pollock".

Our (Fleet Air Arm) Al was a graduate from Cambridge. Al Hickling started later than most in the world of aviation because of his studies. Despite this, RAF Linton-on-Ouse Flying School noticed him immediately, not because of any particular flying skill, although he had many, but because of his car. Al had acquired a 1926 Rolls-Royce, which was remarkable when compared to the well-used jalopies that belonged to the other student pilots.

Linton was situated ten miles north of the beautiful city of York. Apart from the wonderful Minster, Yorkshire had its fair share of lovely pubs. The time the students spent in these attractions was very unevenly shared! After supper in the mess, the cars would stream out of the main gate of the base, each one heading for a favourite local. The journey to the pub was generally reasonable, but return journeys were often slightly more hair-raising. Al Hickling was a passenger in a car that overturned coming back one night, and he had the misfortune to break his right leg—quite a serious fracture that required a solid plaster cast from his ankle to his thigh. It also meant that his flying was suspended and he was back-coursed until he was fit again to fly.

Not being able to fly is perhaps the worst punishment that a pilot can suffer and in our Al's case, frustration became the order of the day. Every evening, when the exodus to the pubs took place, Al stayed behind. None of the small jalopies could accommodate a chap on crutches with a stiff leg sticking out in front of him. Our Al did not lack initiative and one night, after all the others had departed, frustration finally got the better of him.

Pushing himself out of the deep mess chairs, he mounted his crutches and headed out to his own car. The huge Rolls-Royce had the space necessary to accommodate all the accoutrements involved with the broken limb.

His serviceable left leg could operate the clutch and brake. His right leg stuck out under the dashboard of the big old car. His wooden crutch, clutched in his right hand, depressed the accelerator, while his left hand rotated the bus-size steering wheel. Our Al was a very capable pilot and his reactions and anticipation enabled him to successfully negotiate the narrow Yorkshire by-roads to the pub. In fact, he coped admirably on the way back as well, until he rounded the front of the officers' mess on his way to park his car. Behind the mess, the road made a sharp right-hand turn, followed by a short straight of about 20 metres. Sufficient speed had to be built up to carry the car up a short sharp rise onto the students' parking area. The problem occurred during the slight left turn followed by the slight right turn, while accelerating up the rise.

The crutch, depressing the accelerator, was bumped off the pedal during the left and right rotation of the huge steering wheel. It slipped off the pedal to the left and the foot of the crutch ended up under the brake pedal. Careering across the parking area, our Al placed his good left foot firmly onto the brake pedal and applied pressure to bring the car to a stop. Unfortunately, the harder he pressed down on the brake, the more power was applied to the engine by the crutch that was now angled across the accelerator. Before being able to rectify the problem, the car came to an abrupt halt after breaking through the wooden wall of the Nissan huts, used in those days as accommodation for students.

Realizing that he was now in trouble, he decided to hobble off to his bed and report the incident in the morning, on the principle that things always look better in the daylight. He limped off to his room on his crutches, only to find that he could not open his bedroom door. The wall he had crashed through was his own and the front of his car had pushed his bed, wardrobe, and dressing table hard up against the door! Next morning, when he backed his Rolls gently out of the wreckage of his room, he discovered that, just as in a Tom and Jerry cartoon, the complete shape of the stately old Rolls-Royce, including the winged lady, remained as a new opening into his room. That was our Al.

In 1968, a Defence Review in Britain cut huge sums from the Defence Budget, resulting in the loss of numerous RAF squadrons and navy aircraft carriers. Of course, these cuts reduced the country's military capability, and put many servicemen out of a job. Tempers ran white hot, to the extent that a pilot took his Hunter jet and flew at low level down the River Thames passing *under* the bridges close to Parliament, to express his disgust at what the politicians were doing to the military. When the radio announced the report, opinions in squadron crew rooms throughout the country were unanimous that the pilot could only have been one of the Als. In this case it turned out to be their Al, who was then medically discharged from the service.

During 1964, I flew as Number 3 in the 738 Squadron Hunter aerobatics team operating out of the Royal Naval Air Station Brawdy in Pembrokeshire, Wales. Summers in Britain were highlighted by the airshow season. Selected RAF bases held "Battle of Britain" days while the Naval Air Stations hosted Navy Days. For a period of about eight weeks there was a military airshow every Saturday somewhere in Britain. This allowed the public, all over the country, to view their air forces on display. It served a secondary but equally important role, as a successful recruitment campaign. If you were in a display team, however, it meant that every Saturday you flew the same programme at a different airfield. In the aviation business, it was referred to as the "silly season" for good reason!

Pilots are exuberant by nature. These characteristics were well understood by instructional staff at all flying schools who taught restraint and discipline during every phase of pilot training. Then came the "silly season"! For perhaps the first time in his career the pilot was given an aircraft and told, 'Get out there and show off.' It could have been a recipe for disaster!

We had flown up to RAF Leuchars on the banks of the Tay River, just opposite the world famous St Andrews Golf Course. It was a lovely clear day, ideal for flying, and the Scottish crowds were there in the thousands. On the circuit there was great rivalry between the teams and the solo display pilots—everybody endeavoured to get the utmost out of his aircraft. In those days, the Hunter and the Lightning were competing for individual honours.

The Hunter could not compete with the superior performance of the Lightning, so the Hunter pilot concentrated on showing off the agility and manoeuvrability of his aircraft. He consequently performed the majority of his manoeuvres "outside". He flew all his turns pushing negative "G". The Hunter, like all British aircraft, dripped fuel and hydraulic fluid, which showed up as dirty marks under the aeroplane's belly. This particular Hunter was the worst looking aircraft in the entire fleet. The continuous negative "G" caused the leaks to come out the top of the fuselage. At the Saturday night cocktail parties, this Hunter pilot was easy to recognize. He was the man with the pillar-box red eyes. The blood, continually forced into his head by his outside turns, had burst the capillaries in his eyes.

The Lightning pilot had the advantage of power. Two great after-burning engines gave his aircraft stunning acceleration and climb capabilities, which the Hunter could not match. The Lightning pilot, therefore, built his display to show off these capabilities.

During the afternoon of the display, we climbed into our aircraft to wait our turn to taxi out for our performance. Sitting in the cockpit with the radio on, we listened to the chatter between the air traffic controller and the aircraft performing before us.

The Lightning pilot was given permission to taxi and hold at the end of the runway. RAF Leuchars is at sea level where the air is densest, and engines can obtain maximum thrust. On receiving take-off clearance, the Lightning pilot taxied onto the runway as close to the end as he could get. He opened up to full power, and even above the radio noise, we could hear the double explosion as both his after-burners ignited.

Within seconds, his aircraft accelerated rapidly down the runway with the afterburners exhibiting the familiar diamond pattern in the white-hot exhaust. At rotation speed he pulled back the stick to ease the Lightning off the ground. Immediately on breaking clear of the runway surface, he levelled off at approximately ten feet, to gain maximum acceleration in the dense air. Unfortunately, when raising the flaps, the Lightning, like most aircraft, tended to sink initially. From ten feet not much sink was needed before the under surface of the tailpipe scraped the runway. Although the pilot reacted quickly to regain his intended flight path, the scrape was sufficient to rupture the aeroplane's skin.

The Lightning Mk6 had a bulge under the tailpipe that contained a fuel tank, and this tank ruptured. As he reached the far end of the runway, the pilot hauled the aircraft into a 60° nose up climb—a manoeuvre the Hunter pilot could not hope to emulate. This rapid rotation allowed the afterburners to ignite the fuel streaming from the ruptured tank. The Lightning screamed skyward like a comet with a 200-metre long flaming tail.

A truly British characteristic is one of "unflappability". In a cool, calm, and collected voice the air traffic controller called, 'Lightning pilot, you are on fire,' whereupon the Lightning pilot, in an equally dignified voice answered, 'Roger, ejecting.'

What a sight, what an airshow! A puff appeared around the cockpit of the rapidly climbing comet. The canopy came flying off, followed by the pilot attached to the ejection seat. The Martin-Baker chair worked as advertised and the pilot was soon floating down to the earth he had so recently left. Knowing the pilot was safe, the rest of us watched the end of the display.

The aircraft, now without a driver, continued skywards and then, dropping a wing, it arced gracefully over until it was pointing directly towards the ground. All the time the flaming tail was etched against the pale blue Scottish sky. With the help of gravity, the aircraft accelerated downwards. It disappeared behind one of the low hills just west of Leuchars. A few seconds later, great clouds of black smoke billowed skywards signifying the end of a very short, but dramatic, display.

Photographers, both amateur and professional, should never miss an opportunity to attend an airshow. Photographic "scoops" are always a possibility. One of my most cherished memories was of the Red Arrows' performance at RNAS Yeovilton, on the 75th Anniversary of the Fleet Air Arm. They gave their usual polished display and finished by inscribing a perfect heart with coloured smoke, against a dark, cloudy background. Then a single aircraft pierced the heart with a perfect smoke arrow, leaving an unforgettable image etched in the sky.

Unable to match the sheer artistry of the Red Arrows, Fleet Air Arm Air days usually started with an impact of another kind. The programme began to the dull roar and blade clapping of a helicopter under strain. From the far side of the display area, a chopper ascended with an old car dangling from underneath the cargo sling. The noise and the slow ascent ensured the avid attention of the spectators. At a thousand feet above the ground, the pilot "pickles his load" and the car dropped like a stone. Debris and wheels flew in every direction on impact. At RNAS Culdrose in the early 1960s, the drop was particularly impressive. The station commander used one of the old bangers standing outside the wardroom for the demolition drop. He found out too late from a distraught lieutenant that the vintage vehicle was a collector's item due for restoration.

Annually, the Biggin Hill Air Show drew enormous crowds of spectators. The combination of proximity to London and the nostalgia of its Battle of Britain history, proved wonderful draw cards. Two Sea Vixens participated in the show—one flew and the other was on view in the static park. The static park Vixen gave two Yeovilton pilots the opportunity for an extended weekend in London. Willie Hare flew the aircraft to Biggin Hill on the Friday before the show. Mark "Boysie" Thomson was to fly the aircraft back to Somerset on the Monday morning after the show.

Boysie arrived at a deserted airfield. Saturday's thousands had disappeared completely. A solitary squadron leader was there to look after Boysie's requirements, give him the weather briefing, file the necessary flight plan, and answer Boysie's request for taxi clearance over the radio. After reaching runway threshold, Boysie received take-off clearance.

Biggin Hill was named after the hill upon which the airfield was built. The highest point of this hill was roughly in the centre of the airfield. Standing on the threshold, pilots could only see half of the runway. Interestingly, Biggin had two hard-surfaced runways starting from the threshold, and with only a 10° difference in heading. One of the runways was very narrow and the other was big and wide. Having not operated previously from the field, Boysie naturally lined up on the wide runway.

A group of workers, mowing airfield grass, began waving and gesticulating animatedly. Boysie, quite moved by the friendly gesture, waved back as he released the brakes for take-off. Gathering speed slowly, the heavy jet accelerated up the hill. At the crest of the rise, the rest of the airfield came into view and suddenly Boysie realized why the workers had waved so enthusiastically. The broad runway ended abruptly, whilst the narrow one continued far into the distance! The Vixen careered off the end onto the soft, rain-soaked grass and promptly buried itself up to the wingroots.

It was during the "silly season" of 1964 that I flew 50 hours in a month for the only time in my entire flying career. We had normal instruction flights during the day and on some nights. After the daily programme had finished, the Hunter team would practise aerobatics, and on weekends, we would dash here and there across the country to perform at various airshows. September turned out to be a brilliant weather month so we flew a great deal.

My last flight for the month was as a member of a 20-ship Hunter formation flypast, in honour of RNAS Brawdy receiving the Freedom of Haverfordwest. The flypast went well as did the neat return and break into the Brawdy pattern for landing. Approaching as No 13 in the stream to land, I glanced at the cockpit clock. I worked out that if I could stretch this flight for a further five minutes I would have made the magical 50 hours in the month.

Pushing the throttle forward, I broke out of the stream and re-entered the pattern to land at the end of the stream. The boss bollocked [*sic*] me for spoiling the tiddly formation, but I was ready with my excuse. Apologizing profusely, I told him how I had been caught in slipstream from the previous aircraft, and I felt the safest thing to do was to put on power and go round again. The bollocking stopped and he congratulated me instead on using "good airmanship" in a tricky situation! Those 50 hours filled two and a half pages in my logbook, totalling 56 flights.

One cannot leave Wales without mentioning rugby. In 1960, I travelled by train from Yeovilton to Cardiff to watch the test match between Wales and the Springboks at Cardiff Arms Park. The weather was atrocious. Instead of the usual British drizzle, a near tropical rainstorm, accompanied by 50mph winds, blew all day from the west. I managed to get standing room behind the posts on the east stand, face on into the wind.

Within two minutes from kick-off, the 30 players were unrecognizable. The sodden ball grew larger with each succeeding layer of mud. Play was stopped regularly to allow the players to wipe mud from their faces. A penalty in front of the posts gave Keith Oxlee, the Springbok flyhalf, a chance to hoist the heavy ball between the posts for the only score of the game. I cheered momentarily. The quick, menacing glances of the surrounding Welsh supporters stifled further rejoicing and I reverted to the rain-bedraggled, sad sack appearance of the rest of the crowd. Despite the win, this awful day ranks as one of the worst in my life. An hour after the final whistle had mercifully blown, the River Taff burst its banks, and the stadium was flooded in two feet of water.

On a much better day in 1964, I watched Wales beat England at Twickenham, before travelling by train back to Wales. Arriving at Paddington Station, I was amongst hundreds of jubilant Welsh fans. The carriages of the train were of the old design, with separate compartments for eight people, most of which were already half filled. Standing at each open door was a Welshman stating loudly the need for a bass, tenor, or alto to complete the choir in the compartment. What a wonderful journey—non-stop singing from London to Welsh Wales. An unforgettable experience!

Chapter 11

890 Squadron, HMS *Ark Royal*

In mid-January 1965, HMS *Ark Royal* departed for the waters off the north of Scotland for a two-month shake-down cruise. The ship had been refitted in the dockyard and it was necessary to go to sea to rectify any snags that may have developed. Shake-down cruises occurred in home waters so rapid repairs could be carried out if required. Wherever the carrier sailed, the air group accompanied her, even though the North Sea in mid-winter did not have good flying weather.

Eventually the captain sailed into the Moray Firth off Inverness, in the lee of the Cairngorm Mountains, which shielded the worst of the winter weather coming in from the Atlantic. With the cloud base rising to 2 000 feet, flying operations could take place, although the aircrew were not too enthusiastic. Thoughts of falling into the sea under freezing conditions, often occupied one's mind. However, flying continued, interrupted by the passage of alternating cold and warm fronts.

The cold fronts brought embedded cumulo-nimbus clouds that spread sheets of snow over the Scottish mainland. The snow was so thick that the ship lost its SAR helicopter that was hovering alongside the carrier's stern during jet landings. The intakes clogged with snow, the engines flamed out, and the Wessex ditched alongside the ship. Fortunately, the entire crew was rescued.

The warm fronts brought less violent weather but solid cloud cover extended from 2 000 feet up to 35 000 feet. Even at that height the cloud tops remained wispy, leaving no clear horizon. Altogether lousy weather for flying from a ship.

Lieutenants Dave Pickles and Sandy Munro were Sea Vixen pilots on 890 Squadron. Dave had flown Gannet turboprop AEW (Airborne Early Warning) aircraft before converting to the Vixen. One night, while landing-on, somewhere off Hong Kong in the South China Sea, he struck the HI-LO landing aid on the port side of the deck. Most of his aircraft fell into the sea, leaving the tail hanging over the side. This frightening experience left Dave understandably excitable. Sandy was a Scotsman without the characteristic dour, Scot's sense of humour. He was one of the squadron's jokers.

One morning the two pilots were briefed to fly a sortie of AI (air interceptions). The weather was stable, but warm front cloud was continuous to an estimated top of 35 000 feet. The interceptions were to be conducted in the clear above that height.

After launching, each aircraft climbed through the cloud to begin the exercise. Thirty-five thousand feet of cloud requires concentration on the aircraft's flying instruments. The advent of the Vixen had brought new technology to the fleet. Gone was the old mercury-switch levelled, air-driven gyro, and artificial horizons, with all their inherent errors. The Vixen was equipped with an MRG (Master Reference Gyro). The stabilized platform drove the entire instrument suite adorning the pilot's flying panel. Beautiful to look at and use provided it worked.

Excitable Dave was levelling out after his climb to altitude; he was still in high cirrus conditions, without a clear horizon, when it happened. Alarm bells from the audio warning system, drew his attention to the warning panel. An adrenaline rush raised his blood pressure when he realized that his aircraft had suffered an MRG failure. He would have to descend through 35 000 feet of solid cloud, using his tiny emergency AH (artificial horizon) as reference. He called the ship on the radio and notified them of his problems. Without a proper horizon he was already experiencing the onset of vertigo.

Meanwhile, Sandy was being vectored in to intercept Dave's aircraft on the first run of the exercise. He was brought in directly astern and slightly below Dave's aircraft. He picked Dave's Vixen up visually at about a mile range and realized that, coming from behind and below, Dave could not have seen him approach. While Dave was explaining his predicament to the ship's controllers, Sandy accelerated closing range from astern.

Just before he past Dave, Sandy pulled out to overtake on Dave's right-hand side. He then rolled his aircraft upside down and flew past inverted, at the same time saying to Dave, 'Hey Dave, what are you doing upside down?'

It took some powerful persuasion to finally convince Dave which way up was correct. After a ten minute calming down period, Dave joined Sandy in close formation and the two aircraft let down safely together.

Shortly after launching a few nights later, I noticed a large explosion on the flight-deck. Sandy's Vixen had struck the round-down (back end) of *Ark Royal* while carrying out a night-deck landing. Fortunately, his hook remained attached to his aircraft and it caught an arrestor wire and brought the badly damaged aircraft to a stop. Sandy and his observer were uninjured.

After participating in a large NATO fleet exercise in the frigid seas off the Northern Norwegian coast, *Ark* paid a visit to Bergen. Apart from the dramatic scenery, still covered in winter snow, NATO business included the wash-up of the recently completed exercise. As my name had once again reached the top of the list, I had to carry out security checks of the hall where the debriefing was being held. Not normally an arduous task, but, as King Olaf of Norway was to attend as his country's commander in chief, we had to be particularly vigilant.

Satisfied that my team had completed the task assigned, I took time to wander around inside the hall before the crowd started to gather. I was interested in the sort of mini-throne positioned in the front row for the king. This high-backed, wooden seat was covered in delicate and intricate carvings. Studying these works of art, my eyes strayed to the back of the chair. My imagination worked overtime when I noticed, behind the right upper part of the backrest, a lump of chewing gum stuck to the wood. I still like to think of the old king surreptitiously chewing away, until asked to address his audience. I imagine him, like a schoolboy, popping the lump behind the throne before beginning his speech. I guess he must have forgotten it was there!

During the passage back to Britain, I, as the squadron warfare instructor, was to fly an unusual mission. Tactical nuclear weapons had been in storage aboard the ship for a considerable period and the white-coated, thick-spectacled boffins decided it would be prudent to check their condition. To do this one bomb would fly ashore aboard my Sea Vixen. We were to fly an operational strike profile before landing at RNAS Lossiemouth, where a team of experts would check the state of the weapon. Our flight included the catapult launch, a longish navigation leg in the frigid temperatures at altitude, a fast operational speed descent, followed by a 50-mile high-speed dash at low level, before landing.

Throughout the flight I could not keep my eyes from the 2 000 pound green bomb under my port wing. Destruction from the bomb would be akin to that wreaked on Hiroshima. Despite the temptation to experiment, I managed to keep my trigger finger off the release button.

At Lossiemouth, I was marshalled into an area enclosed by security screens. As I shut down the engines, white coats besieged the aircraft, armed with stethoscopes, thermometers, wigglyamp meters, Geiger counters, and the assorted equipment one normally associates with an intensive care unit. Paul and I were ignored except for a brusque invitation to bugger off. Maybe I should have fiddled with the trigger!

After a quick return to Britain to give the ship's company embarkation leave, HMS *Ark Royal* sailed again in June 1965, bound for a year-long cruise to the Far East. Indonesia, under strong Communistic influence, withdrew from the United Nations and began making war-like noises against Singapore and Malaysia. We were to be part of the deterrent force sent out to persuade Indonesia's president, Sukarno, not to do anything stupid. The Straits of Sumatra carried huge volumes of sea traffic, and as one of the world's choke points, it achieved prominence on the Soviet expansion programme.

The almost obligatory stops at Gibraltar and Malta interrupted passage through the Mediterranean. I enjoyed both visits, as it was always a pleasure to have a change from the sight, sounds, and smell of the ship and its male population. Paul Waterhouse and I flew ashore to RNAS Hal Far for a night stop, which included a run around the bright lights and bars where Paul made the most of this heaven-sent opportunity.

Returning to the wardroom, Paul fell asleep as soon as his head hit the pillow. He slept with only a sheet covering him. He awoke at 05h00 to music emanating from the radio, which he had neglected to turn off before falling into bed. Being a Catholic island, each morning's programme began with a beautiful rendering of *Ave Maria*.

The wardroom had been designed with Mediterranean temperatures in mind. Each room had a high ceiling; the tall windows were ornately pointed at the top, and the colour scheme was pure white. Being mid-summer, the rays of the rising sun slanted through Paul's window in a bright shaft of light. Paul, badly affected by the previous night's vino, awoke on his back with his hands neatly folded across his chest, on top of the white sheet. Gradually opening one eye, he slowly took in his situation—pure white, pointed arches, shaft of sunlight, hands neatly folded, and the gentle strains of an organ playing the *Ave Maria*. His first conscious thought was, 'Bloody Hell! Now I really have overdone it!'

Shortly after returning to sea, we entered the Suez Canal. Passage through this waterway, became a game of bluff between the Egyptian Defence Force and the Fleet Air Arm. The Egyptian Air Force had an airfield alongside the canal. Because canal bookings had to be made months in advance, the Egyptian Air Force ensured that almost their entire inventory of aircraft were flown to this field before the carrier passed. They knew that naval intelligence personnel would be counting and photographing everything they possibly could and they wanted to make a major impression of force.

They also put on an air display for our benefit. As the huge ship approached the edge of the airfield, a MiG17 Fresco took off and passed beneath the bow of our ship. The pilot then pulled up into a well-flown, low-level aerobatic show. After landing, a formation of nine ILYUSHIN IL-28U Mascots, light attack bombers, gave a neat flypast.

Not to be outdone, the commander Air of *Ark* played his own little charade. He had all the aircraft brought on deck from the hangar, knowing that Egyptian intelligence agents would be counting their numbers. He then had a Scimitar, Sea Vixen, and Gannet towed in succession up the deck, down the lift into the hangar, through the hanger, and then back up the after lift to repeat the process. This procession kept going during the 100-mile odd passage, and must have filled dozens of Egyptian notebooks and slates! Boys will be boys!

In Singapore, we found the island overflowing with military personnel. Before the ship entered the dockyard, we flew our Vixens and Scimitars to RAF Changi so that we could continue flying. As the RAF officers' mess was full, hotels in downtown Singapore accommodated us. As luck would have it, the Ocean Park Hotel where we stayed, was the same hotel that housed air-hostesses from a number of airlines. From the austere, all male, metal environs of the carrier, it was akin to landing in paradise with girls on tap!

On a later visit, we moved to the Ambassador Hotel, a high-rise building on the main road into Singapore—fortunately still very close to the Ocean Park. I had two interesting experiences in this hotel. I had just put down my bags in my room, when I heard a loud shout outside the door. I flung the door open and looked into the passageway, to see a young Chinese chap walking towards the lift. This fellow, son of the owner, was an under-manager in the hotel. He had been born with an affliction that caused an involuntary shout to explode from his lips at frequent intervals. The rest of the staff, being used to these shouts, ignored them, but they sure kept visitors on the hop!

As a gimmick, I developed the capability of doing the same thing, whilst keeping a straight face. Initially it was difficult, because people react in odd ways to sudden shouts, but with practice it is possible. However, since June and I married I have had to stop telling that little story, under threat of divorce!

The other experience occurred early one morning while I was having breakfast in the dining room on the seventh floor of the hotel. I was to fly the first sortie of the day, so I was the only person in the dining room apart from two Chinese waiters. Dawn was breaking and the sky over Singapore Bay was still misty and grey. With Singapore being on the Equator, the room was open to the elements on the side facing the bay. I kept thinking to myself how lucky I was to have this opportunity and experience, which was completely different to my South African upbringing.

These thoughts strengthened as I watched an elderly gentleman, on his morning constitutional, walking around the edge of the bay. He stopped, lent on the rail, and looked out to sea. It was a picturesque and romantic scene on this lovely morning. I was seated seven storeys up in the air and at least 200 yards from the old man.

Suddenly, I became aware of impending doom. A young man appeared from behind a dense bush and tiptoed stealthily towards the unaware old man. I sensed that a mugging was imminent and could not restrain myself from trying to warn the "victim". Only a powerful voice can carry 200 yards, even in the still of early morning, but at least I tried. I jumped out of my seat and started hollering, hoping to attract the old man's attention and to distract his would-be attacker. On my third shout, I saw the "assailant" swivel gently on tiptoe and proceed to reverse his path using the same stealthy movements. To my acute embarrassment, I later discovered that my "assailant" was a fitness fanatic performing the ritualistic art of Hai-Chi. It is often said that Chinese faces are inscrutable, but I had no difficulty in noticing that both waiters were highly amused at my well-intentioned *faux pas*.

One of the few areas that the Fleet Air Arm tended to neglect was in the retraining of experienced aviators. Often good pilots, who had spent time in non-flying jobs, such as those at the Admiralty, went back to frontline carrier flying, without the opportunity to regain their flying skills. One of our senior pilots found himself in this unenviable position and experienced great difficulty readjusting. His carrier landings, or arrivals, gained him unwanted notoriety. One morning I overheard two chief petty officers discussing the pilot, saying, 'There goes the minister without port oleo!'

Equatorial conditions, particularly off the island of Borneo at night, were not ideal for flying. The high moisture content of the warm tropical air produced what we called the "Fish Bowl" effect. The horizon was never clearly defined—like looking through the opaque glass of a fish bowl. What this moisture did produce in abundance were classic displays of St Elmo's Fire. Electrical discharges illuminated the leading edges of the aircraft's wings, nose and metal canopy bar. Sparks appeared to jump between the tip of the in-flight refuelling probe and the drop tanks. The Vixen windscreen glass would be covered in criss-cross flashes of light in dramatic displays.

One evening, when Lt Colin Lightfoot was flying as my observer, we had an incredible display. Colin had never seen it before as he was always stuck away in the Vixen coalhole; he asked me to describe it for him. I tried my best to convey a spectacular image and he was most appreciative, up to a point. Getting a little carried away by the ethereal display, I said, 'Colin, the entire canopy bar is now glowing like a crown. I really feel like the Lord tonight!' That was enough for Colin. Forever fearful of the carrier deck waiting down below, he stopped my eulogy in midstream, saying, 'Stop that. Don't let's take a chance tonight, OK!'

Borneo was a scary island to fly over. It was mountainous, with tops rising to 6 000 feet and every inch covered by dark green tropical jungle. The green canopy was at least 200 feet above the jungle floor. Ejection would certainly prove fatal. The parachute would probably snag in the trees and leave the unfortunate occupant suspended 100 feet or more in the air. The aircraft wreckage would disappear through the canopy of green, leaving no telltale mark from which to initiate a search and rescue. I always felt uncomfortable over the forbidding island.

The ship carried out an army support exercise with British troops positioned along the jungle frontier, which faced the Indonesian occupied sector of the island. Navigation was extremely difficult, because no feature was visible under the green leafy canopy. Because the Vixen carried a navigator, we flew in to locate the ground troops and lead single-seat Scimitars, whose pilots could not have coped with the navigation. Lt Paul Waterhouse, my navigator and friend of many years, astounded me with his skill. Three times in one day, he guided us to the exact location of the ground troops. Remember, he could not see out of his coalhole and his navigation was carried out using on-board instrumentation. In those days global positioning indicators had not been thought of. It was a masterly display of navigational skill.

An observer serving on 890 Squadron wrote the following poem, which I believe illustrates the task, frustrations, and fears of a Sea Vixen observer. I dedicate it to Paul and all the other Sea Vixen observers.

THE BLOODY O's
The bloody programmes bloody right.
There's bloody flying this bloody night
It's the usual bloody fright
For bloody O's.

The bloody briefings bloody bad.
The bloody D's are bloody mad
And bloody Ops, it's bloody sad
For bloody O's.

Our bloody holes a bloody cuss,
No bloody room to swing a puss,
Who bloody cares for bloody us,
The bloody O's.

The bloody cramp, the bloody heat,
The bloody straps, the bloody seat.
No bloody room for bloody feet,
Poor bloody O's

The bloody cat is bloody 'S',
You're in the air no bloody mess,
All bloody work no bloody rest,
For bloody O's.

The bloody set is bloody duff
The API is bloody rough
The TACAN too, it's bloody tough
On bloody O's.

The bloody hour has bloody gone
Your bloody job is bloody done
Of sign of ship, there's bloody none,
You bloody O's.

A bloody voice it's bloody John
The bloody path, you're bloody on,
The bloody fun has just begun,
For bloody O's.

Four bloody greens, on bloody sight.
The bloody speeds not bloody right
Too bloody late, sit bloody tight
You bloody O's.

A bloody thump, a bloody sigh
You're bloody down and wonder why
You bloody fly.
You bloody O's.

Over centuries Jolly Jack, the typical Royal Navy sailor, and backbone of the service, has built for himself a deserved reputation as a professional seaman. A man who has and still does serve, often under extremely trying circumstances, for little more than knowing he has done his duty. A man to rely on in any situation.

For all that, he is not without humour. On the contrary, Jack has developed Jackspeak, a language peculiar to the navy. It is a masterpiece of brevity and entertainment. This language caters admirably for all situations, particularly when visiting foreign ports. Any Dutchman is referred to as a "Cloggie", presumably because of his national footwear. Foreign currency of any kind is called "ickie"—'How many ickies do you get to the pound in this place?' Under these circumstances the ickie (whether it be a franc, dollar or cruzeiro), is sub-divided into a hundred "klebbies". An ickie store is, of course, a bank.

Females, never far from a sailor's mind, are known as "lumpy jumpers" if they are civilians and "double-breasted matelots" if members of the WRNS. A dim person is a "real Kelvin"—pretty close to Absolute Zero. Naval padres are "Amen wallahs", "God botherers", "Devil dodgers", "Sky pilots", or just plain "Bish". Poorly designed equipment is said to be "as much use as an ashtray on a motorbike".

Naval understatement is nowhere more apparent than in the naming of the Fleet Air Arm's aerobatic teams. Traditionally, the world over, aerobatic teams have adopted eye-catching, commercially attractive sounding names. The Thunderbirds, Blue Angels, Red Arrows, and Silver Falcons are some of the more famous. Royal Navy teams tend to use more mundane names.

Simon Idiens led an excellent five-ship Sea Vixen team in the mid-1960s and called it Simon's Circus. Another equally good team was known as Fred's Five. The Hunter team, which flew out of HMS *Heron* (RNAS Yeovilton) during the 1970s, attempted to buck the trend and called themselves the Blue Herons. However, because the pilots were all experienced and rather elderly, the team was known locally as the Phyllosan Four.

In the mind's eye, the feature associated almost exclusively with Jolly Jack, is the tattoo. From the days of Popeye, the sailor's torso has been adorned with tattoos. Curiously, the tendency is decreasing amongst matelots, while becoming fashionable with modern youth, especially young ladies. However, in the 1950s and 60s, tattooing was still prized by many sailors, keen to display mementoes of trips abroad.

Petty Officer Dean was on board HMS *Ark Royal* during the 1965/66 Far Eastern cruise. He was a flight-deck handler, who drove the tractors that towed aircraft around the flight-deck and in the hangar. The confined space aboard ship, coupled with the movement of a pitching deck, made this job one that required real skill. Dixie Dean was a master at his trade.

In the tropics, when flying was not taking place, the men could remove their compulsory overalls. The dress then favoured by most people working on the flight-deck was navy-blue shorts and sandals. From a health point of view this was encouraged as it exposed the body to the elements. In the close confines of a warship health needs were always considered.

P/O Dean was a well-known collector of tattoos. When I last saw him he had over a hundred, spread evenly over almost his entire body. It had become standard routine for him to acquire a new work of art from every port of call. Strolling around the deck, I spotted Dixie sitting on his tractor. His eyes were staring at the crook of his left elbow as he moved his forearm up and down. 'What have you got this time, Dixie?' I asked. He answered 'Cor, Sir, I've got a beauty! Jump up on the old tractor and have a look.'

Needing no further coaxing, I climbed up to see that he had a door hinge tattooed neatly into the skin covering the inside of his elbow. He was watching the hinge open and close while exercising his arm. He had also insisted that the artist include an oilcan with a long-nosed spout, dripping a drop of oil to lubricate the hinge. He did not want the annoyance of a squeak developing!

Innovation was highly regarded amongst the tattoo fraternity and men were at pains to outdo each other. The British Union Jack, placed above the navel, with the bearer's date of birth underneath, was commonplace. Some added, "Made in England" to complete the picture. Well-proportioned, nude ladies adorned thighs and would dance invitingly when the owner flexed his muscles. "Mild and Bitter" often labelled each nipple. On the soles of feet were the words "THE END". Not visible when the man was awake was the word "SHUT" tattooed on his eyelids, but it could be clearly read when he was asleep.

An unusual sight was a dotted line circling a sailor's neck, under which had been written, "Tear along the dotted line". The phrase "I hate officers" was inscribed along the edge of right-hand palms, on the side that faced officers when giving the obligatory salute. A few wardroom stewards had the same message written along the upper portion of their right hands; to be read as the steward placed a plate in front of an officer. However, these derogatory messages were usually applied when Jolly Jack was filled with the bravado brought on by copious amounts of vino, plonk, or grog.

The recipients of these tattoos suffered a fair amount of discomfort while the punctured skin healed. The scabs often suppurated in the tropical heat. Some "art works" must have been excruciatingly painful. I have seen large eyeballs staring from the cheeks of a man's bottom. Another intricate scene was of flames emanating from a man's behind. On one cheek was a devil shovelling coal into the furnace—on the other side a fireman and hose attempting to douse the flames. How these men sat down during the first week defies imagination.

Perhaps, a sailor, who had just returned from a sentence in naval detention barracks, made the most striking statement. He had two words inscribed across his back, one above the other, in letters three inches high:

**GOVERNMENT
PROPERTY**

May Day 1966, HMS *Ark Royal* headed westwards on fast passage across the Indian Ocean. The unhappy situation that had been festering for so long in Rhodesia reached a crisis when Prime Minister Ian Smith declared UDI (Unilateral Declaration of Independence). Reacting to an uncertain state of affairs, the British government deployed a squadron of RAF Javelins to Lusaka in Northern Rhodesia (now Zambia), and sent the carrier at best speed to the Moçambique Channel. We swapped one confrontation for another!

What a predicament we found ourselves in! There were 24 officers on 890 Squadron; 12 pilots and 12 observers. It appeared likely that we would be placed on a war footing as soon as we reached the station off Beira. Half the aircrew had ties with Southern Africa. I had relatives in Rhodesia; Ron Badenhorst had served in the British South Africa Police in Rhodesia; others had completed their schooling in South Africa; and our sympathies lay with Mr Smith. However, we were in the service and required to do our duty, albeit an onerous one. Fortunately, good sense prevailed and hostilities did not commence.

Nevertheless, the ship did spend many weeks on station, approximately 100 miles off Beira. Our task was to stop oil from reaching Rhodesia. The Royal Navy placed frigates approximately 200 nautical miles north and south of the carrier. The task of these ships was to act as pickets. Using their radar detection systems, they were to identify and track any vessels heading towards Beira, the Moçambique port through which Rhodesia received oil. On spotting a suspicious radar track, the information would pass to the carrier and an aircraft would despatch to investigate. This was tedious business for aircrew, because it entailed many hours of standby duties strapped into aircraft under the burning tropical sun.

At sundown, flying stations were cancelled, and aircrew could relax in the wardroom. As a party was developing one night, my OC, Lt Cdr Tony Pearson, entered the bar. He knew that I was a teetotaller and headed straight to me. After ensuring that I had not had a drink, he told my observer, Paul Waterhouse, and me to get our kit on; he wanted us to fly. The southern frigate had detected a suspicious radar blip moving up the coast towards Beira. Our job was to find the vessel and identify her.

After briefing, Paul and I manned our Sea Vixen. There was no moon and it was a pitch-black evening. Fortunately, the weather was good and we would not be bothered by the huge tropical thunderstorms, so prevalent in the Channel. The catapult threw us into the inky black sky and we set heading for the last known position of the suspicious vessel. It was a long flight and, as we were the only aircraft airborne, the captain sailed the ship southwards to reduce our return journey.

After establishing communications with the frigate, they updated our search area and Paul's task began. Using the aircraft's radar in a look-down mode, it wasn't long before we had the vessel locked on to our radar. I let down to 500 feet above the sea and started running in towards the vessel. Paul adjusted our heading to keep our nose pointed slightly ahead of the ship, which was sailing from left to right ahead of us. At 3.25 miles range, he ordered me to pull up. The aircraft started climbing rapidly and as the range quickly reached 2.75 miles, Paul shouted 'Fire.' I pressed the rocket release button four times in quick succession, sending four, three-inch Glow-worm rockets accelerating away into the night.

These specially designed rockets fly in a huge parabola and burst high in the sky just ahead of the vessel, which then sails into the glare of four million candle-power flares that drop slowly beneath parachutes. I imagine the sudden illumination would scare the living daylights out of a tanker crew carrying millions of gallons of high-octane fuel!

However, this night our target was not a tanker. In fact it was little more than an Arab dhow that would have battled to carry more than two 44-gallon drums of fuel. Reporting our discovery to the frigate, we started the long climb back to altitude for the return flight.

As we were the only aircraft in the sky the radio frequencies were abnormally quiet. Paul and I had a long time to contemplate the landing. Eventually we flew into range of the ship's powerful radar and the controller started directing us to the homing gate, from where our let-down and approach would begin. I was surprised when the controller changed half way through the descent. I was pleased to recognize the senior controller's voice.

The descent pattern positions the aircraft ten miles directly astern of the carrier at 2 000 feet above the sea. The ship heads directly into wind and the CCA (carrier controlled approach) begins. The controller gives you vectors to steer for the centre of the deck. All downwind vital actions are carried out and the undercarriage, flaps, and deck-hook are lowered. At seven miles range, you follow orders to commence a slow descent.

During my entire flying career, this was the action I found the most demanding. Over the sea, on a dark night, you cannot see the surface of the water, but you know it is down below. Enormous faith is required to push the stick forward to get the aircraft descending at a steady 700 feet per minute. As the range to the deck closes, the controller gives the pilot constant height guidelines. 'You are now at five miles, check and adjust your height to 1 500 feet.' These continue down to less than a mile when the aeroplane is only 300 feet above the sea.

At the same time, the controller will order changes of heading all the way down the approach. As the ship is heading into wind, there is very little drift, so these headings are usually not much more than two degrees right or one degree left.

My intercom technique, throughout a normal sortie, was to fly with my microphone switched off. This avoids cockpit noise from entering the earphones and makes for operations that are more efficient. However, once established in the slow descent at night, I did not have time to switch hands to the microphone every time I had to speak. I left the microphone on as I stirred the controls, rudders, and throttles, trying to obey the CCA controller.

This night approach was no exception. I started down the glide-slope and the fun began! I kept my descent quite well all the way down, but I had extreme problems keeping the aircraft on the ship's extended centreline. Instead of two degree heading changes, I had to make five-degree alterations to one side followed by ten-degree corrections the other way.

Night landings are always exciting (most carrier pilots use other explicit adjectives to describe the sensation). As we neared the five-mile marker, my breathing rate increased. Seated in the coalhole, poor Paul had no forward vision at all. He could only see my hands and feet as they flailed about the office, and he could hear my breathing.

Not wanting to scare him unnecessarily, I tried to control my breathing by taking deep breaths. He could hear these as well. By three miles I had lost control of my breathing and was hyperventilating. I can imagine no situation more terrifying for someone than having to sit there and patiently await one's fate. On really bad nights, when he could sense I was having problems, Paul would turn his intercom on and start humming, ostensibly to himself. This made me realize how tense he must have been and this made me relax sufficiently to carry out a good deck landing.

On this particular night, nothing worked and I was still stirring the pot as we came over the round-down. Normally, when the red lights faintly illuminated the ship's deck, one sensed the moment of arrival. The island superstructure seemed to grow out of the blackness on the starboard side. At that moment I would tighten my muscles to prepare for the impact. The moment of touchdown produces a heavy bang, because the aircraft is still descending at 700 feet per minute. Immediately thereafter, if you have landed correctly, the hook catches the arrestor wire and the aircraft is brought to a sudden stop.

I did not have time to brace myself as we flashed over the round-down. An almighty bang underneath the aircraft was followed by the relief of the arrested landing. However, all was not as it should have been. When the Vixen stopped, it was canted over to starboard with that wingtip touching the deck. I had broken off the right-hand undercarriage, and the wheel, drop tank, and missile had all skidded along the deck and over the ship's side.

Apologizing to Paul for the cock-up, I climbed out of the wreck. Despite the adrenaline and the shock, I noticed that the aircraft had stopped with the nose-wheel on the centreline and I had caught number three wire, the target wire. I knew my speed had been correct as we were using the accurate auto-throttle. If these three criteria were correct, the landing should have been perfect. However, the proof of the pudding was lying in the middle of the deck for all to see.

Upset, I walked into our crewroom and hurled my helmet into my locker. I turned to see Tony Pearson, in mess dress, entering the room. Pre-empting the expected bollocking, I said 'Sorry Boss, I've buggered up the aeroplane.' To my astonishment, he told me to forget it and to sit down as he explained what had happened.

After launch, *Ark Royal* sailed south. In so doing, she cleared the southern tip of Madagascar and found herself in the swell from a tropical revolving storm. The weather remained clear, but the swell exceeded normal limits for operating aircraft. We were flying without diversionary airfields, so Paul and I either had to land back on board or we had to eject. A command decision was made not to tell us of the situation, because we did not have sufficient fuel for the ship to move back to the north. Their other decision was to try to get us back on board, because ejection into those seas would have been extremely hazardous. At the time, I was angry that they had elected not to inform us, but in retrospect, there was "method in their madness".

Peacetime flying operations are normally stopped when the flight-deck starts pitching more than 1.25°. On a ship as long as *Ark Royal*, that means the round-down moves up and down 12 feet from the level position—a total of 24 feet. When we landed, the ship was pitching 3.5° and the deck was moving approximately 65 feet. If they had told us, I would never have gotten close to the deck!

A few days later, another long sortie was required. A Sea Vixen, crewed by Lieutenants Alan Tarver and John Stutchbury, was fitted with long-range fuel tanks to cater for the mission. Only when the aircraft was many miles from the carrier, did Alan realize that they had a problem.

At the best of times, the Vixen fuel system was a nightmare. A fuel pump drove each of the four fuel tanks in each wing. Each fuel pump was controlled by a circuit breaker. On a panel on the pilot's right-hand side of the cockpit, were the eight switches and eight circuit breakers, all of them infamously unreliable. The pilot needed the dexterity of an organist to maintain fuel flow and balance when failures occurred. Alan's problem was further complicated by the failure of the fuel transfer system. The long-range tanks could not provide the fuel.

Declaring an emergency, Alan headed back towards the carrier. Scimitar aircraft of 803 Squadron were maintained on standby for exactly this type of emergency. They were configured with the Buddy-buddy refuelling system, from which needy aircraft could top up their fuel.

The Scimitar was scrambled and vectored for a join-up with the Vixen. Monitored by the ship's radar system, the Scimitar was soon in position ahead of the Vixen. The refuelling hose was streamed and ready to pass on fuel. By this stage, Alan's situation had become critical. To conserve fuel, he had shut off one of his engines. As the Vixen flew easily on one, this was not a problem. However, the asymmetric effect interfered with the aircraft's trim, which became apparent as Alan attempted to refuel.

Air-to-air refuelling requires skill and practice. Most fighters are fitted with refuelling probes somewhere on the nose of the aircraft. This positioning allows the pilot to see the probe as he tries to insert it into the refuelling basket—not the British! On the Vixen, some bright engineer fitted the probe halfway down the leading-edge of the port wing. Being a swept wing, this placed the point of the probe 90° to the left of the pilot. Having to formate very closely with the tanker aircraft directly ahead, made things extraordinarily difficult.

On one engine, Alan made his approach to the basket. The Rolls-Royce engine was very powerful so he had no difficulty moving in towards the basket. His first attempt failed—the asymmetric effect of flying on one engine caused the aircraft to skid. This motion was exaggerated as distance increased from the aircraft's centreline. Way out on the wing, the skid caused the probe to miss the side of the basket. As Alan throttled back, to reposition for a second attempt, his engine flamed-out—ironically from a lack of fuel. So near and yet so far!

The Vixen, with its thick, transonic wing, glided well, and Alan started descending to a safe bailout altitude. Both men tightened their seat straps, knowing that an ejection was inevitable. At 15 000 feet, John jettisoned the coalhole hatch, and then pulled the upper ejection handle. Alan would eject after John was safely out of the aircraft. To their horror nothing happened. John tried again, this time pulling the lower seat-pan handle—once again without success.

The only option remaining for John was a manual bailout. He struggled to climb clear of the cockpit, but his upper body was bent backwards along the fuselage by the wind-stream. Alan managed to persuade John to get back into the cockpit. Without power, Alan inverted the aircraft and pushed negative "G" to try to throw John out. Nothing worked. The doomed Vixen was dropping lower and lower. Robin Munro-Davies, the Scimitar pilot, flying alongside, was screaming over the radio telling the crew to eject. Seconds before the aircraft crashed into the water it rolled to the right. Robin put on power to climb away and reported back to the carrier that no one had escaped from the Vixen.

However, on circling the crash scene, he noticed one person in an inflated Mae West, bobbing on the surface. The rescue helicopter was soon on the scene and recovered Alan from the sea. John had gone down with the aircraft. Alan did eject, but so late that the Scimitar pilot alongside never saw him emerge from the Vixen. Alan suffered a broken leg as his body struck the water before the parachute had properly opened. Later, he was awarded the George Cross for his valiant and repeated attempts to save John Stutchbury. The cause of the ejection seat failure was never established.

Our year east of Suez ground to an end as we left the Moçambique Channel and headed towards Suez on passage for Britain. "They" say that things always happen in threes and, as usual, "they" were right! We were asked to delay off the coast of Zanzibar to quell confrontation number three! To the refrain of the well-known old tune, *They're rioting in Africa*, we flew supersonic low-level passes up and down the length and breadth of the island. Our presence, and the supersonic bangs, must have convinced the "bad guys" to stop misbehaving, and we were soon on our way back to Britain.

I was a bachelor, and I had enjoyed every minute of the cruise, but a year is extremely trying on separated families. One really has to doff one's cap to those wives who help, in their own special way, to defend the principles of civilization.

An Ode to 890
Picture, if you can, a Vixen
Rushing through the starry skies,
Picture too, the pilot
Peering through his bloodshot eyes.

Long ago he joined the service,
Said he'd like to learn to fly -
Thought it meant some easy money.
Rich retirement bye and bye.

Thought as well of babes and popsies
And the glamour of the wings.
Of visits to exotic places,
Parties, dances, other things ...

Now he sits in frozen terror,
Bathed in moonlights cheerless glow;
Trying not to think of landing
On that flight-deck down below.

Tiny deck, enormous airplane
Guided by his hands and feet,
In the darkness none to tell him
How on earth the twain shall meet.

His alone the great decisions,
He the Captain of his fate

Life itself the constant wager
'Gainst the snares that lie in wait.

But stay, there is one guiding hand
To lead him in the paths of right.
One voice to lend encouragement,
When fear strikes deep, at dead of night.

For on his right and just behind him,
Shielded from plebeian view,
Dwells within the Vixen's bowels,
A second member of the crew.

This is he they call the looker,
Silent partner of the team,
Thinker extraordinary,
Of the cream, the very cream.

Trained in arts of navigation.
Versed in interception lore;
Master-mind and shrewd tactician
When the Vixen goes to war.

Aided by his electronics
Helped by radar's probing eye;
His vital task the skilled direction
Of the Vixen round the sky.

Master too, of relaxation,
Soothing words and healing balms,
Oft-times in the air he wanders
Wrapt in Morpheus' blissful arms.

Then it is a wrathful pilot
Bellows forth in angry roar,
Only to be answered with
A small observatorial snore.

At last the moment comes for landing,
When the lookers work is done,

Where his special tasks are ended
And his test of faith begun.

Now in turn the pilot needs
Must wake from dreams and concentrate,
While the ATCO talks him gently
Down towards the homing gate.

Through the gate and join the pattern,
Cockpit checks and lights all green.
Throttle back and down the glidepath,
Till the meatballs clearly seen.

Closer still and over the round-down,
Now the time for faith and prayer,
Hold the airspeed, check the line-up,
Nearly down—a bright red flare!

Keep your head now, throttles open!
Take your bolter like a man.
Climb away and keep her level,
Visual circuit if you can.

Downwind leg and check the final,
One more pass and that's your lot.
On the meatball, keep her steady,
Steady, steady, steady, Zot!

Down at last, a perfect landing,
Model of the pilot's art,
Now see the carefree crew emerge
With sweating brow and pounding heart.

See them weaving down the flight-deck,
Twitching gently, faces green,
Reporting to the Senior Pilot:
'Normal sortie—just routine.'
(Copied from the Lines Book of 890 Squadron, Fleet Air Arm)

Next stop, America.

Book Two
United States Navy

Foreword – Book Two

It is a sincere privilege to write the foreword on this section of Dick Lord's autobiography regarding his flying experiences on the Navy F4 Phantom aircraft. Dick arrived with seven other Royal Navy officers on an exchange tour as instructors for VF121 for a period of two years, 1966–1968. During this time, I was an instructor pilot assigned to VF121. The squadron's mission was to train replacement pilots and radar intercept officers for the Pacific F4 fleet squadrons. I also spent many hours socially with Dick. We shared a home with two other instructor pilots—the late Lt USN, Jim Jacanin and Lt RN, Al Hickling. The home we rented resembled a ranch and was appropriately named the "Poonderosa".

Due to involvement in the Vietnam War, the training for F4 crews changed significantly during this period. In addition to all weather interception training, the crews had to become proficient in air combat manoeuvring and air-to-ground weapons delivery. The Royal Navy crews' experience assisted greatly in establishing a training programme for the additional requirements. Dick was the expert in giving air combat ground lectures and fighting the F4 against dissimilar adversary aircraft. His work contributed significantly in the formation of the Top Gun Fighter Weapons programme. This programme is functioning with great success to date.

For the readers, the F4 aircraft was a formidable workhorse in the US Navy, Marine Corps, Air Force and Royal Navy. Being associated with this programme was a memorable and distinguished experience.

Fortunately for Dick, he accomplished this association within the confines of sunny Southern California. His anecdotes regarding his flying and leisure time are of great interest. We appreciated immensely his sense of wit and laughable dry humour.

Commander Theodore Wanner, USN.
Former F14 Squadron Commander, VF114
Former member of the Joint Operations Division, J3, Joint Chiefs of Staff
Retired American Airlines Captain.

Theodore M. Wanner
CAPT Theodore M Wanner, USN, Ret.

Chapter 12

The Big Apple and Beyond

In August 1966, I sailed from Southampton aboard the RMS *Queen Mary*, bound for New York. I received a two-year exchange posting to the United States Navy's VF121 Phantom Squadron, based at NAS Miramar, California. I was thrilled with the idea of flying the Phantom and spending two years in America, and I knew I had to make the most of this opportunity. Instead of flying across the Atlantic and buying an American car in San Diego, I decided to go by sea, take a new car with me and drive across America. Because I was exporting the car, it was exempt from UK tax, making the purchase of a customized Rover 2000 affordable on my Royal Navy Lieutenant's pay. With a sunroof and leather seats, this car was my pride and joy—ideal for crossing the continent.

After we docked in New York harbour, I anxiously waited and watched as my car was lifted out of the *Queen Mary* and gently placed on the quay. Having completed the necessary immigration formalities, I set off on my journey to California. Within the space of three blocks, I learnt to drive in New York with eyes in the back of my head. It took a few anxious moments and lots of concentration to get accustomed to driving on the wrong side of the road. I was convinced that my car was the only right-hand drive car in America. This drew many interested stares from other road users, while making overtaking extremely hazardous. However, these problems virtually ceased once I managed to find my way onto the magnificent American freeways.

My next realization was the immense size of the USA. Coming from South Africa, I was used to long distances—or so I thought! I headed off towards Chicago to join Route 66, because I remembered Nat King Cole "getting his kicks on Route 66". Each State had set speed limits varying between 60 and 65mph, and because by nature I am a law-abiding citizen, I adhered to them. However, nothing is more depressing than driving for a whole day at those speeds and then booking into a motel for the night to check your progress on the map.

Finally, by the time I reached Chicago and Route 66 "Which winds from Chicago to L.A., More than 2 000 miles all the way", I had settled into a daily routine. Before setting off each day, I checked the map and memorized the towns through which I expected to pass. Driving through Illinois in the mid-west, I passed through Springfield before arriving in St Louis. Massive road reconstruction diverted me repeatedly from the security of Route 66. Imagine my chagrin when after a further two or three hours drive from St Louis, I came to a sign announcing, "Welcome to Springfield". Only after a long, hard look at my map did I discover that I was still on the right track and this town was Springfield, Missouri. It is exactly for this reason that Americans say they are going to "London, England", when the rest of the world knows there is really only one London! In America, it is best to confirm one's destination!

After three or four days of driving at between 60 and 65mph, I entered the panhandle of Texas. Here Route 66 entered a small, Wild West looking town. The name escapes me, but it was probably named Shamrock or McClean. Anyway, the speed limit within this town was 25mph. I mentioned previously that I am a law-abiding citizen, but after driving at over 60mph for four continuous days, it is nigh on impossible to slow down to 25mph. I suppose I was still doing around 40mph when I crossed the town's main intersection. Within seconds I heard, and saw, the "black and white" prowl car leap out from the kerb, lights flashing and sirens blaring.

I stopped on the right-hand side of the road and the Highway Patrol vehicle pulled up behind me in a big cloud of dust. I climbed out of my car on the right-hand side and walked back to meet my first Texan. He did not get out of the left-hand side of his car; he unfolded! In true Texas fashion, he was a giant of a man—broad at the shoulder and narrow at the hip. He was wearing a huge white ten-gallon hat on his head and an equally large silver star on his chest. His leather belt was of the same proportions, with gun and bullets to match.

Ignoring my 'Good afternoon, Officer,' he asked if I had a driver's licence. I said I did and handed him my British one. This document was in the form of a small book, which did not contain a photograph. Holding it at arm's length, with obvious distaste, he asked me for my passport and I asked if I could fetch it from my car. He agreed and watched suspiciously as I walked back to the right-hand side door. Returning with the document, I noticed him studying the Rover's registration plates and GB (Great Britain) sticker.

Inside the passport, he found what he had been looking for—a photograph. He compared the likeness to me and seemed satisfied that I was the same person. In a British passport, opposite the photograph, there is a heading marked Profession, which in my case read "Government Service". In certain countries, being military could cause problems. The Texan noticed this entry before turning to the page where one's names are entered. On the first line, Christian names are entered in longhand and underneath, the surname is printed in capital letters and underlined.

Now, my Texan had seen me getting out on the wrong side of a car marked with English number plates and a large GB sticker. He also noted that I was in Government Service and he saw my names entered as follows:

Richard Stanley
<u>LORD</u>

In the twinkling of an eye, his whole demeanour changed. He handed my passport back with a little advisory 'Well you were going a little fast, Sir, but where are you heading?' I told him I was going west, to which he nodded and said he would lead me out of the town. Getting back into our cars, he led me, blue and red lights flashing, to the outskirts of the town. He pulled over, stopped, jumped out, and signalled me to continue on my journey. As I drove past, he gave me a polite salute, which I acknowledged with my impression of a lordly wave.

He obviously thought I was Lord Stanley of the British aristocracy, and I was not about to change his impression! I have often wondered what stories he told the other highway patrol officers about how he nearly booked one of Britain's blue bloods. The remaining 1 200 miles to San Diego were uneventful, except for my arrival in Los Angeles.

Flying jet fighters from aircraft carriers is an adrenaline-junkies idea of heaven. However, this pales into insignificance compared to a first time drive through Los Angeles during the morning rush hour, in a right-hand drive car. On those seven-lane concrete and tar strips, nobody abided by the speed limit. All traffic moved at the same speed and despite law-abiding tendencies and previous experience, one is forced to synchronize speed with the traffic mass.

I remember the terror of being in the fourth or fifth lane, wedged between a 70mph Greyhound bus and an *18-Wheels of Justice* freight truck. The wheels of both vehicles, spinning either side of my head, seemed to dwarf my car. While in this precarious position, my eyes had to flick between the safety of the road surface and the overhead signboards, to ensure that I ended up on the correct freeway for San Diego.

The moment of truth arrived with the same gut-wrenching tension as a night catapult launch, when the San Diego exit sign appeared overhead. Within half a mile, I had to change through five lanes of speeding bumper-to-bumper vehicles to make the required exit, and this in a right-hand drive car! I made it, but to this day I still suffer symptoms of post-traumatic stress!

My first day at NAS Miramar has remained indelibly etched into my memory. Doug Borrowman, the Royal Navy exchange officer I replaced, accompanied me on a tour of the base. He stopped on the landing halfway up the external staircase that led to the offices of VF121—my home for the next two years. Extending his arm, he invited me to look out across the concrete hardstandings in front of the hangars. It was mid-morning and the flying programme had been on the go since dawn. Aircraft were taking off and landing in a continuous stream. Large numbers of fighters were already in the air, exercising away from the base. Despite these absentees, there were still more aircraft standing on the ground than the Royal Navy had in the entire Fleet Air Arm. Some people might say that size does not count, but it certainly made a lasting impression on me.

Naval Air Station Miramar was the permanent home of three training squadrons. VF121, the squadron I joined, was to convert and train navy aircrews assigned to fly the F4 Phantom. To achieve this task, the squadron had 84 Phantoms, 70 instructors and up to 120 students. As soon as the student crews completed the syllabus, they joined fleet squadrons in the waters off Vietnam. VF124 was an F8 Crusader training squadron that operated approximately the same number of aircraft as VF121. The third permanent squadron was VF126. When I joined Miramar, this squadron was equipped with 26 F9 Cougars, two-seat training aircraft. VF126 ensured that all fleet pilots were fully instrument rated. All aircrew had to attend a yearly two-week instrument training course to qualify for their instrument flying rating.

In addition to housing these three permanent squadrons, Miramar was the temporary home of all fleet Phantom and Crusader squadrons whilst they were not at sea. Three or four aircraft carriers could be refitting, or under maintenance, at naval shipyards on the West Coast at one time and their air groups would disembark to their home air stations. All Phantoms and Crusaders were housed at Miramar, hence the vast number of aircraft that so impressed me on that first morning.

My first task on joining VF121 was to sort out accommodation. As a bachelor, I could have opted to live in the BOQ (Bachelor Officers Quarters) on the base. However, space was limited and instructors were encouraged to live off the base. This arrangement suited me and I moved into The Poonderosa, 2574 Grandview Avenue, San Diego. Jake Jacanin and Ted Wanner, US Navy Phantom instructors and Vietnam veterans, were the present incumbents of this well-known bachelor house.

The name was a play on Ponderosa, the ranch made famous in a long-running TV series. The extra "o" in the name came from the slang word Poontang. In Britain, women are known as "Birds". Down-under, a girl is often referred to as a Sheila, as in the famous Australian definition of foreplay, 'Brace yourself, Sheila.' In California in the 60s, Poontang was the in-favour expression for a female. On the road from San Diego to Arizona, way out in the sticks, was the oddly named little hamlet, Plaster City. Because there were girls aplenty in San Diego, it was unnecessary to date women living far away. Jake referred to any girl living outside the San Diego City limits as, a "Plaster City poon". Be that as it may, occupants or tenants of the Poonderosa played host to many Californian girls, so perhaps it was aptly named.

The house had four bedrooms. The lounge and pub opened onto a barbecue area flanked by a kidney-shaped, heated swimming pool with diving board and sunbed. Alan Hickling, another Fleet Air Arm pilot on an exchange posting, occupied the fourth room. The Poonderosa was really a lovely house, and guests often asked for conducted tours. It was a pleasure to show people around our domain. I personally felt a touch of unease whenever entering Jake's bedroom. Being the longest-staying resident, he had graduated, quite rightly, to the master bedroom with the en-suite bathroom. Jake was not a big man but he had the largest bed I have ever seen. This monstrosity was the cause of my unease—it was so big it just looked erotic! This arrangement lasted for the entire two years that I served with the US Navy.

The hit tunes of those days were *Georgy Girl* and *California Dreaming*, which to this day evoke wonderful memories. Whenever people talk about "the good old days", I know exactly what they mean.

One of the perks of being an exchange officer was the duty-free liquor privilege allowed to personnel by the British Government. This enabled people to repay the friendly Americans' hospitality. Four times a year I could place an order for liquor with the British Consul in Los Angeles. They would inform me upon receipt of the consignment and I would drive my Rover up to LA to collect it. At this point, I have to make known the fact that I was, and still am, a teetotaler. However, this did not stop Jake, Ted and Alan from ensuring that we ordered plenty of "the right stuff".

As previously mentioned, my right-hand-drive car attracted plenty of attention in America. Unfortunately, the officers of the law were no exception. On one occasion, I drove out of the Consul premises and within three blocks was pulled over by the occupants of a Californian Highway Police black and white patrol car—presumably to inspect my suspicious looking vehicle. They noticed that the car was riding with its rear-end almost on the tarmac whilst the front wheels were nearly off the ground (the culprits being the crates of Couvoisier, Johnny Walker and Chivas Regal stowed in the boot and on the back seat). Although they let me continue on my way, I am convinced that they never believed my story about being a teetotaler. The Poonderosa pub had the best stocked bar in San Diego, which perhaps accounted for the number of visitors who drifted in and out.

Before flying the Phantom, I had to acquire a US Navy instrument grading. For this purpose, I went on detached duty to VF126 for a two-week course. These weeks proved to be probably the hardest two of my entire flying career. I had no doubt about my instrument flying ability—if it had not been satisfactory, the weather conditions prevalent over England would have taken its toll years before. However, all the procedures were different and it took me a long time to get used to American voices and terminology, particularly over the radio.

Because the American training machine is so vast, there is no time for individual instruction. Every pilot attends the instrument school annually. They are conversant with all the procedures and know exactly what to expect when busy air-traffic controllers rattle off flight-clearances at them. So there I was, the new kid on the block, with eyes as big as saucers, sitting in a classroom with 30 other pilots, listening attentively to the briefing on the requirements of the course.

Exchange posting is not without its hardships. In the eyes of the US Navy pilots, I represented the Fleet Air Arm and Britain. Professionalism ranked high amongst pilots; therefore, it was important to do as well as one could at all times.

I must interrupt my story here to explain something about American aviators. I enjoy and admire them but admit that they tend towards the flamboyant, particularly in their language usage. This is not a criticism; it is to illustrate their different approach from the understatement practised by the Royal Navy.

The first briefing began and my pencil flew over my notebook. But within five minutes it became necessary for me to bury my face in my handkerchief to suppress a fit of the giggles. Two minutes later, the instructor halted his lecture, and focused the attention of the entire class on me. The conversation that followed went something like this:

Instructor: 'Hey! Lieuuutenant, what's bugging you?'

Me (in my best English accent): 'I'm awfully sorry (Englishmen always say awfully), but I cannot understand you.'

Instructor: 'What didn't you understand?'

Me (reading from my notes): 'The part where you said we were to "Ziggy in here, Zap across there then Wiffendale to the right". I'm sorry but I really do not know what a Ziggy, a Zap and a Wiffendale are.'

Much laughter from the rest of the course!

If the ground instruction was difficult, my first flight on 17 August 1966 was an abomination. I still cringe when I recall the circumstances. I dressed in my newly issued flight clothing, which included a torso harness—something we never used in the Fleet Air Arm. All British fighters had the oxygen regulators built into the aircraft. The US Navy mounted their oxygen mini-regulators onto the pilot's mask, which saved a lot of space in the cockpit but had severe disadvantages when pulling "G". The weight of the regulator tended to pull the mask off one's face and nose. The oxygen pipe was solid, unlike the soft rubber hose I had used. The soft hose allowed freedom of head movement, while the solid tube tended to restrict this vital motion. I was feeling vaguely uncomfortable in my new outfit.

Walking out to the TF9J Cougar, Lt Sappington, my instructor, passed remarks like:

'They only select the best pilots for exchange postings.' 'You must consider yourself very lucky to be placed amongst the best,' etc.

We arrived at the aircraft, the first one of its kind I had ever seen. My first flight in America was to be under the instrument hood in the backseat. Strapping in was straightforward, and after checking that the intercom was working, the hood was closed over the cockpit so that I could not see outside. I looked down to acquaint myself with the strange instrument panel and recoiled in horror. The only instrument I truly recognized was the "Rate of Climb and Descent" indicator. The rest were American variations of the standard British instruments. The Artificial Horizon, the main reference point of all instrument flying scans, was exactly opposite to the instruments I had grown up using. Whereas the British instruments used a ground-pointer to indicate angles of bank, the Americans used a sky-pointer. Before we had even started to taxi out for take-off, I had an attack of vertigo—one of the hazards of instrument flying.

The flight called for a SID (Standard Instrument Departure) out of NAS Miramar, a climb to altitude and an entry to an air-route. A couple of legs were to be flown between navigational beacons, a breakout performed from the air-route, followed by a TACAN (Tactical Air Navigation) descent to another airfield, and a GCA (Ground Controlled Approach) followed by an overshoot. The procedure was repeated on the return flight to Miramar. The flying was along air-routes used by all air traffic. Consequently, one's little fighter was often sandwiched between a Pan American 707 and United Airlines 727.

In Britain, civilian and military aviation is completely separate. Many times, I blasted into the air out of RNAS Yeovilton in Somerset without filing a flight plan. I would dial in the required radar control frequency and inform the controller that I was heading for Lossiemouth in Scotland. He would ask if I wanted radar monitoring or control. If I elected to be monitored, I could navigate myself and the radar would watch and inform me if there was conflicting traffic or danger areas. However, if I asked for control, the radar controllers would give me vectors to steer and heights to climb to and maintain. After alerting the Lossie controllers and informing me of the expected weather conditions, they would complete the navigation and place me onto final approach at Lossiemouth. In America, the pilot is responsible for the entire route.

On that first flight in America, the final major problem I faced was one of radio communication. Before departure, the extremely busy air traffic controllers must provide the flight-clearance. A departure clearance is often a long sentence, covering routes, heights, vectors and speeds. Before taking off, the pilot has to repeat this clearance word for word to the controller. These men handle hundreds of flights during each working shift and become as adept as horse-race commentators at giving out these clearances. Being unaccustomed to the drawls and intonations of Americanese, I admit I had extreme difficulty making sense of the radio messages.

The flight was not one of my best and I still wince when thinking about it. Vertigo, from trying to adapt to the odd looking instruments, was my constant companion. It was a feeling of relief when we finally landed. The walk back to the crew room was very different from the walk out. Silence greeted each step; the instructor was at a complete loss trying to make head or tail of this exchange pilot's grasp of simple instrument flying. Looking at my logbook now, I can see an entry, dated 9 September 1966, stating that I successfully completed the VF126 Instrument Course, signed by Lt Cdr RP Alberts. I take this opportunity, 35 years later, to thank him for his perjury.

In truth, I grew accustomed to the system, the flying became easier, and my performance did improve. The volume of air traffic necessitated such a system. People often ask me to compare the pilots' qualities, which is not an easy thing to do. As far as instrument flying is concerned, I would say that the British pilot is possibly the most accurate at keeping the needles exactly where they should be (necessary in the bad weather over Britain most of the year). However, the Americans are past masters of procedural flying and the strict compliance required in the densely crowded skies of America.

I experienced another confusing factor—American aviators converse using figures and abbreviations as opposed to the more "normal" figures of speech. The first flight in my logbook records the following:

TF9J   1A2   1.5   1FGS

The following explanation will indicate the reason for necessary brevity.

The TF9J describes the aircraft flown. The initial letter "T" indicates that it was a Training aircraft. The second letter refers to the category of machine, in this case a Fighter, and the figure 9 refers to the designated aircraft, namely a Grumman Cougar. (American fighters are designated by number as they arrive in service, i.e. F4, F8, F14, F16, etc.) The capital "J" indicates the mark of Cougar that we flew. Initial aircraft are designated 9A. As the aircraft evolves, changes to improve performance and handling are made. The qualification letter indicates these changes.

1A2 comes from the US Naval Flight Classification System, where the first number denotes the CONDITION of flight, the letter indicates the GENERAL PURPOSE of the flight, and the second number the SPECIFIC PURPOSE of the flight. In our case, the "1" shows it was a day visual flight. The "A" indicates that it was used for Unit training and the "2" that it was used for Instrument flying. The 1.5 or 1hr30min denotes the flight time. In British logbooks, flight time is written as hours and minutes, i.e. 1.30, and airborne time is always rounded out to the nearest five minutes.

The 1FGS denotes the number and type of instrument approaches carried out during the flight. In our case, we made one F (ADF) and G (GCA) approach, under S (Simulated) instrument flying conditions.

I often wonder why the British call their aircraft by name while the Americans refer to their machines by designation. Sir Lawrence Olivier, the great Shakespearean actor, or the articulate Rex Harrison, could have made a meal of the word Phantom. By the time they enunciated all the syllables and intonations, a listener would have a good picture in his mind of all that a Phantom could be. These creative possibilities are lost in the American pronunciation *Fannum*, while F4 sounds similar in both versions of the language.

During the Korean War, in the early 1950s, the straight-winged Panther was the mainstay of the United States Navy fighter force. The Grumman Cougar was a swept-wing version of this earlier aircraft. Sweeping the wing allowed the aircraft to achieve higher Mach numbers whilst remaining in the subsonic range. Its contemporaries were British Venoms, French Mysteres, and Russian MiG15s. I enjoyed the Cougar because, like most Grumman aircraft, it was tough, durable and easy to fly.

Chapter 13

VF126, NAS Miramar

Rejoining VF121, with my instrument ticket a thing of the past, I had to return to ground school to learn the technical aspects of the Phantom. At that stage the aircraft, its weapon system and intercept radar, was at the cutting edge of technological achievement. We had to learn in detail every aspect of the complex machine. Simulator training provided us with an excellent grasp of systems, emergency procedures and flight characteristics.

My first and lasting impression of the Phantom was its size. It was high off the ground and the two General Electric J-79 engines enclosed in the fuselage made it bulky. The cockpit, unlike those in European fighters, was enormous. It could carry four Sidewinder and four Sparrow air-to-air missiles, and up to twenty-four 500lb bombs suspended on multiple and triple ejection racks (Mers and Ters) under the fuselage and wings. It carried vast amounts of fuel, produced 34 000lb of thrust when the afterburners were selected and was a dreadful smoker when at 100% dry power. Using full dry power (without afterburner), the engines demanded huge quantities of fuel. To prevent flame-outs, the designers allowed more fuel to be pumped into the engines than they could burn. This excess fuel left a visible "smoke" trail behind the aircraft, which could be seen 20 miles away on a clear day. During take-off, these trails are still visible behind older generation passenger liners.

Ted Wanner, one of my Poonderosa roommates, was the instructor for my first and second flights in the Phantom. This experienced

professional had a relaxed attitude, and he allowed me to fly the
aircraft to its limits. His advice, particularly during approach and
landing, made flying the huge fighter particularly easy. One of the
delights of the McDonnell Phantom was that aerodynamically it was
nearly perfect. It was also responsive to the smallest pilot-controlled
inputs.

During my second sortie, at high altitude, I spotted another
Phantom. We were in the military flying area over the sea, off the coast
of California, with no other conflicting air traffic. I asked Ted if I could
jump the other fighter and he agreed. It was not much of a fight
because the other pilot was busy with his own exercise and he soon left
the area. After landing, Ted discussed the short engagement with me,
and I can remember feeling distinctly disappointed with the flying
characteristics of the much-vaunted Phantom. Pulling "G", the aircraft
began juddering and the bleed-off of speed, due to the high-induced
drag, was exceptionally alarming. I felt that a Sea Vixen on one engine
would have performed better.

Ted patiently explained the aerodynamics of thin-winged,
supersonic aircraft. The reason the Vixen flew so well, even in the
rarefied atmosphere at 45 000 feet, was due to the thick and curved
subsonic wings. They produced enormous amounts of drag,
preventing the Vixen from going supersonic in level flight.
Nevertheless, they also produced vast amounts of lift, allowing the
machine to manoeuvre with comparative ease at all altitudes. Thin
supersonic wings are entirely different. Minimum drag produces high
speeds and Mach numbers; however, they produce only limited
amounts of lift. I learnt that to obtain maximum performance from the
Phantom, I needed to study my aerodynamic notes again, and apply
different flying skills. Two years later, when I returned to Britain at the
end of my tour of duty, I was convinced that the Phantom deserved its
reputation as being the finest all-round fighter of its era.

I was delighted to receive an appointment to VF121, but I joined
the squadron with two major concerns. I knew that all US Navy officers
were college graduates, whereas I had only a matriculation certificate.
I was worried that educationally I might find myself out of my depth.
The other concern was that all the instructors were Vietnam veterans. I
had not seen active service.

My worries were unfounded. I soon discovered that everyone in
America attends "school", whether this is Junior High, High, College
or University. Consequently, everybody is a graduate from

somewhere. While some of the officers had exceptional educational qualifications, others had achieved more dubious accreditation. Some of them held degrees in "Social Recreation", which I took to be the science of throwing a party—they must have graduated Cum Laude. I soon relaxed on the educational score, having had to explain to some of them where South Africa is.

It took a little longer to overcome my professional concern. I had joined a squadron where the entire staff were efficient, experienced aviators. They all spoke, briefed and lectured with authority gained from success in combat.

The squadron was huge to cope with the conveyor-belt of students passing through on their way to Vietnam. The briefing hall was divided into a number of separate briefing cubicles where instructors thoroughly briefed students before and after each training mission. Learning from one's mistakes is probably the most convincing way of understanding the fighter business. The consequences of mistakes are often career and life limiting.

Eavesdropping on these briefings, I realized that the instructors briefed the students according to their own experiences. They usually ended up with statements like 'OK kid! This is the way to fly, because I flew this way in Vietnam and survived. If you don't, you will bust your ass!' (I soon discovered that a major sin in the United States Navy was to "bust one's ass"!) I had no problem with this approach, but each instructor's experience was different and I felt the students could end up confused with the lack of standardization. This vital requirement eventually led to the formation of the Naval Top Gun School.

At that time, I was one of eight Fleet Air Arm officers to join VF121. The Royal Navy decided to purchase the F4K and we were to gain experience on the aircraft before its introduction to the British Fleet. All four pilots and four observers were experienced instructors. Alan Hickling, Bob Jones and I were all graduates of the Royal Naval Air Warfare Instructors Course. This fine course, without doubt the most professional flying and theoretical course I have ever attended, taught us the skills of air weaponry instruction. In VF121, Alan became a leading light in the air-to-ground department, while I was inducted into the Air Combat Manoeuvring (ACM) field. Neville Featherstone was a qualified flying instructor.

The four observers were vastly experienced weapon system and radar operators. Each one soon carved a niche in the instructional field of the Phantom training programme, which I believe was to the benefit of both navies. Paul Waterhouse, Hugh Drake, Nick Child, and Keith Brown added substance to the training of American Radar Intercept Officers (RIOs) before the young officers were deployed to Vietnam.

My first request to the store's personnel was for a box of coloured blackboard chalks. Using a technique taught in the Royal Navy, I recorded on my kneepad, the manoeuvres flown by all of the fighters engaged in aerial combat practice. This enabled me at de-briefing to recreate the fight on the blackboard and to point out cardinal errors that led to a "kill" situation. I used the coloured chalks to differentiate between the involved aircraft. After much leg pulling (chalkboards were on their way out as electronic wizardry began to take over), the ever-accommodating Americans managed to lay their hands on a box of blue chalk. As the technique gathered favour, blue and white chalk dust could be detected on many a flying overall.

With the war in Vietnam becoming increasingly serious, the training tempo gathered momentum. We flew six days a week, which suited the members of the Poonderosa as we were all bachelors. Radio callsigns were personalized because aerial combat had became more involved. Each instructor selected his own callsign, such as Tom Cruise's "Maverick", made famous in the movie *Top Gun*. Fighter pilots, especially American fighter pilots, tended towards the flamboyant. Deadly, dangerous and dynamic callsigns were in vogue, for example: Snake, Cobra, Shark, Lightning and Rattler. British personality is strikingly different. I chose Brit 1 as my callsign for two reasons. First, I am not British and second, it gave me a great kick to have an all-American boy, with a broad Yankee drawl, having to call himself Brit 2 when flying in my formation. Al Hickling, for pretty much the same reason, called himself Spastic 1, knowing that no self-respecting fighter jock wanted to own up to being Spastic 2.

VF121 was a huge squadron and the turnover of students was so rapid that it became impossible to know each one of them. Every student was different, ranging in age, experience and rank (from ensign to commander). Some were brand new, out-of-the-pipeline sprogs, others were carrier veterans returning for requalification or conversion training onto the Phantom. Each flight had to be fully briefed, because it could not be assumed the students had previous knowledge of the subject being taught. This led to long and detailed preflight briefings—a necessary evil.

Shortly after joining the squadron, I was detailed to lead a two-plane air combat sortie. My back-seater was a young ensign under instruction. The student piloting the second aircraft was a senior commander, and Lt Bill Moore, another radar intercept officer (RIO) instructor, sat in his backseat. My briefing was thorough; I covered all the points the commander needed to know about one-versus-one combat, including what he should and should not do during the fighting. Every now and again, as I belaboured a point, I noticed Bill grinning surreptitiously, but I assumed he found my accent amusing.

The flight went well; the "student" commander gave me a tough and professional fight. At the debriefing, I clarified his few mistakes and praised all the good points. He listened, discussed a few details, expressed his thanks upon completion, and wandered off for his shower. Afterwards, I asked Bill what he found so amusing about my briefing. He answered by enquiring if I knew who the commander was. I said no, except that his surname was Page. Bill then explained that Cdr Lou Page, and his RIO Lt JC Smith, was already a MiG Killer. In the early stages of the Vietnam War, he had been the first navy pilot to down a MiG. It amused Bill to hear me telling the commander 'You have to do this,' etc. Lou was doing a Phantom refresher course after a ground tour. I learnt a great deal from his reaction to my briefing. Not once did he look bored or give me the impression I was wasting his time. He absorbed what I told him and, like a true professional, gleaned what he could from the encounter. JC, now a lieutenant commander, was one of the senior instructors on VF121.

One of the other senior instructors was Lt Papa-Joe Driscoll. He had acquired the "Papa" from the fact that he was 42 years old, which was considerably older than all the other "jet jocks" on the squadron. He was an excellent RIO and an accomplished raconteur. His long career in naval aviation included a tour as navigator of an airship. The US Navy operated lighter-than-air dirigibles for a long time after World War II. His account of life in an airship seemed light years away from that experienced in a Phantom. The airships were known as "Poopy Bags" and his descriptions of airship aerobatics included the radical Bag Over—their version of an aircraft Wing Over.

Each instructor was a specialist in one or other aspect of the training curriculum. I was fortunate to be appointed to the Air Combat Manoeuvring (ACM) section, responsible for all aerial fighting training, in old parlance, dog-fighting. It was here that I met my first North Carolinian, my boss in the ACM department, Lt Cdr Sam Flynn. What a lovely man!—also an excellent pilot with a tremendous feel for the hurly-burly of combat flying. He later returned to the waters off

Vietnam and became a celebrated MiG Killer. Nevertheless, it was as a Texan that I remember him best. He had a peculiar habit, quite common I discovered in those from the Tar Heel State, of giving vent to his exuberance whenever he felt the need. In the middle of a briefing, in the pub, or just before walking out to fly, he would place his left hand over his crotch, extend his right arm high into the air and shout a high pitched, 'Wheeeeeeee Haaaa.' This gesture enlivened every situation.

After Sam returned to combat in Vietnam, he was replaced by Lt Cdr Dan MacIntyre, an ex Blue Angel. Whereas Sam had been an extrovert, Dan was calm and calculating. He had a scientific approach to flying. He meticulously thought out and calculated each manoeuvre. In the training environment Dan lost very few engagements and in real combat, none. Of all the fighter pilots I came across in my career, Dan was the best pole-handler of all. I could perform the same turns and manoeuvres as he did, but he always ended up with 50 knots more airspeed on the clock. He was a genius in extracting optimum performance from his aeroplane and his handling was as smooth as silk.

There is a downside to being better than everybody else is. A world champion boxer achieves acclaim but then becomes the target for all other aspiring pugilists. The same situation existed in the ego-rich atmosphere of the fighter pilot's fraternity. Dan would brief a flight, and often finish with the prediction that he would end up on his opponent's tail in a "kill" position. This bland statement irritated and annoyed many of the top jocks. However, Dan never said it as a boast or to gloat, just as a statement of fact, which it invariably became.

Early in 1968, all those involved took the MiG threats in Vietnam seriously. Many other units decided to include basic ACM training in their syllabus to better equip their pilots for operation in increasingly dangerous combat environments. Consequently, I was sent on a lecture tour to give ACM theory instruction to the US Marine A4 Skyhawk squadrons at MCAS El Torro and Navy A6 Intruder units at NAS Whidbey Island. The difference in morale between the two bases struck me immediately.

At Whidbey, the A6 crews had morale as high as any unit that I had ever experienced. They were flying a good aircraft—the Grumman Intruder. Typically Grumman, it was tough, durable and safe to operate from carriers. At that stage, they had not lost any aircraft to carrier accidents, which was an exceptional record. They were flying missions that the aircraft was specifically designed for and their operations were not influenced by political interference.

On the other hand, morale at the Marine A4 Squadron was at low ebb. They had just returned from deployment in Vietnam. During their tour, 12 out of their 18 aircraft had been lost to North Vietnamese anti-aircraft fire. They had flown against some tough targets, over which there were no complaints. Their gripe was that they had lost a number of pilots while attacking "strategically vital targets", such as water buffalo pulling ploughs in Vietnamese rice paddies or the infamous suspected truck parks. The marines, like their counterparts in the navy and air force, relied on the yearly budget funds to maintain and improve their capabilities. The service chiefs felt compelled to sell their service to congress to ensure they received a fair allocation of the budget pie. To do this they had to show that their aircraft dropped a greater tonnage of bombs than the other services—hence the "critical water buffalo" type targets. Political interference cost pilot lives and valuable aircraft; understandably, morale was seriously low.

The ACM instruction did help, particularly the A6 pilots. They even deployed aircraft and crews to NAS Miramar to fly dissimilar ACM against us in the Phantoms. One Saturday morning Dan MacIntyre briefed for the first of a series of these missions. The A6 carried vast quantities of fuel and could remain airborne for great lengths of time, unlike the thirsty Phantoms with their fuel-guzzling afterburners. To optimize training, two pairs of Phantoms would fly against a pair of A6s. The second pair would take off as the first pair ran out of fuel.

Dan and his student flew the first pair of F4s, while I led the second pair. Sitting in my cockpit on the ground waiting for the right time to take-off, I listened in on the fight taking place out over the sea. I heard Dan's clear calm voice calling the Tallyho and his commentary as he talked his aircraft into the attack. Suddenly, I detected a change in Dan's tone and speed of commentary. His wingman came on the air, calling that the A6 was following Dan into the vertical plane—the hunter had become the hunted! Dan, thinking the A6 bombers would be easy meat, had committed the cardinal sin of fighter flying and engaged at slow speed. The straight, thick-winged Intruder, unburdened by its normal huge bomb load, was an excellent aircraft and could turn in exceptionally tight radius turns. This they did as Dan attacked, and within a short passage of time, they were sitting on his tail. This was the only mistake I ever knew Dan to make.

By eavesdropping on their engagement, I was forewarned; I did not repeat the error. When my turn came, I brought my pair of Phantoms in so fast that the A6 crews hardly had time to put on bank before I flashed through and up, to where they could not threaten me. It was a good lesson, fortunately in the training environment.

Chapter 14

VF121, San Diego, California

Checking my logbook, I see I flew an F4J, No 153791 for the first time on 8 May 1967. VF121 received about 20 of these new aircraft, without weapons systems. The airframes, known as lead noses because of the counterweights mounted in the nose, were used in all exercises not requiring functional systems. These exercises included basic aircraft conversions, night and formation flying, carrier qualifications, and some of the basic one-versus-one dogfight and air-to-ground weapon sorties. Because of the lack of electronic systems, these lead noses remained remarkably serviceable. They flew most of the high "G" sorties, and within a year, they started showing ill effects.

Parked on the hardstanding, they would ooze fuel and hydraulic fluid from every orifice. On preflight inspections, provided these leaks were oozes and not floods, the aircraft was accepted as serviceable. Flying the F4, I developed a habit that remained with me for the rest of my flying career. During preflight inspection, as I walked past the trailing edge of the wings and flaps, I would bump the aircraft skin with the palm of my hand. This would cause any popped skin rivets to vibrate. Once again, provided the loose rivets did not strike up a full percussion symphony, I assessed the aircraft to be fully serviceable.

The new AWG-10 weapon system in the F4J improved the capability of the Phantom immensely, however, there were a few airframe and engine modifications as well. A wing bulge was built in to accommodate slightly larger main wheel tyres. This bulge unfortunately decreased the performance of the wing, and allowed the onset of buffet to occur earlier in high "G" manoeuvres, compared to the F4B.

A major aerodynamic advance was the fitting of fixed slats along the entire leading edge of the stabilator. The extra controlled airflow over the elevator surfaces greatly improved slow speed handling, especially in the approach configuration. At light landing weight approaches at IAS, indications as low as 125 knots could be perfectly controlled.

General Electric, makers of the superb J-79 engines, installed -10 engines as opposed to the earlier -8s. The engineers adjusted the stall margins inside the engine to achieve about 900lb extra thrust per engine, a seemingly attractive improvement.

As stated earlier, the F4 was subjected to a tough training environment. During ACM sorties, the aircraft flew to the limit of their performance envelope. This included maximum positive and negative "G" loadings, and Mach 2.1 speeds in addition to twisting and rolling manoeuvres, while operating dive brakes and slamming throttles between idle to full afterburner. The aircraft and engine designers and maintainers deserve high praise for the way the Phantom handled all the abuse to which it was subjected.

As an ACM instructor, one of my tasks was to introduce student pilots to the F4 "envelope". After a suitable briefing, we would invite the student to seat himself in the back seat of the F4. The instructor would then fly the aircraft to explore the boundaries of the performance envelope. This entailed slow-speed handling down to the stall and the incipient stages of a departure, right out to Mach 2.1. We would demonstrate the use of negative "G" flight and maximum instantaneous "G", up to the structural limits of the aircraft. We would show off the incredible low-level acceleration and zoom climb capability up to altitudes of 50 000ft. Overall, an exciting and exhausting flight for both instructor and student.

At this point the situation took a turn for the worse and a large cloud of impending doom appeared on the horizon for the instructor. The student and instructor now changed places, with the student taking the front cockpit, and the instructor, the rear one. In a normal, dual-controlled training aircraft this would not have been a serious problem. However, the rear seat of the navy Phantoms had only a radar set; no dual controls. The instructor had to rely on the intercom to patter the student through the same demonstration sortie, so the student could experience the absolute limits of the Phantom's considerable envelope.

The cloud of doom took on a deeper shade of black when one considered the student pilot's experience level. Some of the "shirt-tales" came straight from their initial flying training with a grand total of 250 hours.

Using the F4B, we perfected a manoeuvre called a "rudder reversal", which we demonstrated during the envelope investigation sortie. This manoeuvre allowed the Phantom to fight using the head-on capability of the AIM 7 Sparrow missile. The manoeuvre involved a 70°–80° nose-up zoom at full afterburner power. At the right moment, with speed bleeding off, the throttles were pulled all the way back to idle and as the Indicated Air Speed (IAS) reached 210 knots, a stall turn was initiated to come back earthwards, head-on to the enemy. The tricky part of the manoeuvre was the fact that, after a supersonic 80° nose-up zoom, the stall turn or "rudder reversal" was started at an altitude between 45 000 and 50 000ft. At that altitude, little air remained to allow the controls to exert aerodynamic force, but if executed correctly, the Phantom responded magnificently.

This lack of air density critically affected the reduced stall margins inside the compressors of the new GE J-79 -10 engines—particularly during the high rates of yaw, induced during the rudder application.

2 June 1967, my day of excitement! The day started in a light grey cloud of impending doom, instead of the usual sombre black. I was programmed to fly the performance investigation with Lt Frank Mezzadri. He was an experienced frontline aviator and an ex-Blue Angel aerobatic pilot—hence the lighter shade of grey! The villain of the piece turned out to be the new F4J 153781 we were to fly, instead of the old reliable F4B.

My initial demo went as advertised. We then changed seats to allow the eager Frank to get to grips with the Phantom. The sortie was perfect until we reached 48 000ft, 80° nose-up with a decaying airspeed falling below 200 knots IAS. Following my patter, Frank reduced power to idle, used aileron to get the nose out of the vertical, and applied full starboard rudder to initiate the reversal. Unfortunately, he applied the boot-full of rudder too quickly, causing a rapid yaw and a roll, which he tried to correct by cross controlling.

The result was a snappy departure from our intended flight path, followed by two loud bangs indicating that both engines had flamed out. So there we were with nothing on the clock but the maker's name; 60 miles out over the Pacific Ocean; close to 50 000ft and gyrating in uncontrolled flight. I mentioned earlier that a cute American trick was to not give the backseat instructor any controls. Now, I discovered their hysterical little joke. Unlike a British or French aeroplane, the Phantom was not fitted with an emergency battery. Without engines, one naturally loses electrical power and the intercom.

Of course, the advantage of the situation was the absolute silence, similar to a glider, incurred by the loss of engine power. Not wanting to prolong our unusual predicament, I utilized the human voice Mk 1 and shouted instructions to Frank in the front seat. Fortunately, being an experienced pilot, he handled the departure and ensuing unusual attitudes with flair, and finally stopped the gyrations and brought the aircraft to an even keel. The rapidly rising pitch of my voice finally persuaded him to extend the RAT (Ram Air Turbine). A switch operated the RAT on the left-hand cockpit wall causing a spring-loaded arm to extend out of the port fuselage into the airstream. A small propeller mounted on the end of the arm starts rotating and generates enough electrical current to return the aircraft intercom and charge the igniters to relight the engines.

After the excitement of the previous few minutes, the flight back to Miramar was an anti-climax. Engine flame-outs were quite common with the F4J. During dog-fighting, experience taught you that if you heard and felt a bang there was no need to take your eyes off your opponent to look into the cockpit to see what had happened. We would run the fingers of our left hand down the back of the throttles to press *both* relight buttons. Whichever engine had stopped would then light up as the fight continued. It was not uncommon, during a dogfight, to suddenly see a broad white trail of unburned fuel curve across the sky behind an F4 on one engine. Fortunately, the J-79 engine relit very easily. Some of the instructors explained that this was the reason McDonnells fitted two engines—in case one stopped! Frank and I were the only pilots to have both motors stop during ACM.

Less than two weeks later we deployed a detachment to the US Marine Corp Air Station at Yuma, in the Arizona desert, for ground attack weaponry instruction. Acclimatization in the desert was necessary as the heat was enervating, but the advantage, in aviation terms, was the 365 days per year of excellent flying weather. By tradition, the first evening played out in the officer's club and it was here that I discovered the real difference between marines and normal military people.

On the shelf, immediately behind the long bar counter, was a large glass jar backed by a mirror. For $1 you could purchase a ladle full of the contents and each marine was expected to start his evening's entertainment that way. The two feet high container was two-thirds full of whisky, and coiled in the bottom of the jar, perfectly preserved, was a full-grown rattlesnake! Nothing on this earth could persuade me to taste the liquid, particularly after the ladle had disturbed the contents. The whisky then became a little cloudy and the odd scale swirled round the pickled corpse. I would not, could not, have qualified as a marine pilot!

Early mornings and evenings in the desert were lovely. Two early morning memories of Yuma remain with me. Both occurred just as dawn was breaking, after landing on the long main runway. Because of the heat, it was customary to open the canopy during taxiing. Alongside the airfield were irrigated citrus orchards and the freshness of the morning filled the air with the exquisite scent of orange blossom. A never-to-be-forgotten sensory experience.

My second memorable experience was strangely enough associated with a popular cartoon character. It is a peculiarity of military personnel—they tend to follow fashion in the world of cartoons. I can remember going to the cinema in England when *Tom and Jerry* featured before the main screening. You could always tell when other Royal Navy people were in the audience because loud shouts of "Good old Fred" were heard every time Fred Quimby's name appeared on screen; Fred Quimby being the writer of *Tom and Jerry*. In later years, *Yogi Bear* and *Boo Boo* became the flavours of the month.

In America during the mid to late 1960s, the *Roadrunner* dominated proceedings. It was so addictive that weekends only began after 12h30pm on Saturdays, because at noon one of the main TV channels broadcasted 30 minutes worth of *Roadrunner* cartoons. People did not leave their houses until the programme ended. The speedy little bird always outwitted the sneaky old coyote.

Once again, rolling down the long taxi track at Yuma, with my cockpit open and my oxygen mask hanging from my helmet, I was surprised and delighted to spot a real life *Roadrunner*. He must have thought the coyote was up to one of his sly tricks and disguised himself as a Phantom. He ran onto the taxi track, stopped on the centreline, and looked over his shoulder at the approaching Phantom. Of course, I could not hear, but I imagined he gave his famous "Beep-Beep" before disappearing at great speed into the scrub. My RIO thought I had gone crazy as I suddenly weaved the aircraft. While trying to keep the bird in sight, I shouted into the microphone telling him where to look.

Two of my Poonderosa roommates, Jake Jacanin and Al Hickling were on the same deployment, which turned out to be fortuitous for Alan. Jake, as well as being an F4 pilot, used to fly the propeller driven T28 used for weaponry spotting and Forward Air Control (FAC) training. After a previous detachment to Yuma, Jake flew his T28 back to Miramar at low level, revelling in the superb, clear flying conditions. On entering California, he had to cross the Sierra mountain range. Recently back from a tour in Vietnam, he decided to practise contour flying through the mountains. At extremely low-level he skimmed mountain ridges and valley floors, enjoying the opportunity away from the populated areas where strict low-level restrictions applied.

Inverting his aircraft after clearing a ridge, he pulled down into a valley, rolling level just above the ground. A new road, which did not yet feature on his chart, was being constructed through the mountains. Directly in front of his spinning propeller were the tin sheds occupied by the tea-drinking road construction gang. A touch of rudder allowed him to skid between the two sheds and disappear down the valley. During the remainder of the flight back to San Diego, Jake had time to contemplate the consequences of his low pass.

On landing, he noticed a small tear in the fuselage and a nick in one of the propeller blades. Asking the maintenance officer to touch things up and file the nick, he dashed in to see the skipper and inform him of what he had done. He then rushed back to the Poonderosa and changed into his khaki stepping-out uniform with medals attached. He drove out in great haste to the mountains and eventually found his way to the construction camp.

He was met by an enraged group of workers who told him that an aircraft had flown through their only telephone wire strung between the sheds, so disrupting their communications with the outside world. Worse than that was the trauma suffered by all the inhabitants of the sheds, when out of the blue, in the tranquil surroundings of the high Sierras, they had been fiendishly attacked by this inconsiderate %$#&! harum-scarum pilot. After their tirade had ended, Jake, in his most conciliatory manner, clinked his impressive row of medals before explaining that he was the perpetrator of this most dastardly deed.

Clinking his medals again, he explained that he had just returned from Vietnam where everybody in North Vietnam had been trying to kill him. After a further clink of medals, he asked for a cup of tea and sat down. Within minutes, he was telling the awe-inspired group war stories, emphasizing the necessity of flying low as the only way to stay alive. The cup of tea turned into two, with a dash of whatever construction crews add to their brew. After a well-spent morning, Jake paid $124 for a replacement telephone cable. Instead of lodging complaints with the Federal Aviation Authorities, the leader of the construction team wrote a "To whom it may Concern" letter for Jake. In the letter, he explained how the atrocious weather had forced Jake to fly with utmost care through the only open gap in the mountains. He strongly recommended Jake for the way he had controlled his aircraft and added that he was the sort of pilot America needed to carry on the fight against any, and all, foes. Just before Jake left, they measured the height above the ground of the broken telephone line; it was 28 feet!

Luckily, Jake survived the consequences of the incident, but breaches of air traffic regulations are taken extremely seriously and it was not uncommon for pilots to lose their wings. With these thoughts always in the back of his head, Jake returned from a weapons sortie to land at Yuma. Coming up to the initial point, he heard ATC give take-off clearance to Spastic 1, roommate Al Hickling. Take-off clearance was straight ahead on runway heading for three nautical miles before a turn could be commenced. This procedure ensured that the noisy jets avoided over-flying Yuma town.

Al was weaned at RNAS Lossiemouth in northern Scotland, where the sparse population allowed immediate turns after lift-off. With a sudden rush of blood to his head, Al rotated his after-burning Phantom and cranked it into a steep turn directly after getting airborne. He completely ignored the three-mile restriction. The accelerating Phantom blasted its way virtually down the main drag of Yuma, to the astonishment of the good citizens of the town and the anger of the air traffic authorities.

Jake, by this time overhead the field, had watched the entire performance from the grandstand. Realizing the consequences of this action, he interrupted the radio call from the tower by repeating in a loud voice: 'Spastic 1, confirm you have just experienced hydraulic control difficulties' until the penny dropped and Alan replied: 'Affirmative, control difficulties.' The obligatory after-landing checks of the systems could not detect any anomalies, but Jake's quick thinking had extracted Alan from a very difficult predicament.

On another occasion, Jake gave me the mother of all frights. I was fighting a one-versus-one against a student pilot out over the Pacific Ocean. He ran out of fuel through overuse of the thirsty afterburners and I sent him back to Miramar, while looking for someone else to fight. As it was after sundown, the air space was empty and I decided to head for home base as well. Enjoying the serenity of a lovely evening, I cruised back at 20 000ft with my mind in neutral.

Unbeknownst to me, Jake had flown a similar exercise and his student was also sent home short of fuel. Jake spotted my aircraft and realized that I was not watching my six o'clock, the area from which any threat could appear. Accelerating to supersonic speed, he overtook me from directly astern and immediately below. I was quite literally shocked out of my reverie by the shockwave from his aircraft as he zoomed up in front of me. Against the dark sky, I glimpsed the two long flames from his afterburners. After landing, my legs were still like jelly.

While at Yuma, I flew three sorties with Lt Cdr Jim Flatley, another experienced pilot on a Phantom conversion. Jim, son of an admiral, had previously qualified as a naval test pilot, at NAS Patuxent River. During that tour of duty, he performed a feat that is now recorded in aviation history. One of his test projects was to evaluate the Lockheed C130 Hercules for use in the US Navy inventory. Taking a lead from the famous Jimmy Doolittle, he planned, and then flew the huge transport aircraft onto and off the deck of an aircraft carrier.

Not having an arrestor hook, he knew that stopping after landing on the shortened angle-deck was going to be hazardous. He, therefore, elected to land the monster using the straight portion of the deck. This alternative certainly allowed him an extra 300ft of landing run, but it created another problem. The starboard wingtip of the big aircraft would be within a few feet of the carrier superstructure during landing and take-off. Therefore, lining the aircraft up on the selected centreline was crucial.

The ship was able to steer exactly into wind, and so eliminate crosswind problems. Landing speed was calculated to the final knot. In the non-turbulent air over the sea, this speed could be accurately attained and held. With the ship moving at 25 knots into a headwind of 20 knots, this effectively reduced the aircraft's relative landing speed by 45 knots, making the entire operation feasible.

Apparently, the project went very well. On the day in question, Jim carried out a number of touch and go landings followed by further full-stop landings. After each stop, Jim selected reverse thrust and the aircraft taxied backwards to the stern of the deck to give sufficient space for the next running take-off. After a very sweaty hour or two,

Flyco (Flying Control) invited him to reverse back to the stern and shut down the aircraft so that the ship's staff could discuss the operation with the aircrew.

After completing his after-landing checks, the front door opened and Jim stepped out to check that his aircraft was properly chocked and lashed to the deck. To his complete surprise and embarrassment, as his flight overall was drenched in perspiration, he discovered a red carpet had been rolled out to the steps of the aircraft. The ship's band formed up neatly under the wing. As he stepped out, the ship's captain greeted him and pinned an immediate award of the Distinguished Flying Cross (DFC) onto his chest.

If there are slight inaccuracies in this story, the intervening 35 years since Jim told me about it are to blame. In the event, as any pilot with carrier experience will understand, it was a wonderful achievement and well worthy of the award.

In August 1967, I flew another envelope performance sortie, this time with Captain Jack Heffernan, USAF. Jack was an experienced air force pilot doing, like myself, an exchange tour with the US Navy. I like to think my instruction was good, because Jack left us for Vietnam after his course, and "got himself a MiG".

Lt Robert Benjamin (Bob) Jones joined the Fleet Air Arm at around the same time as I did and, as our career paths crossed many times, he became one of my closest friends. He was a good pilot whose other interest was Johan Sebastian Bach—he knew every note the composer ever wrote. We served at Linton-on-Ouse, Lossiemouth, Brawdy, and Yeovilton. We flew together on 738, 891 and 890 Royal Navy Squadrons and were together again in San Diego.

The Royal Navy did things with style and dignity. Every year when a pilot had to undergo his annual medical, the examination took place privately between the aviator and the flight surgeon. A flight medical was probably more intensive than usual medical examinations and, because there was a good deal of poking and prodding, it seemed only right that privacy was maintained.

The United States Navy, without the hundreds of years of Royal Navy tradition to guide them, adopted a different, more democratic approach. Every man serving at NAS Miramar, and there were over ten thousand of them, had to report to the medical establishment at 08h00 on the morning of his birthday. On average, 20 to 30 men reported daily. Ranks could vary from the base commanding officer to the newly joined national serviceman conscript. Precisely at eight, the doctor appeared and ordered the whole group to strip to their underpants. There was probably nothing more revolting than 30 men standing around in their skivvies. Old, young, fat, thin, smooth-skinned and hirsute bodies presented an unfortunate spectacle. The privilege of rank was removed and all were treated in the same democratic manner.

Most of the Royal Navy officers, whilst not enjoying the situation, made light of their predicament. Not Robert Benjamin, who was acutely embarrassed by the entire scene. He joined diffidently at the end of the queue to have his height, weight and blood pressure measured. He felt slightly more isolated by separating himself slightly from the mass of bodies in front of him.

An occupational hazard in the fighter pilot fraternity was haemorrhoids. Constant high "G" manoeuvres forced blood to the lower half of the body playing havoc with most flying behinds! The US Navy took these things seriously and had no hesitation in whipping out anything offensive that they may have detected in the rear. The doctor armed himself with a powerful, four-cell flashlight, to track down the offending "bunch of grapes". In a stentorian voice, he ordered the line of persons to drop their skivvies and bend over. From the head of the queue, he marched behind the stooped line of men shouting, 'Spread your cheeks,' while peering closely with his flashlight. (I have often wondered what the doctor told his children when they asked, 'What did you do when you were in the navy, Daddy?')

Disliking this whole ugly business, Bob was stooping, slightly aloofly, at the end of the line. When the doctor's feet appeared behind Bob, he shouted again 'Spread your cheeks.' Not getting the desired reaction, he tapped Bob on the back and repeated his command. Still receiving no response, he went around and looked at Bob's face. Robert Benjamin was doing his best to obey the doctor's commands and had both little fingers hooked into his mouth, spreading his cheeks as wide as possible!

Like all of us, Bob did not enjoy giving instruction from the rear seat where there were no flying controls. Being a training squadron, we would receive newly qualified pilots, straight from *ab initio* training establishments, with extremely limited experience. Our job was to teach them to fly the "top of the range" Phantom. The squadron was equipped with procedure trainers and simulators to fully prepare the students for their first flight in the beast. Unlike many other aircraft, no dual seat trainer version existed in the navy. This meant that the student had to fly solo on his very first introductory flight in the aeroplane. To assist the youngster, the "navy" decided that a qualified instructor pilot should fly in the back seat on these solo flights. (I believe the "navy" who made this decision, was some desk bound maintenance puke in the Pentagon.) The fact that there were no controls in the back that the instructor could use to recover from any potentially dangerous situation, was the little trick Bob abhorred!

Bob soon noticed that by studying the flying programmes very carefully, he could take a few days leave at critical times and so avoid the first solo flights of each new course. As none of the instructors really enjoyed these flights, they made sure that they were scheduled to fly no more than any other instructor. Keeping a careful eye on the situation, Lt Donald L (Sid) Schneider, officer in charge of flight scheduling, soon cottoned on to Bob's little ploy!

Each student's history accompanied him throughout his career. The instructors studied these files with interest to ensure they flew with the better students. Towards the end of our two-year tour a student pilot arrived who had had a checkered career. Before receiving his "wings", he had to repeat his basic flying training. After animated appeals by the programmer scheduler it seemed that no instructor wanted to volunteer to fly with this youngster. Bob, as usual, put in for a few days leave to avoid the possibility of ending up with the short straw.

The flight programmer solved the problem by allowing the whole course to go solo, except the suspect youngster. He saved the lad for Bob's return to work! Having no choice, Bob was committed. He used all his considerable experience to brief and rebrief the boy. He checked him through the procedure trainers and the simulator before the two of them headed out to the flight line. This attention to detail paid off because in no time, the youngster had started the engines, taxied out to the holding position and was granted clearance for take-off.

Both great J-79 engines were brought up to full dry power. As the young man released the brakes, all four stages of afterburner were applied and the aircraft accelerated rapidly down the runway. It was about here that things started to deviate from the briefing. The pilot had been briefed to hold the stick right back into his tummy. As airspeed built up, airflow increased over the tailplane, which raised the nose of the aircraft. As the correct take-off angle was reached, the pilot was briefed to move the stick forward to maintain the correct attitude.

Those were exciting moments for every youngster, because the acceleration was quite unlike anything experienced up to that point in their short flying careers. To our boy, with his uncertain pedigree, it was just a bit too much. He failed to react quickly enough to stop the nose-up rotation and the Phantom's nose reared up like a cobra. This huge increase in angle-of-attack lifted the aircraft prematurely into the air.

When a Phantom stalls, it signifies its intentions by initially entering a wing-rocking motion. It rolls 40° to starboard followed by 60° to port before the aircraft departs from the intended flight path into a spin. Robert Benjamin, an experienced instructor, had experienced this often, but only when he was doing the flying and was at a safe height thousands of feet above the ground. This is exactly what occurred on take-off. Bob realized that the aircraft was virtually stalled only 20 feet above the ground. He yelled to the youngster to eject before he pulled his own ejection handle.

When Bob came flying out strapped into his seat, the aircraft was in a steep bank to port. The ejection sequence worked, the parachute deployed and dumped Bob on the end of the runway in a great cloud of dust, with nothing worse than a sprained ankle.

The student meanwhile, thinking this was a normal take-off, had completely missed Bob's call to eject. Somehow the aircraft, thanks to its excessive thrust and suddenly reduced load, managed to stay airborne and the makee-learner pilot got it under some semblance of control as it passed 5 000 feet.

Regaining some of his composure, he spoke to Bob on the intercom, not realizing that Robert Benjamin was no longer there. 'That was some take-off, Sir,' he said, but he received no reply. After a second or third call, he looked into his rear view mirror to see if he could see his instructor. Imagine his shock when he saw a completely empty cockpit, with the canopy, seat and instructor missing, and the extended ejection seat gun sticking up like a thick fishing rod.

It then dawned on him that his instructor would not have left the aeroplane unless he knew something that he, as a student, did not. Before he could create any more havoc, Joe Brantuas, another instructor, who had witnessed the whole escapade, joined him. Joe flew up alongside the youngster and gave him good instructional patter. He calmed the boy down and talked him down to perform a reasonable landing.

The ambulance recovered Bob and drove him off to the sickbay. While the emergency was taking place, base personnel were kept informed of the situation over the loudspeaker system. As a result, a huge crowd gathered to watch the landing of the unusual looking Phantom. By this time, many of the instructors were mumbling that Bob jumped out because he was so scared of flying with student pilots, etc.

It was only when the Phantom stopped that we realized that Bob had done exactly the right thing by ejecting. The vicious rotation on take-off was so severe that the tailplane, with its acute dihedral, struck the runway with such force that the port mainspar broke. The under surface skin was completely torn and it was only the upper skin that had kept the tailplane in place. The student was lucky to have survived a potential disaster and Robert Benjamin Jones continued flying for many years.

Lt Joe Brantuas, hero of the incident, was another exceptional pilot and an interesting personality. A short, pugnacious looking man accentuated by a previously broken nose, Joe spoke with what I took to be a broad Bronx accent. These features gave rise to his nickname, Joe Bananas. I remember playing golf with him on the Miramar course. Standing on the driving tee, he interrupted his swing to look up into the air to see what kind of aircraft was making the disturbing racket overhead. A push/pull, twin-engined, twin-boomed Cessna 337 was labouring past, with both propellers in fine pitch. 'Holy smoke, look at that,' said Joe, 'a formation of spare parts!' On completing his instructional tour on VF121, Joe, along with another outstanding instructor, Lt Cdr Sam Leeds, became commanding officers for F14 Tomcat squadrons in the US Navy.

Chapter 15

F4J Phantom

During a number of training sorties, the aircraft demonstrated its ability to reach its restriction of Mach 2.1 using maximum acceleration techniques. The Phantom was a terrific aircraft and it could easily exceed this limit. The aircraft climbed in full afterburner at Mach 0.9 to altitudes of around 38 000 feet. Temperature at altitude determined the optimum height. At that altitude, we pushed forward on the stick to reach 0 "G". This gentle, bunting manoeuvre effectively removed the drag associated with gravity. Maximum acceleration through the transonic zone then occurred. During the transonic phase, the movement of the shockwave affected aircraft aerodynamics; therefore, it was best to avoid flying within this zone and to pass through it as quickly as possible.

After Mach 1.1 was reached in the bunt, gentle positive backpressure was applied to the stick to raise the nose just above the horizon. With both burners going, the Mach number increased rapidly. At Mach 1.6, the nose of the aircraft wagged gently back and forth, but this movement ceased by Mach 1.7. I believe this distinctive nose wag was probably caused by the expansion of the splitter plate in front of the engine intakes. Mechanical jacks pushed this plate, with hundreds of tiny holes, outwards from the fuselage at high Mach numbers. This controlled the shockwave around the engines, and ensured laminar or streamlined flow of air into the engines. The pilot experienced a peculiar sensation from this outward movement. From the edges of his peripheral vision, he would detect his aircraft apparently growing larger, like a person hunching his shoulders. Up to Mach 2.1, acceleration was smooth and rapid.

During debriefing, after one of these flights, my RIO remarked on what he thought was a strange phenomenon. Could I explain why I vanished from view as the Mach number increased?

On one of my first flights out to Mach 2, I was sitting in the cockpit enjoying the sensation when the hydraulic jack controlling the port splitter plate collapsed. The terrific bang, close to my left shoulder, gave me a fright I still vividly recall. Experienced pilots understand these "change of underpants" type frights. The memory of the incident brought about a modification in my cockpit checks on these high-speed runs. At around Mach 1.5 I placed my hand on the ejection seat motor and ran it all the way down. I disappeared into the bowels of the aircraft and completed the run on instruments—as far from that hydraulic jack as possible!

Towards the end of 1967, Rear Admiral Louis Le Bailly, Royal Navy attaché in Washington, invited me to be his *aide-de-camp* at the Trafalgar Night Dinner he was hosting in Washington DC in mid-October. I thanked him for the privilege and stated that it was difficult for me to get all the way across the continent just for a dinner, but that I would ask my boss, Cdr Marland "Doc" Townsend. The admiral replied that he was sure it would be no problem as he had invited the commander as well.

On 17 October 1967, I found myself sitting in the backseat of a Phantom flown by the skipper (RHIP—Rank Has Its Privileges), as we headed east across America. We landed at AFB Tinker in Oklahoma to refuel before continuing to NAS Patuxent River, the US Navy Test Pilot School, close to the nation's capital. The sheer size of the United States is illustrated by the 4.5 hours it took to complete the flight—remember too that the F4 cruises at around Mach 0.9, or 9 miles per minute.

Trafalgar Night was a tremendous success. It was held in the Army Navy Club in downtown Washington DC, and it was attended by nearly 120 of the highest-ranking officers. Naval admirals of the USN and the RN were two a penny; marine and army generals, and air marshals completed the exalted throng. Medals, Decorations, Orders, Garters and gold braid made it a spectacular and glittering occasion. The standard of speeches and toasts made me consider how fortunate I was to attend.

At the end of the function, Admiral Le Bailly invited a few special guests to his house. One group of four very distinguished C in Cs arrived full of laughter, having obviously enjoyed the evening. While ridding themselves of their capes, coats and caps in the entrance hall, I heard one of them ask with a chuckle: 'What has happened to old So and So?' Five distinguished gentlemen set off from the club in one large car, but only four arrived at the house!

The mystery was soon resolved. Apparently, they decided to play "Chinese Firemen" on the way. In this game all occupants of the car shift one place in a clockwise direction as the car halts at each traffic light. The occupant of the right-hand front seat must move to the back seat as the opposite occurs on the left-hand side of the car. After each evolution, the car has a new driver. Somewhere, at one of the many intersections, old So and So had not been quick enough to reboard the car before the lights changed to green and his absence was not noticed. It still amuses me to think of this bejewelled, bedecked and gold-braid encased figure left stranded in the middle of an intersection, without his cap, in the wee small hours of the morning. His face was often seen on television when grave cold war and nuclear problems were debated and the well being of the world was being planned. It was refreshing to see that these men also knew how to relax when the opportunity arose. One tended to forget that they were all 2nd Lieuts at one time.

Back at Patuxent River, before our return flight, I discussed the flame-out problems of the F4J with Lt Ausley, the test pilot in charge of that investigation. I had previously explained our rudder reversal manoeuvre to him on the telephone, but the pilots at Patuxent River had not experienced any engine flame-outs. He decided to fly with me to study the manoeuvre. Those who know the East Coast of America will also know how humid conditions can be and it was on a particularly moist morning that we blasted into the air. From 30 000 feet upwards the engines left distinct and lasting condensation trails.

I pulled up steeply into the first rudder reversal, the standard manoeuvre we were all teaching at Miramar. As the nose got higher, and the IAS got lower, conversation on the intercom became quieter. The F4 was such a good aircraft aerodynamically that we performed a perfect rudder reversal. As we plummeted earthwards we were exactly alongside the contrail we had made going upwards. These trails were still visible when we landed a few minutes later. Ausley explained that our telephonic descriptions were nowhere near as graphically illustrated as the flight. Fully understanding the requirements of aerial combat the engineers and test pilots cured the flame-out problem shortly afterwards.

In San Diego, I noted that a combined band of Her Majesty's Brigade of Guards was touring America and was to perform indoors at a San Diego arena. Banter between the Brit and American occupants of the Poonderosa included the differences between our services, our countries, our sports and the Beatles versus the Beach Boys. I used the arrival of the guards to emphasize my point on the need for proper tradition by inviting Jake Jacanin and Ted Wanner to accompany Al Hickling and me to a performance.

I am a lover of military music and the guards were terrific. We all sat there enthralled at their precision drilling and wonderful music, which was full, resonant and loud inside the closed arena. At one stage, the marching stopped, and the lights dimmed until the hall was in full darkness, as the band played Tchaikovsky's moving 1812 Overture, symbolizing Napoleon's battle for Moscow. The music included violent battle crescendos, and silently in the dark, cannons moved into the entrance passageways of the arena. At the appropriate moment, these cannons fired with wonderful effect. The noise almost raised the roof and the long flames exhausted out the gun barrels, creating a realistic battle scenario.

Our seats happened to be alongside one of the entrances. As the cannons fired, Ted, seated alongside me, rose straight out of his seat like a Mercury rocket and landed virtually in my lap. Jake's jaw hung wide open as he gaped like a fish out of water. Alan and I used the situation for months afterwards to take the mickey out of our American roommates.

Many years later, after I had become seriously involved in the air battle of South Africa's border war with Angola, this story took on new significance for me. War, in any form, is an ugly, dangerous business. No one, not even the most gung-ho individual, is immune from the psychological effects. Ted and Jake had recently returned from seven-month cruises off Vietnam where they had been involved in the war. Even today, elderly veterans of the Battle of Britain still receive counselling by an association specially set up to deal with cases of post-traumatic stress. In a street full of people, it is easy to tell which ones have served in the infantry—if a motorbike backfires, all ex-infantry men immediately duck their heads. Post-traumatic stress is a subject that needs in-depth study. All veterans suffer from it and all handle it in different ways; some handle it better than others do.

Serving on VF121 was an elderly, round hat sailor, who kept our crew rooms and offices spotless. Everyone knew him fondly as Pop

Swazey. What an interesting and lovely man! It was 1967 and he was 68 years old. He was born in 1898 and was still an ordinary seaman. He enlisted in the US Navy and served in coal-burning battleships during World War I. After demobilization, he tried his hand at many jobs until the Japanese attacked Pearl Harbour on that infamous day, 7 December 1941. He re-enlisted for the duration of World War II. He was hardly back in civilian clothes after that conflagration when the Korean War broke out. Again he re-enlisted, and this time he decided to eliminate the constant upheaval of resorting to civilian life and stayed on in the service.

In a very nice gesture, Alan Hickling strapped Pop into a Phantom and flew him through the sound barrier. The incident was recorded in the base newspaper and Pop proudly received a photograph of himself in the Phantom. It was just here that the incident turned sour. A paper-pushing s.o.b. decided that the 68-year-old sailor should have retired years before and promptly set out on corrective action.

A decade and a half later, in the mid-1980s, I landed in a helicopter deep inside the enemy territory of Angola, to converse and plan with Major Corrie Meerholz who was leading a team of South African reconnaissance force commandos. After the planning session, I spoke to a grey-haired sergeant, who conversed in a broad Scottish accent. I had served in Scotland and I loved that country; I was naturally interested to hear about the sergeant's background. His name was Jock Hutton. He had dropped with the British paratroopers into Arnhem during World War II. He performed the same deeds in the Rhodesian services during their war and here he was with the South African Recces on their frontline at age 60. Militaries and countries can be justly proud of men like Pop and Jock; they are the solid foundation on which military traditions are built.

The ACM syllabus included dissimilar air combat. The intention was to expose student crews to the varying capabilities of different types of fighter aircraft. The MiG17 and MiG21 posed a threat at that stage in Vietnam. Although the 21 had better speed, and sustained "G" and zoom climb performance, in the hands of a good pilot the MiG17 was often the more formidable opponent because of its superior turning capability. Fighter pilots know that the aircraft that can turn in the smallest radius has the biggest advantage in aerial combat.

In 1968, the American A4 Skyhawk compared very favourably to the MiG17 in turning performance. VF126, the Instrument Training School at Miramar, was equipped with TA4Fs. These brand new aircraft were tandem seat trainers fitted with command ejection systems and the Douglas Escapac rocket ejection seats. To assist our dissimilar ACM programme, a number of F4 ACM instructors checked out in the TA4F to act the role of the aggressor squadron in the "Top Gun" idea.

On 30 April 1968, I flew Skyhawk 153472 against a student crew flying a Phantom. Because of the crowded airspace over Southern California, our exercise area was out over the Pacific Ocean, away from all civil air traffic. The sortie proceeded as planned. GCI vectored us onto each other and we successfully completed three engagements. In the fourth engagement, I rolled in about 1 200 metres astern of the F4, in a good position for a Sidewinder shot. Before I called the missile away, my aircraft began to buffet—not a clear air turbulence buffet or a high frequency stall warning type, but an extreme, heavy buffet. The vibration was so severe that I had to physically hold the instrument panel in both hands to read the instruments.

Nothing was wrong—according to the instruments! JPT, oil pressure, RPM were all normal. Not really enjoying the situation, I turned the aircraft onto a heading for Miramar. As I rolled out of the turn, my oxygen suddenly stopped flowing and I had to remove the mask from my face to breathe. This was not a problem at 11 000ft. The next occurrence followed almost immediately. The aeroplane nose reared up like a cobra. I tried the stick and the trimmers, but I could not gain any control. Under the right-hand side of the instrument panel was a T handle, rather like the one in a car, which opened the bonnet. In an emergency, one could pull that handle to change from hydraulic powered control to manual control. Well, I pulled and nothing happened, so I pulled again. When one is anxious, one has the strength of ten men and I very nearly pulled the instrument panel out of its mountings, but still nothing happened.

By this time, the aircraft had commenced a roll to the right and it dawned on me that now was the time to get out. Before I pulled the ejection handle, I pushed the mask against my face, called my F4 opponent and asked him if he could see me. He replied 'Yes' and asked if my problem was serious. I had time to answer in the affirmative and told him I was ejecting. This sequence of events happened quickly, and I left the aircraft inverted.

I can remember pulling the handle, feeling the bang of the ejection and smelling the cordite, but then the law of physics took over. Being inverted, I now had weight, gravity and the propulsion of the rocket, accelerating me towards the centre of the earth. The British Martin-Baker ejection system had a gentlemanly device that deployed a stabilizing drogue parachute to stop the seat tumbling and slow it down before the main canopy deployed. Not the Douglas Escapac! At the end of rocket-burn, come hell or high water, it deployed the main parachute. The effect was to rapidly alter my mean attitude of advance from head first to feet first. Apart from parachute riser burns on the back of my neck, I also fractured one of my spinal vertebrae and thus do not recollect anything further of the parachute descent.

The 12° Centigrade water must have revived me and my first conscious thought was to spread my parachute out for ease of recognition from the air. The only problem was that I was not on dry land but 40 nautical miles out into the Pacific. I disconnected my parachute and it sank without dragging me under. I unknowingly disconnected my dinghy, which I never saw again. I can remember saying to myself that I was in America not Britain, while trying to inflate my Mae West. The British Mae West inflated when the knob was pulled off on the gas bottle situated under the left lobe of the vest. The US Navy Mae West was rather like a kiddie's rubber tube, and it inflated by pushing down on two strings either side of your belly button.

I was now floating easily in quite a large swell. As I bobbed up and down, I could see a smoke float nearby, dropped by an S2F Tracker aircraft that was circling my position. After what seemed like a long time, but was really only about 25 minutes, a Sea King helicopter arrived, lowered a collar into which I climbed, and winched me into the chopper. The flight back to the sickbay at NAS Miramar took another 25 minutes. My back was sore by this time and the seawater was stinging the burns on the back of my neck. They laid me on the floor of the sickbay to cut the torso harness I was wearing off my body, before picking me up and placing me in the bed.

The American media services are quickly onto anything newsworthy. As I was deposited into bed, the local radio suddenly interrupted its transmission with a series of bleeps. This was followed by the announcer, in real American style: 'Hi folks, we just want to tell you that a British flier has just ejected over the Pacific Ocean and we hear he is OK.' Aching all over, I thought: 'You lying bugger.'

This was not the end of the story because, as I stated earlier, I ejected in the ACM area. In this airspace, any aircraft was fair game and could be attacked. If you were busy with instruction and did not

The author relaxing at The Poonderosa, the famous US Navy bachelor-pad in San Diego.

Four F4J Phantoms of VF121 "Pacemakers".

Observe the size of the Phantom. Standing next to the author on the extreme left is Lt Nick Child, the observer who was with the author when he was "caught short" in a Sea Venom. Third from the right is Lt Cdr JC Smith; he was famous for bagging the first MiG for the US Navy in the Vietnam War. Extreme right is Lt Jake Jacanin, the author's colleague in the Poonderosa and the perpetrator of a supersonic close pass that nearly forced him to repeat his follies from the Sea Venom incident.

The author wearing the tropical khaki uniform.

San Diego, Wednesday, April 24, 1968

BRITISH FLIER IS RESCUED AFTER BAIL-OUT OVER OCEAN

A British Royal Navy flight instructor ejected from a disabled jet training plane 30 miles west of La Jolla yesterday and was fished out of the water minutes later by a helicopter operating in the area.

Lt. Richard S. Lord had taken off from Miramar Naval Air Station where he is one of a group of exchange pilots. He gave ejection time as 12:04 p.m., and said the plane apparently had failure in the hydraulic system.

He was promptly rescued by Lt. (j.g.) Michael Schloz, of 2231 Hemlock St., Imperial Beach, pilot of a helicopter from Squadron 2, Imperial Beach, which was operating with the fleet nearby. Lord, uninjured, was returned to Miramar. Lord is assigned to Fighter Squadron 121, training in the F4B Phantom jet and used by both the United States and British navies.

The report on the author's ejection from a TA4F Skyhawk, which also appeared in the San Diego Tribune.

The Fleet Air Arm contingent that served in VF121 at NAS Miramar 1966 – 1968. Left to right: Alan Hickling, Neville Featherstone, the author, Paul Waterhouse, Nick Child, Hugh Drake, Keith Brown.

Half a wing overlap for a Change of Command ceremony. Lt Cdr Dan MacIntyre led this formation. The author was in the box position.

want to be disturbed, you just waggled your wings and your would-be attacker would wander off looking for some other prey.

On this particular day, Lt Cdr Bob Kirkwood was training a new wingman before returning to combat duty in Vietnam. Bob had already shot down a MiG on his previous tour, so he knew exactly what it was like. He came upon this unsuspecting A4 and, calling his wingman to follow him and cover his tail, he rolled his F8 Crusader into a dive and came into range behind my Skyhawk. As he moved into the firing bracket, I pretended to take evasive action by pitching up violently. He tracked me as I rolled to the right and then he squeezed the trigger. As he did this, the A4 "exploded" in front of him, exactly as the MiG had done in Vietnam. When I pulled the ejection handle, my Skyhawk had virtually exploded. The command ejection system ejected the canopy, then the backseat (which was unoccupied), and I followed fractions of a second later.

Unknown to me, he let out a howl of anguish on the radio and told the world that he had shot down an A4 and could they please send rescue teams to the scene. It took a lot of talking to persuade him that it was pure coincidence. Bob's F8 Crusader had his name painted under the cockpit rail and his MiG kill was proudly displayed. The following morning the groundcrew added the silhouette of a Skyhawk.

There was also a little story attached to the helicopter pick-up. Miramar was nine miles north of San Diego. NAS North Island, the base from where the S2F Tracker anti-submarine aircraft operated, was on the edge of Mission Bay in downtown San Diego. NAS Ream Field was the huge navy helicopter field just a few miles south of the town. It was a large base, housing hundreds of helicopters, and on hearing the *mayday* call, they all rushed to be first on the scene. They told me it was similar to a Durban July handicap of choppers all racing to pick me up. I must say I could not have chosen a better place to eject. The US Navy laid everything on.

Discharged from sickbay, I walked into VF126, the squadron from whom I had borrowed the aircraft. To enter the crewroom, one had to walk under a semi-circular banner, which previously boasted: "VF126 HAVE FLOWN 70 000 ACCIDENT FREE HOURS". Everyone knew the "Brit" because of the funny accent, so I poked my head round the crewroom door and asked if they would lend me another A4. I ran for safety, followed by books, flying boots and anything they could lay their hands on to throw at me.

I could not tell what had caused the accident, except that the only failure had been to the oxygen system. However, before I completed my two-year tour, the USN had lost five TA4F Skyhawks, including a couple with fatal consequences. They were a brand-new mark of aircraft and, in fact, mine had only flown 10 hours total time. The failure was finally established as an explosion in the LOX (liquid oxygen) converter. The LOX bottle was situated in the tail and the exploding converter was similar to a gas bottle blowing up. In my case, it had virtually severed the tail from the fuselage. In retrospect, the decision to eject was a good one.

Chapter 16

ACM, the Pacific and the Bed

Intensive instruction was the bread and butter of VF121. Only occasionally did two instructors end up in the same area of sky, when all the student pilots had returned to Miramar short on fuel. These opportunities were welcomed with open arms and some serious fighting then took place. On just such a day, Lt Dave Hoffman jumped me. We were both flying TA4F Skyhawks, which were magnificent flying machines when stripped of all external pylons, tanks and pods. With a tiny wingspan of less than 28 feet and leading edge slats, they could hold their own against most adversaries, particularly in a slow speed fight. Our fight degenerated into a slow speed battle of wits as we both tried to dominate the favoured six o'clock position. Neither of us gave or gained an inch. We called the fight off below Bingo fuel (the amount needed to return safely to base), with both aircraft gyrating closely around each other in a downward, descending scissors. A year or two later, Dave returned to the combat arena over Vietnam. He was shot down and spent the rest of the war as a guest of the North Vietnamese in the "Hanoi Hilton", the infamous prison where hundreds of downed US aircrew were kept, tortured and humiliated.

Without doubt, the hardest fight I flew in occurred during the final ACM sortie of the Phantom ACM syllabus. I had a student crew as my wingman and we were vectored onto a pair of F8 Crusaders under GCI control over the Arizona desert. Like our formation, an instructor flew the lead F8 with a student pilot as his wingman. This dissimilar sortie was also the culmination of the Crusader ACM programme. For me the sortie held added spice as Lt Cdr Tooter Teague flew the lead F8. Tooter was, and I'm sure still is, a famous US Navy fighter pilot and at that time he was the acknowledged master of the F8 fraternity. He later went on to achieve a MiG kill in Vietnam flying a Phantom.

Under radar control, my wingie and I vectored onto the two F8s. They crossed our nose at 90° travelling from left to right. Accelerating, we entered a starboard turn and rolled into their six o'clock at about two miles range with good closing speed. The set up was perfect; I split my wingman onto the right-hand F8, whilst I moved in for the kill on the formation leader. Just before simulated missile launch, I almost felt a little tapping on my shoulder. It had been just too easy. Although I could clearly see both F8s growing bigger as we closed range, I felt uncomfortable. I glanced over my left shoulder and there, positioned at no more than a hundred metres from my exhausts, was the menacing shape of a Crusader. The large under-nose intake seemed ready to swallow me whole. Instead of a two-versus-two as we had briefed, Tooter had launched a three-ship formation. He had sacrificed his two students, but he had suckered me completely. I had committed the cardinal sin in air combat of not checking my six before moving in for a kill.

Leaving the students to sort themselves out, I broke to the left, using maximum instantaneous "G". Tooter followed with nonchalant ease. I climbed; I dived; I used full afterburner; I tried idle and dive brakes; I went over the top in a high "G" barrel roll; I scissored and reversed, all to no avail. Tooter clung to me like a leech. Finally, after pitching up sharply from a high-speed descent, I throttled back from full afterburner to idle. The rapid deceleration caught Tooter unawares and he overshot close on my port side.

The boot was now on the other foot. In a reversal of the situation, I jumped into a close six o'clock position behind the Crusader. Now it was his turn to sweat. Until he ran out of fuel and called Bingo that was exactly where I was going to stay. Apart from my fundamental mistake on the initial engagement, I believe the fight ended up a creditable draw.

I suspect there is not one military pilot in the world, young or old, who, on hearing the acronym TAFFIOHHH, will not immediately be able to sing out, 'Trimmers, Airbrakes, Fuel, Flaps, Instruments, Oxygen, Hood, Harness and Hydraulics.' These, or slight variations thereof, are the checks required to be carried out before take-off. At each stage of flight, acronyms assist the pilot in completing the checks that are the hallmarks of safe flight. Flying instructors throughout the world agree that those students prone to forgetfulness, or who have demonstrated a slipshod approach to completing their checks, often end up as spectacular front-page news stories.

Some of us, in fact all of us (if we are honest), have been guilty at some time in our careers of missing a check or two. How often have we ridiculed the pilot who has taxied back to dispersal with his flaps still down or his landing light burning brightly, hoping that we would not be in his shoes the next day? We always remembered TAFFIOHHH because we wanted to get into the air—it was usually the other routine checklists that caught us out.

At NAS Miramar, a student crew took off for a night familiarization sortie in an F4 Phantom. This involved a climb to 35 000 feet, some night navigation and then a return to base. The pilot and Gib (Guy in the back) were youngsters straight from the training schools, and both were in awe of the mighty Phantom. All went well for the 50 minutes at altitude and then they headed back for a TACAN descent into Miramar.

The outside air temperature at 35 000 feet was a frigid minus 45° Centigrade and the metal aircraft surface cooled down appreciably. The steep rate of descent, required for the initial part of the TACAN pattern, took the aircraft through a thick cloud layer between the tops at 19 000 feet and the bottom at 10 000 feet agl (above ground level). This penetration should have been without difficulty, especially as the cloud base was so high.

Shortly after entering the cloud, with the pilot concentrating on his aircraft attitude indicator, the Gib told the pilot that the airspeed was falling. To compensate for this the pilot increased his nose-down attitude. This steepening of the dive had no effect and the Gib, all his attention now focused on the ASI (airspeed indicator), called the pilot in a higher pitched voice to say that the speed was still falling. The pilot realized that some drastic action was needed, so he pushed the nose further forward and applied full throttle. The airspeed kept falling dangerously, approaching the Phantom's stalling speed.

Pushing the nose down violently, the pilot then ignited all four stages of afterburner. Even this drastic action had no effect on the falling airspeed that was rapidly approaching zero. The Gib knew that the Phantom could not stay in the air below stalling speed, and he decided to leave the deteriorating situation. Using a fear induced soprano voice, he yelled, 'Ejecting' into the intercom, and then he disappeared in a blaze of flame into the black night.

At the same instant, the aircraft broke out of the bottom of the cloud layer. It was pointing almost vertically downward, with both afterburners accelerating it towards solid earth. The pilot realized that although the airspeed indicator registered zero his aircraft was damn near supersonic. Using all his strength, he hauled back on the stick, bottoming out perilously close to the tops of the hills on the approach to Miramar, before zooming back up through the cloud layer. Regaining control of his aircraft and settling it into level flight, he clicked in the autopilot to give himself a few minutes to calm down.

On rechecking his cockpit switches, he found that the pitot-head heater switch was OFF. The pitot measures dynamic pressure, which is fed as indicated airspeed to the cockpit dial. Because of the extremely low temperatures at altitude, the pitot-head heats up to avoid icing on descents through cloud. A gentle flick of the switch to the ON position and the airspeed soon reached the correct readings. The chastened pilot could re-enter the approach pattern to carry out a safe landing at Miramar, without his Gib. This unfortunate youngster returned on the rescue helicopter after a heavy night parachute landing 20 kilometres short of the Miramar runway.

Mike Maughan, a South African who had joined the Fleet Air Arm in the early 1960s, was nicknamed Noddy because of his penchant for falling asleep at any opportunity. Despite this characteristic, he was an excellent pilot who recently retired after a long and successful career as a Boeing 747 airline captain.

We served together in 890 Squadron on HMS *Ark Royal* during a year-long cruise to the Far East. 890 was an all-weather fighter squadron equipped with Sea Vixen Mk1s. Our job was to protect the fleet in bad weather and at night, when the Scimitar "day fighter" pilots were enjoying the duty-free facilities in the wardroom!

Night flying from a ship was not the easiest job in the world! The aircraft was arranged on deck so that the tail stuck out over the sea and the wings were folded. It was chained to the deck to prevent it from trickling over the side each time the ship rolled. In the mid-1960s, deck lighting was minimal. The captain did not want his ship illuminated in case enemy submarines saw it. Completing the external check before climbing into the cockpit was not simple. Even strapping in had inherent difficulties that required the assistance of a flashlight. In addition to the technical difficulties, each crewman had his own battle coping with the stress factor accompanying each night mission. On our squadron, tension was not eased by Noddy singing a popular

Rolling Stone's hit as you left the crewroom on your way to fly. He would sing: 'This may be the last time …' but only when he was not on the night flying programme himself!

On that night, it was Noddy's turn to do battle with the elements. The catapult launch and the entire mission went well until he was told to put down his undercarriage by the CCA (Carrier Controlled Approach) controller. He moved the large selection lever to the down position. Usually indicator lights came on— three red lights glowed while the undercarriage was in transit, followed by three green lights when the wheels were down and locked. To Noddy's horror no green lights appeared. In fact, no green or red lights showed, although the undercarriage lever was firmly down.

The ship was in mid-Pacific and no diversion airfield was within range. In answer to Noddy's request about what to do next, the controller told him to continue his approach but not to land. He was to make a slow flypast of the carrier while the ship's searchlight scanned his undercarriage. Observers would then give Mike a report on the state of his wheels.

Mike's Sea Vixen appeared out of the black and he banked gently to port to allow the viewers to get a good look at the underneath of his aircraft. In the light of the blinding illumination, the wheels were visible and appeared normal. Noddy received permission to carry out a missed approach and then to return to land, which he duly did.

On investigation, they discovered that the entire indicator had been removed from the cockpit that afternoon for servicing, and it had not been replaced. Noddy failed to notice the missing instrument during his prestart checks. He gave up singing after this incident!

In fairness, I hasten to add that Mike did have extenuating circumstances. His assigned aircraft for the flight was not ready as launch time approached. At the last minute he was told to take the spare (the aircraft held in readiness for just such an occasion). There was a mad scramble to carry out a quick preflight inspection and to strap in securely, before he was ordered to start engines. In his haste, by the light of his torch, he failed to notice the missing instrument.

Flying from the deck of HMS *Victorious* in 1962, I also became the victim of a "Take the spare" decision. It was a 22h00 launch and the carrier was steaming off the island of Pulau Tioman in the South China Sea. Two Sea Vixens, led by Lieutenant Simon Thomas, father of actress Kristin Scott Thomas, were to carry out a session of low-level interceptions, before landing ashore at RAF Tengah, on the island of

Singapore. For some crazy reason, known only to him, the commander (Air) requested that we perform a formation flypast over the ship, before departing to Singapore. At 23h00, no one would be outside to watch the flypast and no one would be able to see the aircraft in the dark either, but orders were orders!

On start-up my aircraft developed an unacceptable fault, hence the decision to take the spare. This meant rushing across the deck and repacking my overnight kit, uniform, cap and shoes into the spare aircraft. Unlike transport pilots who could take three suitcases, a steamer trunk and their golf trolleys with them where ever they went, the fighter jock was restricted by the lack of space in his aircraft. Everything fitted into the cockpit—into every available space at the sides and behind the ejection seat. To complicate matters, the spare had been parked as the first aircraft "on the angle". This position was at the very front of the angled part of the flight-deck, which protruded over the port side of the ship just short of the bow. While all that may seem a little technical, it meant in essence that the spare received the brunt of sea spray that always blew back from the bow wave of a carrier.

Eventually I launched off the catapult into the black of a humid, tropical night. Under radar guidance, I vectored towards Simon's aircraft and gained a visual sighting. He then told me to join into close formation on his starboard side. At night, depth perception is lost. Many times pilots have followed a bright star thinking it was the taillight of the aircraft ahead; it is easy to make that mistake. You joined up by placing the leader's taillight out to the left of the front windscreen, and then overtaking until the green navigational light came into view. You then adjusted your speed to match that of the lead aircraft. Once settled, you could start moving towards the leader by banking gently to the left. At this stage, you kept your aircraft below the lights of the leader. This gave you an escape route if your rate of closure was too fast. You stabilized your aircraft in the proper position again, but below the leader. Once settled, you lifted your aircraft gently into the correct close formation position.

On this occasion, I had difficulty getting into formation. I stabilized my aircraft out on the starboard side and could see both the tail and wingtip lights, although they looked faint. While trying to move closer, the lights did not appear to get any brighter. Simon, who was steering away from the carrier, called me to hurry things up, as he would not be able to make the briefed flypast time if we remained on this heading. Having battled to get close to him, I now put on port bank to close the distance. Fortunately, I had positioned my aircraft below his, because within seconds I flashed underneath Simon's Sea Vixen. If I had opened the cockpit and put my hand up, I could have touched the underside of his fuselage. The upswept tail of my aircraft must have passed within a few feet of the tailplane of Simon's aircraft. After a pregnant pause, Simon called me up on the radio and asked, 'Dick, did you just pass underneath me?' His aircraft lifted bodily as the airflow passed over mine. We cancelled the flypast and headed for RAF Tengah.

We discovered the problem after landing. The spare, my aircraft, had been tethered on the angle for hours before launch. Salt spray from the bow wave had dried on the port side of the aircraft. Salt thickly coated the left side of the canopy, reducing visibility to the left to almost zero. Like Noddy Maughan, I had been a victim of the spare, with almost catastrophic results. Beware the spare!

In the mid-1960s, the Phantom was the biggest, best, hottest, highest, fastest fighter in the inventory and it could certainly perform. One omission from this list of superlatives, which I seldom mentioned, was that it was also possibly the noisiest aircraft from the outside and inside. Three huge, efficient, pressurization motors inside the cockpit created the noisiest cockpit imaginable.

One of the few difficulties I experienced while on exchange duty with the United States Navy was attuning my ear to the American's version of English. Until the day I left, take-off clearances were always a problem for me. First, they were always long and the air traffic controller read them at high speeds with the flamboyance for which Americans are world famous. The high noise level inside the Phantom cockpit made it difficult to pick up what the ATC was telling me. On approaching to land, I solved this problem by "dumping the pressurization" (Americanese for turning off the fan motors) when down to a safe height. This stopped the noise while I negotiated joining and landing clearances with the tower.

To save time and money we often flew "double-bubble" sorties. The aircraft would be prepared and the crews would brief for two missions. To save on aircraft turn-around times we would complete the first sortie, taxi into the pits after landing and refuel while the engines were still running. On completion, we would take off again for the second sortie. An efficient use of the aircraft—but hard on the bum!

I completed the first half of an ACM double-bubble. After topping up the fuel, I blasted straight back into the air where the GCI controllers vectored me directly back into the fighting. My first interception was from head-on. I accelerated to supersonic speed at about 20 000 feet above the sea, but well below my unsuspecting opponent cruising in towards me at 35 000 feet.

At the correct range, my RIO called me to pull up into a steep climb. The wonderful thing about the Phantom was that even at 20 degrees nose-up, the speed did not bleed off and it virtually rocketed skywards. Passing behind the opponent, I converted the attitude to 70° nose-high, before coming down in a rudder reversal. This manoeuvre was performed at around 45 000 feet. To assist the pilot, who dared not take his eyes off his opponent throughout the evolution, the RIO called out the indicated airspeed, which fell quickly in this exaggerated attitude.

The moment my RIO started calling out the speeds, I realized that I had forgotten to do all my pre-take-off checks. On the first half of the double-bubble, I dumped the pressurization, but I had neglected to turn the dump valve back on. We rapidly approached 50 000 feet without pressurization and my Gib sounded like Mickey Mouse. The lack of pressurization causes the human voice to sound more like a cartoon character the higher one goes. Apologizing to my RIO, I broke off the interception and descended as quickly as I dared, with both of us having to use the "hold the nose and blow" technique to help equalize the pressure within our ears. I never forgot that check again!

Despite the similarities between the RN and the USN, I experienced small differences when scheduled to do night flying. Reporting at the maintenance office to sign for my aircraft, I asked the chief if I could borrow a torch to assist me on my preflight check. He obviously misunderstood my question and, to my increasing irritation, made me repeat it two or three times. I explained in simple language that I needed to check the intakes and wheel wells. A broad grin suddenly crossed his face. 'Oh! You mean a flashlight, Sir,' he said handing me an instrument. A torch in America is synonymous with those flaming branches used by the Ku Klux Klan and, always a little suspicious of the Brit, he could not imagine what I needed one of those for.

Another difference that made the Americans uncomfortable was uniform. In the USN uniform was exactly that, identical! This should also have been the case in the RN, but small irregularities crept in to permeate the system over the years. Some officers insisted that the points of a white handkerchief showed out of the top of the breast pocket. There was a well-known non-aviator at RNAS Yeovilton whose handkerchief showed out of his left sleeve, like Little Lord Fauntleroy! This was an anathema to the Americans.

While at Miramar, VF121 had a change of leadership. Cdr Doc Townsend took over from Cdr Scotty Lamoreaux. The change of command proceedings called for a parade and a six aircraft flypast. With the stroke of a pen, they solved the uniform problem by scheduling all eight Royal Navy officers to fly in the formation.

Dan MacIntyre, the ex-Blue Angel pilot, briefed and led the formation, which was to be a Vic of five with me as number six in the box position. My other task was to be the "whipper-inner" during form-up and before run-in. Dan briefed that he wanted us to fly in the very close formation that had made the Blue Angels famous, with half a wing overlap. We joined up in the non-turbulent air over the sea. While flying straight and level, I flew above the other aircraft and coaxed them into the close positions. Just before we flew over the saluting dais, I ducked into the box and eased into position.

Unlike the Blues, we were not flying aerobatics. Nevertheless, for pilots unaccustomed to flying with overlapping wings, the formation was extremely close. In my proper position, my head was probably only eight feet away from the wingtips of the aircraft in the Vic on either side, and I was staring at the huge exhausts of Dan's Phantom.

We held good positions for the flypast, which extracted favourable comments from all the onlookers. As we reached the dais, Dan made a spectacular, full afterburner, vertical exit from the centre of the formation to symbolize the departing commanding officer. I understand that it looked magnificent from the ground and luckily all eyes focused on Dan's zooming aircraft. His rapid departure was, in the parlance of the day, "something else!"

He rotated his aircraft as he lit full-afterburner. From my position beneath his tail, the effect was electrifying. Two long flames suddenly swirled round my canopy and the turbulence from his sudden rotation and full-afterburner application gave me an unequalled adrenaline rush. Fortunately, his speed of departure was so rapid that I only had to "stir the porridge" for a few frantic seconds to stay in formation.

The United States Air Force equipped their Fighter Weapons School at Air Force Base Nellis with F4C Phantoms. These Phantoms had dual controls in both cockpits. With the North Vietnamese Air Force displaying an increasing willingness to intercept American strike forces, the USAF were wondering if they would be at a disadvantage by manning their Phantoms with two pilots, instead of a dedicated intercept officer in the rear seat. An evaluation team deployed from Nellis to NAS Miramar to fight against the VF121 instructors to gather the data they needed.

For a wonderful week we flew our best ACM instructors against those of the USAF. The structural limits of the USAF aircraft were higher than the restrictions placed on the navy carrier-borne aircraft. They pulled eight "G" compared to our seven "G". The results were pretty even, although we usually managed to get our missiles away fractionally ahead of the air force crews. The reason was put down to the experience of the dedicated radar intercept officer in our back seats. The difference was judged not to be that significant to warrant changing the configuration of their aircraft.

The USAF received their new, swing-wing F-111 fighter-bombers. They were wonderful aircraft, although they suffered terribly from initial teething pains. Most fighters were refined developments of previous aircraft; this eliminated many design problems. In concept, the F-111 was brand new in all aspects, including the modular cockpit, swing-wings, terrain clearance radar and autopilot. It was an electronic marvel when it all worked, but a nightmare when it did not.

In a USAF Safety Magazine, I read of an incident where superior airmanship, skill and a good measure of prayer allowed a USAF crew to safely recover a miss-behaving F-111. During flight, a hot air duct broke loose and pumped hot air directly into the aircraft's avionics bay. This bay was normally cool to control heat build-up from the electrical components. The popping of a circuit breaker confirmed the sudden temperature rise. A circuit breaker was a safety device installed to protect components from overheating. Of course, when the breaker popped out, that component stopped working.

The second, third and fourth circuit breaker quickly followed the first popped circuit breaker in rapid succession. Wings started to spread, the autopilot kicked out, instruments fell to zero, and the emergencies increased. The pilot tried to cope with each in turn while the navigator had his hands full trying to reset the buttons as they popped out. By the time they landed, 76 circuit breakers had popped, indicating 76 components which had ceased to function. The crew did an outstanding job, but I suspect that 35 years later, they still awake at night from bad dreams.

Shortly before Christmas in 1967, a crew had to ferry a Phantom from Hawaii to NAS Subic Bay in the Philippine Islands. All the

Americans had been to Hawaii, and they had already made plans to spend Christmas with their families. Being a bachelor, I volunteered with alacrity. A tanker was provided, because the long flight required air-to-air refuelling. On one particular flight I had carried out 14 plugs—this qualified me for the task. The next day I flew from California to Hawaii, courtesy of United Airlines. On the airliner, I met Lt JG Lou Biosca, the RIO who was to accompany me across the Pacific Ocean. He had recently returned from combat in Vietnam, and he was a bachelor. His squadron, all married men, had volunteered him. He was a pleasant, swarthy, laid-back youngster, with longish sideburns.

We landed in Hawaii and made our way to NAS Barbers Point, the US Navy air base on the island. After reporting in, we were told that the Phantom would be ready for test flying the next morning. We quickly headed into Honolulu and took a room at the military establishment, whose name escapes me (Fort something or other), for a price I do remember. We stayed right on Wakiki beach, perhaps the most famous beach in the world for $1 per night. We made the most of the opportunity; we did all the touristy things; we saw the famous "Tiny Bubbles" singer and show; and we ended up in the Pearl City Tavern, outside Pearl Harbour. This tavern was an interesting place housing about four different restaurants. While waiting for tables to become available, patrons sat at the central bar counter. This long counter was backed by a glass cage filled with dozens of monkeys—an ideal place to wait. As if understanding the need to entertain the customers the monkeys carried on as monkeys do. Many patrons spent all night watching the amusing antics of these primates.

The test flight the next day was unsuccessful. The huge, 600-gallon centreline fuel tank would not transfer fuel, so a replacement tank was ordered from America. The further delay meant further tours round the island and a visit to the huge military cemetery, plus another visit to the Pearl City Tavern. The new tank would also not transfer and it was established that the fault lay in the aircraft, not in the tank.

The Phantom had been one of the aircraft on a "Transpac". Every so often, a large group (20–30) of navy and marine aircraft assembled in California, to fly out to the Philippines as replacements for aircraft lost in combat. This Transpac included Destroyers or Frigates positioned along the route to act as navigational guides and rescue ships. A fleet of tanker aircraft would accompany the formation to provide fuel for the thirsty fighters en route. It was a big, involved organization.

We had just two Navy A3 Skywarriors to assist us. One to provide us with fuel and the other as a navigational leader. Both these crews wanted to be in America for Christmas. Understandably, they were getting edgy the longer it took to get our Phantom serviceable. Eventually, the commander in charge of the tanker approached me with a request. Would it be possible for me to take the Phantom even though the main 600-gallon external fuselage would not transfer?

To my knowledge, this had not been done before. All three, under-wing fuel tanks were necessary for the safe completion of the long flight across the ocean. Sympathizing with their need, I asked him to give me time to do some serious flight planning before I gave him my answer. After very careful consideration I agreed to go, provided they could supply me with exactly the fuel I required at exactly the time I needed it. Relieved, we set a take-off time for early the next morning from Barbers Point. Exactly on time, the two A3s lifted off, followed by my Phantom. The navigator devised a dogleg to the left to over-fly Johnson Island. Two refuellings were vital for us to complete the flight to Wake Island, a tiny atoll in mid Pacific. These tankings were to take place shortly before Johnson and then again after flight over the island. I had calculated the positions and amounts of fuel needed in the finest detail.

Approaching Johnston Island, and at just about the time I wanted to refuel, I heard Lt JG Lou Biosca say on the radio, 'OK Bill, could you give us 6 000?' Bill happened to be a commander, USN, who I would never have addressed without the prefix "Sir". Nevertheless, the hose came streaming out of the pod under the wing of the tanker, so I moved into position and accepted 6 000lb of fuel.

While waiting for the next all-important refuel point to come up, I took Lou to task. I told him clearly that I, who had done the detailed planning, would decide on the details of the next tanking. Completely unfazed, Lou answered, 'No problem.' The crucial time arrived; we took on exactly the correct amount of fuel and we were off on our own for the rest of the flight to Wake. We had to cruise-climb the Phantom to a more economical altitude and accelerate to a more efficient speed. We had to leave behind our tanker and navigational leader. My logbook recalls that it was a 4.9-hour flight with nothing but blue sea and sky for company. There were no navigational aids and in those days, we did not have INS or GPS—only good old-fashioned DR.

Passing 37 000 feet in the cruise, I had my map out, which like the sea below, was just plain blue. I tried not to look at the watch fixed to the canopy rail. Minutes seemed like hours as my bum started objecting to being firmly strapped down and my bladder began exerting all kinds of real and imaginary pressures.

Like a magnet, my eye was constantly drawn towards the slowly ticking watch. As I glanced up, I caught a movement in the rear mirror mounted alongside. Staring into the glass, I was horrified to detect a cloud of smoke swirling around the back cockpit. I shouted, 'Lou' into the intercom. I saw the reflection of his head appear in the mirror, wearing a yellow peaked cap. He said 'What?' Knowing the dangers of fire in the 100% oxygen environment of the cockpit, I told him about the smoke I had seen. Nonchalantly he told me that he always smoked in the back of the aircraft, so I reluctantly let him have his way.

A minute or so later I called him again. 'What?' was his standard reply. It dawned on me that when I had seen his face in the mirror, he was not wearing his helmet or mask and I knew oxygen to be essential at that altitude. He then explained his modus operandi for long flights. He would unstrap from his seat so he could lift his legs to one side of the radar. He would take off the heavy helmet and replace it with the yellow peaked cap to protect him from the fierce effects of the sun at that altitude. He would place his helmet and mask alongside the radar set, take out his paperback and settle down to a good read. Whenever his eyes lost focus through oxygen depletion, he would raise his mask to his face and take a deep breath of the life giving gas. Well if this was good enough for Lou it was good enough for me and we flew on to Wake Island.

We found the atoll and landed. It was so small that the runway took one complete side of the rim of land that barely rose above sea level. The A3s arrived and after all three aircraft were prepared, we took-off on the next three hour flight to Guam, needing one tanking on the way. From Guam, we set off again on the final leg to NAS Subic Bay. Once again, we required one refuelling and it was at this stage that a moment of crisis arrived. When the pilot selected his hose to stream, nothing happened; the basket stuck inside the housing. Without hesitation, I started to climb for best performance while the A3 crew pushed and pulled positive and negative "G" in an attempt to dislodge the basket. Luckily, they were successful and I could gratefully descend to take on the "lifeblood" I needed.

After a long day, made longer by the nervous tension, we landed at Subic Bay and delivered our aircraft. The tanker crews flew back to the USA the next morning to spend Christmas with their families. We had flown 11 hours and had been strapped in appreciably longer. We had flown westward, travelling with the sun, so we had been in bright sunshine the entire trip. Relaxing in the bar that evening, I learnt a little more about Lt JG Lou Biosca. Although still a young man, he had already completed two tours of combat duty flying from carriers off Vietnam. He was the recipient of 15 Air Medals. Before I knew better, the thought of being awarded so many medals was amusing. Americans seemed to award medals almost indiscriminately. As I said though, that was before I knew better!

Vietnam was divided geographically into four regions for purposes of awarding mission points. A mission in South Vietnam, where no MiG or anti-aircraft missile threat existed, was worth one point. Inside the Demilitarized Zone (DMZ), between South and North Vietnam, a mission was worth two points. Flights over North Vietnam, where the threat from missiles and MiG aircraft was serious, carried a loading of three points. Going downtown to the real danger areas of Hanoi and Haiphong was worth four points. Twenty points qualified the recipient for an Air Medal award. To be awarded 15 medals meant that Lou had accumulated 300 points from either that many sorties over South Vietnam, or more likely, he had been downtown more often than was good for anyone. This explained his casual approach to the flight over the Pacific!

As the war in Vietnam grew in intensity, the training programme expanded to keep up with the demand for properly trained crews, especially in the art of carrier deck landing. The United States Navy monitored each pilot through every stage of preparation for this skilful task. The secondary runway at NAS Miramar was in operation around the clock, with pilots carrying out dummy deck landings. Landing sight officers (LSOs) watched, recorded, and commented on every landing. At the end of each session, the student pilot was told if he had any dangerous tendencies and what to do to correct problem areas. After performing successful day approaches, he progressed to night approaches before being sent to the ship where carrier qualifications were flown.

The turn round of ships and squadrons going back and forth to Vietnam meant that time and space in each deck programme was limited. I greatly appreciated the sacrifice the US Navy made in allowing me to qualify on the USS *Constellation* as she cruised in the Pacific Ocean off the Californian coast. It was like going First Class, after flying off the smaller British carriers! The ship was so big and spacious that landings were relatively easy, particularly as the Phantom F4J, with the slotted stabilator, was rock steady on approach. The catapults were twice the length of the British ones, giving a smooth gentle acceleration to flying speed.

One must give credit where credit is due; so, I must state how impressed I was at the professional level of American deck operations. The flight-deck teams were well drilled and efficient. From the captain down, everyone knew exactly what he had to do, and when and how to do it. It is precisely for this reason that the carrier remains the ultimate global force-multiplier.

During my final weapons deployment to MCAS Yuma, I had the opportunity to visit the Grand Canyon by air. With Keith Brown, one of the other "Brits" in the back seat of a Phantom, we flew at high level to overhead Flagstaff, Arizona. The reason for this was to look at the magnificent 300-million-year-old meteor crater close to the town. From altitude, one is able to get a wonderful view of the mile-wide circular crater, the 600-foot deep central hole, and the 150-foot high rim wall.

We let down to low level to view the Grand Canyon, a titanic gorge cut by the Colorado River through the high plateau region of Arizona. It is over 200 miles long, varies in width between four to 18 miles and in places is over a mile deep. It is perhaps the world's most spectacular illustration of the accumulated results of erosion. We initially flew level with the rim while passing through the more populated areas of the National Park. However, once away from prying eyes, we went lower until the Phantom was just above the river. We regained a respectable altitude before crossing the Hoover Dam on our return to Yuma. It was a wonderful, thought-provoking flight through breathtaking scenery. One can understand why poetry is often used to describe the beauty of flight.

At the end of July 1968, two wonderful years in the United States Navy ended. I was given the opportunity to fly superb aeroplanes with outstanding people and it was with genuine sadness that I left VF121. My departure from NAS Miramar occurred a week later. My last official function took place in the Base Chapel on 10 August, when I married June Beckett. She was an airhostess with BOAC when I met her two years previously. I was on HMS *Ark Royal* in Singapore when she flew through on a trip to Australia. Two years of long distance telephone calls had secured her place by my side in front of an audience of Phantom aircrew. It was a great day for us, despite the fact that neither family could attend.

Many years later, on a visit to South Africa while stationed in South West Africa (Namibia), *Top Gun* was showing at a cinema in Pretoria. During a meal, after the screening, June asked me how I had enjoyed the performance. I told her that I loved the flying sequences, which were very realistic. I can remember Tom Cruise remarking 'Shit,' with just the right sort of feeling as a fighter passed down his port side at supersonic speed. I added that the story was real Hollywood and that the characters were unrealistic. She looked away in one of those gestures married couples recognize. I asked her if she agreed with my assessment to which she answered an emphatic 'No!' She said that all the chaps at our wedding were exactly as depicted on the screen; in retrospect, maybe she was right. We were all completely involved in fighter flying with an intenseness only experienced during a war situation.

Driving across America may not be considered an ideal honeymoon by many couples, but for June and me it was superb. Northwards from San Diego, through Disneyland in Los Angeles; the lovely Monterey peninsula; the delights of San Francisco; the magnificent Redwoods; wine-tasting in the Nappa Valley—the list of attractions never end.

However, it was an extremely long drive, particularly as we wandered into Canada and skirted the northern banks of the Great Lakes, before making the obligatory stop for newly-weds at the Niagara Falls.

Our route took us back into America as we headed south through Pennsylvania towards Washington, DC. Travelling in the States was very easy. The roads were excellent, service stations frequent, and accommodation after a long day's driving was easy to find at the many roadside motels. These establishments all advertised on large, sometimes huge, neon signs. One could choose between double, queen and king-sized beds; swimming pools; colour TV's with umpteen available channels; and restaurants or diners.

We chose the Valley View on Route 15 in Mansfield, because it offered "relaxer" beds. America and Americans were into every new gimmick to increase the commercial attractiveness of their product. This "relaxer" turned out to be a vibrating bed that supposedly had therapeutic effects after a long day on the road. By placing a quarter (25 cents) into the slot of a meter next to the bed, the entire bed would then gently vibrate for ten minutes, inducing a soporific, drowsy sensation, which soon encouraged deep and restful sleep.

On entering our allotted room, I decided to watch a bit of television, before we went to the restaurant for dinner. Unfortunately, the TV set and bedside lamps did not work. This was not a crisis, but I decided to mention it to the motel management on our way to dinner. The receptionist, the wife of the motel manager, was, like most Americans, very obliging and she said she would get her husband to rectify the fault.

The meal was good and we retired to bed. Shortly after midnight, our room came alive! Both bedside lamps came on and our bed started to gyrate. The husband must have returned from night shift and with typical American efficiency, immediately repaired the reported electrical fault. Turning the lights out, we waited for the bed to stop moving. The electrical circuit had been out of order for quite a considerable time. Being transients, none of the previous occupants had bothered to report the fault, although many of them had pushed quarters into the slot machine. For what seemed like hours, our bed happily vibrated until it had used up all the money. Like banging one's head against a wall, it was wonderful when it stopped!

Book Three
South African Air Force

Foreword – Book Three

Outside of South Africa, the SWA/Namibia Angola war is not well known despite the fact that it lasted over 20 years.

In the course of those 20 years the war, which started in the guise of a small-scale guerilla war, transformed into a full-scale conventional war with ongoing embedded guerrilla conflict. With the help of Russian, East Bloc and Cuban surrogates, the air defences of Angola improved with well-prepared and linked early warning radars, and MiG21 and MiG23 interceptors.

The South African Air Force, with its proud fighting record in World War II, had last been involved in waging war more than a decade before, during the Korean conflict. They once again emerged with great honour from a war that saw the introduction of "jet-age" warfare.

The war they were now involved in required the SAAF to redevelop its former aerial prowess. It would also need to develop all the skills required of an air force conducting its own air war, supporting the army's mobile warfare and conducting wide ranging air mobile operations against guerrilla forces over vast expanses of featureless, difficult, hostile terrain.

The SAAF's use of helicopters in this scenario depended largely on an evolutionary development of skills. They learnt by observing and adapting, or adopting, tactical methods used in Vietnam and elsewhere. The SAAF's inventive helicopter crews rapidly mastered the operational demands in their own particular way to become a formidable airmobile force.

The development of the SAAF's fighter combat skills required a different approach. The cold war and South African isolation ensured that the complex subject of air combat manoeuvring, electronic warfare, evasion tactics, aircraft and missile performance, and many other vital aspects were not readily available to the SAAF.

As the saying goes: "Cometh the time, cometh the man". It was into this capability void that Dick Lord stepped. His huge reservoir of knowledge and tremendous ability to impart his contribution with skill, understanding and tact, was exactly what was required at this time. He rapidly made his presence felt in the fighter community and the competence and confidence that he instilled in his fledglings transformed them into a highly professional band of eagles.

During my own involvement in the South West Africa/Angola conflict, I derived a great deal of professional insight from Dick. His great sense of humour and professional collegial manner, until today, leaves me with a profound sense of gratitude for having been afforded such an association. I am sure that you, the reader, will equally enjoy the sharing of the experiences, the insight and the humour that characterizes this book.

There were a number of stars in the development of the SAAF's most recent aerial warfare capabilities. Shining most brightly amongst them was Dick Lord!

Major General Winston H. Thackwray SM, MMM (Ret SAAF)
Former Officer Commanding Western Air Command

Chapter 17

2 Squadron, AFB Waterkloof

Although it was a pleasure to return to South Africa after 12 years in the Royal Navy, I did feel an element of uncertainty. The navy looked after all my needs, allowing me to concentrate on flying—the task I loved. Now, I had to make a new career for myself. My first step was to attend the Durban Aviation College to qualify for a commercial flying licence. My previous training stood me in good stead and after passing all the exams, I was invited to join the staff. While I contemplated future career moves, instruction brought in the much-needed money.

I finally realized I was back in Africa while giving ground instruction at Virginia airfield, on the northern outskirts of Durban. Standing with my back to the chalkboard, I could talk to the class and keep an eye on activities out on the airfield. One afternoon, the noise from a sudden burst of throttle caught my attention, and I was in time to see a Rocket Maule shoot out onto the airfield from the refuelling area. This light, high-winged, nose-wheeled aircraft gained speed rapidly under full power. Propeller torque soon swung the nose to starboard causing the machine to perform two ever-increasingly tight ground loops. On the third rotation, the starboard wing tip struck the ground; the propeller dug into the turf and the aircraft flipped over onto its back.

The light plane belonged to an order of missionaries who carried out their good work high up in the Drakensberg Mountains in Lesotho (formerly Basutoland). On this particular day, there was high excitement and expectation at the mission. A brand new missionary from Belgium was arriving in South Africa to swell their numbers. The resident missionary flew down to Virginia that morning, and then he drove across by car to Durban International to meet the new man. They returned to Virginia for the flight back to Lesotho.

While the pilot was away, the Maule was towed to the refuelling area and topped up. Apparently, after the refuelling was complete, the battery master switch was on and the battery was flat. Hand-swinging the propeller usually fired up the motor. The new missionary was strapped into the right-hand seat while the pilot set the necessary magneto switches, throttle, and prop settings. He then swung the prop but nothing happened. After opening the throttle a little bit more he tried again. This time the engine dutifully coughed but it did not start. The pilot opened the throttle a little more knowing that on the next attempt, the engine would catch. He explained the situation to the new missionary who was understandably a little excited about all the activity, or lack thereof, on his first day in darkest Africa. The pilot briefed the new boy to bring the throttle to idle once the engine started. He received an excited nod of agreement.

Third time lucky, with the throttle now set half-open, he swung the prop. A great roar and a cloud of smoke indicated that the engine had started. Unfortunately, the wheels of the little aircraft were not chocked and with a rapidly spinning propeller, it began rolling forward. Not wanting to be struck by the whirling blade, the old missionary threw himself sideways to the ground as the wing passed over him. The sudden engine roar sent a complimentary surge of adrenaline through the new missionary's veins. Remembering his instructions, he tried to move the throttle back to idle, but without success. The old missionary had forgotten to explain the workings of a vernier throttle and the requirement to depress the locking button to retract the throttle.

By now, with the Maule gathering momentum by the second and finding himself in sole command of the runaway aircraft, the new missionary took charge. If the throttle did not move backwards, it might move forwards. This burst of power was what drew my attention to the unfolding drama. The sudden surge of energy caused the new missionary, on his first day in Africa, to lose all semblance of control. At this stage, I realized that he was indeed a missionary. Each time the circling aircraft passed our building I could hear the poor man screaming for help and I am sure he was not blaspheming!

The fuel attendant closely followed by the pilot was chasing the aircraft. All's well that ends well! Although the Maule was damaged, neither missionary suffered any physical damage. Nobody said Africa would be easy!

Although I enjoyed teaching, I kept my eyes open for a way to return to the cockpit. Two events influenced my decision. One of the big events on the South African aviation calendar was the annual State President's Air Race. A huge variety of aircraft entered, ranging from Cessna 150s to executive twins. Theoretically, any aircraft could win the two-day race, as each type was handicapped according to its published performance figures. The navigational and airmanship skills of the aircrew were the ultimate determinant. The course varied each time the race was held and on this occasion, the finish line was Virginia Airport in Durban.

A colourful, 200-yard tape stretched between the tower and the windsock indicated the finish line. Aircraft passed over this tape to qualify. Around mid-afternoon excitement built to a fever pitch as the radio calls were broadcast over a specially erected loudspeaker system to the waiting spectators. Suddenly, over the ridge to the west of the airport, aircraft appeared. Pushing the noses down to extract the last knot out of their straining aircraft, the pilots aimed for the tape. Only then did the penny drop! If the handicappers had done their job correctly, then all the aircraft should appear over this 200-yard tape at exactly the same time, and this was precisely what happened. In a parody of Churchill's famous speech, 'Never, in the field of human conflict, have you seen so many aeroplanes in so small an airspace, at the same time!'

It was horrific! Slow aircraft, flying at just over 100 knots, were bustled out of the way by heavy twins flashing in at nearly four times the speed. All the pilots had eyes only for the finishing tape. Near misses were two a penny, not only over the tape. All the pilots had to land at Virginia, so they broke onto a downwind leg. The turning circle of an aircraft flying at 400 knots is much greater than that described by a 100-knot aircraft. Approach speeds differed by as much as 70 knots and all aircraft were in the circuit together. Reared in a flying-safety conscious, military aviation milieu, I was appalled. Although it was most entertaining for the onlookers, I decided that "civvy" flying was not really for me. In fairness, I must report that I did not witness any aircraft crash—but my eyes were shut most of the time!

Shortly after the race, HMS *Eagle* visited Durban. It gave June and me the opportunity to see and entertain old friends, and the sight and smell of the carrier touched a cord deep in my soul. The following week I paid a visit to AFB Durban and asked to see the commanding officer of 5 Squadron, South African Air Force (SAAF). This Harvard equipped unit was an Active Citizen Force (ACF) squadron tasked with training and maintaining a pool of reserve officers for the regular air force. The HMS *Eagle* visit prompted me to enlist to retain my skill as a military pilot. Major "Blondie" Cillier, the commanding officer, arranged the necessary interview for me at Air Force Headquarters in Pretoria. Lt Ev van Rooyen flew me up country in one of the Harvards.

The interview conducted by General Ray Armstrong in Pretoria was similar to the one I underwent before joining the navy. However, the general seemed to lose all interest when I admitted to being 34 years of age. Seeing this reaction, I explained that I did have a bit of experience. I went down the list of courses I had completed and aircraft I had flown. Even this long list failed to animate him until I mentioned the magic word Phantom. He suddenly blinked and asked me to repeat what I had said. Certain that I had said F4 Phantom, he stopped the interview, told me to stay where I was, and promptly walked out. A quarter of an hour later he returned, invited me to accompany him upstairs, and ushered me in to meet General Verster, chief of the air force.

This tall, distinguished looking man, showed me to a chair, pressed a button summoning his steward and ordered a pot of tea, which he personally poured for me. Unaccustomed to this reaction from senior officers, I was suitably impressed. Being a blunt man, he came straight to the point. 'You don't want to join the citizen force,' he said, 'you want to join the permanent force!' He then immediately offered me a position in No 24 Buccaneer Squadron. He was a little miffed when I refused the offer saying that, if I were to join permanently, then I would rather fly the Mirage III as I was a fighter pilot at heart. 'All right,' he said, 'you can fly the Mirage.' Then we negotiated rank. I was a lieutenant commander in the navy, but he thought it would be only right to bring me in as a captain. Having not applied for the permanent force, I told him I could not afford to go backwards. 'Oh! All right,' he said again. 'You can join as a major.' I was ushered out and Col "Bossie" Huyser then settled the details.

Bossie was probably the most dynamic man I ever encountered. He had been commanding officer of No 2 Mirage Squadron; he won the Top Gun trophy at the annual weapons meeting, and he was now senior staff officer fighters. Bossie explained that it was necessary for me to pass language tests in English and Afrikaans before I could enrol as an officer. He arranged for me to sit the tests there and then. I did not have a problem with English. Afrikaans, however, proved a much sterner test. I learnt Afrikaans in high school as a compulsory subject 16 years earlier, but to me it had been rather like learning Latin. I grew up in Johannesburg and I did not have Afrikaans friends. I had never conversed in the language.

I took the test and knew I could not have passed. I left pages of the exam sheet untouched, often not even understanding the questions! Reporting to Bossie, I told him this, and I said I would return to Durban. He made me wait for the result, talking hard and fast on the telephone to the examiner in the language I did not really understand. Twenty minutes later, without a blink of his eye, Col Huyser announced that I had successfully completed both language tests, and I must now wait for joining instructions enlisting me in the South African Air Force.

Although serving one's country in the military is a honourable duty, it is certainly hard work for a wife! My decision entailed another pack up and another move to another house. In the SAAF, the saying goes that one can always tell a military family by the naughty children and the broken furniture! Certainly, during my career, we had our fair share of moves and all of them were traumatic.

I was appointed to 2 Squadron, operating out of AFB Waterkloof, near Pretoria. This prestigious unit gained numerous battle honours from service with the Desert Air Force during World War II, and for distinction in the Korean War. The squadron was better known as the Cheetah squadron because of the winged-Cheetah emblem that adorned its aircraft. As the only Mirage equipped unit, it was a large squadron. Inventory included 16 Mirage III CZ interceptors, 16 EZ ground-attack fighters, three BZ dual-trainers for the CZ, three DZ trainers for the EZ, and four RZ photo-reconnaissance aircraft. The suffix Z indicates that the aircraft were supplied to South Africa. A large proportion of the maintenance personnel attended courses in France, so the expertise level was high and serviceability figures good.

Although Waterkloof was a good airfield, it had its limitations. First, like Johannesburg International, it was nearly 6 000 feet above sea level, making for hot and high operations. Second, it was close to the Johannesburg terminal and was continually squeezed for air space by the voracious demands of civilian air traffic control authorities. Third, like most military airfields, when it was originally built the site had been carefully selected far away from the city and suburbs to avoid unnecessary conflict with residents. Urban sprawl round Pretoria surrounded the base and complaints from the locals of noise pollution were two a penny. Apart from 42 after-burning Mirage fighters, Waterkloof was home to squadrons of Buccaneers, Canberras, C130 Hercules, C160 Transalls, and the HS125 Mercurius VIP jets of 21 Squadron—so maybe the complainants had a point!

The delta-winged Mirage III was a delight to fly and a handful to land. Without trailing edge flaps, the approach was made at high speed and a large nose-up flare was required before touchdown. This high nose attitude made visibility of the runway difficult, with the pilot having to look around the left-hand side of the nose. The high-speed touchdown required the deployment of a drag chute to save wear on the braking system. In a crosswind, like those generated by the frequent summer thunderstorms, the pilot needed good anticipation.

Once away from the ground, it was a real fighter pilot's aircraft. French cockpits were small, neat and ergonomically years ahead of the random scattering of instruments, gauges and switches found in contemporary British aircraft. The delta construction provided a robust machine very suitable for the punishing environment of fighter operations. It was agile, fast, and it had an incredible 420° per second rate-of-roll. Perhaps its major problem was the limited amount of fuel it carried. The fuel flow and content gauges required constant attention. Flying sorties often lasted only 40 minutes. This proved to be a considerable tactical limitation in a country as large as South Africa.

Unlike the Americans, who built their Phantoms without controls in the back seat or emergency batteries, the French incorporated their little tricks in the fuel system! To ensure the Mirage III was fully refuelled between flights, a lever situated under the wing opened all the fuel lines. If no fuel lines were opened, only the fuel tanks above the valves would fill and, although visually the aircraft would appear to be full of fuel, a nasty surprise could await the pilot.

I can remember Maj "Spyker" Jacobs climbing steeply out of AFB Waterkloof in Pretoria in full afterburner. He had to convert his climb to a loop by rolling off the top and setting his aircraft into a glide back to base. The Mirage had the gliding characteristics of a brick, and Spyker landed back with just enough fuel to turn off the main runway. A very similar situation occurred when Maj Roelff Beukes, future chief of the air force, made it back into Durban with only fumes in the tank. I suspect the French Air Force must have had similar experiences, because when they built the Mirage F1 the fuel system did not have this peculiarity.

Inside, the engine intakes were streamlined semicircular bulges, known for some unexplained reason as "mice". These mice were movable and performed the same function as the splitter plate alongside the Phantom intakes. Instead of a hydraulic jack pushing the mice outwards, electrical power motored them forwards as high supersonic Mach numbers were reached, so controlling the shockwave ahead of the engine intake.

Although acceleration was slower than the F4, Mach 2.1 was easily attainable. As a safety precaution, because of limited fuel reserves, these high-speed runs always occurred heading back towards base—not ideal for an air defence fighter!

The Mirage was a delight but the flying lacked variety. Tasked with air defence duties, the squadron was linked with the underground command bunker at Devon Ground Control Intercept (GCI) radar site in the Eastern Transvaal. Our normal daily activities were restricted to taking off in pairs, climbing to altitude, splitting for a session of radar controlled intercepts called "hook-ups and hiccups", followed by a close formation recovery to base.

Twice a year the squadron deployed for live weaponry training—once to AFB Langebaanweg in the Cape for air-to-air firing over sea and once to Bloemfontein in the Free State to use the De Wet ground attack weapons range to the west of that town.

Personally, I felt that the SAAF had fallen into the trap of becoming a "peace-time" air force. There were no ex-Korean War pilots left in the cockpits so flying had become rather like the activities of an exclusive aviation club. I hasten to point out that this is not a criticism; peace encourages this malaise. One only has to think of the sorry state of the RAF between the World Wars and the debacle in Lebanon in December 1984 when the US Navy lost an A6 Intruder to a Strela SA-7 missile, to understand how quickly and easily this happens.

After a year on the squadron, I was posted to Central Flying School Dunnottar to learn to become an instructor, even though I had been instructing in the navy since 1963! Nevertheless, I enjoyed the course but more so the opportunity to fly the Harvard A6. It was fun to handle a tail-dragging, propeller-powered aircraft again. My only previous experience had been on the Provost. Aerobatics in a piston-engine aircraft is always enjoyable, even though I never really mastered the normally aspirated carburettor on the Harvard. My engine always coughed when I applied forward pressure on the stick at the commencement of a slow roll or Derry turn.

Like most flying establishments, the pub was well used and the centre of much amusement. One evening, after a few toots, Capt Basil Newham said his goodnights and headed for the exit. Less than two minutes later, he was back asking for assistance because he had over-turned his car. Not believing this unlikely story, we duly trooped outside. There, exactly as he had explained it, was his car on its side. He had reversed with a flourish out of his parking spot. Unfortunately, he had failed to notice a wire hawser, supporting a telephone pole. This cable stretched between the top of the pole and the ground at an angle of about 60°. The impetus of the car was sufficient to lift the rear end and tip the vehicle gently onto its side. The damage was no worse than a few scratches and Basil's red face.

Central Flying School Dunnottar was a busy airfield in the 1970s. Pupil pilot courses ran twice a year to feed the expanding squadrons of the SAAF. Within every course were those with a natural talent for flying and others who, perhaps, were never meant to fly. This second group always required the most attention from the instructors. The staff, who had the awesome responsibility of sending pupils solo, had to ensure the safety of students.

All people are different, making the world the interesting place that it is. At any military Flying School, the instructors endeavoured to ensure the pupils went through exactly the same mould. Their aim was to produce ideal flying "clones". Human personality, being what it is, avoids that dreadful state and so the pupils do differ.

Like pupils, the instructors also varied. Only a special few had sufficient patience to handle the slow-learning students. These men were tasked with the responsibility of carrying out final handling and pre-solo checks on the problem children. Captain Renier Keet, who later became a Mirage III pilot on 2 Squadron, was selected as one of these instructors. He had the extraordinary ability to extract the very best out of slow, or problem, pupils.

On one particular course was a youngster who, although he could fly quite well, could just not remember all his checks and vital actions. His instructor became incensed at this lack of memory and as a last resort, he asked Renier to try and help. After flying a sortie with the youngster, Renier realized what he was up against. He spent long hours in the ground school, repeating over and over the list of checks that the young man had to remember.

Finally, the great day dawned. Renier, strapped into the back seat of the Harvard, listened with amazement as the youngster rattled off, without a hitch, the cockpit check, pre-start check, and the after-start check. The engine was running smoothly, the pupil pilot had asked for and received his taxi clearance from Air Traffic Control, and they were ready to taxi out to the duty runway. The groundcrew man had the chock rope in his hand awaiting the signal to remove them from the wheels, so that the Harvard could start moving.

Unfortunately, that was as far as the youngster's memory could take him! He completely forgot the next item of his procedures, which was to wave to the crewman by crossing both hands in front of his face and so indicate to him to remove the wheel chocks. They waited until, finally, Renier decide to prompt the pupil. He told him, over the intercom, to give the groundcrew man the sign. What an unfortunate choice of words! The youngster, obeying the legal order from his instructor, leant his right arm out of the cockpit. He then proceeded to point, with his thumb firmly between his fore and middle finger, at the astounded groundcrew man!

Realizing the hopelessness of the task, Renier shut the engine down. After apologizing to the mechanic, he suggested to the pupil that it would probably be better, as well as safer for all concerned, if he considered a drastic change in career direction.

On completion of my course, I returned to 2 Squadron and the lovely Mirage III. Before flying solo, I had to carry out a dual-check under the watchful eye of Maj Barry Moody. During this flight, we spotted another Mirage flown by "Spyker" Jacobs. He was passing from right to left below my nose and we were in an ideal position to jump him. Receiving permission from Barry in the back, I peeled over and dived into the attack. Spyker saw us coming and broke into a steep left-hand turn. I was in danger of overshooting when he reversed as I slid through under his tail. I cranked on the "G" to bleed off excess speed in order to stay behind the other aircraft. At about this stage I thought I heard a wailing over the intercom. The harder I manoeuvred the aircraft the more insistent and louder the wailing became. Ignoring the noise, I secured the "kill" and headed back to Waterkloof to land.

At debrief I mentioned the wailing noise on the intercom. Barry owned up to being responsible, but in mitigation he mentioned that it started when the *adhemar* turned pure red. After being away from the aircraft for five months, I had missed one of my pre-start checks. I neglected to lift the night flying cover on the angle-of-attack (*adhemar*) indicator. Because the delta-winged aircraft had unpredictable spin characteristics, nose-up attitude was limited by reference to the angle-of-attack indicator that consisted of three coloured lights. As in normal traffic lights, green indicated safe angles and amber indicated caution. Red was forbidden, outlawed, prohibited, tabooed, and according to the pilot's notes was absolutely *verboten* under peril of death, destruction and annihilation.

Not seeing these lights, I attacked with gay abandon. Apparently, from the first turn, our *adhemar* went straight to bright red and stayed that way throughout the engagement, prompting Barry's wail! We proved that provided we flew the aircraft smoothly and without harsh cross controlling, it was an excellent platform. In fact, a quick pull into the red raised the delta wing and bled the speed quickly—a handy tactic to force a high-speed attacker to overshoot.

A few days after this flight an electrical fire in the GCI command centre at Devon put the facility out of action for three months. Their flying programme was based on radar controlled "hook-ups and hiccups". The flight schedulers were at a loss trying to decide how to fill the gap. I looked on this fire as divine intervention!

South Africa has an unfortunate history of "transformations". Rather than adopting a live and let live policy, the political masters have all blundered blindly along the "change for change-sake" path. After the Anglo-Boer War, up until 1948, English was the flavour of the month! This changed radically when South Africa came under Nationalist Afrikaans domination. The historic De Klerk/Mandela negotiations led to the 1994 electoral victory of the African National Congress. Since then, in the natural course of South African politics, everything has turned black.

In the 1970s, parts of the population, with long memories, viewed the British with suspicion and distaste. Coming from the British Fleet Air Arm, I was taken to be a "Pommie", despite being born and bred in Johannesburg. During my first year, I learnt from the experience of other pilots who had returned from Britain to the SAAF. I was hesitant to offer any suggestions as to how they could improve their flying efficiency. Earlier, I sat in during a briefing at 24 Buccaneer Squadron and heard the new commanding officer state, 'That's how the *Souties* flew the Bucc in England. I am going to change all that!' He did alter the tried and tested techniques of the original Buccaneer crews and for a number of years thereafter the Buccaneer in SAAF service had an abysmal safety record.

However, to my knowledge, I never suffered because of this bias. I do know that I was referred to as "daardie blerrie Engelsman" on a good day and "daardie f... Engelsman" on bad days. I saw the fire as a golden opportunity, and I offered to initiate a programme of ACM. Barry's wide-eyed stare after the red *adhemar* flight, lent credence to this type of flying. The authorities agreed and I immediately started giving lectures of ACM theory.

The flying programme began with instruction on one-versus-one fighting. Having to give all the dual instruction, the programme took a while to get into its stride, but it caught on like wildfire. Suddenly everyone was clamouring to get on the flying programme. Within a few short weeks, the pilots had grasped the essentials and aerial engagements were becoming increasingly intense. South Africans, probably because of the countries long history of conflict, are naturally aggressive. This characteristic is an ideal ingredient in the make-up of a fighter pilot.

Flying safety was of paramount concern. Replacing aircraft was becoming more difficult as South Africa sank deeper into the mire of world isolation. Balancing both these needs was tricky, but we succeeded. The ACM programme expanded from one-versus-one to two-versus-one, to two-versus-two, and then to four-versus-two. After that, ground attack strike progression missions were flown. A flight of four would simulate an air-to-ground strike on a selected target. Two other pilots with the chosen route and times would jump the formation en-route—the forerunner of the famous Red Flag exercises!

Chapter 18

85 ADFS, AFB Pietersburg

The growing threat of terrorist war with SWAPO in South West Africa and their host country Angola was beginning to influence national policy. Teams of air force personnel went overseas to survey the market for new military hardware. Britain's Labour government lost a number of jobs in the British aircraft industry when they refused to honour their commitment to sell a further 16 Buccaneers to South Africa. France eagerly took over the traditionally British role of arms supplier and South Africa went French!

Eleven Mirage III D2Zs equipped a new Mirage flying school at AFB Pietersburg in the Northern Transvaal. Sixteen Mirage F1CZ interceptors were bought for 3 Squadron and 32 F1AZ ground-attack aircraft replaced the Canadair F86 Sabres of 1 Squadron. The Sabres moved to the combat school at Pietersburg in a training role. Four Mirage III R2Z photo-recce aircraft supplemented the four RZs already in service and gave 2 Squadron a greater reconnaissance capability.

During the same hectic era, single-seat, light, ground-attack Impala Mk2s re-equipped all the Citizen Force Harvard squadrons, and supplemented the Italian Aeromacchi 326 Impala Mk1 jet trainers. This rapid expansion required the formation of an advanced combat flying school at Pietersburg. This unit consisted of an Operational Conversion Unit (OCU) equipped with a mix of 27 Impala Mk1 and Mk2 aircraft. A Sabre flight was used for advanced instruction to qualify experienced pilots as Pilot Attack Instructors (PAIs). The third flight, equipped with 16 Mirage III EZ single-seaters and 14 Mirage III DZ and

D2Z trainers, presented the Mirage OCU. All pilots destined for Mirage III, Mirage F1, Canberra, and Buccaneer squadrons had to graduate from this course. All three flights presented two six-month courses per year. Aspirant fighter pilots progressed from gaining their wings to the Impala OCU. Postings to an Impala Mk2 squadron, gained them frontline experience. The Sabre flight appointed suitable candidates and after further squadron experience, the candidates eventually made it onto the Mirage OCU. 85 Advanced Combat School provided the training and honed the skills of pilots who performed active service during the border war until 1989.

ACM training formed a large part of the fighter-training syllabus and within a few short years, most SAAF fighter pilots were proficient in this "art form". During this training, a sequence of events occurred which I described in Nyala, the SAAF Flying Safety Magazine. I repeat this story in its original form.

A COMEDY IN THREE ACTS

(SETTING THE SCENE)
The year: 1975
The place: AFB Pietersburg
The cast: Staff and students of 85 Advanced Flying School
The aircraft: Four Mirage IIIs
The training phase: Air Combat Manoeuvring (ACM)

CAST (in order of appearance)
Brit Lead: Cmdt Dick Lord
Brit Two: Cmdt Bertus Burger
Boer Lead: Cmdt Willem Hechter
Boer Two: Lt Thys Muller
SATCO: Maj H Venter (Oom Hennie)

ACT 1
STAGE: NORTH
SCENE: Two supersonic Mirages
                      Northern sky over bushveld backdrop
CAST: Two fighter pilots
PROPS: G suits
                      Gloves
                      Dark "dobies"—the whole bit!

Brit Lead, with his wingman tucked in close, blasts off Runway 01 in full afterburner and they rapidly disappear out of sight, heading north of Roodewal Weapons Range. Once in their allotted sector, they level off at medium altitude and separate, prior to their first engagement.

Fuel is a critical item in a Mirage. So, after the dogfight, Brit Lead asks for a "Fuel check". Brit Two answers immediately, indicating plenty of fuel still on board. Brit Lead, with a puzzled expression, asks Two to confirm the amount, which he does with alacrity.

Now this situation is slightly unusual, as the student always tends to use more fuel than the instructor. Brit Lead displays prescience by orientating the next engagement heading back towards Pietersburg. The second fight ends up 22 nautical miles north of the air force base. Lead calls for a fuel check. Two answers and once again the amount he reports is more than Lead has. Alarmed by this rare occurrence, Lead asks Two to recheck both detotalisor and fuel gauge. Two radios back a satisfactory reply, but within two seconds he bursts back onto the frequency to say that he has in fact only 12 gallons!

A surge of adrenaline courses through Lead's body; the kind that ages one instantly. Lead instructs Two to head for Runway 19 at Pietersburg, while he leaves the "chat" frequency to inform Air Traffic Control at Pietersburg.

ACT 2
STAGE: SOUTH
SCENE: Two supersonic Mirages
                         Southern sky over a mountain range and poort
CAST: Two fighter pilots
PROPS: Steely eyes
                        Square jaws
                        Big watches—the whole bit!

Two Mirages in close formation are heading south to Chunies Poort flying sector. At medium altitude Boer Lead splits his formation to start an ACM engagement. The heated action is called off halfway through the first fight when Boer Two levels out, telling his Lead that he has an oil malfunction and is battling to control the engine. An oil failure is one of the most serious problems that can occur in a Mirage and requires the stricken aircraft to land in the shortest possible time.

Boer Lead displays good airmanship and sets his number two up for a straight-in approach onto Runway 01 at Pietersburg. Chunies Poort is approximately 22 nautical miles south of the airfield! Boer Lead leaves their "chat" frequency to inform Air Traffic Control at Pietersburg of the emergency.

ACT 3
STAGE: CENTRE
SCENE: SAAF Air Force Base Pietersburg
                  Quiet air-conditioned ATC tower
CAST: Jovial, elderly ATC major

Enter four aircraft. Two approaching from stage north and two approaching from stage south. Normal activity in the glass house of the ATC tower with feet up and mug of coffee to hand.

The tranquillity of the morning is suddenly broken by an urgent call on tower frequency.

Boer Leader: 'MAYDAY—MAYDAY—MAYDAY! I have Boer Two with serious oil problems. Request you clear the circuit of other traffic. I am setting him up for a straight in on Runway 01.'

SATCO: 'Roger your Mayday.'

The tower frequency loudspeaker immediately erupts again to other strident tones.

Brit Leader: 'MAYDAY—MAYDAY—MAYDAY! I have Brit Two on high finals for a straight in on Runway 19. He is out of fuel. Request you clear the pattern of all other traffic.'

SATCO: 'Can't you wait your turn? I am already busy with a Mayday!'

A hurried discussion takes place between Boer and Brit Leaders. A decision is made to leave Brit Two on 19, while Boer Lead shepherds his number two around onto Runway 05.

SATCO interjects: 'I agree with the decision, but PLEASE don't collide on the intersection!'

FINALE
STAGE: CENTRE
SCENE: Two Mirages
                  Runway 19 and Runway 05, Air Force Base
                  Pietersburg
PROPS: Nervous tension
                  Anxious expressions
                  Beads of sweat

> Instantly greying hair
> Confused fire engines (not knowing which runway to attend to)

A Mirage III lands off a high, fast final approach on Runway 19 and deploys his brake chute.

A Mirage III lands off a slow, low approach on Runway 05 and deploys his brake chute.

Brit Two heading southwards crosses the runway intersection one hundred metres ahead of Boer Two, who is slowing down on Runway 05.

Boer Two shuts down at the end of Runway 05. Brit Two flames out as he turns off Runway 19.

ALL'S WELL THAT ENDS WELL!

Postscript

This improbable coincidence occurred exactly as described above. Both student pilots carried out successful and safe emergency landings. Both instructor pilots and SATCO aged appreciably in the time it takes a Mirage to fly 22 nautical miles! I am sure an aviation record was established that day. It does not happen very often in an aviator's lifetime that he gets to initiate a genuine Mayday. Imagine how peeved I was when my big chance arrived, only to be told to 'Wait your turn!'

While at Pietersburg, I received a call from a group of aircraft-modellers requesting permission to view a Mirage III. Meeting this excited group of middle-aged gentlemen at the main gate of the base, I drove them out to the hardstanding where I had arranged for a Mirage to be on display. Almost beside themselves with anticipation, they scrambled out of the combi. They did not stop to view the beautiful fighter but immediately dived under the wing and peered into the undercarriage main wheel-well. Triumphant shouts rang out and I heard one man exclaim excitedly, 'I told you there were four hydraulic lines, not three!' These men obviously argued about this during the long drive all the way from Johannesburg. I, as a conscientious pilot, looked into the wheel-well as part of my preflight inspection every time I flew and I had no idea how many lines were in there! To these enthusiasts it was crucial that every minute detail was correct.

Aircraft equipment was continually updated and improved as technology advanced. Instrumentation and test installations also became extremely sophisticated and sensitive. According to the test engineer, the new completed electronic installation at Pietersburg was supersensitive. He was worried that aircraft noise and vibration nearby could harm the calibration. Before accepting the installation, he asked that a Mirage engine be started up and run outside while he monitored the instrumentation carefully. This test was completely successful.

Having a "Doubting-Thomas" personality, the engineer was still not satisfied. He asked for a high-speed run over the airfield as a final assurance that his beloved test equipment would perform flawlessly. The pilot, Capt Mike Weingartz, was briefed to pass at low-level at high speed, close to the building containing the test instrumentation. In retrospect, the briefing should have included stricter guidelines and limitations. Pilots, especially fighter pilots, are very willing to fly low and fast—which Mike did. Keeping a watchful eye on his Mach meter, Mike approached the field at low level. Unfortunately, from that height, Mike could not get a good view of the approach. As he reached the airfield fence, he realized that he was a few degrees off the correct heading. Racking the delta into a quick turn, he passed exactly over the desired spot.

At high subsonic Mach numbers, shockwaves start forming around the thicker parts of the aircraft, such as on top of the canopy and around the engine intakes. A sudden application of "G" increases the angle-of-attack and intensifies the shockwave. With the customary double bang, Mike flashed across the airfield. After landing, the base commander escorted him through a swathe of destruction and devastation. Ceilings had fallen down; glass from shattered windows was scattered all over the base; light fittings lay in crumpled heaps where they had ejected themselves from the roof; lady secretaries were sobbing uncontrollably, and one man who had been sweeping a hangar floor had disappeared. He was last seen heading west into the veld. Mike was the benefactor of a rare stroke of good fortune. Most perpetrators of similar deeds suffered severe consequences. Mike pointed out that he had only carried out what was asked for in the briefing, albeit very enthusiastically. His bar privileges were only stopped for two months! The electronic test gear was unmoved by the entire episode. However, the engineer now has a permanent nervous tic in his eye and neck, and he has a tendency to burst into tears at sudden loud noises.

In January 1977 I received a promotion to commanding officer of the school, following in the footsteps of two illustrious officers, Commandants Zach Repsold and Willem Hechter. The latter eventually became chief of the air force. Extracting the utmost out of the old saying, "rank has its privileges", I immediately carried out a conversion onto the F86 Sabre. This classic beauty was for years on my wish list of aircraft to fly.

Having had previous experience of American ejection seats, I was suspicious of the old Weber seat in the Sabre, but apart from that, the aircraft was all that I had envisaged. It had a big, comfortable cockpit. The bubble canopy was superb; the designers knew the advantage it gave in combat. The finely balanced controls allowed the pilot to carry out every manoeuvre without undue heaving or pulling. From my very first familiarization flight, aerobatics were a delight to perform—the aircraft had no vices.

I had flown and loved the Hawker Hunter, the English built contemporary to the Sabre. I was keen to compare the machines. Both were superb aircraft and I could understand the preferences of both sets of adherents. For me the deciding factor in choice of fighter was the comparison of the aerodynamic leading edge slat on the Sabre to the notched-flap selection system fitted to the Hunter.

When the Sabre was stationary on the ground, the aerodynamic slat hung forward, opening the slot between slat and wing. Under aerodynamic pressure, this slat lifted to run back flush with the wing so that drag did not adversely affect high-speed performance. However, during air fighting the centre of lift on the wing moved forward as the angle-of-attack increased, and at high angles-of-attack it would draw the slat out of its housing. The open slot would permit a flow of air to re-energize the boundary layer on the wing, allowing the pilot to pull additional "G" before the onset of aerodynamic buffet.

I came across this superb type of slat on the A4 Skyhawk, but one had to know how to extract optimum use from them. Operating aerodynamically, they had a tendency to work slightly out of synchronization. In a rolling manoeuvre, the upper wing generated more lift than the lower wing, therefore the upper slat left its housing fractionally before the one on the bottom wing, causing a minute period of instability. I overcame this situation by giving the stick a sudden backward pull in a turn to unhouse both slats together.

The Hunter did not have leading edge slats, but a tiny flap lever situated forward of the throttle, making it easy and quick to get at during a dogfight. This lever moved in a groove that had five or six detents in it between fully up to fully down. The trailing edge flaps could be set at any of these settings. This capability of controlling exactly the amount of lift generated by the wings produced the feature that weighted my choice in favour of the Hunter. Sitting in astern of an opponent during a tight-turning dogfight, the Hunter pilot could "milk" the flaps to bring his sight onto the opponent for a kill. The superb turning Sabre had that little moment when something, other than the pilot, controlled the lift. I preferred to keep positive control of my aircraft.

During my tenure as the "boss", I had occasion to deliver an aircraft to the Atlas Aircraft Industry facility at Johannesburg International Airport. Walking into operations to sign off the aircraft, I bumped into Lt John Inggs. John had completed the Impala OCU with us and was serving on 4 Squadron at that time, but he was due to return to the school in the near future to complete an advanced course. Speaking to him, I noticed that his hair was slightly longer than I liked it to be. His commanding officer at 4 Squadron was Commandant Piet Roos, nicknamed Sir Peter Rose because of his famed sweeping locks. I told John I was looking forward to having him back but that he would have to be more conventionally shorn.

A week or two later he arrived and his flowing, curly locks were trimmed but still too long. John was a tremendous youngster who had impressed us with his latent flying ability on his OCU. One morning, shortly after he rejoined us, I paid a visit to his flight. On entry, everyone stood up, as was customary in the service. I motioned them all to sit, except John. I looked him straight in the eye and asked him if he thought he could beat me in a one-versus-one ACM fight. He looked straight back at me and said, 'Yes Sir!' I then made a deal with him in front of all the others. We would go off and fight and if he won, he could keep his hair as it was. However, if I won, I would give him a suitable haircut. Donning our flying clothing and "G" suits, we walked out to our Impala Mk2s.

John gave me a fantastic fight. We flew three long engagements before low fuel lights forced us to return. During the debriefing John reluctantly agreed that I had won two engagements and he had won one. Using a set of electric clippers, I gave him a haircut that those present still remember. John later died in a civilian aerobatic aircraft accident—the sad loss of a lovely person and great pilot.

My tenure as commanding officer of the Advanced Fighter School seemed, at the time, to be the apex of my career. I incorporated all the lessons I had learnt in the Fleet Air Arm and the US Navy into the curriculum of the courses we ran. The pilots were eager to learn, and the expertise among the entire operational fighter force grew in leaps and bounds.

I was fortunate to receive Captain Hubert (Hubbs) Füss, ex-French Air Force, as an instructor on my staff. Like a character in an Agatha Christie play, Hubbs, with his straggly beard and Maurice Chevalier accent (which seemed to get broader with time), was the epitome of a Frenchman. His hands and long expressive fingers became a necessary part of his briefings, bridging the conversational divide. Hubbs gained exchange experience on a tour with the Canadian Air Force, and he had operational exposure during the French fighting in Algeria. His forte was low-level reconnaissance. He initiated a highly successful recce course as part of the school, which benefited later operations during the Angolan border war.

While talking about his tour with the Canadians, we discovered that we had experienced similar difficulties in comprehending North American English. My torch/flashlight incident in America was due to pure language variations, whereas Hubbs had experienced an Anglo/French culture difference. Hubbs grew up under the strict disciplinarian regime in the French Air Force, where the general said, 'You will' to the colonel, who said, 'You will' to the major, who said, 'You will' all the way down to the pilot who then did!

Not long after his arrival in Canada, he was enjoying the warmth of the crewroom on a bitterly cold, snowy, northern day. His flight commander, using the Anglo-Saxon method of command, approached Hubbs and said, 'Would you like to get your kit on and go and fly.' Not recognizing the subtle difference in technique, Hubbs took a quick look at the terrible weather outside and declined the offer, to the chagrin of the Canadian.

I have another reason for remembering Hubbs. Years later, when I was in charge of the air war in Owamboland, South West Africa, I tasked Hubbs on numerous armed reconnaissance missions into Angola. His skills were such that he was the only pilot who never brought back any live weapons.

A command position required decision-making, some of which were difficult and others unpleasant. Perhaps the worst duty of all was to look an eager young man in the eye and tell him that he did not have the necessary attributes to qualify as a fighter pilot. In a career as inherently dangerous and demanding as fighter flying, there could be no compromise. There could be no doubt whether the youngster would make it or not. If there was the slightest doubt in his ability, he was suspended from training; the consequences were simply too severe.

When serving as a Hunter weaponry instructor at RNAS Brawdy in Wales during 1964, I flew with a student pilot who I considered to be below average. However, at our weekly progress meetings, the other instructors thought this lad good enough. As it turned out, he qualified and went to RNAS Yeovilton to convert to the more demanding Sea Vixen. Entering the landing pattern one night, he crashed on the downwind leg, killing himself and his observer. This accident could have, and should have, been avoided if the right decision had been made. This tragedy guided my thoughts throughout the rest of my flying career.

During my welcoming address to each new course, I explained to the pilots that the academic side of the course was no harder than the matriculation examinations they had all passed at school. As they all had acquired this standard, I told them that the only reason for anyone failing a theoretical examination at the school would be through a lack of motivation. A lack of motivation was completely unacceptable in anyone desiring to become a fighter pilot. A failure in any ground school subject meant automatic suspension from the course.

My resolve was tested in a most unfortunate manner. One of the students failed an exam and, in accordance with my instructions, came in to see me. This youngster was an excellent pilot with considerable latent ability. He came from a family in the Orange Free State; almost all had gained national and international acclaim as glider pilots. To make things even more difficult, he was a superb young man who I got on very well with. I made the interview a short one. I asked him to repeat to me what I had told them about exam failures. I then shook his hand and sent him on his way. In my time, I never had another ground school failure.

The delta-winged Mirage III was a testing aircraft to fly in the take-off and landing pattern, particularly for young pilots coming from the straight-winged Impala. The Mirage Course flight commander asked me to fly the pre-solo check flights with problematic students in the dual seat Mirage. Within months of taking over the school, I failed two Mirage students.

Shortly thereafter, I found myself on a DC4 heading down to the Cape to attend a Flying Safety conference. I was offered a seat alongside a senior air force officer and we engaged in social chitchat for half the fight. He then explained to me, as a newcomer to the air force, about the political set-up pertaining then to South Africa. Finally, he mentioned that since the SAAF had received Mirage aircraft ten years previously, no one had ever failed the conversion course. He then pointed out that within two months I had failed two students and added, '... they both happen to be Afrikaans speaking!' He said that I would face deep trouble if it were ever established that I had failed these two pilots because of their Afrikaans heritage. Nothing had been further from my mind! I explained my previous experience in the Royal Navy and told him that it really did not matter to me if the pilot was blue, black, yellow, or green, if he was not up to standard, he would not qualify. The senior officer is still a very good friend of mind, but I cannot say that I was not upset by the implication.

In 1978, during my tour at AFB Pietersburg, I was sent up to the border on a three-month ground tour in charge of air operations. The low intensity of the war meant that air force personnel could rotate through the operational area to gain experience. It was while serving at the Joint Army/Air Force/Police headquarters that my lack of fluency in Afrikaans became evident.

Amongst the captured SWAPO terrorists was one who had served in their "Air Defence" unit as an anti-aircraft gunner. After Army Intelligence personnel had questioned the detainee, I wanted to interrogate him. I felt it was important to try to glean exactly how these men trained and how they applied lead to affect aiming solutions against fast flying aircraft. Although the man was an Owambo, he had worked on the diamond mines in Oranjemund and could converse in Afrikaans.

Throughout my questioning, the Army Intelligence major kept glancing at me with an accusing, baleful look on his face. After completing the questioning, I asked him what the problem was. Afrikaans does not have an exact translation for the English word "Sir". Usually they use the word *Meneer* (Mister). However, in normal conversation, when talking directly to a person, they use the word *jy* (you). However, when talking to your superior, in refined Afrikaans you substitued *U* for *jy*. The major was upset because I had continually addressed the Terr as *U*!

I explained that I had learnt Afrikaans at school in Johannesburg, much as a student learns Latin. Not having Afrikaans associates or friends, I never had cause to use the language. Replying to a question in class one day, I answered our Afrikaans master with '*Jy, Meneer,*' my literal translation of 'You, Sir.' Approaching my desk from the back of the classroom, he smacked my right ear, knocking me completely out of my desk, and I ended up in a crumpled heap beside the wall. He then explained to me that I must NEVER use the word *jy* only *U*. I guess it was the one Afrikaans lesson I never forgot. To this day, everybody is still *U* to me!

The other incident occurred during Mr Matie Atasari's visit to South West Africa on behalf of the United Nations. He flew down to Opuwa in Kaokoland, an arid, scarcely populated area of western South West Africa, resembling in places the face of the moon. A number of journalists flew down as well in a light twin communications aircraft. This aircraft crashed during take-off for the return flight and a number of the passengers were slightly injured.

I was sitting in the operations room late in the afternoon, when the high frequency (HF) radio, renowned for its static interference, started to crackle. It was an army signaller from Opuwa wanting to report the accident to headquarters. HF, notoriously fickle during the changing ionospheric reflective layers at sunset and sunrise, was the only communications available at that time. The signaller spoke in Afrikaans and the HF interference reached its most disruptive peak. I attempted, quite successfully, to copy the contents of his message.

To my horror, I received one sentence that referred to the injuries sustained by one of the journalists. This poor man lived in Cape Town, and I thought it important to inform his family as soon as possible. The Afrikaans message relayed that this chap had been taken to the hospital in Opuwa and that his injuries included an *af been*. Translating it literally into English, I phoned the man's wife, expressed my sympathy at the circumstances of the crash, and said I was sorry to have to inform her that her husband's leg had been amputated. To me, *af* means off and *been* is leg. After suffering terrible hours of distress, I phoned her to apologize for my mistake. I discovered that in Afrikaans an *af been* means a broken leg, not one which is off!

Over the years, language has caused much mirth in our family. When we returned to South Africa, after the completion of my 12-year commission in the Royal Navy, I spent a lot of time explaining to my English-born wife about the peculiarities of living in a bilingual, multi-cultural country. By law, all notices were published in all official languages. One day, while house hunting in Durban, June pointed out that one agency seemed to have the complete monopoly of the housing market. Every "For Sale" notice had *Te Koop* written underneath and she assumed these were the agents. She did not realize that *Te Koop* means "For Sale" in Afrikaans. In a similar vein, she imagined that the chain of Curry Motors showrooms in Natal were Indian garages!

During the course of the war, I paid many visits to the little town of Opuwa. One of these happened to coincide with payday, when the soldiers of the ethnic battalion received their monthly reimbursement. In South West African terms, these men became wealthy when they joined the SWA Territorial Force and their status in the local community soared.

My driver stopped the vehicle and pointed out one of the soldiers going off on weekend leave, pushing a bicycle laden with crates of beer. My guide told me that each month this man converted every cent he earned into beer. I commiserated saying it was tragic how these rural people could become so addicted to alcohol and what a hardship it must be for the family and children. Laughing, my driver interrupted to explain that the soldier was the local entrepreneur. He gladly pushed his bicycle back to his local village where he proceeded to sell his beer at three times the price he paid for it!

Opuwa used to be known as Ohopoho, but whichever name is shown on charts of Kaokoland, the place is still difficult to find. When the United Nations Peace Force arrived to oversee the transition at the successful conclusion of the war, the Malaya contingent was based at Opuwa. On a pre-deployment tour by helicopter, the UN contingent commanders were shown their areas of responsibility. On landing at Opuwa, the Malayan commander just wrung his hands in grief and repeated, 'Oh! My poor people,' at everything he was shown. It was just that kind of place!

Chapter 19

1 Squadron, AFB Hoedspruit

The annual posting list arrived, and in December 1978 I was appointed to the new SAAF base at Hoedspruit close to the Kruger National Park in the Eastern Transvaal. My appointment was as base operations coordinator. I was 42 years of age, and I thought that my active flying career had finally ended.

Hoedspruit was being built as a hardened fighter base incorporating all the latest defensive techniques and technologies. Individual concrete-hardened shelters housed each aircraft. Readiness shelters were constructed at either end of the main runway to allow alert fighters to scramble in the minimum time. All the base buildings and facilities were placed amongst the thick bush, which abounded in the area. The buildings were widely dispersed to reduce the chances of damage during an enemy attack. My old mentor, Bossie Huyser, was running the entire project.

Bossie drove the civilian contractors like he drove 2 Squadron—full steam ahead; wide open throttles; maximum afterburner; 24 hours a day! It was a great base to be on if one's flying career had come to an end. The first squadron to arrive was 2 Squadron, equipped with Mirage III fighters. The drone of jet engines echoed in the bushveld.

Colonel Pierre Gouws, the base commander, was detached for six months to the Senior Joint Staff Course in Pretoria—I deputized for him during that period. Roads were still under construction, outside communications and telephone lines were non-existent, and we were very short staffed. The large scale construction affected the bushveld environment, which had been undisturbed for centuries. Virgin bush was cleared, scraped, and dug, disturbing the long-time residents. Jackals, antelope, and flocks of the lovely, speckled Guinea Fowl scurried to new pastures. Other species, obviously irritated by all the activity, slithered off to find new hiding places. These creatures became the focus of everyone's attention.

The bushveld is renowned for its snakes, and at Hoedspruit they were two a penny! Most of them were highly venomous mambas, cobras, boomslang snakes, and puff adders. All of the human residents of Hoedspruit adopted the fighter pilots' habit of continually scanning the surroundings—swivelling heads became the order of the day. While working in the garden one Saturday morning, an explosion shattered the peace. I looked up to see Captain John Orr, a 2 Squadron pilot, standing with a smoking shotgun in his hands. He had seen a boomslang snake in the overhanging eaves of his house and he knew that if it disappeared he would never be able to persuade his wife Rina to re-enter the house. He had no option but to blow it away along with four or five roof tiles.

Major Hennie Venter removed a baby python from a gutter pipe near the stop where children caught the bus to school. Oom Kerneels, a local farmer who played tennis at the base club, capped them all by bringing a 14-foot python in the back of his bakkie to my house to show my wife. Kerneels thought it would be nice for June, who was born in England, to get a close up of things African!

The worst, by far, were the mambas. Second Lieutenant Les Carlisle, a national serviceman security officer, rode over a two-metre black mamba on his 350cc Honda scrambler motorcycle while carrying out a security patrol. He watched as the obviously confused snake slithered away to seek refuge in a hole in a nearby tree. Les, realizing that the reptile could not see him, because its face was buried in the tree, seized the snake behind the head. He brought it back to the security camp, where he kept it in his clothes locker. The "kept" part was short, because as soon as we discovered what he had done, we told him clearly to get rid of his pet!

Despite their proliferation, I can only recall snakebites to two people. The first was the lady doctor who opened her garage door, disturbing the serpent lying along the bottom edge. The reptile took umbrage and sank its fangs into her foot. The other was Flight Sergeant Quintus Knobel who ran over a puff adder while driving back to base. Instead of leaving well alone, he stopped and picked the flattened body up by the tail. This bugger, with his last ounce of strength, struck out and grazed Quintus on his knee. Although only a graze, the venom was strong enough to lay Quintus low for a considerable period.

Late one Sunday evening, I heard a knock on my front door. I opened it to find a police constable from the police station down town. Apparently, Air Force Headquarters in Pretoria needed to contact me urgently and the police had the only telephone line in the area. Thanking the messenger, I told him I would drive down to his office as soon as I was suitably dressed. Pulling on shorts and shirt, and slipping my feet into a pair of rubber flip-flop sandals, I jumped into my car.

As I drove out, I noticed a large thick puff adder, slithering across the sand road straight for my back garden. I accelerated over the snake, spinning the wheels in the dust, before reversing and repeating the process. Unfortunately, the sand was soft and these manoeuvres had little effect on the supple body of the snake. Eventually, I succeeded in killing it as it tried to escape over the little sand wall left at the edge of the road by the grader. All this time I had been eyeballing the evil thing from a distance of less than a metre out of the driver's window. Finally satisfied that it no longer posed a threat, I continued down to the town with reptiles at the forefront of my mind. I parked outside the police station and ran down the concrete path to the charge office.

It was late at night and in the dark, I did not notice the garden hose lying stretched out across the path. Stepping on it with flip-flops, I felt the round, curved shape with my foot, and I felt the spongy effect of the rubber hose give slightly under my weight. I launched into a leap that would easily have broken the Olympic long jump record. I came back to earth in a heap at the door of the charge office. Hearing the noise, the constable opened it to find an undignified, jittering bundle of humanity. Hard as I tried, I did not succeed in regaining the dignity one would expect from the local representative of the air force!

As compensation for the snakes, Hoedspruit had many other charms. Before the officers' mess had been built, functions were held in one of the houses of the original game farm. This charming building had a traditional thatched roof and was referred to as the *grasdak*, (Afrikaans for grass roof). One evening, Oom Jan du Plessis met us in the entrance hall. Oom Jan was a local game farmer employed by the air force to manage the conservation programme at the base. Suddenly two little creatures came scuttling out of the kitchen between

June and me and vanished onto the patio. June, my English lady had only caught a quick glimpse of the animals; she asked Jan what type of dog they were. With a piercing whistle, Oom Jan called the creatures and the pair came hurrying back. They were introduced as Heidi and Pinocchio, two orphaned Warthog babies. Like puppies, they followed Oom Jan everywhere. Although they lost their charm when they were fully-grown, they remained on the farm and earned their keep as four-legged lawn mowers. Warthogs have a peculiar way of folding their front legs to kneel while grazing. They were very fond of the green shoots on the Kikuyu lawn.

Hoedspruit fitted the description of an outlying base to a T. It was outlying and miles from anywhere! The Mariepskop Primary School was 16 kilometres away, while the nearest high schools were over 70 kilometres away in Tzaneen and Phalaborwa. The nearest shopping centres were also that distance away. To help resolve the distance problem from the official air force point of view, the base acquired a high-winged Cessna C185 light communications aircraft. Naturally, I felt it was imperative that the base OPS CO be qualified to fly it, so I promptly carried out the conversion course. It was not quite what I was accustomed to, but it was a pleasant change from being chair-bound. Interestingly, of all the aircraft types I ever flew, this little Cessna was probably the most exciting to land.

The aircraft was a taildragger with a fixed undercarriage. The fixed undercarriage did not incorporate any shock absorber systems, but the sprung-steel legs gave sufficient flexibility to take up normal pressures on landing. However, there was, and still is, a trick to landing similarly configured aircraft. At the moment of touchdown, the stick or yoke must be right back in the pit of the stomach. If only partially backwards, particularly when landing on a hard runway, the weight of the aircraft will be absorbed by forcing the sprung-steel legs apart—so far so good! However, spring-steel, like elastic, incorporates the property of hysteresis and always tends to return to its natural state. The bowed legs of the C185 spring back to normal after absorbing the initial landing shock, which flings the light aircraft back into the air. The rest of the landing run resembles a damped fugoid (for Australians—kangaroo bounds) until the pilot pulls the stick all the way back.

One of the many tasks that fall on the shoulders of the operations coordinator (OPS CO) at any base is that of "Meeter and Greeter". It is customary, and polite, for visitors to a base to be formally welcomed, whatever time they decide to arrive. On the first Sunday of August 1980, I was at home preparing to sit down to lunch, when the duty air traffic control officer (ATCO) phoned to tell me that a light aircraft had just requested landing instructions. The aircraft was en-route from Pretoria and had already started its descent. Apologizing to my wife, I jumped into my car and sped off to the base. On entering the main gates, I called the ATCO on the car radio and asked him which dispersal the aircraft would taxi to. He told me the passenger was in a hurry and did not want to bother with the extremely long taxi tracks. He requested that I meet the aircraft as it cleared the main runway onto the high-speed turn off. As it was Sunday, with no other expected traffic, I agreed and arrived at the meeting place at the same time as the aircraft.

I was curious and surprised at the demands of the aircraft passenger, but when Colonel Bossie Huyser emerged from the cabin, the mystery was revealed. A fighter pilot to the core, he always operated in this manner! I imagine we did say hello to each other, although I can only recall that he immediately got down to the reasons for his visit. Normal greetings start with mundane small talk such as 'How are you? Hot for this time of year,' etc. But not Bossie! Standing on the runway, he opened with, 'Dick, how would you like 1 Squadron?' After considering the proposition for all of five seconds, I answered that I would like it very much. With that he clambered back into the aircraft, shouting over his shoulder as he closed the door, 'Good, you start tomorrow.' The aircraft engines burst into life and moments later Bossie was winging his way back to Pretoria.

Lunch was barely cold when I returned after the briefest of meetings, but it took the rest of the afternoon to explain to June how our life had changed in those few, wonderful moments on the runway. To be given, virtually out of the blue, the opportunity to command the premier squadron of the air force was beyond my wildest dreams. In retrospect, my time in 1 Squadron was the culmination of my flying career in fighters. I would happily repeat it, if that were possible!

We felt the alteration to our pattern of life immediately! The next morning I set off on the long drive to Pretoria to become a weekly commuter until the end of the year. The squadron was based at AFB Waterkloof but it was scheduled to re-deploy to AFB Hoedspruit over the Christmas period. Even today, if I close my eyes, I can picture every bend of the 492 kilometres through the Strydom Tunnel, over the Abel Erasmus Pass, through Ohrigstad, Lydenburg and Dullstroom, and finally onto the freeway to Pretoria.

The South African Air Force bought 48 Mirage F1s (16 F1CZ interceptors on the inventory of 3 Squadron, and 32 F1AZ ground attack aircraft for 1 Squadron). Both types had common airframes and engines; the differences were in the on-board avionics suites. The entire nose-section of the CZ housed the intercept radar. The AZ nose was home to a simple, on aircraft axis, radar-ranging system; immediately underneath the needle-shaped nose was an oblique window for the air-to-ground laser optical head; bombing computers and roller-map avionics crammed the remaining space. Among the pilots, the CZ was known as the PC (Piss-Cat), while the sophisticated AZ was proudly referred to as the F1 GT (*Gran Turissimo*).

I loved the aircraft from the very first take-off. She was responsive, easy, and delightful to fly. Unlike the Mirage III, one felt in complete command from brakes off. The cockpit was small and pilot friendly, with good all-round visibility and well-balanced flying controls. The roller-map made navigation easy provided the set-up procedures were correctly carried out. One of the better improvements over the Mirage III was in fuel specifics. Although one still had to keep an eye on the remaining fuel, it was nowhere near as critical as in the older aeroplane. The landing was "a piece of old *takkie*" compared to the high nose-angle, high-speed, poor-visibility approach in the old Mirage III. First impressions are lasting impressions, and today I think back with fond memories of the Mirage F1.

By mid-September the ground theory course, familiarization flights, and Mach 2 runs were complete and I was absorbed into the normal squadron programme. One day I flew down on my own to Mafeking (now Mafikeng after the latest transformation, but it is still the little town that was made famous during the Boer War siege and the heroism of Baden Powel). A parade was to be held there the next morning and 1 Squadron was tasked to perform the flypast. I went to seek out the landmarks, turning points and holding positions necessary to ensure a spot-on time and place flypast. Professionals never cuff it!

The following morning, after a thorough briefing to the rest of the four-ship formation, we manned our aircraft at the required time for a 09h30 take-off. Everything went perfectly until after start-up, when the ground crew signalled me to cut my engine because of a hydraulic leak. Notice how cunningly Murphy selected the only member of the formation that had been to Mafeking! I told Frans Pretorius to take-over as deputy leader; I shut down as fast as I could and ran for the spare aircraft. Frans and the other two took off and headed westwards. Time was critical and I rushed to get airborne. A professional would have taken the deputy leader with him the previous morning—I had not. Frans would now have to cuff it if I could not get there in time.

ATC gave me clearance to blast off immediately and after a Michael Schumacher drift onto the runway, I was into full afterburner and away on runway 01. Straight after take-off, I made a steep turn to port onto the heading for the Western Transvaal (now the North West Province). Unfortunately, the visibility was extremely poor as I came up for Hartebeespoort Dam at 500 plus knots. Suddenly, out of the gloom, at what seemed like the speed of light, appeared a Frelon helicopter. It was so quick I did not have time to take any avoiding action, but thanks to God, I passed directly underneath the chopper with one or two feet to spare. Only "Os" de Waal, the chopper pilot, and I know how close we were to disaster that gloomy morning.

After a gulp, a deep breath, and a quick 'Sorry!' over the radio, I concentrated on getting to Mafeking quickly and safely. I arrived as the three-ship was on the run-in to the saluting dais. Frans and the others opened up formation for me to drop in as leader and we passed over on time and in position!

Another difference between the F1 models was the ability of the AZ to carry out in-flight refuelling. The probe was superbly positioned just to the right and forward of the windscreen. When extended, it made things relatively simple for an experienced pilot to enter the tanker aircraft's trailing basket. My logbook records that I had a success rate of 7/9, and 5/6 plugs on my first two sorties, emphasizing how controllable the aircraft was even under slow speed handling conditions. With experience, the squadron plug-in success rate rose to well over 90%, even at night.

However, before that standard was achieved, there was a tendency for new pilots to over-control immediately before entering the basket, and we had our fair share of "panty rippers" in the squadron! A canvas spreader surrounds the edge of the open basket. Its aim is to stabilize the basket in flight. A desperate stab of the probe by a pilot who made a poor approach to the basket, sometimes resulted in the ripping of this canvas, known in the squadron as the "panty".

By 7 January 1981, the squadron had moved lock, stock and barrel, to AFB Hoedspruit. From a living point of view, I enjoyed the fact that my commuting days were over and I could spend more than just the weekend with my family. The settling in process for the squadron was a tremendous challenge. We were used to operating out of a maintenance hangar with our aircraft alongside each other in a line. We were now completely dispersed. An individual hardened shelter housed each aircraft. They were spread out over a distance of two kilometres. Vital maintenance equipment, previously shared between aircraft, now had to be specifically allotted to each revetment. The load on the maintenance personnel was also increased. Instead of one or two armourers being able to service a whole line of aircraft, sufficient personnel were needed to service each shelter group. Ground servicing equipment, which had previously been used on both F1CZ and AZ aircraft at AFB Waterkloof, had to be divided between the two squadrons. Additional purchases from France made up the deficits, and South African equivalents were manufactured.

All this occurred during a period of escalation in the border war. Between 1975 and the late 1980s, the South West Africa/Angola border war smoldered along as a low intensity terrorist incursion. SWAPO terrorist gangs, using Angolan soil as a base, carried out mine laying and ambush atrocities inside South West Africa, before scuttling back to the supposed safety of their host country. Helicopters and light fixed-wing aircraft contained this military activity. However, in the final two years of the 1970s, the conflict drew in fighter aircraft and bombers as the war escalated.

A great rivalry sprang up between 2 Squadron, the famous Flying Cheetahs, and 1 Squadron. Each squadron—quite correctly—thought they were the best and they went to great lengths to prove which one was superior. Commandant Mac van der Merwe, their officer commanding, was an excellent sportsman, so their sports results perhaps tended to overshadow ours.

The truth, as recorded here, was that 1 Squadron was always first at flying, while 2 Squadron, by virtue of their name, always remained second! Nevertheless, they did try manfully, especially Captain "Jeronkie" Venter, a good, keen fighter pilot. The two squadrons arranged "Battle of Britain" type contests over the lowveld. Under GCI (Ground Control Interception) radar control, we were brought into ideal firing positions, and we proceeded to simulate all sorts of missile "kills" against 2 Squadron. At the debriefing, Jeronkie, who had been shot to pieces, opened with his stock phrase: 'Now this is where you made your mistake!' Fighter pilots the world over never lose their training fights! It is for this reason that I suspect if Jeronkie or Mac were writing this 2 Squadron might have emerged the winner!

Grim statistics at the end of 1980 revealed that 1 447 terrorists had been killed at the cost of 100 South African/South West African soldiers—the heaviest yearly casualty figure of the border war. Despite their grievous losses, SWAPO again embarked on an incursion into South West Africa during the rains of 1981. In an effort to expand the war, they sent infiltration units into Kavango and Owamboland. This SWAPO move achieved the desired result, effectively doubling the length of border to be defended. By April 1981, 365 of these terrorists had been killed. The first week of July became the bloodiest of the year, when a further 93 SWAPO insurgents died.

The situation prevailing along the South West Africa/Angola border became intolerable. Escalation in the expanded area and in the intensity of the war was unacceptable. Defence force capabilities and resources were being stretched unnecessarily. SWAPO, using the protection and often the logistics capability offered by the Angolan Army, could approach close to the South West African border with impunity. From temporary bases, they carried out quick forays into South West Africa to lay mines, intimidate local population, abduct school children, and kill headmen, before slipping safely back into Angola.

With limited resources, in equipment and particularly manpower, it made little economic or military sense to attempt an impossible task. Imagine a 1.2-metre high, broken, four-strand wire fence, stretching from Brussels to Milan, in northern Italy. The combined NATO forces in Europe would have extreme difficulty in trying to stop determined people from crossing from one side to the other! In South West Africa, the dense bush compounded the problem; visibility was often reduced to less than 30 metres.

While politicians on both sides prevaricated, a military option to solve the problem was required. The answer was to prevent SWAPO from using the "shallow area" in Angola (up to 50 kilometres from the border), from which to launch their raids.

At a highly secretive briefing at Air Force Headquarters, I was informed, along with the other fast jet commanding officers, about Operation Protea. The aim was to destroy SWAPO's military forces and logistical supply lines in the central theatre of the Cunene Province of Angola, in order to safeguard our long borderline. Planned Air strikes would enable the army to take the key towns of Ongiva and Xangongo. Air attacks on the enemy's air defence radars at Chibemba and Cahama were also sanctioned. The operation was to take place in the dry season—late August into September—so mechanized vehicles could be used.

Security was extremely tight and we were told—almost under pain of death—that no one else in our units was to know. However, we had to ensure that all aircraft were serviceable and properly configured by mid-August. What a daft instruction! What naïveté! I had to return to Hoedspruit; cancel all leave for August and September; and ensure that all aircraft were fitted with drop tanks, rocket pods, multi-ejection racks (MERs) and twin-ejection bomb racks (TERs), 30mm cannon ammunition, and the pièce de résistance, live V3B air-to-air missiles! When asked why we were doing all this, I had to look at the ceiling, whistle a little, and tell white lies. Live missiles could only mean border duty!

While the ground forces made their approach to the key towns, the air force carried out independent strikes to destroy and disrupt the enemy air defence installations to gain air superiority over the battle area. Once that had been achieved then air strikes were to be used against selected targets in support of the ground forces.

The helicopter, light aircraft and transport units had shouldered the burden of the war for many years. Now, as conventional operations were envisaged, they were to be complemented by Mirage IIIs, Canberra and Buccaneer bombers, and the Mirage F1s of 1 and 3 Squadrons. Protea was the biggest SAAF operation since the Second World War. Another step up the escalation ladder!

On the morning of 21 August 1981, 12 F1AZs flew to AFB Grootfontein via a refuelling stop at Upington. Fuel and weather considerations dictated the route. Nevertheless, very heavy weather ensued and three of the aircraft suffered hail and turbulence damage. Radar warning receiver (RWR) radomes, navigation lights and missile heads were broken or cracked. After aircraft repairs and lunch, we flew on to the forward airfield at AFB Ondangwa.

We spent the rest of the afternoon and evening in briefing and preparing for a strike the following morning. The target was the radar installation at Chibemba, code-named Elephant. This revetment-protected site consisted of radar ramps housing Sidenet, Spoonrest and Flatface radars. The names were standard NATO code-names for the Russian height finding and early warning radars supplied to Angola.

The combined attack would begin with an AS-30 (air-to-surface guided missile) strike by low flying Buccaneers against the radars. The

Buccaneer pilots were to call if any SA-2, SA-3, or SA-6 missiles launched, and they were to call off the next strike if they encountered any of these missiles. The F1s would fly formation with Canberra bombers to saturate the Elephant site with bombs. The F1 pilots would release their bombs on command from the Canberra bomb-aimers.

At 10h30 the next morning, I led 12 fully loaded F1AZs off the short strip at Ondangwa. The rendezvous with the Canberras over Ruacana was successful and the "bomber-stream" then set heading for the target. At 20 000 feet (the release altitude), the heavily loaded F1 was difficult to handle at the Canberras slow flying speed. Each Canberra had two Mirages in close formation on each wing. Navigation turns, particularly for the Mirage pilots on the inside of the turn, were extremely demanding. Pilots used dive brakes, flaps and afterburner in quick succession, trying to find a reasonable solution to the situation!

The target came up and passed directly under the nose. The formation flew on until the call came and the bombs dropped. Looking backwards, the crew could see the bombs detonate in the bush, kilometres away from the target. The Canberra leader had opened his bomb-bay doors too late; hence, all the bombs were way over the target.

On landing, Bossie Huyser, now brigadier in charge of Western Air Command, was hopping mad! The secret to survival in aerial combat was never to carry out a second run on a target that had just been attacked. Bossie had the decency to ask me, as I stepped off the cockpit ladder, if I would mind going back to repeat the strike. I agreed, but on condition that I took only the Mirage F1s.

After the armourers had re-armed all the aircraft (a mammoth, backbreaking task), we re-flew the mission. This time the aircraft were easier to handle, because the correct Mirage speeds were flown. We repeated the route, except that it was flown at low level to minimize radar warning, with a pitch-up to enter an attack dive on the final leg. The flight ranks in my memory as one of the best that I ever flew in an AZ. The aircraft I was flying had just come out of the rigorous ESDAP testing programme. Everything worked perfectly!—navigation computer, roller-map, bombing computer and "Sir Ponsonby" (the automatic pilot).

The Mirage F1 autopilot was so sophisticated that the pilots refused to call it George, the traditional name for an autopilot. This clever piece of kit was a cut above the normal so it was christened "Sir Ponsonby" or "Sir Pons" for short.

A solid layer of medium-height cloud covered the target, stretching eastwards as far as the eye could see. Luckily, however, the edge of the cloud began directly over the radar installations. As we attacked out of the sun from the west, all the pilots had a perfect view of the target until after the bombs released. We pulled out up and through the solid cloud layer into the clear air above.

Pilots reported that 70% of the bombs exploded within the target area. Electronic warfare (EW) operators, who reported that at strike time, all enemy radars at Chibemba went off the air, confirmed these results. Brigadier Huyser was all smiles in the pub that night. Eight days later, an enemy Flatface radar finally came back onto the air, this time operating out of the Cahama area. An air strike subsequently eliminated it too.

During the following 18 months, I led 1 Squadron to Cahama so often, I felt that if we ever captured that town, I should be made mayor! To be truthful, I had really set my sights much higher and fancied myself for the post of governor of the entire Angolan Cunene province. Fortunately, history precluded the attainment of my political ambitions!

After heavy air and ground bombardment, both towns were taken and occupied. All the jets participated on close air support sorties to attack pockets of stubborn enemy resistance. It was during one of these missions that a heat-seeking, shoulder-launched, SA-7 Strela missile struck the tailpipe of Rynier Keet's (of the sign fame) Mirage III. Despite damage, he managed to land safely at AFB Ondangwa, where the battle scars were repaired.

On 28 August, we were tasked to attack a SWAPO logistics base in the bush, northeast of the little Angolan town of Mupa. The briefing was excellent. Each pilot received a photograph of the target. Ten AZ and four CZ aircraft were armed and ready to fly. Ground forces, under command of Commandant Deon Ferreira, were positioned just west of the target. They would attack immediately after the air strike, while the enemy was at their most vulnerable.

At 09h00, I led 14 Mirage F1s into the air. After impeccable low-level navigation, the formation rose as one to reach the perfect roll-in point. The photos easily identified the target. A quick radio call to Deon ensured that the ignition of white phosphorous grenades faultlessly marked the frontline of own troops (FLOT). Pilots dropped all their bombs spot onto the aiming points. The target was saturated. After release, while the aircraft returned to perfect battle formation, Deon called me on the radio to confirm a flawless strike. However, he added that during the entire attack, no enemy fire was seen. He later confirmed that his troops swept through the area without encountering any opposition. SWAPO had obviously received wind of the attack and had disappeared during the night! Deon and I were immediately elected as directors of the Citrus Board for carrying out a combined attack that turned out to be the "perfect lemon"!

At this stage of the war, the enemy had not introduced mobile surface-to-air missile (SAM) systems. The threat posed by Angolan SA-2 and SA-3 batteries was nullified. The positions of these static sites were known and avoided. If aircraft were tasked to strike targets close to these sites, low-level, high-speed profiles were used.

However, SWAPO cadres were equipped with SA-7 Strelas and these could appear anywhere in the operational theatre. Light aircraft, transport planes and helicopters reduced the threat by flying very low. The Strela operator usually had insufficient tracking time to achieve a successful launch out of thick bush.

The tactics we employed in the Mirage fleet involved flying above 15 000 feet at 450 knots, the maximum height and speed of the missile. During strike sorties, targets were attacked using a 30-degree dive, releasing the stick of bombs at 10 000 feet above the target. The aircraft bottomed out of the ensuing pullout at around 7 000 feet. Although this was within Strela range, theoretically the missile could not overtake the aircraft if the aircraft's speed was above 450 knots. It was a good tactic to keep our aircraft safe, but it did raise the pilots' blood pressure.

Heat-seeking missiles lock onto the hot jet pipe exhaust plume given out by the aircraft's engine. The missile then follows a curve of pursuit profile, chasing the aircraft. All pilots in a formation strain their eyes watching for the telltale trail of smoke that signifies a missile launch. Immediate radio calls alert the rest of the formation. Time is critical as missiles travel at very high speeds. During training, pilots learn to call immediately a missile is sighted: 'Missile, seven o'clock low, three miles.' At this warning, all pilots swivel their heads around to the seven o'clock position (12 o'clock indicates straight ahead and six o'clock, directly astern). The pilot looks below the horizon and focuses his eyes at a three-mile focal length.

On spotting the missile, the pilot turns into the smoke trail. The reason is twofold. First, the manoeuvre increases the missile's tracking problem. Second, and more importantly, it allows the pilot to ascertain whether the missile is locked onto his aircraft or not. If the missile is locked on, the pilot will notice the distinct kink in the missile's smoke trail as it follows the turn of the aircraft.

During pullout from an attack on Cahama, this type of call alerted me to the SA-7 locked onto my aircraft. As I turned, the missile turned, getting ever closer. At this stage, the flame from the rocket exhaust of the missile appeared as an incandescent tip to the curving, approaching missile. I pulled the nose up into a steep climb and at the same time selected full afterburner. Although this increased the exhaust plume from my engine, it helped keep the airspeed above 450 knots. During this hectic manoeuvring, my eyes remained glued on the missile. The missle followed the aircraft's every move.

Two thousand feet below me, the smoke trail and the light suddenly disappeared—the missile motor had reached all-burnt range. However, the speed and energy of the missile allowed it to continue its flight. This was the most frightening moment of the encounter, not knowing where the missile was. Within a few seconds, which felt like a few minutes, I saw the missile detonate below and behind me. The theory had worked!

Our experiences during Protea made me aware of how fatigued all personnel become during sustained operations. The burden was particularly heavy on aircrew. The US Air Force were clever when they ordered their Phantom F4 fighters. Unlike the US Navy, the air force fitted dual controls into their Phantoms. Pilots had to fill all these cockpits—providing the air force with a huge pool of pilots to call on during operations. The SAAF, like the US Navy, had a smaller inventory of pilots, hence the burden and fatigue that became part and parcel of operations.

Nervous tension is present on every cross border mission. I can well remember the sudden quickening of heart rate as the cutline flashed beneath the belly of the Mirage on my first operational sortie. It affects everybody. One SAAF classic occurred on 1 Squadron on an early mission. Just after entering Angolan airspace, one of the pilots started to whisper when he used the radio. Another Mirage pilot, working with 32 Battalion deep in Angola as the mobile air operations officer, whispered, 'It's a MiG!' while seated under camouflage netting at the mobile headquarters as jets screamed overhead. These are amusing stories to recount in the bar, but they do illustrate the level of stress people operate under.

This poem, written by Captain Neil McGibbon, Buccaneer pilot on 24 Squadron, illustrates people's mixed emotions under the stress of operational conditions.

Dawn Strike
Pale slice of morn
as we ride on the dawn
A herald of fire
out there in the east

Friends silhouetted
dark knights here on high
Helmeted heads, tall
and proud as they fly

Canopies glisten
on black pregnant birds
Visors glint as heads twist
quartering the sky

This moment transcends
our fear of what's hence
For one brief instant
we are gods in suspense

A terrible beauty before
the casting of sense.

In between operational deployments to the border, training remained our prime responsibility. Early in 1982, we flew to Bloemfontein for two weeks Forward Air Controlling (FAC) work with the army on the nearby weapons range. Army officers learnt how to "talk" pilots in to attack targets in close proximity to the land battle. Training changes the mind-set of the soldiers from the slow grind of an infantry assault, to fighters moving at close to 14 kilometres per minute.

The army officer positions himself on a suitable vantage point overlooking the battlefield, hence the traditional value of "the high ground". When he has selected suitable targets that require immediate attention, he requests air support. Fighter-bombers, armed with the correct weapons, fly to predetermined holding points within close proximity of the battle area. While the aircraft orbits the holding point, the FAC describes the target and its defences to the pilot. The FAC then passes a carefully worked out heading and time for the pilot to fly, from his holding position. Immediately after the pilot pitches up, the FAC describes the target and surrounding area. The FAC tries to orientate the pilot to acquire the target visually so he can carry out the desired attack.

This training is vital for success in the heat of battle. However, on the training range these flights often result in extreme pilot frustration. Trainee FAC officers often suffer from "first night nerves" the first time they find themselves in charge of jet fighters. Instead of the fast, accurate commentary that the pilot requires to find his target, the trainee frequently comes up with statements like: 'As you pitch-up look for the tree in the big green field.' Little does he realize that from 5 000 feet the pilot can see a million trees in hundreds of green fields! A good FAC can make the difference between life and death on a battlefield, hence the necessity for training.

Every year we deployed to Durban for a supersonic ACM training camp. Mobile GCI radar sites were sent along the Natal coast and their fighter controllers were responsible for controlling our aircraft as we operated way out over the Indian Ocean. Passed 30 nautical miles from the coast, the land-based restrictions of supersonic flight only above 30 000 feet disappeared and the aircraft could fly to their performance envelope limits. These deployments were a direct result of my first flight in a Phantom, before I fully understood the aerodynamics of thin, supersonic wings.

On one occasion, Captain Hennie Louw could only fly to Durban from Hoedspruit the day after the rest of us. The Durban folk greeted our arrival with interest and local press photographers always wanted to take interesting pictures for their newspapers. Knowing from experience that the novelty of noisy jets usually wore off quite rapidly, I decided to add a bit of sensationalism to the news stories. I told Hennie that when I arrived in Durban, I would tell the news-hounds to gather there again the next day to greet his arrival. I tasked Hennie to take-off from Hoedspruit, climb to over the required 30 000 feet, accelerate to supersonic speed and pass directly over the Hoedspruit Air Traffic Tower, starting his cockpit clock. He was to stop the clock as he passed overhead Durban. He would set a record for the flight, which I thought would make a good story. It happened exactly as briefed; Hennie's record was 28.5 minutes and there was excellent coverage in the press.

Two weeks later, at the end of the deployment, I had to return one day earlier and as the old saying goes, 'When the cat's away the mice will play!' The remaining 11 pilots decided to return individually to Hoedspruit to try to set the record for the Durban/Hoedspruit leg.

In my office the next morning, I enjoyed the unusual solitude while catching up on paperwork before the aircraft returned. The strident ringing of the telephone suddenly shattered the tranquility of the moment. A lady resident of Pinetown, a northern suburb of Durban, complained about a series of "explosions", which had just rocked her house. Telling her that I would investigate, I replaced the receiver, which immediately rang again. This time it was the commander of the South African Police station in Cato Manor, 20 miles north of Durban, with the same complaint. The morning went on with calls coming quick and fast from Greytown, Vryheid, Paulpietersburg, Piet Retief, Barberton, Nelspruit, White River and Hazyview—following my pilots' route exactly as they skimmed around Swaziland in their quest to be fastest back to Hoedspruit. By the time the last aircraft landed, I was hoarse from all the talking.

As it turned out, all the pilots had flown supersonic legally above 30 000 feet. When an aircraft exceeds the speed of sound, a cone shaped shockwave forms with the aircraft at its apex. For the entire period that the jet remains above the speed of sound this cone is dragged behind it. Wherever the cone edge contacts the ground, people will hear and feel the passage of the shockwave as a distinctive double bang. Eleven shockwaves moved over the residents of eastern South Africa between Durban and Hoedspruit and, understandably perhaps, they were a trifle agitated. I cannot remember what the record time was for the trip, but I know that during the rest of my period in charge there were no further attempts to break it!

An interesting and unusual event occurred, which helped lift the burden of recriminations off the shoulders of the squadron. A minute or two after taking off on an ACM training flight, Frans Pretorius and record-setter Hennie Louw, spotted a fast moving jet streaking round towards their stern. Turning to investigate, they recognized the unmistakable shape of a MiG17. In quick time, they manoeuvred into a firing position, while initiating radio calls to alert the air traffic authorities and all other aircraft. It turned out to be Lieutenant Bomba of the Moçambique Air Force. This young man, tired and frustrated by the restrictions of living under a Communist regime, had risked his life on both sides of the border, trying to defect to South Africa. The two Mirage F1AZs escorted him to a safe landing at AFB Hoedspruit. After the South African test pilots had flown it, the elderly Russian-built fighter was eventually returned by road to the Moçambique authorities.

Our Frenchman, Hubbs Füss, produced a wonderful crop of enthusiastic, professional reconnaissance pilots for this demanding task. Of all the aspects of combat flying, reconnaissance work probably requires the most concentration. Photographs brought back attest to the accuracy of their flying. The majority of targets photographed are dangerous, defended by anti-aircraft artillery (AAA) and SAM batteries. Because the photo-reconnaissance (PR) aircraft were unarmed, escort fighters were provided. Usually these were interceptor Mirage F1CZ aircraft, but occasionally we were tasked to provide escort in F1AZs. To keep up with the PR aircraft, we dropped all external pylons and flew with 30mm cannon and two V3B air-to-air (AAM) missiles.

During a training flight, Leon Burger, flying a Mirage III RZ, selected Hoedspruit airfield as a target for a low-level, high-speed photographic run using the sideways looking oblique camera. From low level at 600 knots, he pulled up and rolled inverted to level off at 400 feet above ground level (agl) for the pass at the correct distance from the side of the airfield. At the end of the run, he inverted his aircraft, lowered the nose, and then rolled out almost immediately at low level for the escape from the target area. This profile exposed his aircraft to enemy fire for the minimum amount of time. At these very high speeds, accuracy and judgement had to be perfect to safely achieve the necessary results, hence the need for constant practice.

On one of these runs, Leon's timing was out by a few seconds. At 600 knots, a few seconds equates to a considerable distance covered over the ground. At the end of the filming run, Leon inverted his speeding Mirage, lowered the nose, and then rolled out at extremely low level. On completion of the roll, he looked up and saw high-tension wires of the national electrical grid stretching out on either side of his front windscreen. Raising his nose slightly, he had no option but to fly through them.

With a series of lightning like flashes and bumps, the cables touched the aircraft skin. He flashed up into the clear blue sky to discover that he was alive and his aircraft was still flying, albeit not as smoothly as normal. A quick radio call to the tower obtained him clearance to land, which he did. At first glance, his aircraft appeared fine apart from structural damage around the engine intake. However, on closer inspection it was discovered that most of the removable aircraft panels had been spot-welded together by the electrical discharge as he flew through the cables. Hoedspruit and surrounding areas of the Eastern Transvaal and Kruger National Park were effectively blacked-out while the cables were repaired.

Captain Otto Schür, also flying a Mirage III R2Z, was tasked to take post-strike damage assessment photography of a target near the Angolan town of Omapande. At 600 knots and 190 feet agl, Otto began his filming run. Seconds later he was struck by AAA that caused a total electrical failure. Clearing the target, he zoomed to gain altitude as he turned back towards base. Passing 8 000 feet at 500 knots, the Mirage flicked into a high-G, right-hand descending spiral, from which he could not recover. He ejected, evaded capture and was recovered to AFB Ondangwa by Puma helicopter, in a daring rescue. The pilot, Major Polla Kruger, gained a bullet wound in the neck, 22 holes in his helicopter, and an award of the Honoris Crux.

My time in charge of 1 Squadron and my career as a "pole-handler" ended in December 1982. I admit with pride to shedding a tear as the band played *Auld Lang Syne* at the change of command ceremony. Hoedspruit saved one final trick for my finale. I saluted as the guard of honour marched past and watched as they turned to disappear between the high revetment walls. A military parade is always a moving spectacle and all sorts of emotions rise to just under the skin. This one, however, was different. As the immaculate column entered the gap, a large snake, which had obviously been sunning itself on the edge of the revetment, must have awoken with a start at the loud banging of the base drum and it had fallen into the gap. To the consternation of the marchers, the reptile, now very much awake, slithered off at high speed between the feet of the marchers. Without waiting to be dismissed, the immaculate column dispersed at high speed, in all directions.

Chapter 20

310 AFCP, Oshakati, SWA

In January 1983, I was promoted to colonel and appointed back to Oshakati, this time on a permanent basis. I could take my family with me. On arrival, I had a distinct feeling of *déjà vu*. I had occupied this post for three months nearly five years earlier. The major difference was in the increased intensity of the war.

Back in 1978, I had been on my first bush tour. The war had been simmering since 1975, in a low-key way, after the South African forces had withdrawn from Angola at the completion of Operation Savannah. Air force involvement up to that time consisted of helicopters, light reconnaissance and transport aircraft, flown in support of army and police ground forces. The escalation that led to the inclusion of jet aircraft in the ORBAT (Order of Battle) had not yet taken place.

Having been a dedicated *vlammie*, (jet pilot), I was thus the new boy on the block when I reported for duty as commander of the air force Command Post at Oshakati in Owamboland. Over the previous 20 years, I had been involved in the intense, competitive, and exacting world of fighter flying. It was thus an interesting and novel introduction to the world of the bush war.

My duty was to allocate, control, task, and plan all air force involvement in the war. Naturally this was a very busy but also an interesting appointment. It took only a few days to familiarize myself with the scenario, assisted by Commandant Theo de Munninck, the officer I was to replace. His hand-over was expeditiously carried out, because he could only leave when I was competent to take over.

I accompanied him to AFB Ondangwa to see him safely on board the C130 "Flossie" on his first step back to his home in the Cape. Driving back the three kilometres to Oshakati, I realized that I was now "solo"—the buck stopped at my door!

As I entered the office, my operations officer, Captain "Lappies" Labuschagne presented me with my first problem. In the services, all Labuschagnes were known as "Lappies", therefore each was given a prefix so that people understood which Labuschagne was being referred to, such as "Black" or "Lang". In this case, he was "24 Lappies", from 24 Squadron Buccaneers.

An army patrol urgently required a helicopter to airlift a section member to hospital. Casevacs (Casualty Evacuations) were always at the top of the priority list, so of course we immediately tasked a Puma helicopter to rush to the scene. In a war situation, Casevacs are daily occurrences. I always felt it was important to get feedback on the condition of the patients, so that I could inform the aircrew who had carried out the task.

At the order group the next morning, I asked the doctor about the condition of this particular man. He told us that just about everything that could be broken in a human body had been broken. The good news was that, being young and fit, the patient would recover fully after a lengthy period of rehabilitation. The doctor then explained exactly how the injuries had been inflicted.

The boy, for that was what he really was, was only 19 years old. He had started his national service straight from school and, like me, this was his first bush tour. Being in the PBI (Poor Bloody Infantry), his introduction to the war was as a member of a ten man section, assigned the laborious task of patrolling a designated area of the border. He was a city boy, raised in the bright lights of Johannesburg. The novelty of being in the bush, like the anxiety associated with a first live patrol, soon palled as they trudged kilometre after kilometre through the sand and heat, to be replaced by the fatigue only foot soldiers really understand.

Silence is a prerequisite for a patrol. No metallic clinking or other noises are permitted. The enemy must not be forewarned—surprise is a principle of war. Towards noon, the sun's heat was nearing its maximum, exacting its toll on the soldiers' stamina. Walking quietly, in a tactical spread formation, they entered an area of thick bush in search of a place under the shade of the trees, where they could take a much-needed rest.

"Sol" or "Spike", as the sun was referred to by the troops, also sapped the energy of wild animals and they too sought refuge from the burning rays. A lone elephant found an ideal spot in the shade of a kameeldoring tree and went to sleep. Unlike humans, elephants sleep standing upright; only the slightest to and fro sway of their enormous bodies indicates their state of repose.

Approaching soundlessly, the soldiers discovered that the elephant already had first choice of the available shade. Not wanting to awaken the slumbering behemoth, the patrol leader made signs to his men to withdraw, which they duly did. Once out of audible range, the soldiers discussed their discovery. They knew that no enemy would be in the vicinity and so they could relax for a while. During their break, our "Casevac" produced an automatic camera from his rucksack. Cameras were forbidden in the operational area for security reasons, but our city boy wanted to record all his experiences for posterity.

He decided he needed a photograph of the pachyderm, but he wanted desperately to be included in the picture. Mom, or the girlfriend, was bound to be impressed! He asked one of his buddies to hold the camera and take the picture, but only when he mouthed the word *Now*.

Approaching from the rear, he crept towards the creature, making sure that he remained downwind. The midday heat is intense in those latitudes and Jumbo was sound asleep, allowing our boy to creep right up behind him. Excitement amongst the rest of the soldiers was reaching fever pitch, as our boy got closer. He reached a position that was in the eyes of the rest of the section much too close for comfort or safety, but they could not shout to tell our boy, lest they awakened the monster.

The excitement and success of his stalk aroused the daring spirit of our boy. To the rest of his section's dismay and horror, he lifted the elephant's tail whilst turning round to pose and silently articulating the word, *Now*. I agree it would probably have made a wonderful snap shot, but I was not there. The elephant, however, disagreed with the whole silly idea. He awoke immediately his tail was lifted. Presumably, this rare occurrence has that effect on wild animals!

The elation of the moment was spoilt by the elephant's spiteful reaction; the elephant proceeded to extract revenge on the would-be model. The rest of the soldiers, firing into the air, chased the animal back into the bush, but not before the beast had broken "just about everything that could be broken".

It is with relief that I can report that not only was my first "Casevac" successful, but the doctor's prognosis of a full recovery, also turned out to be correct.

From a staff of four in 1978, the complement of the Command Post now grew to 45. A new operations complex was built where the air force was co-located with the army—the only way to successfully run joint operations! The air force developed a new command and control structure, based on the Israeli Air Force structure. Dedicated communication lines ensured immediate access and response to bases, units, and aircraft under control. Air force operations ran in real-time for the first time ever, as electronics replaced the delays associated with telephone exchanges, teleprinters, and HF radio. The Command Post at Oshakati was used as the guinea pig to test the theory and installation, before the entire air force was converted to this method of command and control.

An added bonus was that the new complex was fully air-conditioned. This luxury was for the benefit of all the electronic equipment. Unfortunately, in our houses and accommodation blocks, personnel still endured the extremes of the harsh climate. Temperatures above 40° C were common for weeks on end during the summer. The glaring white sand exacerbated these trying conditions, making sun hats and dark glasses essential items of protection.

For over 300 hundred kilometres in every direction, the countryside was as flat as a pancake. Owambo school children learnt about hills from textbooks, never having seen a real one. Our children attended the local school that catered for government employees. Children from outlying areas were conveyed to and from school every day in convoys of mine-protected armoured vehicles, but only after the roads had been swept for terrorist-planted mines. At critical times, we even supplied air cover to these convoys to prevent the possibility of ambush attacks. Outside the school classrooms, bomb shelters were built and part of the school routine included periodic "attack drills". Between Oshakati and Tsumeb, the nearest town where a wife could shop, stretched the only tarred road in the entire province of Owamboland. This 250-kilometre road was completely straight except for one 20° kink halfway, where the builders avoided a corner of the Etosha Nature Reserve.

Civilian traffic was always at considerable risk on any of the side roads. Many of the worst incidents occurred on these sand roads as Owambo locals moved between their homes. These unfortunate people, like civilians in most wars, all to often become the victims of the so-called "liberation fighters".

Earlier peacetime residents of Oshakati scraped a nine-hole golf course out of the sand. There was not one blade of grass on the course. Tee boxes and fairways consisted of sand so there was no need for bunkers. The "greens" were also built, naturally, with sand, the only commodity in plentiful supply. This sand was mixed with oil to give substance to the "green", or more correctly the "slightly black!" After pitching the ball onto the "green", usually with a sand-wedge, the most useful club in one's bag, the putting ritual began.

You lifted your ball from the plug mark, dragged a flat iron between it and the hole, and then putted on the smoothed surface.

I played a few times on this course because there were not many other forms of entertainment in the vicinity. Some wag, using a technique copied from the major circuits around the world, produced name boards for each hole. It was one of these boards that drastically reduced the active membership of the club. The hole at the far end of the course, where the players were furthest from the town's defensive perimeter, was named POMZ CORNER after one of these devices was found there. The Soviet POMZ-2 was the notorious, anti-personnel widow-maker! Having taken so many chances during a long and exciting flying career, I felt that this was just one risk too many, so I temporarily hung up my clubs!

All the operations I had flown in during the previous three years seemed to have had little effect on the SWAPO insurgents. Every year they came over the border in droves, intent on sowing mayhem and death. Our job was to track, attack, and disrupt their efforts until normality could be restored to the troubled area. In the Command Post, we were busy running all the daily operations necessary to counter these activities. Army and police patrols needed aerial support. Light aircraft on our side of the border, and Impala jets flying into Angola, constantly carried out photo and armed reconnaissance patrols. Transport aircraft re-supplied the forward bases, and Puma helicopters were on continuous alert for casualty evacuation (Casevac) duty.

Alouette gunship crews and sticks of parabats were also on immediate call for fireforce operations. Whenever an army or police ground patrol found spoor left by SWAPO insurgents, they notified us by radio. We passed the information to the helicopter crews and brought them to a higher state of readiness. Often we moved the entire team forward to an advanced base to reduce reaction time once contact was made. The fireforce then entered the fray. Parabats dropped as stopper groups and the gunship Alouettes, armed with sideways firing 20mm cannon, controlled the fight from the air.

Whenever Intelligence identified or pinpointed a SWAPO base inside Angola, we planned suitable autonomous air strikes or combined ground/air assaults. We often requested that additional Canberra, Buccaneer, or Mirage aircraft deploy from South Africa. These planning sessions could become very involved. Strikes over the border, beyond the "shallow area" had to have cabinet approval. The politicians were not averse to changing their minds and decisions at the drop of a hat, often causing delays and even cancellations of proposed strikes.

The advent of night-sight equipment extended our working hours to a non-stop 24-hour a day routine. In earlier years, the terrorist enjoyed complete freedom at night, but his "happy days" were now at an end. Suitably equipped gunship helicopters flew Lunar operations, light reconnaissance aircraft scouted for targets, and Dakotas orbited, ready to drop parabats into night engagements. Impala light strike fighter-bombers flew Moonshine and Darkmoon patrols inside Angola, and they dominated the routes the enemy utilized to re-supply their ground forces near the front. Any vehicle displaying headlights was attacked and destroyed.

The majority of air force operations were carried out in radio silence. We knew that, like ourselves, the enemy monitored VHF and HF radio frequencies. Only during emergencies were pilots cleared to use open text messages over the radio in an effort to expedite rescue operations. One night, however, I broke my own rules—temptation got the better of me. We briefed a Kudu pilot to carry out a night mission and his route brought him very close to Oshakati. As I entered the Command Post, I heard the distinctive drone of the Kudu as he approached the overhead. Picking up the microphone, I made a transmission that would follow me for the rest of my career. Captain Mark Moses was flying the Kudu and I could not waste the moment. 'Moses,' I said, 'This is the voice of the Lord!'

Oshakati had developed into a garrison town. At the main centre of rural Owamboland, a small civilian community were responsible for the administration and economy of the vast territory. The officials of ENOK (the Afrikaans abbreviation for the First National Development Corporation), schoolteachers, "Cashbox" van der Merwe who ran the bank, engineers from the Department of Water Affairs and the Post

Office made up the bulk of the non-military personnel in the little town. Later, this population dwindled further when a number of postal workers departed after the Post Office blew up!

The population had grown since the first armed clash with SWAPO insurgents in 1966. The police, and later the army, deployed counter-insurgency personnel. By 1983, the air force, medical services, engineers, signallers, and workshop artificers, had joined the swelling ranks of South African and South West African Territory Force soldiers and police officers, transforming the settlement into a military garrison.

In an operational area, where ambushes, anti-personnel and landmine detonations, and stand-off bombardments were everyday occurrences, daily activities for the population took place within the confines of the town's defended perimeter. This curtailment of social, sporting, and leisure opportunities led to a conservative lifestyle.

Without museums, theatres, cinemas, or discos, life was pretty much a humdrum affair—except for Tosca! Tosca was the star attraction and focus of conversation in that war-torn town. No visit to Oshakati was complete without a drive past Tosca's house. Tosca was a full grown, magnificent male lion—and, yes, he did live in a house in the main street of Oshakati!

A patrol on operations came across an abandoned lion cub in the bush. Separated from its mother and suffering injuries to its hindquarters, the animal was in a desperate state. Realizing that the minute bundle of fur could not survive on its own, the men brought it back to Oshakati, where they christened him Tosca. All kittens are adorable and none more so than a lion cub. Captivated by the little lion, his master approached the Department of Nature Conservation and explained the predicament. He asked if he could keep the lion instead of having it put down. The injuries were such that it could not be released back into the wild.

Nature Conservation agreed to his keeping and rearing the animal provided he followed the proper rules of conduct and safekeeping. Abiding by all the regulations and guidelines, he raised Tosca to manhood in Oshakati. The entire backyard was enclosed, but the lion also had the run of the house. He grew up with humans and probably thought he was also a human. Apart from a slight limp, he matured into a magnificent specimen.

As air force commander, we moved into a house that backed directly onto that of the army commander, Brigadier Joop Joubert. Tosca lived two back gardens away on the left. Coming directly from Air Force Base Hoedspruit, close to the Kruger National Park, we thought we were accustomed to the presence of wild animals. Accustomed or not, when Tosca roared at night 60 metres from your open window, you awoke with your hair erect and a palpitating heart.

Tosca loved company and enjoyed his many visitors. Friends of the family allowed their children in to the yard to play with, and pet, the beast. He was huge, with enormous paws and a long, thick, dark mane. I often stroked him and permitted my two boys to do the same, but always through the bars of his enclosure. Tosca was not only the king of the beasts, but also of Oshakati, and I felt he deserved the right to roam his kingdom on his own.

The intensification of the war in the early 1980s necessitated the need for additional personnel to handle the increased load. The air force solved this problem by seconding personnel from their home units and sending them to the operational area on bush tours. These tours were usually three months in length resulting in an ever-changing work force.

Each new member was fully briefed and trained to ensure the maintenance of standards. Each briefing contained at least a passing reference to Tosca, as was the case when Flight Sergeant Nicky Havenga arrived from the Cape to commence his tour at 310 Air Force Command Post in Oshakati.

Nicky was a specialist cryptographer, and as the majority of the signal traffic was classified, his services were in great demand. He arrived in Oshakati late one Friday afternoon, with just sufficient time for the briefing before suppertime. He was accommodated with all the other air force personnel in the bungalows alongside the Oshakati runway. To get to work in the Command Post, he had to walk one kilometre up the main street past Brigadier Joubert's residence. His house was two doors away from Tosca's kingdom.

At 22h00 on Nicky's first evening, a Top Secret signal arrived and he was sent for to decode it. He walked rapidly up the road to the office wondering where this lion lived that he had heard about. He arrived at work and decoded an extremely long signal. He started his walk back to the airfield around midnight.

To avoid being a target for a SWAPO stand-off bombardment, no lights illuminated the town. The roads were not tarred and the surface consisted of thick sand, making movement very silent. So there he was in the pitch-dark silence, walking back down the main road. Once again, Tosca was on his mind and he knew he must be close to where the lion lived.

Brigadier Joubert lavished tender loving care on his large collie dog, Oubaas. This beautiful animal had a coat like Lassie with the long mane around his neck that is so typical of that breed. Oubaas slept outside, serving as a faithful watchdog. He was a lovely big friendly animal, whose greatest desire was to be made a fuss of. The hundreds of troopies he met petted him daily. However, Oubaas did have one bad habit!

He liked to greet people by running out and bounding up at passing pedestrians. Nicky was pacing silently down the street in the pitch black thinking about lions. Oubaas, never one to miss an opportunity, raced out of the brigadier's garden, silent as a shadow on the powdery sand, and sprang into the air and onto Nicky. Moments before the dog landed, Nicky glimpsed the long flowing mane around the collie's neck and thought it was Tosca.

He ran the remaining kilometre back to his bungalow, even after discovering that his lion was nothing more than a big friendly dog!

Brigadier Joubert applied an army solution to all crises. Such a crisis faced the garrison when the barber's tour of duty ended and he returned to South Africa. Without batting an eyelid, the brigadier appointed a young, 18-year-old national serviceman to the position. I learnt about this posting from Major Daantjie Beneke, my helicopter warfare specialist in the Command Post.

He sent his young son to have his hair cut the previous day, which happened to coincide with the national serviceman's first "solo". Aghast at the result, Daantjie asked his son to explain what had happened. Haupt answered, 'I don't really know, Daddy, except that every time the barber brought the electric clippers close to my head, I heard him say, "Shit!"'

Personality clashes occur in all walks of life, including the military. One of our forward bases in Owamboland was a place called Eenhana. It was an army base, but it also housed elements of the police and a detachment of air force personnel. An interservice problem arose on the base that required the army and police commanders from Oshakati and me to fly out to the base. On our return, in an Alouette helicopter, we overflew a Koevoet police unit, busy with a spoor follow-up. Our pilot brought the chopper down so we could talk to the policemen on the trail.

A group of between 20 and 30 SWAPO terrorists had just passed through a local kraal; their tracks disappeared amongst those of the locals. A short delay occurred while the trackers circled the kraal to pick up the trail again. Never having seen a spoor, I asked the policeman in charge to show me a terrorist track. Calling one of his Owambo trackers, he took me to a spot in the long grass, where the tracker pointed at the ground. From a standing position, none of us could see any disturbance at all. Eventually, the two brigadiers and I were on our knees in the dust, and the tracker, using a stem of dried grass, outlined a perfect barefoot print, which he could see from an erect position and while running!

With a flash of brilliance, I remarked to the tracker, through an interpreter, that the print he showed us could just as easily have been from one of the locals. He looked at me as if I had just crawled out of the cheese. The tracker placed his hand, palm down, on the ground. With the fingers widely splayed, he explained that local feet, unused to being restricted inside a boot, resembled the spread hand. Feet recently removed from boots, had the toes close together. Terrorists use the trick of removing their boots when crossing trodden ground. The ploy might delay a good tracker, but very seldom did he lose the spoor completely.

Early one afternoon, the orderly calm of the Command Post was disturbed by the entry of Captain Sakkie van Zyl of the South African Police. He explained that during a necessary culling programme an elephant had escaped from the Etosha Nature Reserve and was rampaging northwards through a densely populated area of Owamboland. It was a rogue elephant, destroying kraals and crops, and it was now endangering human life. It had to be shot.

A week earlier, I took my son to the firing range at Air Force Base Ondangwa, to teach him to shoot. Also at the range was Major Bernie Sharp, my operations officer, who was shooting-in the telescopic sight of his Winchester 300 Magnum. The name Magnum suitably impressed me. Clint Eastwood, playing Dirty Harry, always carried a Magnum, which was supposed to be the biggest handgun available. The second impressive fact was that the muzzle velocity of this rifle was 3 100fps, only 100fps less than the 30mm Defa cannon I had fired from the Mirage fighter.

This elephant had to be shot, and I immediately thought of Major Sharp and his Magnum. I asked him if he would like to go on an elephant shoot and he jumped at the chance. I asked Capt Van Zyl if he owned a big rifle. He said he did, so he was elected as the hunter for the expedition. I arranged for an Alouette helicopter to pick us up at

Oshakati and I went along as operations coordinator to record the event on camera. The Alouette crew consisted of the pilot and flight engineer/gunner; a four-barrelled light .303 Browning machine gun armed the aircraft. I donned a headset and sat in front to direct operations; the two hunters sat in the back with their rifles.

We found the area and the rogue elephant. From the air, we could see that both his tusks were broken off from where they protrude from the skin. Two police Casspir vehicles stopped near a school and hundreds of local Owambo surrounded them. The elephant was striding backwards and forwards in the thick bush about 300 metres away. After making a quick tactical appreciation, we dropped Major Sharp in a clearing approximately 200 metres from the elephant, and then we hovered the chopper directly above the animal while Bernie made his approach.

The close-up view of the elephant flapping his ears and striking out with his trunk at the helicopter was a sight to set the adrenaline pumping. We watched as Bernie stalked to within 70 metres of the agitated animal before he took careful aim. We saw his shoulder recoil from the shock as he fired. The elephant collapsed backwards onto his haunches and my immediate thought was one of relief. One shot, one elephant!

To our consternation, the elephant stood up and glared around. If he was agitated before, he was now downright furious. I shouted to the pilot over the intercom to keep the chopper in front of the elephant to distract it, while Bernie fired again, this time without any apparent effect on the animal.

Our appointment with fear now began in earnest. Bernie realized that his bullets were having little or no effect. He decided to move in closer. From the chopper we watched aghast as he crept within 40 metres of the huge creature. From our seat in the grandstand we could see that he was much too close, but there was no way we could communicate that fact to him. As if in super-slow motion, we saw him raise his rifle, aim, and fire again. The elephant did not bat an eyelid. Instead, he turned his massive, angry head and glared straight at Bernie. He knew that this was the perpetrator of all his annoyance. He flapped his ears and charged directly towards the major.

Give Bernie his due though. He stood, leaned into the shot, aimed, and fired deliberately at the charging elephant. To our horror, the elephant did not falter and continued straight for the stationary figure. Deciding at last that discretion was the better part of valour,

Bernie turned tail and ran. The monster was now only 10 metres behind him, trunk outstretched, trying to seize the man.

Bernie is a tall man with long limbs, and the picture I carry in my memory was of the frantic whirling of his arms and legs as he literally ran for his life. When the elephant started his charge, I dropped the camera as all thoughts of photography vanished. The pilot started an anguished wail over the intercom and all I could hear was a loud, continuous AAAHHHHH!

In a straight gallop, Bernie was no match for the elephant and it was gaining at every stride. At this crucial stage, fate intervened in the form of a large, tall Owamboland ant-heap. Bernie took a sharp left around this two metre tall obstacle. The elephant followed but due to its enormous inertia, his turning circle was larger than Bernie's was. Dust clouds started to rise as the left-handed scramble around the ant-heap built up momentum.

I persuaded the pilot to manoeuvre his machine to a position directly above the animal, and I gave Sakkie the order to fire from his side of the chopper. At the speed that things were happening, we only managed to hover over the huge head for a fraction of a second. In all the excitement, Sakkie forgot to cock his rifle and the opportunity was lost.

The pilot moved away from overhead and we managed to get an oblique view of the closing stages of the race. I ordered the flight engineer to open fire with his machine gun. He had anticipated this and immediately let fly with a prolonged burst. The elephant collapsed in a cloud of dust but it still took me a while to get the adrenaline-charged gunner to cease firing.

With the elephant immobilized, we landed the chopper and as the engine shutdown, I heard a single shot ring out as Bernie finally put the poor animal out of its misery. Within minutes a seething mass of locals surrounded the huge carcass all exclaiming the characteristic "augh" as they clapped their hands together. They were also all anxious to reap the benefit of this unexpected windfall. Through the throng, I noticed a police Casspir driver and he related what had occurred before our arrival.

The Casspir is a mine-protected, armoured personnel carrier, built for off-road bundu bashing, while tracking and chasing terrorists. It is immensely strong and weighs over 13 tons. Interestingly, the name Casspir is an anagram of the initials SAP (South African Police) and CSIR (Council for Scientific and Industrial Research), the two groups who combined to produce this excellent vehicle.

During the course of the morning, the elephant had charged one of these vehicles and put it out of action. The other Casspir stopped to give assistance once the elephant had left the scene. While all the occupants were standing outside the stationary vehicles discussing the problem, the rogue returned. It came storming out of the bush and ran into the side of the second Casspir. This 13-ton vehicle was physically moved about eight metres sideways by the force of the collision. The policeman I spoke to was the driver of this second vehicle. Although this incident took place three hours earlier, his face was still chalky white!

I told this story in the pub to General Dennis Earp, chief of the air force, about a month after the event. I spoke about the vision I had had of Bernie's limbs whirling all over the place while he was running. On completion of the narrative, I felt a tap on my shoulder. It was Bernie, who then explained the whirling action of his limbs. During his sprint, he tried to shoot backwards over his shoulder as the elephant rapidly gained on him!

During the planning of an operation, I had occasion to visit Omega, the Bushman Battalion base in the Caprivi Strip of northern South West Africa. Colonel Brian Adams, commander of the base and an old friend, met me at the airstrip and drove me down to his officer's mess. We stopped to watch one of the splendours of that remote part of the world—the sun set in a blaze of glorious red, orange and blue. During the conversation, he told me about the newest inhabitant of Omega—an elephant.

Fortunately, this one turned out to be a baby! One of the patrols found the abandoned orphan and, not wanting to leave him to die in the bush, brought it back to Omega. Of course, I expressed a desire to see the creature, and Brian said he would arrange a meeting when we arrived at the mess. Built in an open-plan design, with a thatch roof, the officer's mess was a pleasant place to enjoy a sundowner. Without side walls, the air could circulate freely and it was most refreshing after the heat of the day.

Suitably equipped with long, cold glasses in our hands, Brian called for the regimental sergeant major (RSM) and asked him to arrange for the elephant to put in an appearance. Stamping his foot and exclaiming loudly, 'Yes, Sah!' he stepped outside and hollered 'McClaren, bring your elephant!'

It turned out that McClaren, a national serviceman, was the lad who had caused the RSM the most grief. The RSM saw the arrival of the baby elephant as a godsend and installed McClaren as the baby's mother, nursemaid, friend, and cleaner. McClaren arrived out of the darkened bush, looking like a modern day Quasimodo. His left arm was dangling misshapen away from his side, while his right arm stretched across his chest to the left. As he walked into the light, we could see that the tiniest, most charming, infant elephant imaginable was closely following him.

The resourceful young man accepted his new role as mother and applied considerable thought to his unusual position. Realizing that most babies need constant nurturing, he armed himself with cardboard cartons of long-life milk. He made an opening in the top and poured the milk in a steady trickle down his left forearm. His left hand dangled downwards and his fingers acting as teats pointed backwards. The elephant followed him wherever he walked, suckling on his fingers, and oblivious to barstools, tables, or anything else that was in his way. He was no more than a metre tall and the characteristic bristles of newly born elephants still covered his hide. I have witnessed many unusual, macabre, amusing, and crazy scenes in my military career, but none could match this delightful little elephant. Unfortunately, he could not stay long; the repair bill would have been exorbitant.

Omega was always an interesting base to visit. It was established to accommodate an entire Bushman community. During South Africa's earlier forays into Angola in the mid-1970s, interestingly at the bidding of the United States, all the warring factions in that strife-ridden country used the opportunity to rid Angola of the Bushmen. South African forces came across bands and groups of these little people, wandering aimlessly around Angola in an attempt to avoid conflict and stay alive. In an act of humanity, the South Africans protected these groups and gave them sanctuary inside South West Africa. Bushmen maintain strong family ties and often families included grandparents and up to eight or ten children. Therefore, their sanctuary at Omega grew in leaps and bounds.

These men had skills that our own ground forces could utilize. Therefore, in the British tradition, they raised an ethnic Bushman Battalion. The men enlisted in the South African Army, receiving the same pay and benefits as any other member. After basic army training, they were set to work as trackers in infantry patrols. They were magnificent in the bush and their skills soon led to an increase in engagements and contacts with the enemy. They ran down an enemy spoor and gave accurate estimates of how old the tracks were from days and hours, to minutes. Ground troops could tell when a firefight was imminent by watching the little men at work. They would indicate the direction of the enemy while changing places with the regular soldiers and taking up position in the rear. They knew their own strengths and weaknesses—fighting was an unfamiliar skill for these gentlefolk.

Omega, where the total Bushman community exceeded 10 000 souls, covered a vast area. The army erected a large open-air cinema screen on which nightly movies played. Apart from the army vehicles and the airstrip alongside the base, these people had been exposed to nothing else. They had never seen a mountain, train, double-storied building, snow, or a neon light—all the things they now watched on the screen. They could not follow the dialogue, but they stared at the moving images. Of course their reactions were understandably different to those of more sophisticated audiences.

There were no chairs in front of the screen; the people sat in the sand, as they had done for centuries. An area was de-bushed to provide sufficient space for the nightly gatherings. The entire area was needed, because they were a "moving" audience. With all their limitations, they could still recognize the good guy from the bad. Whenever the good guy or the beautiful girl was on the screen they all edged nearer to the front. However, when the bad guy appeared, they all scampered into the protection of the surrounding bush, until "the coast was clear"! This description is not meant to be patronizing, but an attempt to illustrate the lovely innocence of a people uncontaminated by so-called civilization.

Unfortunately, in true life, not every story has a happy, Hollywood ending. In a sincere attempt to save the little people from annihilation and to improve their standards of living, the South African Army tried their very best, but they did not achieve the results they had hoped for. The Bushmen, who did not know what money was and had never needed any, suddenly discovered that with their army pay they had become wealthy overnight. They bought fridges and TV sets, not realizing that they needed electricity to make the appliances work. They discovered that with money they could buy hard liquor or beer, substances that they had no previous experience of. Within a relatively short time, the people began losing their traditional bushcraft skills and becoming dependent on, and in some cases addicted to, western material goods and brews. Although well meaning, the experiment was not the desired success story.

1 Squadron, Mirage F1AZ, AFB Hoedspruit, in final camouflage livery.

"Boots hanging, probe out, landing lights on". 1 Squadron Mirage F1AZ aircraft perform a final slow flypast on the decommissioning of the squadron.

A dramatic photograph of a Mirage F1AZ, carrying self-defence wingtip missiles. Escaping after a low-level attack, it fired infrared flares.

Himba inhabitants of Kaokoland in front of their dwelling. The arid terrain was rugged, like the face of the moon.

Apart from the river there were no navigational features to aid the pilot. The border war terrain in SWA/Angola was as flat as a pancake!

South African Army Base Okangwati, Kaokoland, South West Africa.

A clean Mirage F1AZ landing at AFB Waterkloof in original gloss camouflage scheme, which proved to be too conspicuous during operations. The radar ranging nose and the laser ranging window below it can be easily seen.

Every milestone in a pilot's career is celebrated with some suitable beverage. Even these occasions are competitive; the slowest drinker had to repeat the process!

Two fully-loaded Mirage F1AZ fighter-bombers pose for the camera over the foothills of the Drakensberg Mountains.

Mirage F1AZ on approach in final operational livery.

Mirage F1AZ on approach in original gloss camouflage.

Perfect plan view of Mirage F1AZ pulling wingtip vortices during a tight turn.

Moçambique MiG17 parked at AFB Hoedspruit, after the pilot defected from the Communist state.

Mirage pilots of 1 and 2 Squadrons pose alongside Lt Bomba, the Moçambique pilot who defected to AFB Hoedspruit. The author is wearing the cap.

General Constand Viljoen, Chief of the SA Defence Force, and Jonas Savimbi, leader of UNITA, pose for the author outside the UNITA headquarters at Jamba, Angola.

Mirage F1AZ leaving the readiness shelter at AFB Hoedspruit.

A sequence showing a Mirage F1AZ approaching the refuelling basket trailing from the starboard wing of a Boeing 707 tanker. The good positioning of the probe made the task relatively simple.

The author, with a terrified Major Norman Bruton in the backseat of an Impala Mk1, formatting at low-level over the Kavongo River, which separates Angola from South West Africa (Namibia).

The author standing in front of an Angolan Air Force An26 at Ongiva in Angola during the failed peace negotiations of 1984.

The author displaying the Tarpon presented to him by Major Manuel Dias of the Angolan Air Force during one of the peace negotiations.

Two young elephant, two Springbok, and a Wildebeest at the SA Police Counter-Insurgency Unit (Koevoet) "zoo" in Oshakati. Orphan animals, innocent victims of the border war, were cared for in this "haven of peace".

Inadvertent low-level supersonic flight caused extensive damage to property!

Captain Wassie Wasserman, a SAAF panty-ripper, displaying his handiwork in front of a Buccaneer tanker of 243 Squadron.

The rear half of a light delivery van, which was completely severed from the chassis after detonating a landmine. Innocent civilians were the usual victims of this type of random terrorism.

A line-up of 1 Squadron Mirage F1AZ fighter-bombers at AFB Waterkloof.

Plan form of Mirage F1AZ carrying four 68mm rocket pods. By the end of the border war, this type of weaponry was obsolete.

The pilots who flew the famous "Fifty Mirage Aircraft Flypast" over Pretoria. The aircraft consisted of the full SAAF range of Mirages, including Mirage III B, C, D, D2Z, E, R and R2Z models; and the F1CZ and the F1AZ ground-attack "Mudmovers".

The author leads the distinctive 1 Squadron formation flypast of Mirage F1AZs.

A diamond of Mirage F1AZ aircraft fly past "slow, low and dirty".

The end of Shackelton Mk3 1716. A night crash landing in the
Sahara Desert—all 19 on board survived!

An Impala Mk2 light strike fighter firing a full salvo of rockets. A successful aircraft in the SAAF bush war.

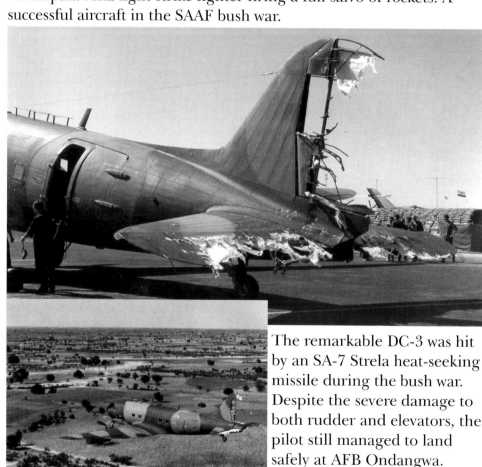

The remarkable DC-3 was hit by an SA-7 Strela heat-seeking missile during the bush war. Despite the severe damage to both rudder and elevators, the pilot still managed to land safely at AFB Ondangwa.

A Sabre pilot dances with the clouds.

A SAAF Canadair Sabre 6 at low level over the Drakensberg escarpment in the Eastern Transvaal.

The author after landing from his first flight in the legendary Sabre.

Fortunately, a distant view of the results of an air strike.

Rugged Kaokoland—like the face of the moon.

The inhospitable Namib Desert, just inland from the notorious Skeleton Coast.

A SAAF Puma and crew after landing on the Skeleton Coast.

A Mirage F1AZ "Mudmover" leaving its lair at AFB Hoedspruit. This aircraft was on a test flight; hence, it was "flying clean".

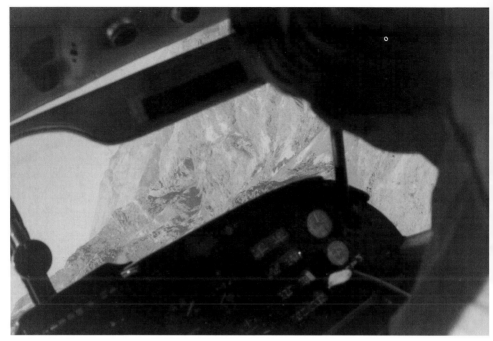

Winding down the Cunene River in the rugged mountains of Kaokaland.

The Mirage III fleet at 85 Advanced Flying School at AFB Pietersburg in the late 1970s showing off the symmetry of their camouflage!

The ice-shelf surrounding Antarctica.
This spot was on latitude 70° South.

Pancake ice, Bergy bits, and
an iceberg broken from the
Antarctic ice-shelf.

A glacier on Bouvet Island, the remotest spot on earth, half way to
Antarctica.

An also-ran in the beard competition.

Entering Cape Town harbour, with Table Mountain providing the magnificent backdrop.

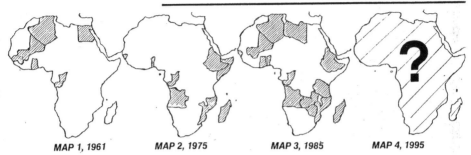

MAP 1, 1961   MAP 2, 1975   MAP 3, 1985   MAP 4, 1995

PAINT AFRICA RED. Map series shows Soviet penetration into Africa over past quarter-century, a period when many states came under Soviet influence, while others shook it off. MAP 1, 1961: Six nations under Red influence — Algeria, Congo, Mali, Egypt, Guinea, Ghana. MAP 2, 1975: Now 11 states — Mozambique, Angola, Benin, Congo, Madagascar, Guinea-Bissau, Sao Tome, Cape Verde, Comoros, Somalia, Ethiopia. MAP 3, 1986 — figure crept up to 18 states in the Red camp. Vanguard states — Angola, Mozambique, Congo-Brazzaville, Ethiopia, Benin. Military governments: Burkina Faso, Ghana. Broad national fronts: Madagascar. Multi-party system: Zimbabwe. Mass parties, strongly slanted towards communism: Guinea-Bissau. Cape Verde, Sao Tome en Principe. Slanted towards Marxism: Algeria, Libya, Tanzania, Zambia, Seychelles, Mali. MAP 4, 1995 — ?

Africa outlines illustrating the advance of Communism since 1961. Map 3 vividly displays the threat surrounding South Africa during the "Border War".

Reaching the ice-shelf on the run to the SANAE Base in Antarctica. The Puma colour scheme aids visibility in the white environment. Skids are fixed to the undercarriage to support snow landings. Floatation bags around the nose and undercarriage housing offer protection if the chopper has to ditch into the frozen waters.

Nelson Mandela takes office as president of the new South Africa in 1994. Exultation can be seen in the wildly waving forest of hands.

A tribute paid by two old crew mates, the author and Keith Brown, To Able Seaman Just Nuisance in the graveyard above Simonstown in South Africa. Just Nuisance was a legendary Great Dane, who officially enrolled into the Royal Navy as an Able Seaman during World War II. Perhaps a fitting finale to a wonderful military career.

The last thing I want to mention about Omega was the large water tower built on pylons that dominated the camp area. It would supply water pressure to the spread out community. On the sides of this steel tank, in huge white letters, was painted the word "OOPS". It appears that the reservoir, erected by the Public Works Department, had been built in the wrong place, far from the water source, and people wanted a permanent reminder of the folly.

Interruptions to the routine of the Command Post occurred almost every day by the necessity to cater for critical situations. We attached absolute priority to casualty evacuation. The "golden hour" between injury and hospitalization drastically affects the chances of survival. A Casevac callout during wartime is a very involved procedure. The standby helicopter crew is briefed of all the circumstances. A doctor and his orderly must ensure they have the correct equipment on board. A section of parabats accompany them to secure the helicopter while it is on the ground. In some situations, top cover gunship helicopters must accompany the ambulance chopper as protection from ambush during the critical pick-up. Long distance flights require additional fuel, which can be taken in extra fuel tanks loaded inside the helicopter cabin, or the helicopter has to land at forward bases or Helicopter Administrative Areas (HAAs) to be topped up. All these arrangements have to be made after the flight has been thoroughly planned.

In South West Africa, we worked hard to reduce the average Casevac time to about 40 minutes. Worldwide, the Israeli Defence Force was the benchmark used to compare efficiency; they had a remarkable reaction time of about 20 minutes. When we considered that their theatre of operations was about the size of the Etosha Pan, we felt we were doing pretty well recovering most patients within the "golden hour". Unfortunately, situations existed where wounded soldiers waited hours before recovery. Often we had to wait for cover of darkness to protect the unarmed and vulnerable choppers.

During major terrorist incursions, SWAPO sent up to 14 or 15 detachments across the border at the same time. The incursion routes covered almost the entire border from the Kaokoland in the west, through to Owamboland and Kavango—a distance of nearly 900 kilometres. Each group consisted of between 40 and 100 men carrying the ubiquitous AK-47 rifles, vehicle and anti-personnel mines, mortars, Katusha rockets and, almost always, a number of Strela SA-7 shoulder-launched, SAM missiles.

Our aircraft were at considerable risk wherever they flew in this vast theatre of operations. Constant adherence to safety regulations was a prerequisite. If it was not possible to fly above the 15 000 foot Strela limit, we tasked the pilots to fly at low level. The incredible flatness of the entire area helped our strategy, allowing pilots to fly at 50 foot above the tree canopy with comparative ease. At this low altitude, SA-7 operators had insufficient time to acquire the aircraft, gain lock-on and fire, before the low flying aircraft disappeared from view. Like contraception, this method was not 100% safe!

A Dakota C47 returning to AFB Ondangwa from western Owamboland was one exception that proved the rule. The relatively slow-moving transport aircraft presented an ideal target for the right length of time to a lucky Strela operator. His missile streaked away and exploded as it struck the tail of the Dakota. The pilot heard the explosion and felt the strike, and he lost the balance of his aircraft.

The fabric-covered, vertical tail fin was destroyed and his aircraft immediately started to yaw, as directional control was lost. The horizontal elevators, peppered with holes, made height control difficult. With great difficulty, the pilot managed to keep control of his badly damaged aircraft. Little did he know that the holes in the elevator fabric were gradually tearing in the air-stream. He experienced this effect while trying with difficulty to control his height.

He eventually solved the porpoising problem by manoeuvring the position of his passengers. Getting out of their seats, they moved in a closely packed group backwards and forwards, adjusting the aircraft's centre of gravity, and thus allowing him to keep the aircraft more or less level. Fortunately, the passengers included the chief of the navy and his entourage. These men, accustomed to a pitching deck, were quite adept at dancing up and down the fuselage at the behest of the pilot! After a great demonstration of flying skill, the pilot landed safely at his destination.

Major Hojan Cronje is an extremely tall helicopter pilot with years of experience in operations. His nickname was given to him when he arrived at the Central Flying School to learn to fly. It turned out that there were three youngsters called Johan on his course. The chief instructor solved the problem by re-christening two of them. Hojan received the anagram of Johan!

Hojan, a Puma helicopter pilot, was tasked to ferry much needed ammunition into a battle zone where 32 Battalion, under command of Commandant Eddie Viljoen, were engaged in a serious firefight with

SWAPO forces. Sneaking in at extremely low level, Hojan landed in the open area of a *shona*. The troops rapidly unloaded his aircraft. Lifting off moments later, Hojan spotted a baby donkey standing forlornly in the *shona*. Disturbed by the thought of this poor creature having to endure the trauma of battle, Hojan pressed his radio transmitter button and called Echo Victor, the callsign of Col Eddie Viljoen. In the heat of battle, Hojan persuaded Eddie to send a few men to capture the donkey and load it into the cabin of the helicopter, which they did.

The following day, Hojan flew the Puma back to South Africa for a major service carrying a passenger, the donkey! Twelve flying hours later, a very tired Hojan landed at AFB Swartkop in Pretoria just as it was getting dark. Hojan loaded his equally weary passenger into the front seat of his car and drove home. As he passed through the main gates of the base, the guard drew to attention and saluted. Hojan says the entire event was made worthwhile by the sentry's expression of disbelief when he realized that he was saluting a donkey!

Another interesting Casevac also involved 32 Battalion, perhaps the most effective anti-terrorist unit involved in the border war. This time the flight was not for a war wound. A group of soldiers had been swimming in the beautiful, crystal clear river running past the Buffalo Base in Caprivi. One of the regular river inhabitants, a smallish crocodile, had taken exception to this human disturbance and vented his annoyance by taking a bite out of Sergeant Major Koos Kruger's leg as he was climbing out onto the riverbank. His shout alerted his buddies, who grabbed Koos's arms and heaved, while the crocodile pulled in the opposite direction. The situation was resolved when 2nd Lieutenant Jurie Groenewald leapt onto the reptile's back and pushed his fingers into the animal's eyes. Releasing his grip, the crocodile disappeared with a sweep of his great tail. Koos was Casevaced and recovered fully with just a name change! To this day, he is referred to as Koos Krokodil.

Africa is famous for its animals and they certainly played their part in our wars. On one occasion, Puma helicopters were flying back to base after a very long day supporting the ground forces in battle deep inside Angola. Flying westwards into the late afternoon sun made the tired crews very drowsy. Two of the SAAF's most experienced pilots, Crow Stannard and Breyty Breytenbach were flying the lead chopper. Breyty's head was lolling against the port window and Crow was monitoring the autopilot through half closed eyes. Suddenly, a cry of

"JUMBOOO" over the radio broke the serenity of the droning chopper engines. A brand new, eager, young co-pilot, had spotted a herd of elephant among the trees below, and he wanted to share his joy with the rest of the flight.

To a snoozing crew "Jumbo" sounds very much like "Tallyho", the call that would alert everyone to the presence of enemy MiGs. Crow disconnected the autopilot and dived for the safety of the trees. The sudden alteration of power caused the chopper to yaw. The rapid change of airflow around the fuselage pulled the flimsy port window open. Breyty awoke from his slumbers to feel a sudden roar of air in his ears as the chopper descended frantically. Recovering from a series of self-induced attitudes, it dawned on them that as Shakespeare had written, there was really "Much ado about nothing!"

Talks between political masters on both sides of the boarder, brought promises of peace. Unfortunately, politicians have earned themselves an extremely poor record of keeping promises and the war went on. The lull during negotiations gave me a much-needed break and I flew with my wife and youngest son to England, to visit her family. We left Ondangwa on the afternoon C130 "Flossie" flight for Pretoria. That same evening we flew out of Johannesburg International Airport on a South African Airways Boeing 747 for London. I knew both airline pilots, and I was invited into the cockpit and from there, via the radio, I was able to talk to my Command Post staff as the airliner headed out towards the Atlantic Ocean.

It was summer in Europe and at 05h00 the cabin crew raised the shutters covering the aircraft's windows so that they could serve breakfast before we landed at Heathrow in London. Michael, my eight-year-old son, had the window seat, and I sat next to the aisle. Pointing out of the window towards the 7 o'clock position, he asked, 'Daddy, what is that?' Leaning forward to peer in that direction, I received the fright of my life. There, curving around towards our tail was the grey smoke trail of a SAM missile. At its head was the bright incandescent tip of the burning motor. My reaction was as instantaneous as it was embarrassing! With a shout, I dived out of my chair and landed in the aisle!

Michael promptly disowned me; June put on that nonchalant look as if to say 'Oh! My husband does these sort of things regularly'; and I returned self-consciously to my seat.

In the split-second before I hit the floor I realized that the smoke trail I had seen was the contrail of another airliner circling in the busy approaches to London. The rising sun, reflecting brightly off the aircraft's nose, reminded me momentarily of a burning missile rocket motor, but realization came too late to avoid the embarrassing dive!

A few days later, we were in Bristol visiting June's sister, who kindly took us on a tour to see the sights of the old city. Michael was engrossed, particularly when we stopped to let him have a close look at the statue of Queen Victoria standing outside one of the impressive buildings. He had never seen a statue before and he walked around taking in every detail. Eventually the inevitable question came, 'Daddy, what is she doing with the hand-grenade?' pointing towards the sceptre clasped in the royal hand.

Amusing as both incidents are, it proves that the unnatural environment of a war zone does have an effect on people. Driving to Johannesburg airport in home-going traffic, Michael asked, 'What time do they close the roads?' In Owamboland, he was accustomed to the nightly curfew that had been instituted to hinder terrorists from moving their heavy mines and mortars by vehicle.

Late in November 1983, we launched Operation Askari. This operation differed from our previous forays into Angola. In an attempt to disrupt SWAPO before their yearly incursion into South West Africa began, a motorized semi-conventional force advanced across the border. Usually we did this during the dry season because the heavy armoured vehicles experienced extreme difficulty in muddy terrain. We wanted to achieve surprise by breaking the cyclical nature of the war.

Our extra-curricula activities in Oshakati included planning Operation Askari. My air plan supported the army ground plan. Once again, Cahama, "my town", was targeted. The intention was not to capture the place, so my chances of mayoral office were negligible, but we did devise a plan to capture a battery of Russian built SA-8 missiles that had recently made their appearance near the town. The SA-8 was an excellent missile that posed a serious threat to any low flying aircraft. Its capture would be a first for the Western world. Previously, Russia had not allowed these sophisticated systems to leave.

The idea was to use the SAAF to bomb, and the artillery to bombard, in a set sequence and pattern against the launching sites of this mobile missile. These attacks began in the north and worked gradually towards the south. Our intention was to force these batteries to move southwards for their own safety. Ediva was a little spot on the map south of Cahama that was home to an aggressive AAA battery. These gunners fired at every SAAF aircraft within visual range, whether they had a chance of success or not. Once the SA-8s were near Ediva we planned to launch Special Force Commando units into the area to capture an SA-8 intact.

This ambitious plan began and it was working exactly as we thought it would. By Christmas, we had chased the SA-8s to sites well south of Cahama. The aircraft dropped obsolete General Purpose (GP) bombs that would otherwise have been dumped at sea, making it a cost-effective campaign. In the true spirit of Christmas, I sent a stream of Canberra bombers to drop their bombs from 24 000 feet on selected aiming points. The strike time for the first attack was 23h59. By my reckoning, the fall of the bombs would take one minute, and would therefore arrive on Christmas Day. I entered freely into the festive spirit by allocating Santa, Claus, Dasher, Dancer, etc., as the callsigns of the individual aircraft.

The uproar in the United Nations over South African advances during Askari proved that the operation was achieving success. Unfortunately, perhaps, our politicians got an attack of cold feet because of the opposition they were receiving, and they promptly changed their minds about the plan they had approved. By New Year's Day, we had to cease all our activities around Cahama and withdraw further eastwards. The Angolan commander saw this withdrawal as a victory over the *Boere*, and our hopes of capturing an SA-8, after all the effort and expense, vanished at the stroke of a pen.

Early in January 1984, Operation Askari reached its climax during the battle for possession of Cuvelai, a town in southern Angola's Cunene Province. During the afternoon of January 3rd, the actual attack took place. It commenced with a coordinated air attack aimed at all the known artillery and AAA sites. Each pilot was equipped with up-to-date enlarged photography of his particular target. Ten Impala MkII light strike fighters led the raid, followed by four English Electric Canberra bombers. Between them, they dropped 60 x 120kg bombs, 18 x 250kg bombs, 2 x 450kg bombs, and 600 Alpha bombs.

On completion of this air strike, we intercepted a desperate radio message from the Angolan commander in Cuvelai. He pleaded with his Lubango headquarters to send help. The gist of his message stated: '75% of my artillery has been taken out by the South African Air Force.' However, the undisputable success was not without cost!

The Impala strike formation leader was Captain Joe van den Berg, the senior Impala pilot at Ondangwa. His target was the Firecan radar-guided 57mm AAA site situated just east of Cuvelai. During the pullout, after bomb release, he observed missile firings and proceeded to fly evasive manoeuvres. One of the missiles, later identified as a SA-9, struck Joe's aircraft in the tail section, completely removing the starboard tailplane and elevator.

His aircraft entered the incipient stage of a spin directly above the target he had just attacked. Displaying superb flying skills, he recovered to a normal flying attitude and discovered that by reducing speed to below 150 knots, he could control the induced roll to starboard. Joe also found that he ran out of elevator control if his speed decayed below 130 knots. Having established that he was able to fly his aircraft within that narrow speed band, he set heading for Ondangwa, his home base.

After the excitement of the previous traumatic seconds, he had time to reappraise his predicament. To his consternation, he discovered that in the configuration he was forced to fly, he could not maintain height and his rate of descent was close to 2 000ft per minute. Reaching Ondangwa was out of the question and he diverted to Ongiva. The SAAF had recently repaired and resurfaced this Angolan airfield for exactly this kind of emergency.

Further calculations showed that with the given rate of descent, the Impala would not even reach Ongiva. Just then, physical science began to exert its influence on events. As the aircraft lost height the air closer to the ground became progressively denser. The thicker air provided the engine with more thrust and improved the aerodynamic qualities of the wing by giving more lift. Therefore, the Impala's rate of descent decreased from 2 000ft per minute to 1 500, 1 000, 800, 700, and eventually to approximately 400ft per minute. The shallower angle of descent enabled Joe to stretch the glide and with very little height to spare sneak over the threshold at Ongiva to perform an excellent touchdown.

On two occasions during Askari, I had the chance to study men's reactions under threat. The first time occurred during a long-range artillery bombardment of Cahama. Having visited "my town" so often by air, I took the opportunity to accompany the army commander to witness the bombardment. We looked at the battery of guns as we moved to within seven kilometres of the little town. We were in a party of senior officers being transported inside Ratel armoured vehicles. The vehicles stopped in a safe location and most of us climbed onto the top of the vehicles to watch the bombardment. It really was not much of a spectacle, because the ground was too flat to offer a decent vantage point.

It was nevertheless exciting to hear the rumble of the guns as a salvo of shells was fired. We could hear them whistling overhead followed seconds latter by the "crump" of the explosions. The novelty began to wear off after a while; far-off dust clouds were the only visible effect of the bombardment. Suddenly, awareness returned to peak levels. A new series of noises began, identical to the first, but this time coming from the opposite direction, as the enemy opened up with a counter-bombardment.

Their shells did not land near us, because they were aiming at our artillery battery. However, the telltale "crump" of exploding shells was a lot louder and it gained everyone's attention. Here was an exercise in human reaction. Only the *dominee*, the Afrikaans padre, showed any real sense. At the first enemy shot, he dived into the cavernous interior of the Ratel and slammed the door. The rest of us feigned bravado and refused to scuttle for shelter—we would rather die than be accused of being afraid! Preserving the male macho image is akin to madness!

The same situation existed the day after the battle in Cuvelai. Once again, a group of senior officers wanted to go forward to witness the battle scene. Standing in the main street of the little town after the briefing on the fighting, a Russian built PT-76 tank suddenly fired its main gun from roughly 50 yards away. None of the generals ran for cover, but I did notice that suddenly we all just happened to be standing nonchalantly behind the cover of our armoured vehicles.

After the successes achieved during Operation Askari, the Communist MPLA government of Angola agreed to cease hostilities. Traditionally, whenever Communist forces are in trouble, they use this ploy. South African and Angolan military and political delegates formed a Joint Monitoring Commission (JMC). A combined JMC force of South African and Angolan troops would monitor "peace" activities. South Africa agreed to leave southern Angola and the Angolans were to ensure SWAPO terrorists did not fill the vacuum.

During the regular meetings of the JMC, we had the unusual situation of hosting our Angolan enemies in their own country. Most of the discussion was of a political nature, but I did get the opportunity to meet my opposing Angolan air force commander face to face. Interestingly, the two of us got on very well. Both sides arrived for these meetings in helicopters and in a matter of a few minutes, the opposing aircrew were swapping stories, mementoes, and Aqua Vit, a menacing looking liquid that the Angolan pilots carried in their choppers. It appeared that members of both military organizations bore little or no malice toward their opponents. Each man did his duty as his superiors required. Perhaps politicians should be made aware that it is their inability to solve problems that results in the ugliness of war.

Away from the negotiating table, Major Manuel Dias and I had interesting and friendly discussions, and we exchanged gifts. I supplied him with a few Cape grapevines to plant outside the Angolan Air Force headquarters in Lubango. Knowing how much I enjoyed fishing, he brought a magnificent fish as a present for me. This monster was a Tarpon or Silver King, described in the encyclopaedia as a "great and powerful fish". Standing on its head, it was nearly as tall as I was and it provided sufficient meat to satisfy the hunger of the 35 staff in my Command Post. We *braaied* the fish over the open coals at the Oshandira—the SAAF pub at Oshakati. And in their absence, we toasted our opponents who had thoughtfully given us this wonderful gift. Unfortunately, despite the best efforts of the military, peace was not to be.

It has been my experience that Western ethics are no match for the Communists' deviousness. One has only to think back to Stalin in WWII and the cold war immediately thereafter, the protracted negotiations over the 38th Parallel with the North Koreans between 1950 and 1953, and the vicious Tet offensive launched in the middle of peace negotiations in Vietnam to realize that Westerners have always come off second best. I put the problem down to the use of the French word *détente* in political negotiating circles. The exact meaning of the word according to the dictionary is "Relaxing of tension between States". To westerners, this means ceasing conflict and sitting around a table to resolve issues with the aim of returning to "normality". However, Communists see *détente* as an excellent opportunity to seize positions of power while the military heat has been conveniently removed.

In Angola, the situation again developed according to Mao's "Little Red Book". The South Africans relinquished all their gains in Angola and withdrew according to the terms laid down by the JMC. Angola blatantly ignored every restriction placed on her and in fact logistically encouraged and assisted SWAPO in reoccupying the territory vacated by South African forces. By mid-1984, it was "back to the drawing board".

Chapter 21

Western Air Command, Windhoek, SWA

Life in the military is one of constant upheaval. After two years in Oshakati, I was appointed as the senior staff officer operations (SSO OPS) at Western Air Command in Windhoek. This was my very first staff appointment and initially I felt it was a step backwards from the direct involvement in the war. After a career of frontline aviation and command appointments, I had developed a feeling for staff officers that was only fractionally better than that of my pet aversion, politicians. Overnight I changed from being "one of us" to "one of them".

The first thing I learnt was how dependent the staff is on the character and personality of the commander. In this regard, I was extremely fortunate to work under Brigadier Winston Thackwray. Thack was a long-time friend who I respected as an aerophile with an incredible knowledge of all aspects of aviation. His initiative and drive eventually produced the "Rooivalk" attack helicopter now in SAAF service. He differed from many other commanders in that he was unafraid to make decisions. He trusted and encouraged me to get on with running operations. Instead of stepping away from the war in Owamboland, I could now get actively involved in the battle on all three operational fronts, Sector 10 Owamboland, Sector 20 Kavango, and Sector 70 Katima Mulilo.

From a personal point of view, living in Windhoek was easier than living on the border. It is a lovely town with a strong German influence. It is within three hours drive of Swakopmund, the resort town on the Atlantic seaboard. My entire family benefited, because we could relax.

My arrival in Windhoek in 1985 coincided with a change in the nature of the border war. SWAPO lost all chances of gaining power through "the barrel of the gun". Militarily, they knew the organization had been effectively neutralized. We had beaten the terrorists at their own game. Terrorist or insurgency wars are wars of attrition. They rely on the cumulative effects of terror to erode the resistance of the government they wish to overthrow. A terrorist war is therefore a long war of murder, mining, maiming, abduction, ambushes, and stand-off bombardments aimed mostly at the soft-targets, the local population. In South West Africa, the positive and continuous efforts of the South African and South West African Defence Forces outlasted SWAPO and brought it to its knees.

It is necessary now to digress from my story to explain the situation prevailing in Southern Africa at that time.

World history, like beauty, is in the eye of the beholder. In the mid-1980s, the cold war was reaching a critical point. The comparatively enlightened views of Gorbachev threw Russian Communism into turmoil. Their avowed struggle for world domination was seriously dented by the failure of their Imperialistic adventure into Afghanistan. The increasing loss of Russian lives in that forbidding part of the world was causing a ground swell of opposition against authorities in Moscow.

In a bid to regain expansionistic impetus, Moscow agreed to give large-scale support to the Communist MPLA regime in Angola, which had seized power after the withdrawal of Portugal in 1975. After subjugating that mineral-rich country, the ultimate Russian goal was the acquisition of the strategic minerals of South Africa and its position astride one of the worlds "choke-points". Russian studies showed that between them, South Africa and Russia controlled 16 strategic minerals, on which Western high tech aero-industries depended. A monopoly of these would place Russia in an enviable position of power.

Control of the "choke-points" around the world would give Russia the power to effectively control world trade. Since the early 1950s, the Communists had made significant advances in this direction. Under the disguise of liberation struggles, they had fomented the conflicts around the Suez Canal, Malta, Persian Gulf, Panama Canal, and the Straits of Sumatra. If they could dominate the important Cape sea-route, they would have almost achieved their aim.

A third facet of the conflict in Angola was that it was never meant to be the launching pad for the final push into South Africa. The Russians tried for a long time to woo Mugabe of Zimbabwe, who had been weaned on the Chinese brand of Communism. The vast arsenal of weapons poured into Angola was to be a symbol to Mugabe of what he could also receive if he aligned himself with Russia. The springboard of the final Russian advance was envisaged to be on the much shorter path from Zimbabwe, through Botswana, straight into the heart of South African power in Johannesburg and Pretoria.

The Russian military assessment was correct in another detail of their long-term plan. They had established that the SAAF was the major obstacle to their expansionistic plans. They also knew the extreme difficulty the SAAF had in replacing aircraft losses, because of the international arms boycott instituted against South Africa. The vast array of sophisticated air defence radars, SU-22 and MiG23 aircraft, anti-aircraft artillery, and SAM systems were deployed for that specific reason.

The anti-aircraft missile systems included SAM-2 and -3 static systems; SA-6, 8, 9 mobile systems; plus thousands of shoulder-launched SA-7, 12 and 14s. The muscle was to by supplied by introducing Cuban surrogates to the African theatre—Russia could ill-afford further losses of her own troops. The border war now moved into a conventional phase.

The Angolan Army, backed by Cubans and commanded by Russians, attempted to advance into South East Angola in 1985 and again in 1987. Their announced intention was to annihilate the Western-orientated South African and American supported UNITA resistance movement, under its charismatic leader Jonas Savimbi. To achieve this they needed to capture and occupy the little village and valuable airstrip of Mavinga. They would then have a suitable stepping-stone from which to control the entire south-eastern corner of Angola.

Using force levels and tactics laid down in the Russian warfare manual, they advanced in a typical pincer movement. Both times they were savaged near the headwaters of the Lomba River, and they had to retreat in disarray, leaving the wreckage of entire brigades on the battlefield. On both occasions, UNITA forces harassed the enemy during the advance and retreat phases of the expedition. The final battle of each campaign was fought against South African artillery and ground forces. However, the decisive factor that lead to both crushing defeats was the unleashing of SAAF destructive firepower at crucial moments in the battle.

The airstrip at Mavinga was as important to us as it was to the enemy. The single, sand runway was vital to our logistic effort. Transport aircraft were vulnerable to roaming MiGs during daylight hours, effectively preventing re-supply operations. At nightfall, Mavinga came to life; a shuttle service of C130 and C160 transport brought in the vital materials of war. Only one aircraft could use the strip at a time because it had no taxiways or loading ramps. It was a strip with turning circles at either end, built for light aircraft during the Portuguese colonial period. Motors stayed on to avoid the possibility of restart problems. We could not leave the aircraft on the ground during the day because it would invite attention from the MiGs.

The loading parties at Mavinga developed a slick routine to off-load the freighters in the minimum amount of time. They then removed the cargo, ammunition, or food from the dumb-bell so that the next aircraft had space to turn and unload. It was extremely hard physical work, but the aircrew appreciated it. They felt very vulnerable while the aircraft parked on the ground. This procedure occurred every night of the seven-month campaign, with an average of three to four flights off-loading every night. During intense periods, six or seven flights were made, with the last flight sneaking home in the rapidly breaking tropical dawn.

Any electricity that Mavinga may have had in the past was non-existent in 1987. Normally, when approaching to land, the pilot used homing instruments to guide him to the airfield, which he spotted visually by reference to the lights of nearby towns. In Mavinga's case, there was no electricity, town lights, or navigational homing beacons. The deployment of a mobile beacon would have eased the problem for our pilots, but the Angolans could also have used it, so they dismissed that idea.

To find the airfield at night was a difficult task and the aircrew had to rely on on-board systems to get them onto an extended long final approach. Only then could they ask, over the radio, for illuminated runway lights. These lights shone long enough for the aircraft to land, after which they immediately extinguished. Prowling MiGs were a constant threat. The lights would illuminate; the pilot would hopefully spot them visually, adjust his flight path, and then land. On touchdown, the propellers were put into reverse thrust, and power was applied to slow the heavily laden aircraft. This reverse thrust caused clouds of dust from the dirt runway to billow into the air, which was another reason why the strip could not be used during daytime. Dust clouds attracted the attention of fighter-bomber pilots.

Unlike Heathrow or Johannesburg International, Mavinga runway did not possess the luxury of row upon row of lead-in lights. Lining-up, in the blackness of darkest Africa, was extremely difficult. The lack of a visual horizon often caused an induced oscillation in the yawing plane, because the aircraft tended to move from side to side as it approached. The pilot flew visually using outside references, while the co-pilot closely monitored the flying instruments and pattered the captain on the aircraft attitude. All the landings were successful—some being harder than others—but no aircraft was damaged to the extent that it could not fly out of Mavinga the same night.

In later stages of operation, a generator and mobile landing lights improved the situation, but initially these were not available. Beer and cold drink cans, half-filled with sand and soaked in paraffin, were placed at equal intervals alongside the runway. UNITA soldiers operated these cans and when the pilot requested the lights, the soldiers would light their cans.

This worked very well—for the first landing! Unfortunately, when the pilots applied reverse thrust, dust blew into the air, and the cans dispersed everywhere, to the disgust of the soldiers. The tins had to be retrieved, refilled, and repositioned for the next take-off. To alleviate this tedious task, the UNITA runway illuminators decided to modify the system. They tied the cans to shoulder-height sticks, which they could hold onto while the aircraft passed, thus preventing the frantic search after every landing. This evolutionary step seemed initially to solve the problem, but no R & D (Research and Development) was carried out on the new modification.

With the introduction of the new "UNITA Flare-path Illuminating System" (UFIS), the pilots started reporting severe cases of spatial disorientation and even vertigo when on final approach to land. After an in-depth investigation, the cause was established. Invariably, after the lights were illuminated, the pilot found his aircraft to be off centreline. They had to bank the aircraft to fly towards the centreline, and then apply opposite bank to stop the crossing movement. This is straightforward and happens on every approach to land—BUT—now put yourself in the position of the man holding the stick on the edge of the narrow runway!

After setting fire to his can, he looked up in the direction of the approaching aircraft. He saw the aircraft landing light and detected that instead of coming straight down the middle of the flare path it appeared to be heading directly towards him. This perception magnifies when you remember that there is no depth perception on lights at night. Holding onto his pole, he moved away from the runway, until he noticed the aircraft making the bank correction onto the centreline, where after he moved back to the edge of the runway. The soldiers on the other side of the runway were quite happy when the aircraft seemed to be heading towards the far side. However, when the pilot banked to get onto the centreline, it suddenly appeared that the aircraft was going to fly towards them. They in turn, holding their poles, also moved away from the runway. They returned to their original position when they could detect that the danger had passed.

The aircrew's spatial disorientation problem was induced by this "ebb and flow" of the moving flare path. The poles were then anchored firmly into the ground. This modification Mk3 remained in use until the arrival of the generator and mobile lights brought a vestige of civilization to that dark corner of Africa.

There was no doubt that Mavinga was the logistical key to the regional conflict in the entire south-eastern theatre of Angola. I am personally convinced that in global terms, Mavinga was far more important. Unlike most other observers, who considered our border war to be simply a regional tussle, I firmly believed that world issues were being contested.

The Angolan battles were primarily Russian inspired and planned. The Angolans followed Soviet military doctrine to the letter. Russian fighter policy stated that air operations must only take-place undercover of own radar systems. This was an excellent policy, but one the SAAF could not abide by, through lack of resources. However, I strongly believe that this was one of the reasons why Angolan fighters seldom participated on offensive missions against South African aircraft.

For years, Angolan radar coverage extended over the airspace of AFB Ondangwa, but still the Angolan Air Force never attacked this major South African air base. I believe the reason was that AFB Rundu, further to the east, was beyond Angolan radar cover, leaving them open to a counter attack. If the Angolans had succeeded in capturing Mavinga, radar installation there would have given them the coverage they required to stay within Soviet military policy; air attacks could then have been expected.

Under Soviet guidance, a radar chain was built to provide coverage of the South West African and South African northern borders, which extended from Angola, through Zambia, Botswana, Zimbabwe, and Moçambique. The only gap remaining was that around Mavinga. A study of these radars showed that in typical Russian fashion radar coverage extended southwards in the recommended saw-tooth manner, giving the redundancy desired by Russian staff manuals. Completion of this radar chain would have enabled Soviet expansionism to advance towards South Africa; South Africa was their ultimate goal.

Conventional weapons were necessary to oppose the mass of Russian supplied armaments that accompanied the Angolan brigades advancing on Mavinga. As a counter to the Russian D-30 artillery piece, South African-designed and built G5 and G6 155mm cannons were deployed. These magnificent guns outranged the enemy and delivered their fire with superb accuracy. During critical periods, the out-numbered South African forces relied heavily on these artillery pieces to maintain the balance of power. Continuous bombardments caused wear and tear on the weapons and servicing schedules had to be rigidly enforced.

An urgent appeal from the front informed us that a small component in a G5 breech block mechanism needed replacing. This delicate operation could not be performed at the front. Only someone with factory experience could make the necessary precise adjustments. Not wanting to withdraw the gun from the frontline, an expert from the factory in Pretoria was dispatched in all haste. This poor chap received his instructions when he returned to his workbench from lunch. He had time to collect his toolbag, the required component, and an overnight case before speeding off to AFB Waterkloof. At the huge air base, he rushed out to a C130 whose propellers were already spinning. Moments later this excited civilian found himself on the long haul to AFB Rundu in South West Africa.

It was already dark when the freighter landed. As soon as the engines stopped, the man, clutching his toolbag, G5 component, and overnight case, walked across the hardstanding to a Puma helicopter. The rotors were turning and engine noise made conversation difficult. However, his guide did manage to give him the instruction: 'Make sure you get out on the third landing,' before he strapped in to a canvas seat and the chopper lifted off.

A few short hours previously, he had been going about his daily business in the serenity of peacetime Pretoria. Now he was crossing the border in a darkened helicopter filled with fully armed, fighting men. Some of the soldiers offloaded at Mavinga on the first landing within half a minute. At this time, the helicopter answered a request to urgently lift a seriously wounded soldier. Casualty evacuation took precedence over everything else, so the chopper re-routed. At the next stop, the second landing, a medical doctor climbed aboard before the helicopter set heading for the frontline. At the third landing, stretcher-bearers, ready to load the patient, waited while a bewildered passenger dressed in civilian clothing alighted. No one had informed the unfortunate man about the change of route!

All these activities occurred in almost complete darkness; the enemy's proximity precluded the use of illumination. Everyone apart from the civilian was dressed in camouflage, their faces covered in "black is beautiful", and they were heavily armed. Only after the chopper had disappeared into the night did the man discover to his horror that he had alighted in the wrong place. He was not at the artillery deployments, but he was now with the infantry who were face to face with the enemy on the frontline! He spent a most uncomfortable and anxious 24 hours dodging bullets and explosions, waiting for the following night's helicopter to arrive to rectify the problem!

It was during these battles that we deployed a detachment of Remotely Piloted Vehicles (RPVs) to assist in the identification of suitable targets as the Angolan brigades advanced through the dense bush. Despite overhead foliage, tanks and armoured vehicle tracks were easily identified. The Angolans placed these intelligence-gathering vehicles at the top of their list of targets to destroy. Using SA-8 missiles, they achieved success, shooting down three of the unmanned aircraft.

Two days after the first RPV was destroyed, a signal arrived in our headquarters from UNITA. Their message was one of deep sorrow, expressing their grief at the event that they had witnessed. They heard the SA-8 explode and saw the aircraft fall to earth. After a lengthy search, they found the wreckage. They then spent two days trying to find the pilot without success. We thanked them for their efforts and concern and explained that fortunately, these aircraft were unmanned.

A number of years earlier we deployed the system at Xangongo Airfield to carry out surveillance of my town, Cahama. It was during this deployment that we discovered for the first time that mobile SA-8 batteries had entered our war. I can vividly recall watching video footage taken from the RPV while it was on a pass near the town. The drone received the attention of a salvo of three SA-8 missiles. Fortunately, all three missed by the narrowest of margins. Everybody in the room automatically ducked as the video showed the missiles flashing past the seeker dome. This intelligence led us to our abortive attempt to capture an SA-8 vehicle during Operation Askari.

The main Angolan thrust came from the town of Cuito Cuanavale, across the bridge spanning the Cuito River just east of the town. This bridge, the only structure capable of supporting armoured vehicles, was vital for the logistical back up for the advance. The South Africans also noticed the importance of the bridge. An audacious plan called for a team of reconnaissance force commandos to be flown in to a safe area about 40 kilometres north of Cuito. This happened at night without compromising the team. At last light, the following evening, the combat team entered the water and after a combination of swimming and rowing reached the bridge about five hours later.

The placing of demolition charges did not proceed without problems. The low state of the river and the unexpected alert state of the bridge guards combined to compromise the swimmers. A firefight ensued; the enemy used small arms and hand-grenades to drive off the team, but not before the charges had been set. Withdrawing down the river, the team was pursued and fired at, but in the ritual of the special force commandos, this was all in the day's work!

Enter Murphy—this time in the guise of prehistoric crocodiles! Having had their slumbers rudely disturbed by grenade explosions in the water, they were understandably upset by this unusual invasion of their privacy. They extracted their vengeance on the rapidly fleeing swimmers. They bit frogmen's flippers, and in the worst case, a knife fight ensued between a scuba-breathing soldier and his three-metre assailant.

Despite gunshot wounds, hot pursuit from enemy soldiers, and crocodile bites, the team managed to evade their pursuers temporarily. Carrying their equipment and assisting their injured, they had a further 20 kilometres to trek through the bush before reaching the designated helicopter rendezvous point. Re-enter Murphy, this time in the form of thunderstorms during the dry winter months!

Flying in to fetch the swimmers at 150 feet agl, the chopper pilots encountered severe thunderstorms with headwinds that reduced their ground speed from 120 to 45 knots. Running out of fuel, they had no option but to return to Rundu. The pick-up was rescheduled for the following evening; enemy MiGs precluded a daylight rescue attempt.

The enemy's persistence now aggravated this pick-up attempt. Using Mi8 and Mi24 helicopters, they kept on the track of the commandos by leap-frogging pursuit troops. The commandos had to vacate the pre-planned rendezvous point. It was very difficult for the commandos to provide a grid reference for a rendezvous because they had been running through thick bush. Fortunately, the runners heard the sound of Puma engines in the distance and illuminated an Instant Light, which the chopper crews saw and homed on to. As the helicopters approached, the soldiers fired a pencil flare parallel to the ground to indicate a landing zone. They did not fire it up into the air because of the Angolan's close proximity. After a brief touchdown, the helicopters whisked the grateful commandos into the air and onto their way home.

Far away to the west, another combined force operation was underway. This time a team of reconnaissance force commandos deployed deep into the south-western corner of Angola. Okangwati was the obvious place from which to run the operation, a military base in remote northern Kaokoland. Fixed-wing aircraft could use the sand runway and there was a strategic fuel store of Avtur (helicopter fuel) and Avgas (aviation fuel for piston-engined aircraft).

The operation was planned in Oshakati, but the tactical force of three Puma helicopters and a Bosbok fixed-wing light reconnaissance aircraft was under command of an air force major. Two choppers could perform the required task while the third was available as back up. The Bosbok would fly in a holding pattern at 10 000 feet over the Cunene River, the border between South West Africa and Angola, to act as the Telstar (airborne radio relay station). Penetration would occur at low level below Angolan radar cover. VHF radio range is limited to line of sight only, hence the necessity of a radio relay facility. Most clandestine missions were flown in radio silence, but a back up was required in an emergency.

The selected route went northwest to the Marienflüss,and then north across the Cunene River, into Angola. The choppers inserted the commandos at last light and recovered them in the dark. The flying conditions were typical of those associated with the Inter-Tropical Convergence Zone (ITCZ)—the area between the tropics of Cancer and Capricorn, where the trade winds from both hemispheres converge. This convergence causes huge upward development and results in a line of cumulus-nimbus clouds extending roughly west to east over thousands of miles. Airline passengers travelling between South Africa and Europe are often woken and instructed to fasten their seat belts somewhere over mid-Africa. This is invariably caused by conditions in the ITCZ.

The weather did not hamper the choppers en-route, because they flew below the cloud base, necessitating only a few minor deviations from the planned track to avoid the heaviest rain showers. After the successful insertion, the choppers returned. The choppers maintained radio silence, but every 20 minutes the leader broadcasted a quick "Ops normal" call on VHF radio. The Telstar Bosbok relayed the call so that the Command Post could keep track of the operation's progress. The post also gave an area to search if an emergency arose.

The Bosbok, flown by a young pilot on his first bush tour, climbed to 10 000 feet and orbited in its holding pattern. Unfortunately, the ITCZ weather seriously affected the light aircraft at this height. The moisture content of the cloud mass was high and the freezing level had dropped to around 8 000 feet. Icing on the aerials degraded the reception and transmission power of the radio, making it difficult for the pilot to hear the calls from the choppers and to transmit them to the Command Post. In addition, the piston-engine aircraft was very susceptible to carburetor icing. Engine manufacturers know this and all similar aircraft are fitted with a carburetor de-icing facility. The drawback of using "carb heat", however, is that the fuel consumption is greatly increased.

Crossing the Cunene River back into South West Africa, the leader of the two Pumas realized that the weather had deteriorated while they were away. Low cloud completely socked in Okangwati and they could not return; they decided to land in the flat, sandy expanse of the Marienflüss and overnight there. Apart from the geological wonder of the Flüss, the rest of Kaokoland closely resembles the face of the moon. Rugged mountains, steep-sided valleys, and the absence of any vegetation, make it one of the most inhospitable areas in the world.

Approaching to land, the Puma leader called up the young Bosbok pilot who was still circling in his holding pattern and suggested he divert to Opuwa for the night. After a slight delay, the young pilot called back, asking, 'Where is Opuwa?' After receiving the explanation and finding Opuwa on his map, the youngster realized, to his horror, that because of the increased fuel consumption while using carb heat, he did not have enough fuel to reach the diversion field.

The Puma leader remembered seeing the outline of a sand runway marked with old petrol drums, which had been laid out in the Marienflüss many years before, and he suggested this as the only alternative to the Bosbok pilot. He described the area: high mountains to the east and west, and the valley ran south to north. He determined the height of the valley floor and passed the altimeter setting to the Bosbok pilot.

While he was talking, both choppers, still airborne, were air taxiing across the valley trying to find the runway in their landing lights. Normally a runway is easy to find. In the Flüss, however, an infrequently used sand runway is the same colour as the valley floor. At night, under the illumination of the aircraft's landing lights, the search was extra hard. Finally, they spotted the windsock and using it as reference, they eventually located the runway.

The Bosbok pilot, following the instructions given by the Puma leader, performed a spiral descent out of the clouds. On breaking through the base, he spotted the helicopter landing lights, which orientated him in the valley. The two choppers employed a technique utilized by ground vehicles assisting light aircraft landing on bush strips. They hovered on either side of the runway threshold, with their landing lights pointing at 45° angles in the landing direction. The Bosbok pilot made his approach between the two helicopters and landed safely. The two Pumas followed. The Puma crews' quick thinking demonstrated the South African knack of adapting in the classic *'n Boer maak 'n plan* tradition.

Chapter 22

AFCP, Pretoria

After a long career in the military, I should have recognized the signs! As a family, we were very happily settled in Windhoek. We lived in a nice house; we loved the town and the country; the schools were excellent; we had made many good friends; I loved my job; and there were definite indications that a conclusion to the war was in sight. This happy state of affairs is an anathema to military career planners. So, in January 1988, they posted me back to SAAF Headquarters in Pretoria.

My new post was as SSO OPS (Plan) in the Air Force Command Post. It was a natural progression from my previous post in Windhoek, only this time the range of responsibility covered all air force operations, so I was delighted. We moved into our own home for only the second time in 20 years—a pleasurable change from moving in to rented accommodation!

The 23-year-long border war reached a stalemate. The Angolans, and their Cuban helpers and Russian advisors, retreated to the Cuito River. They experienced a terrible lose of men and equipment. Our Intelligence estimated that they lost between 4 000 and 6 000 men, dead and wounded. Fidel Castro, addressing his parliament in Havana, put the figure at between 6 000 and 8 000. He had General Ochoa, the Cuban commander in Africa, executed for this humiliation. Cuban propaganda mentioned an involvement with drugs as their cover story!

The battlefield situation remained static until late March. South African logistic lines were now long and tenuous and the theatre was at the extremity of air support range. The Angolan Air Force controlled the air over the battlefield, and their base was at Menonque, only nine minutes flying time away. Their radar coverage extended from ground level upwards. To reach the area, SAAF Mirages flew for 43 minutes. Little combat fuel was available should they be jumped by MiG23s patrolling the area. SAAF radar, positioned in Rundu, could only see aircraft operating above 24 000 feet, making the situation far from perfect for SAAF operations. It was a situation akin to playing with a lion's testicles!

Despite all the disadvantages, Mirage F1AZ aircraft still pounded enemy positions around the clock, with little intervention from the MiGs. A SAAF Mirage F1CZ interceptor did take a hit from a MiG23-launched AAM-8. The pilot managed to fly his badly shot aircraft back to Rundu, where it crashed on landing. The aircraft had lost hydraulic pressure to the brakes and the braking parachute had been shot off; the pilot could not stop it on the runway.

The Cubans launched a powerful thrust in the southwest of Angola in an attempt to relieve pressure on the stalemate. They made threatening moves towards the South West African border in an attempt to draw South African forces away from Cuito. A small South African battle group and a show of force by the SAAF in the west was sufficient to persuade the Cubans to abandon any further adventures. Castro later proclaimed this thrust a glorious victory for the forces of liberation and Communism, using Communist propagandist terms and flamboyant gestures. However, they never came within 40 kilometres of the border. If they had had enough bravado to do so, I am convinced they would have suffered a similar fate to all the other "advances" made from Angolan soil during the previous 23 years—but of course, that is just my opinion.

After all those years of bloodshed and toil, our political masters finally succeeded in getting their act together and seriously negotiating a peace agreement. The Russian dream for African domination had failed. One of the tenets of Communist expansion, espoused by both Russian and Chinese camps, was based on their slogan, 'Where you strike butter, go right through. Where you strike steel, withdraw!' Their bid to foment revolutionary change in Africa had failed. In Angola, as in Afghanistan, they had struck steel. The last conventional battle around Cuito Cuanavale, which ended early in 1988, had been their final throw of the dice in the cold war. Within a year, the hated Berlin Wall fell. The Russian economy was in tatters and the citizens were ready for a change in ideology. I believe that, but for our effort and determination in South West Africa and Angola, the world might well have been very different today.

By mid-1988, South African forces finally withdrew from Angola. Shortly afterwards, South West Africa received her independence and her name changed to Namibia. A feature of African politics is the insistence on spending large sums of much needed money on name changing! Imagine Piccadilly Circus becoming Blair's Roundabout or Times Square becoming Bush's Block! Tradition, heritage, and history have little significance in this part of the world.

In terms of United Nations Resolution 435, UNTAG, a composite military force, arrived to oversee the transition from South West Africa to Namibia. The British component was a highly professional unit from the Royal Corp of Signals. Literally within minutes of deploying from the transport aircraft in Windhoek, they had set up mobile communications from their Land Rovers. We were delighted, because communications in that vast territory had always been a headache. Congratulating them on their rapid response, we asked them to assist us in contacting the Kenyan force that had deployed a few days earlier. 'Sorry, Sir, we don't speak to them, we only speak to London,' was the surprising answer. Within the United Nations organization, insularity was the common feature!

Brigadier Oosthuizen, the chief of army logistics, accompanied a team of Australian army officers on their orientation visit to all the bases bordering Angola. During the long flight to Mpacha, the brigadier told the Aussies about SAAF City, the renowned air force pub in Katima Mulilo, and he promised them a visit. With temperatures approaching 40°C, they welcomed the suggestion. The brigadier warned them about the pub's special Ströh Rum, liquor with an exceptionally high proof rating. Perhaps that was like waving a red rag at a bull!

The pub rang to the usual chorus of 'Gedday, Mate,' as the group entered. The host customarily ordered the first round. Oosie had a pronounced tic in his eye, which, once you knew him, was easily disregarded. However, his constant winking usually perplexed newcomers. The SAAF sergeant barman, a little overwhelmed by the sudden influx of high-ranking officers, listened attentively as Brigadier Oosthuizen ordered six Ströh rums. He had never met the brigadier before, so he never knew about the man's affliction. During the ordering, Oosie explained how the Australian visitors had been looking forward to tasting Ströh rum. During the entire conversation, the brigadier continually winked at the barman.

One can not blame the sergeant for using his initiative. He knew that Australians tend towards brashness, so he naturally assumed that Brigadier Oosthuizen wanted to show them a thing or two! He produced six tumblers of the milky looking liquor and was astounded when, after a quick, 'Cheers, Mate,' five empty glasses were placed back on the table. Oosie sensibly sipped at his glass.

Within a minute, their foreheads beaded with sweat, their eyes began to water, and their speech became slurred. With a quick, 'Feeling a bit doggo, Mate,' they disappeared to their beds. The following morning they appeared at the breakfast table, tottering in on wobbly legs. One by one they said, 'No tucker for me, Mate, just a glass of water.' One sip of the cool liquid renewed the fire in their bellies and, to put it candidly, they were pissed again! In fact, they completed the three-day trip in a haze of semi-consciousness. Everywhere they stopped, they pleaded for water to sate their raging thirsts.

The cessation of hostilities came as a welcome change. The air force used the opportunity to catch up on all the modification and rectification programmes that had taken a backseat during the fighting. Ironically, many of these modifications were to enable our aircraft to handle the increasingly sophisticated threat that had faced us in Angola. They were incorporated "after the horse had bolted"! Long overdue career development courses became fashionable and I was appointed to attend the Senior Joint Staff Course.

The most beneficial part of this course for me was the chance to meet and get to know my counterparts in the other services. Joint operations are so easy when you work amongst friends. Only lecturers of the highest quality participated and it was usually a pleasure to listen to them expound their views—but not all! One morning, we attended a double period of labour relations, or work-study, or some equally dull subject, presented by an appalling professor. Having rapidly lost interest, I looked around for other possibilities and my gaze fell on the bald pate of Colonel Spike Conradie, seated in the tier below and in front of me.

Pretending that I had a bad cold, I started sniffling and sneezing loud enough for Spike to hear. Then, with a flourish, I coughed into my handkerchief, and depressed the button on my spectacle cleaning spray at the same time. This fine mist descended gently onto the shiny bald head in front of me. The more uncomfortable he became, the more I coughed and sprayed. By the end of the second period, Spike was sitting on the edge of his seat leaning his body forward to get his head as far from me as possible. Only later, after suffering severe discomfort, did I show him the spray.

The SAAF shifted their emphasis from war to more beneficial humanitarian operations. President De Klerk, realizing that dialogue is always better than confrontation, started negotiations with Nelson Mandela, even while that famous man was still incarcerated. This glimmer of light in the tunnel soon became the ray of hope to most South Africans that the political impasse of the past would soon normalize. Unfortunately, no baby is born without a fair amount of pain and these trials and tribulations still awaited us.

In the meantime, the SAAF provided assistance to neighbouring countries. Mount Mlanje, near Blantyre in Malawi, started to collapse from the effects of continual tropical rain. Huge mudslides brought down thousands of tons of earth and rubble all the way round the conical shaped peak. People living on the lower slopes evacuated their villages. All forms of communications were severed, and the road, the logistical lifeline for thousands of people, was destroyed in dozens of places.

We flew up to make a survey of the damage, and then we sent in a team of helicopters and army engineers with earth moving equipment. We were the first nation to supply some sort of aid in Malawi's time of need.

A short time later, I visited Kinshasa in Zaire, this time to assess what assistance South Africa could offer in an attempt to clear mines. A group of parachute battalion troops later flew in as advisors to train the Zaire Defence Force in this hazardous task. The South African Navy also performed a mammoth operation clearing the shipping ports trying to get them back into working order.

Then came our erstwhile enemy Angola's turn. Their government decided to register the entire population in order to hold "democratic" elections. At the behest of the United Nations mission in Luanda, South Africa once again offered help. I flew up to Luanda to find out from the UN officials what help they required. The SAAF deployed a ground team to support a large force of South African helicopters and fixed-wing Cessna Caravan aircraft. Their task was to fly in registration officials to all corners of Angola to enable these people to complete the enormous task.

The task was not without difficulty and danger. Much of the country was still under UNITA control and although there was supposed to be a truce in the civil war, many troops were still gun-happy. The MPLA government chose the priority of each registered centre, and they made sure that MPLA strongholds were top of the list. The task was so successful that after 700 flying hours, we were able to start flying to UNITA controlled areas. Now our troubles really started in earnest. I believe the MPLA did not want their likely opposition to receive the same opportunities to register and we found obstacle after obstacle in our way.

I was summoned peremptorily to the office of a MPLA minister. On arrival at the stipulated time, I was made to wait the stipulated hour and 15 minutes as laid down in the manual of non-elected government officials. Finally, he used the opportunity to berate, scold, and verbally abuse me; the SAAF team operating in "his" country; South Africa; and then, using the "hotgun" technique, included all western, capitalistic countries. The registration of the MPLA parts of the country was complete and now suddenly it was abhorrent to this chap that our helicopters flew in the camouflage livery the Angolans had hated during the war. When he finally tired of the game, I was asked to leave "his" office and withdraw the SAAF team from "his" country, which we did. Ten years later there is still little democratic progress in that unfortunate land, so perhaps this gentleman saved us further fruitless expense.

I flew up to Nairobi, Kenya to assess once again if South African assistance could fly in to aid victims of the terrible genocide in Rwanda and Burundi. This visit included a landing at Mwanza in Tanzania to study the state of the airport facilities and runway to see if they could accept SAAF C130 and B707 aircraft.

I visited Kenya in the 1960s while serving in the Fleet Air Arm and was very impressed by that lovely country. I enjoyed Mombasa and the beautiful beaches along the coast. The overnight train trip between Mombasa and Nairobi remains one of my treasured memories, especially waking up in the morning as the train wound its way through the Nairobi National Park. Nairobi was delightful with its broad streets and superb hotels, and it was an ideal centre from where to visit the Great Rift Valley. It was Africa at its most magnificent.

For 30 years, I cherished the memories of gentle, smiling people, safe cities and towns, and wild animals roaming free through panoramas of unspoilt African bush. Thirty years had wreaked huge changes. Politics had not changed the landscape, which was still beautiful, but it had destroyed the wonderful feel of Africa. Most of the vast animal herds were gone, as were the smiling people. A withdrawn and sullen appearance replaced the expected smile and open-handed wave. Walking in the streets was a discomforting experience. Nairobi had lost its charm and had begun to take on the run-down, neglected appearance that was becoming common in Africa.

I had never visited Kinshasa or Luanda before, so I had no means of comparing them to how they had been in the past, but both were in terrible condition. Kinshasa must have been a magnificent city. It was built on the banks of the enormous Congo River, offering superb vistas of Brazzaville on the opposite bank. Broad streets and large European-type buildings lined the centre of the town. Huge mansions stood side by side along the riverbank. Unfortunately, not one lick of paint had been applied during all the years since the Belgians had departed. In the tropics, white-painted buildings soon lose their appeal if they are not properly maintained. The roads were potholed, making driving an interesting and perilous experience.

The ubiquitous Toyota minibuses plied a busy trade; public transport seemed non-existent. Each little bus had had the sliding door removed to allow the transport of the absolute maximum number of bodies. Drivers employed "pusher-inners" who hung precariously outside the door. At each stop, this lad would use his foot to squeeze extra fare-payers into the interior of the cab. I noticed that grease coated the rear-view mirror supporting struts on the sides of larger vehicles (those that still had them). I was reliably informed that this was to discourage unwelcome hitchhikers.

Kinshasa Airport was a sight to behold! Aircraft of all types covered the hardstanding and grass verges. It seemed that aircraft flew until they broke down. These hulks were then pushed to the edge of the parking area. With the next installment of foreign aid, they would purchase new aircraft as replacements, until the same fate befell them. There were French-built Caravelles, Russian Antonovs and Tupolevs, British Viscounts and Britannias, and early model American Boeing-707s, none of them airworthy. In the military hangar were C130s and Mirage IIIs, all in the same condition.

They did have a small number of serviceable piston-engined SIAI-Marchetti SF260 training aircraft. I heard the engines firing into life and watched as two aircraft taxied out, one behind the other. I was keen to see them fly, but I was disappointed on that score. They stopped at a refuelling point and topped up their tanks. Another start-up sequence followed, they taxied back to the original dispersal, stopped, and the pilots climbed out and walked away. Apparently, this was a daily routine. Once the aircraft returned to the hangar, the fuel tanks were tapped, and the fuel bled into cans. They sold the fuel to the local motor industry to supplement the air force members' meager pay.

Luanda International Airport was much the same, except here, nearly all the derelict aircraft were of Russian manufacture. Among the airliners and freighters stood a number of MiG21s, as well as Mi8 and Mi24 military helicopters. Like Kinshasa, Luanda must have been a beautiful city. Situated around a huge bay, it provides magnificent sunset views over the Atlantic Ocean. An ancient Portuguese fort dominated the southern end of the town. Here the Angolans proudly displayed the wreckage of South African aircraft shot down during the war, alongside some captured vehicles. Along the front, one service station stood out like a beacon from all the others—it had been recently painted!

Luanda had stunning buildings, many of them quite tall. The upper stories must have had phenomenal views, but they were not sort after as places in which to work or live—the lifts had not worked since the Portuguese left hurriedly in 1975! Sewage ran in streams across the main roads, and driving rules and regulations appeared non-existent. Clearing passport control, filing flight plans, getting aircraft refuelled could only be achieved after the number of notes, preferably green and marked with $ signs, had been pocketed.

Another interesting similarity existed between these two, once beautiful, cities. Both had huge structures, reaching half way to the sky, apparently celebrating or commemorating the glories and ideologies of Communism. I used the word apparently because both of them were unfinished. The cost of both monuments must have been enormous. These countries desperately needed to use available resources on projects that were more beneficial.

Driving carefully down to a beachfront viewpoint, someone in our vehicle asked, 'I wonder if Johannesburg will be like this in 20 years time?' We all laughed then, but times have changed and some portions of Johannesburg strongly resemble the decay I saw in those African capitals. As I write, the lovely land of Zimbabwe may have felt the hammering of the final nail. By allowing Mad Mugs another term as president, the citizens have set that country into an ever-increasing downhill spiral.

I am an African, born, bred and raised on the highveld of South Africa. I have always been proud of my country and my continent. As part of my marriage proposal to June, I explained that on the completion of my service in the Royal Navy I wanted to return to South Africa. Very fortunately, she agreed! As I write these derogatory statements about Africa, I have the uncomfortable feeling of being a turncoat—like telling tales out of school. Sadly, that is how I saw and experienced them and my visions for the future of this continent have lost the rosy glow of optimism.

During the years of isolation, South Africa built up strong ties with Taiwan. June and I accompanied General Wen Chi Lin, chief of the Taiwanese Air Force, on a week long visit around South Africa. Among the memorable moments was a flight in an Oryx helicopter around the lovely Cape peninsula followed by a landing on top of Table Mountain. After touching down gently, within about 40 metres from the precipitous face of the mountain, I heard General Lin say in awe, 'Now we have landed on the moon!' Although these visits were hard work, they were superb and every arrangement and function was in the five-star bracket.

General van Loggerenberg, then chief of the SAAF, requested (Anglo Saxon for "told") that I extract and compile a document detailing the "Lessons Learnt" during our long border war. It took a year of research and writing, but what an interesting job it turned out to be! I wrote it in an abbreviated book form and titled it *From Fledgling to Eagle*, because it documented how the SAAF had expanded and developed from a peacetime air force to an operational, efficient arm of the service.

After a long hard grind, I completed it shortly before taking Christmas leave. Needing something to occupy the lazy days at home, I decided to read. The war in the North African desert has always appealed to me, mainly because of the fall of Tobruk where my father was taken prisoner of war. I came across the autobiography of General Montgomery and decided to read just the section that dealt with the desert war. However, once I commenced reading I became increasingly engrossed in the book. Because the book belonged to me, I picked up a pencil and started marking important statements, in a chapter entitled "My Doctrine of Command". Remember that in his career Monty had led everything from a section, platoon, company, and regiment to divisions, corps and armies. I marked lessons that he had learnt from his years in operations, and they were identical to those that I had just spent a long, hard year trying to extract. If only I, and I think I can safely add we, bothered to read, perhaps the same mistakes in war would not reoccur so regularly.

There are few things more alarming than a middle-of-the-night telephone call. The strident tone sounds louder than normal, more urgent, and chillingly ominous. Everyone, who has raised a family, knows how the rude awakening of a night call induces anxiety and images of potential disasters. My call came on Saturday, 3 August 1991.

Two days earlier, I received promotion to brigadier and appointed officer commanding of the air force Command Post in Pretoria. A decision had been made to split the functions of the director of operations (D OPS) and to leave him to deal with staff functions, while the Command Post would have the sole responsibility for carrying out actual operations. My suitability for the post was about to be tested!

All the resources in the entire inventory of the air force could be utilized for operations, and the Command Post had top priority whenever personnel, aircraft, or equipment was needed. Apart from normal air force or interservice operations, the Command Post was also responsible for handling any emergency that arose. Understandably, the Command Post was staffed around the clock, year in and year out, to handle these requirements. My mid-night caller turned out to be the senior duty officer, Commandant Dawid van Rensburg.

Dawid was a very competent and conscientious young officer and this fact registered on my sleep-befuddled brain—he would not phone me unless there was a serious problem. He apologized for waking me and then told me that we had a ship in trouble off the coast. I can remember thinking to myself that he was probably going to tell me that the damn thing was sinking, and those were precisely his next words. Problems at sea, around the South African coast, were common and our maritime personnel at Silvermine in the Cape were geared to assist wherever possible. Under normal circumstances, they performed this duty and then informed headquarters the next day. Dawie added that the sinking ship was an ocean liner with 600 people on board. The adrenaline reaction I experienced was second only to the call, 'Missile at 7 o'clock closing,' over a target in Angola.

I told Dawie to call out all the duty helicopter crews and expect me at work in 15 minutes. Headquarters was 17 kilometres from my home and I still had to dress, but I made it with a few minutes to spare.

During the high-speed dash into Pretoria, I tried to anticipate all that would be required to assist in a rescue at sea. Dozens of thoughts flood through your brain. Only once you have the details of the nature of the emergency can you make any worthwhile decisions.

Dawid briefed me on what had occurred and what actions had been taken up to that point. At 22h30 that Saturday evening, the port captain at East London picked up the distress call of the MV *Oceanos*. This call was relayed to all the maritime rescue agencies, including Southern Air Force Command Post at Silvermine. This establishment, nestled in the hills behind Muizenberg and overlooking Tokai, Constantia, and the Cape Flats, was the unit whose prime task was to look after the maritime requirements of the air force. Brigadier Theo de Munnink, a navigator with vast experience in bush war and maritime operations, was the commanding officer who coordinated all maritime search and rescue activities in which the air force might become involved. His Command Post assumed responsibility for initiating the rescue attempt.

The duty staff called in Colonel George Hallowes (SSO OPS), who conducted activities throughout the rest of the night. Col Hallowes, known perversely as "Tiny" because of his towering six-foot plus stature, was also an officer with tremendous knowledge and experience in the maritime scenario. His first action had been to activate the two standby Puma helicopters from 30 Squadron at AFB Ysterplaat in Cape Town.

As the emergency progressed, he realized that the situation was very serious indeed and that resources greater than he had at his disposal were needed to cope. He notified the Command Post in Pretoria and requested assistance; hence, my midnight phone call.

The critical problem facing rescue services, during the initial stages of any emergency, is the lack of accurate information on which to start formulating a rescue plan. This was the situation in the small hours of that night. We knew that the MV *Oceanos* sailed from East London earlier that day, bound for Durban, with 581 souls on board. The ship encountered bad weather and was in difficulties. This lack of information became the priority task whilst activating emergency personnel.

Emergencies seldom occur on weekdays during normal working hours and immediately outside general hospitals or major airports! It is the very nature of an emergency to occur away from any helpful infrastructure, outside of working hours—thus aggravating the task of gathering a suitable rescue team—and away from any reliable form of communication. This was precisely the scenario when the *Oceanos* transmitted its SOS at 22h30 that evening.

If a theoretical exercise was carried out to select the most remote area along the entire 1 700 kilometre coastline between Cape Town and Durban, the most likely spot would be the Transkeian coast, between The Haven and Coffee Bay. Both little hamlets were accessible from Umtata, about 90 kilometres to the northwest, on single-track road renown for its poor condition. The village hotels only opened during the holiday seasons. The majority of dwellings in the vicinity were holiday homes closed up and sealed against the winter elements. Overhead mounted telephone cables connected the isolated communities with the outside world. These cables were susceptible to the vagaries of the weather.

Residents along South Africa's southern coastline understand why Sir Francis Drake's "Fairest Cape in all the world" was also dubbed the "Cape of Storms" by seafarers who navigated these waters during winter. On Friday, 2 August, a severe winter storm buffeted the Cape. An intense cold front brought the storm up from the southern Atlantic Ocean. Tremendous seas and high winds made shipping difficult all along the coast. This particular cold front moved up the coastline in a northeasterly direction and reached the East London area at noon on the Saturday.

East of East London, the predominantly southern coastline curves up towards the northeast. This curve has a significant effect on the warm Moçambique current that flows down the East Coast of South Africa. The curve, like the upper surface of an aircraft's wing, creates a venturi effect. The compression of the current around the curve increases the speed of the flow. Off the Transkeian coast, this current increases up to a very strong six knots. This flow, opposing the gale force southwesterly winds moving up the coast, causes the development of huge swells. An additional hazard was the possibility of these swells synchronizing, and causing the freak waves for which this particular coastline is notorious. Lloyds of London, the maritime insurers, add additional premiums on vessels passing through these waters for this very reason.

During the afternoon and evening, this severe front passed through the disaster area from southwest to northeast, accompanied by frontal cloud and rainsqualls. Gale force southwesterly winds replaced this frontal system, blowing between 90 and 110 kilometres per hour. At the height of the storm, the opposing natural forces caused the development of 10 to 12 metre swells. The decision to sail the *Oceanos* from East London into these conditions at the height of the storm was to prove critical.

This stretch of water is dotted with mysterious disappearances of ships and yachts. A notable incident was the disappearance of the liner *Waratah* in 1909. The incident occurred in broad daylight with other ships on passage ahead and behind the *Waratah*, but no trace of the ship or of the 211 people onboard was found. Encounters with freak waves and unaccountably deep troughs have caused considerable damage to shipping over the years, leading to this stretch of sea acquiring a reputation akin to the notorious Bermuda Triangle.

The *Oceanos* transmitted her initial emergency call around 22h30 on the Saturday evening. This call, picked up in East London, was routed routinely to all emergency service agents. This is a common occurrence, as it is a recognized procedure for any vessel, or aircraft, experiencing problems of any nature, to notify controlling agencies. The emergency services can then start preparations in case the message upgrades to a distress call. The appropriate services are then activated.

Shortly before midnight, the *Oceanos* crew transmitted the SOS, the international distress call, indicating that they had lost control and the ship was in imminent danger of foundering. They gave the ship's position, which was approximately five kilometres off the coast. The ship had lost steerage way, was listing to starboard, and the gale-force winds were drifting it towards the rugged, rocky coastline.

The main characteristic that separates the air force from the rest of the defence force is one of speed. The ability of an aircraft to reach the scene of an emergency quickly has made the air force the prime emergency service. Command and control of these aircraft has to be in "real-time" for two main reasons, speed of reaction and the problem of fuel. To cope with maritime emergencies, the air force, in 1991, based aircraft at Air Force Base (AFB) Ysterplaat in Cape Town and AFB Durban. Defence cuts and shrinking budgets forced the closure of AFB Port Elizabeth in 1990, significantly reducing reaction times to emergencies between Cape Town and Durban.

At each base, two Puma helicopters and crews were on standby duty every night of the year. The frequency of maritime and mountain rescues, veld and forest fires, and motor accidents necessitated this requirement. Various fixed-wing aeroplanes were also available for casualty and medical rescues.

Tiny Hallowes and his staff, on receipt of the SOS, called out both Pumas at Ysterplaat and Durban and tasked the crews to make all haste towards the scene. My previous experience in the Royal Navy told me that four helicopters would be insufficient for the task. I then ordered the two standby Pumas from 19 Squadron at AFB Swartkop, outside Pretoria, to head to the scene. The Swartkop helicopters responded regularly to inland accidents and rescues, but they had never been tasked to go to sea before! Captain Anton Botha, one of the pilots, called me on the telephone before he took off to ensure I wasn't joking! When I confirmed my seriousness, he said that the largest stretch of water he had ever flown over was Hartebeespoort Dam, but he would give it a go. Maritime helicopter operations require specialized training. Hovering over the sea, without stationary references, is not the easiest task in the world. However, realizing the need of those on board the endangered ship, I told Anton to go.

The acute problem facing us all was still lack of on-scene knowledge. We therefore tasked a C160 Transall from AFB Waterkloof, near Pretoria, to fly to the scene to act as the initial on-scene commander and to relay real-time messages to the various headquarters. Rationalization, international sanctions, and boycotts affected the SAAF's capability. AFB Port Elizabeth was closed, and the long-range maritime Shackletons were withdrawn from service, hence the tasking of the Transall transport aircraft. A crew had to be found in the early hours of Sunday morning and the aircraft prepared for an over-water flight. Around 04h00, this aircraft lifted off and shortly after 05h00 it started relaying information from the scene.

During the hectic activities in the Command Post hundreds of telephone calls were made and received. One of my early calls was to Navy Headquarters in Pretoria, where I spoke to Captain Piet Potgieter, their officer in charge of operations. He and I are good friends and as such discussed the problem facing us. He told me that the navy had three strike-craft available in Durban, and they had immediate sailing orders to proceed to the scene to offer assistance.

I have always admired that decision. A strike-craft is only 62 metres long; it has a tonnage of 430 tons, and it is manned by seven officers and 40 ratings. The navy ordered three of these tiny vessels to sail into the same atrocious conditions that had just claimed an ocean liner. A brave decision made in headquarters by personnel who well understood the horrendous conditions that could prevail onboard the ships.

The next problem was one of medical care for possible survivors. The duty officer at the South African Medical Services (SAMS) Headquarters in Centurion told me that five medics were available in Port Elizabeth and four more in East London. We arranged for the helicopters transiting from Ysterplaat to pick these medics up en-route. Nevertheless, this small group would be insufficient if the ship foundered. I explained the problem to their duty officer and told him that a C130 Hercules would take-off from AFB Waterkloof at 08h00 bound for Umtata. It would be available for medical personnel and equipment.

As mentioned earlier, an aircraft has unique characteristics, one of which, unfortunately, is that when it arrives at its destination it is usually out of fuel! This was the next problem we had to grapple with. We tasked the Durban Pumas, the closest to the scene, to take drums of Avtur (Jet fuel) in the passenger cabin, so that the rescue could get underway. The nearest available fuel was stored at Umtata Airfield, but this was also a problem.

In 1991, Transkei was an independent country ruled by General Bantu Holomisa. Relations between South Africa and Transkei were poor; in fact, the Transkeians were nervous that South Africa was intent on taking over their country. We, in the Command Post, now faced a major disaster inside the borders of a country that did not belong to us, and whose citizens were politically hostile to us. Experience is a good teacher! While it might be expedient for political parties, and spouses, to ignore each other during disagreements, this luxury cannot be afforded during operations. Commanders must talk!

I picked up the telephone and rang Minister Pik Botha's Department of Foreign Affairs—they also had a Command Post open 24 hours a day. The duty officer acknowledged my call and told me that they were aware of the impending disaster. I then gave him my list of demands and asked for a rapid response. My demands were:

The Umtata Airfield be made available to SAAF aircraft for the duration of the emergency.

All the fuel at Umtata be reserved for SAAF use.

If any fuel was stored in drums, then these drums were to be loaded onto road transport and taken immediately to Coffee Bay for SAAF use.

A restricted flying area be imposed immediately with a radius of five nautical miles around the *Oceanos* and up to a height of 5 000 feet above sea level.

With a nervous half-laugh, the duty officer said he would try to get me what I wanted. Within 10 minutes, the duty officer phoned back to say that all my demands had been granted. He rang Mr Terblanche, the South African ambassador in Umtata. He, in turn, explained the problem and reasons for our demands to General Holomisa, who then granted authority for all we had asked for. Sometimes it is handy to have a military man as head of government—he understands operational problems straight away! In addition, the air traffic personnel at Umtata were to cooperate fully with the SAAF.

Most of the passengers were elderly. To get in and out of a hoisting strop is not easy without the benefit of instruction. Physically tough young men were required aboard the ship to assist the passengers. The navy had a small team of divers available for emergencies at Durban and Simonstown and these men were ideal for the job. They arranged with Captain Potgieter for six divers from each base to be transported to the scene by the helicopters.

Normally a Mobile Air Operations Team (MAOT) deployed to the scene if a number of aircraft were going to be involved. Safety and effort coordination are prerequisites for all air force operations. Major Louter van Wyk, an experienced maritime helicopter pilot, was appointed as commander, and together with his radio operators, operational clerks, and equipment he was dispatched with the helicopters to the scene. His job was to select a suitable sight on the shore, erect his radio equipment and antennae, and control all air activity within the restricted zone.

During the early hours of that Sunday morning, Tiny decided to send three Dakota aircraft to assist with the visual search for survivors should the ship sink. A similar thought crossed my mind and I tasked two Alouette light helicopters to leave Durban at first light for Coffee Bay. If necessary, these choppers would scour the rocky shoreline for survivors or, in the worst case, bodies.

By 03h00, the planning and tasking of aircraft and personnel was complete and the frantic activity in the Command Post started to decline. The worst part of any operation now began—the wait! Desperately, you try to think of any other form of assistance that you might have overlooked. You re-examine your plans and you consult with the other commanders by telephone, hoping that this action will prompt further ideas. Eventually you try to imagine the scene. I served 12 years in the Fleet Air Arm of the Royal Navy and spent a fair proportion of that time at sea on aircraft carriers. We encountered some violent storms that made life aboard the huge carriers unpleasant, while our 2 000 ton escorting frigates became virtually unmanageable; so I could picture the scene.

As news came in concerning the increased starboard list, the complete loss of power, and the drift towards the rocky shoreline, I imagined that by first light on that Sunday morning, South Africa would have a national catastrophe on her hands. I pictured floating bodies, flotsam and jetsam, shark frenzies, and all the horrors that the small hours of the morning exaggerate in one's mind.

At about this time, Commodore Johan Retief, now admiral and chief of the navy, joined me in my Command Post. He was working in the office of the minister of defence. I decided to seat him as close to the action as possible so he could keep the minister informed. While discussing the situation, Johan told me of an incident he had experienced along that same coastline. He had been the captain of a strike-craft making passage to the Cape. Just after 23h00, while in his bunk, the watch keeper had called him to the bridge. It was a perfect night with weather that gave no cause for alarm. On the bridge, which was only two paces from the captain's bunk, the watch keeper explained that something unusual was approaching the ship from ahead. The radar showed a long white line across their path.

Johan only had time to alter heading to meet this line head on, when an enormous wave appeared out of the dark. The angle of the wave's leading edge was so steep that the strike-craft's bows lifted sharply upwards. The weight of the ship then forced the bows through the crest of the wave and the ship plummeted down the back slope, but not before the tops of the wave removed the ships uppermost aerials. Immediately, the ship regained her posture as if nothing had happened. This encounter with a freak wave did not cost any lives, but the story reiterated that anything was possible along that unpredictable coastline.

Close to 04h00, I phoned Piet Potgieter again and asked him if his three strike-craft had sailed from Durban. He answered, 'Yes, all four of them.' Thinking I had misheard, I asked him again and he explained that somehow the navy personnel in Durban had managed to get a fourth ship ready. Each ship had a crew of 47, which meant that in the early hours of a Sunday, the navy had managed to gather together 188 men and four ships, even though we had requested only three.

On that Saturday afternoon, Western Province played Natal at Kingsmead Rugby Stadium in Durban. By pure coincidence, three

Cape ships were in port at the same time and after the match the crews set about celebrating, as only sailors know how! A round up of the clubs and bars had proved to be very successful.

The navy's fantastic reaction made me think that I had better check on the air force's progress. I heard the two Pumas lifting off from Swartkop and knew they were on their way; I rang 15 Squadron at AFB Durban. I asked their duty officer if their two Pumas were airborne and he answered, 'Yes Sir, all four of them.' Then I rang 30 Squadron at AFB Ysterplaat and asked the same question. This time the reply was, 'Yes Sir, all five have already left Cape Town.' Instead of six Pumas, we were now in the fortunate position of having 11 machines hurrying to the scene. In addition, the C160 Transall was just about overhead the *Oceanos*; three Dakotas were ready for take-off from Cape Town; and the two Alouette helicopters would leave Durban when it was light enough for them to fly.

Commandant Gawie Steenkamp, commander of the C160, was nearing the scene and relaying accurate weather information. On arrival at the given position, he could see the *Oceanos*. He put his large aircraft into a low-level orbit around the stricken ship. He notified us that a number of merchant ships were near the liner and that the *Oceanos* had already lowered all her lifeboats. The merchant ships were trying to get the survivors aboard, but locating the tiny boats in the huge sea swells was a real problem. The Transall aircrews then dropped smoke and flare markers close to the lifeboats to indicate their position.

Shortly before 06h00, I received a telephone call from Brian Suckling, an ex-SAAF officer now flying for South African Airways. They had heard about the emergency and understood the magnitude of the task facing the air force. They kindly put a Boeing-737, plus crew and paramedic team, on standby at Durban airport. We did not need to utilize them, but it did illustrate the willingness on their part to offer their assistance.

The 15 Squadron Pumas from Durban were the first to arrive at Coffee Bay. The first formation of two aircraft landed at 05h55 and the second pair at 06h10. All the aircraft were unloaded and configured for rescue. The two helicopters with the most experienced pilots lifted off and headed straight for the ship, which was visible from the coast. The second pair started refuelling. By 06h30, the first pair was over the ship and only then did they realize the magnitude of the task. The ship listed approximately 30° to starboard and was noticeably down at the bow. Long rows of passengers donned in their red life jackets hung onto the upper rail of the steeply sloping deck.

A cable strung between the bow, the two masts, and the stern created the most serious problem. Coloured lights decorated the length of this cable to make the ship look attractive at night. In this situation, however, the cable assumed lethal proportions. Hovering over the stern or bow became virtually impossible, because this cable was rising and falling over an eight-metre distance, and rolling from port to starboard. It was imperative that this cable be cut. Helicopters carry the cable-cutting tools and the navy divers lowered the tools and themselves onto the ship. Rescue hoisting began after the cable was removed.

The choppers had to use an extremely long hoist line to compensate for the eight-metre movement of the ship. Without the slack, passengers would be plucked from the deck as the ship pitched, whether they were ready to be hoisted or not. This long line made the hoist up into the helicopter a lengthy tedious business. An alternative plan had to be devised if all passengers were to be recovered. The ship's position in the water continued to deteriorate throughout the rescue and it was obvious to the pilots that speed was essential.

Instead of hoisting one passenger at a time, the hoist carried two collars. As the other helicopters became available, a rescue pattern developed. The helicopters would hover in position, while the navy divers placed passengers in the collars. As soon as the lift began, the chopper moved out over the sea to continue the long lift while the next helicopter moved into position for hoisting. As soon as each helicopter was full or running short of fuel, it departed the scene to deposit the survivors on shore and to then refuel.

Hoisting started shortly after 06h30, and initially the recovery rate was agonizingly slow. This rate increased once the other choppers from Cape Town and Pretoria arrived. At one stage during the early morning, all the drums of fuel brought by the Durban Pumas had been used up and the helicopters had to commute to Umtata, 15 minutes flying time away, to refuel. This caused a few moments of panic aboard the *Oceanos*. The helicopters' arrival had caused a surge of hope amongst those on board. This hope increased as the passengers were lifted off. All of a sudden, the passengers saw the helicopters fly out of sight instead of lifting the remaining survivors.

Gawie Steenkamp, still orbiting in his Transall, realized the problem, and relayed by radio to the ship the reason why the choppers were going to Umtata. He convinced the people to remain calm and to stay on board, because some passengers were contemplating a jump into the sea. Lifting people out of the water would have been a far more difficult and time-consuming task.

At exactly 08h00, the C130 Hercules lifted off from AFB Waterkloof bound for Umtata. On board were 48 doctors, nurses, medical personnel, and mountains of survival equipment, stretchers and blankets. The South African Medical Services responded with the same enthusiasm as the rest of the service arms. A further 35 volunteers were turned away at Waterkloof because the aircraft was full.

Shortly after 08h00, the Cape Town Pumas arrived and landed at The Haven. Major van Wyk, the MAOT, unloaded his team and their equipment. Within minutes, he had his VHF and HF radios set up, and he had started controlling the operation of all aircraft within the Restricted Zone. By this time, the *Oceanos* had stopped drifting towards the cliffs and was now wallowing about three kilometres offshore. The centre of operations moved from Coffee Bay to The Haven. Survivors, medical personnel, and equipment were uplifted by chopper and moved to the new position.

Back in headquarters, the situation had improved now that the rescue had begun. Reports from the scene started arriving regularly, which was a blessing. It was amazing how many people felt they should be kept informed of exactly what was going on. Heads of the air force and navy had to be in a position to answer questions if the chief of the defence force asked them. The chief in turn had to have his statements ready if the minister should ask. The minister needed to be able to inform the state president so that he could make meaningful statements. On top of all this, was the media!

Reporters from the newspapers, TV, and magazines, declared it their right to be told what was going on so that they could, 'Keep the public informed.' Now this was probably true, although one suspects that the possibility of a "scoop" might also have been a strong motivational factor. From the earliest hours, media personnel from all over the world started telephoning the Command Post for information. Before we activated our air force media liaison officer to handle these queries, this burden fell on the shoulders of the staff, who were busily engaged in organizing the rescue. The American media were by far the most persistent and insistent. Their audience wanted an update every half an hour. This required staff time that in the early stages of the rescue could have been better spent on the task.

On reflection, the media people did an excellent job. Coverage of the rescue was widespread and generally accurate. With the exception of the initial problems, the conduct of the media personnel throughout was very professional. Many reporters hired aircraft to fly them to the scene to take aerial photography of the stricken ship. The air force installed the Restricted Zone for the exclusive use of SAAF aircraft actively engaged in the rescue. The pilots of these hired aircraft obeyed instructions and stayed outside the Restricted Zone, allowing the rescue to proceed unhindered. One aircraft, however, with an American TV team on board, ignored all instructions and flew through the area at below 500 foot, straight over the *Oceanos*.

I imagined that particular TV station's head office and the MD giving the intrepid team a pat on the back, presenting them with a bonus, and entering their photos in the annual "Press photo of the Year" competition. In reality, their actions were selfish and extremely dangerous. Between the coastline and the ship was a constant shuttle of helicopters.

Two Alouette choppers searched along the shoreline for bodies that may have washed against the rocks. Over the *Oceanos*, a pattern of four Pumas were engaged in the difficult task of hoisting survivors. The C160 Transall was still orbiting the ship looking for people who had perhaps jumped into the sea. Three Dakota aircraft performed the same function. All the pilots were occupied with their tasks but still conscious of the other rescue aircraft in the vicinity by the constant chatter on the radio.

Suddenly the entire rescue was disrupted, when an air force pilot yelled, 'Lookout for a civilian aircraft entering the zone at 500 foot.' Hoisting stopped and all the aircraft scattered to avoid collision with the civilian aircraft that had penetrated the active airspace unannounced; they were not even on the appropriate radio frequency. In the interests of flying safety, all activities ceased until the intruder had left the area. When the Beechcraft Baron finally departed, Louter van Wyk gave clearance for rescue activities to resume. One of the Dakota aircraft had flown away from the *Oceanos* and was at its greatest distance away when the recall was given. On lowering the wing, to turn back towards the ship, an observer in the Dakota spotted a red object in the sea, directly below the aircraft—it was a person in a lifejacket! A helicopter responded and the person was winched to safety. Perhaps divine intervention made the Dakota fly so far from the scene and enabled them to rescue this man.

Hoisting continued all morning and the weather conditions improved, although the sea swell remained a problem throughout. The condition of the *Oceanos* deteriorated; the ship listed further and further to starboard. The weight of water, which had entered the vessel, was forcing the bow lower and lower into the sea. The people still onboard were finding it increasingly difficult to maintain their position in the queue for hoisting. They had to grip the ship's rail tightly to avoid sliding downwards across the steeply sloping deck. It was obvious that the ship was in imminent danger of sinking and no one knew when that fateful moment would be.

The various ships offering assistance recovered all the survivors in the *Oceanos* lifeboats. The critical factor was ensuring the survival of the passengers and crews still onboard the liner. The only way they could be saved was by air. An incident occurred mid-morning when a husband and wife were put into the lifting collars. When the couple finally lifted off the deck, the collar slipped off the shoulders of the husband. He grabbed hold of his wife while she tried to grip him with her legs. The flight engineer working the hoist saw the man's difficulties and informed the pilot that the man was slipping. The pilot immediately started decreasing height to reduce the impact of the imminent fall. When it happened the man dropped nearly 12 metres into the sea.

An 18-year-old navy diver, Able Seaman Paul Whiley, who was loading the passengers into the collars, saw the man plummet into the water. Without hesitation, he ran to the side of the ship and dived into the sea. He swam to the passenger who was by this time face down in the water. He turned the man onto his back, revived him, and then dragged him to a ship's boat that had been lowered into the water to look for survivors. With assistance from those onboard, Whiley managed to get the passenger inside the boat.

Whiley then swam back to the liner, which was now lying almost with its starboard side parallel to the surface of the sea. After repeated attempts to catch ropes and rope ladders, which were washing down the port side, Whiley managed to clamber back onto the *Oceanos*. In the process of climbing up the ship's side, huge swells dragged and buffeted Whiley. He had to use immense physical strength to retain hold on the ropes. He made his way once again to the head of the queue to help with the loading of the passengers. Later, one of the survivors told me that Whiley had asked the passengers if he could take a few minutes rest, before continuing the rescue.

The excitement in all the involved Command Posts was reaching fever pitch as the total of people brought to safety increased. Reports of the ships' seaworthiness showed that the end of the drama was nearing. The American media phoned every half an hour. I gave them the figures of those saved and those still onboard, but their overwhelming desire was to know the number of fatalities. Towards the end of the rescue, I apologized profusely that so far the worst I could give them was a sprained ankle.

By 11h20, the last people on the upper deck of the *Oceanos* were brought to safety at The Haven. During the entire morning, the MAOT staff, with assistance from the medics, tried to compile a list of people recovered. This list was then compared to the ship's manifest to establish whether all the people onboard had been accounted for. 350 people were taken on board seven merchant ships all heading to different ports, and many of them were not conversant in the English language. After a headcount, it appeared that perhaps 10 to 14 people were still missing. The MAOT decided to take the divers back to the ship to search inside the vessel for the possible missing persons.

The choppers loaded up and headed back to the liner. It was obvious to the crews that the ship was rapidly nearing the end of its fight to stay afloat. The divers needed no urging to make it a thorough, but quick, search. No further survivors were found and the divers were lifted off the hulk just after midday that Sunday. The ship finally slipped nose first to the bottom of the sea an hour later.

Numerous awards and decorations were presented to the rescue crews, including an Honoris Crux (Gold) to AB Paul Whiley. This decoration for valour is the South African equivalent of the George Cross.

Colonel George (Tiny) Hallowes was, at one time, the commanding officer of AFB Bloemspruit. He ensured that he personally greeted all VIPs visiting his base, which included members of the government. Standing at the steps of an executive jet, he saluted smartly as Minister Pik Botha stepped out of the aircraft. Tiny extended his right arm to shake hands and at the same time introduced himself, by saying, 'Hallowes.' Minister Botha, thinking perhaps that Tiny was being a little informal, replied, 'Oh! Hullowes.'

Everyday the staff of the Command Post processed intelligence reports, aircraft requests, logistic requirements, and dozens of miscellaneous inquiries. They were authorized to deal with all routine affairs, but they had to raise unusual matters at the morning meetings.

This gave me the opportunity to make decisions on further action, or to relegate the subject directly to "File 13". In this way I was able to sanction a number of very interesting projects.

A couple of civilians requested permission to attempt to break the world height record for kite flying in the Johannesburg/Pretoria area. They required verification of the height by radar, which they knew we had in this area. Because of the high density of air traffic in this region, I did not hesitate in refusing their request. Nevertheless, I am an ardent kite-flyer myself, so I arranged for these two to come see me, which they did.

Two interesting chaps were later shown into my office, both driven by a desire to have their names entered into the Guinness Book of Records. One was a kite "fundi" and the other an engineer. They had worked out that they should be able to reach well over 30 000 feet using a "stack" of kites. Allowing for the inevitable bow in the flying line, they would require an electrical winch to handle 15 kilometres of flying line. The physical load exerted by the kite-stack was so great that they needed a Kevlar flying line. Kevlar is the tough fibre used in the manufacture of bulletproof vests.

They test-flew their kites on a number of occasions, all of which resulted in modifications to the electrical winch. On early flights, the winding drum collapsed under the pressure exerted by the kites. I never found out where they conducted these test flights, but I politely reminded them that South African Air Navigation Regulations sets a height limit of 30 metres for any object extending vertically upwards. To venture above that height requires permission in writing from the Directorate of Civil Aviation.

I always enjoy enthusiastic people and these two fell into that bracket. They were obviously disappointed, but they understood the reason for the regulations. I then offered them the use of defence force facilities at Riemvasmaak, the weapons range bordering the Kalahari Desert. The area was remote and in a Military Danger Zone, which prohibited civilian air traffic, so there would be no breech of regulations. The South African Artillery used the range for training exercises and it was ideally suited to cater for the 40-kilometre range of the G5 and G6 cannons. To achieve pinpoint accuracy over these vast ranges required the computing of accurate prevailing weather and wind conditions. The meteorological section, an integral part of an artillery battery, supplied this data. By attaching a radio-sondé transmitter to the kite-stack, a very accurate trace of the entire flight, including height, could be recorded. This would be ideal verification for claiming the record.

With all this information, the excited pair went on their way with the instruction to call me when their project was ready to "get off the ground". To my knowledge, they still have not made the attempt; technical problems with the winch and the huge length of Kevlar are the probable reasons. However, it may have been the additional information I gave them about high altitude conditions that stopped further attempts. There is an almost permanent jet stream situated over the western parts of southern Africa. Above 30 000 feet, wind speeds often exceed 100 knots. I imagine the thought of trying to hang onto a stack of kites under those conditions added almost insuperable problems to the project.

Since my ejection way back in 1968, I had always rued the fact that I was unconscious throughout the parachute descent into the sea. I missed what must have been a spectacular view and experience. Over the years, I built up a close and professional relationship with the Parachute Battalion and in particular MacGill Alexander, their commanding officer. Having a drink in their mess one evening after a joint exercise, I told the group of experienced paratroopers the story of my one and only jump. Once again, I voiced my regrets about missing the experience—this turned out to be once too often!

A month or two later Mac phoned and reminded me about my, 'Wish that I had been awake to experience the thrill,' etc. He explained about 44 Parachute Brigades annual water jump taking place on the coming Saturday. He told me that he had set aside his top instructor to give me ground instruction, and I was to report to the airfield on Saturday at "O"crack sparrow, the time all army events seem to take place.

At the appointed time and place they explained the theory. I was inserted into a parachute harness and persuaded to take my place at the open door of a Dakota. As the wheels started rolling for the take-off run, the other seasoned occupants began a rhythmic clapping and chanting. 'One, two, one-two-three, one-two-three-four, let's go!' Not wanting to miss out again on the experience, I joined in and found that it helped to dampen, but not quite eradicate, the unease circulating through my brain and body.

Within minutes, I was standing in the open door with the slipstream tearing past. Then things happened in a blur of activity. The green light came on; the dispatcher shouted 'GO' in my ear; I think I jumped—but he may have booted me out. I found myself tumbling through the turbulent slipstream. A satisfying jerk was followed by the noise of the canopy breaking open, and then unbelievable peace! Suddenly, I was suspended in space; the noisy Dakota rapidly disappeared. I had time to look around an unobstructed view for the first time in my flying career and it was breathtakingly beautiful. All too soon, I had to concentrate on the landing. We chose the Bon Accord Dam, north of Pretoria, as the target and I was pleased to see I was right over the middle, far from solid ground.

Doing all the correct things, I positioned myself for splashdown, but I was still surprised by the velocity at which I entered the water. Within a few seconds, recovery motorboats rushed alongside and willing helpers pulled me from the water. At last, I knew what a parachute descent felt like, and I could now make the decision, based on experience, that once was quite enough.

The distribution of emergency food aid during emergencies always created a problem. First, there was often a scramble between the suppliers, because each contract was greatly sort after, particularly a United Nations' one. Ironically, companies can, and do, make large sums of money providing aid to the needy. Aircraft, ship, and road transport delivery is usually expensive. Distribution is often problematical, because of weather conditions or political factors. In Third World countries, warlords and administrative corruption hinder and sometimes even prevent aid getting to those who really need it.

A certain gentleman conceived a method of aid delivery to solve many of these inherent problems, and he approached the SAAF with his idea. The most attractive feature of his proposal was that it could "almost" ensure that aid went directly to the needy. After the cessation of our border war, SAAF policy encouraged greater involvement in humanitarian actions. This proposal was therefore worth looking at.

Instead of transporting aid in bulk to a distribution point, aid would be dispersed by air over the emergency areas directly to the threatened population. Hermetically sealed plastic envelopes contained a nutritionally balanced cereal. Each envelope, filled with sufficient food for one good meal, weighed only a few grams. Recipients had to mix a little water into the cereal, which could be done in the plastic envelope, and then the meal could be eaten.

The envelopes stacked into one metre square cardboard cartons were loaded into delivery aircraft. The cartons had loose bottoms and tops. Once placed in the aircraft, the packing straps and the carton tops were removed. Over the selected dropping zone, the rear door of the aircraft would open and, at the right time, the cartons would slide backwards out of the aircraft. The loose bottoms would blow away in the slipstream and the plastic envelopes would fall out. The aircraft's slipstream would then gently disperse the envelopes.

Using a C130 Hercules, the SAAF did a number of dropping trials to perfect the technique. The project was aptly called "Snowflake", because that was exactly what a drop looked like from the ground. The higher the release altitude the greater the dispersal area would be. I notice with dismay that since then the system has only been used worldwide on a few occasions. The only reason I can think of is that probably not enough money is made by all parties in the aid chain when "Snowflake" is used, hence the apparent unpopularity!

On our first trial drop, we discovered a snag that led to the loose modified carton bottoms and tops. On the first trial, the cartons opened, but they still had solid bottoms. We expected the tumbling motion of the released carton in the slipstream to disperse the contents. On a number of boxes, this did not happen and they hit the ground like exploding bombs—not ideal if dropped in among the local population. The modification solved the problem.

Watching the first drop, I vividly remembered an event that occurred a few years previously in the Cape. Captain Charlie Bent, one of the SAAF's colourful pilots, flew his Alouette helicopter over the mountains near Du Toit's Kloof, after a particularly heavy winter snowfall. Although Cape Town was clear and sunny, the mountaintops were pure white. Charlie Bent, known by many as Karel Krom (the Afrikaans literal translation), decided it would be a noble gesture to allow the people at AFB Ysterplaat to also enjoy the snow.

He touched down gently on a rocky outcrop and his flight engineer filled a sack up with snow, and then, before it could melt, he set heading for base. He radioed ahead informing the tower to warn the inhabitants of Ysterplaat of the approaching snowstorm. Everybody rushed outside to watch the Alouette approach. At what he judged to be the right height and distance from the crowd, Charlie ordered the flight engineer to empty the sack, which the engineer did. Unfortunately, physical science affected the snow. Instead of lovely, loose snowflakes, the snow had congealed into a huge, solid rectangle of ice, which came flying out of the sky at tremendous speed. Charlie's release conditions were spot on and the ice block smashed into the concrete at the feet of the awed spectators. Only one person suffered serious injuries and the rest survived with smaller cuts and bruises. To this day, when Charlie enters an air force pub, someone is heard to say, 'Behold! The Ice-man cometh!'

Animals are to Africa as the Alps are to Switzerland—consequently, their preservation and well-being is important to the economy and image of South Africa. Requests to the air force for assistance in this regard usually received favourable attention, because "Green" stories were always viewed as valuable public relations operations. Elephants were perhaps the "biggest" offenders, because of the damage they caused to crops. Each year we deployed helicopters to herd these gentle giants back into their reserves. South of the Kruger National Park, a lone elephant crossed the Crocodile River to enjoy the sugar cane near Malelane. After the animal had run through the two-metre high cane fields, the tracks of his successful return to captivity were visible from the air. These tracks were definitely not the mystery circles in the wheat fields of England!

Herds of up to 20 elephant were shepherded back across the Limpopo River into Zimbabwe, near the Madimbo Army base. A similar herd, further to the west, moved back into Botswana. Each of these events required careful planning, cooperation, and coordination with the game rangers on the ground. Occasionally, our efforts were unsuccessful and the game rangers had to kill an animal. A sense of failure affected all those involved; each person grieved as if it was a personal loss.

Maritime disasters and oil spillage, often from the intentional cleaning of tanker ballast tanks, cause environmental pollution along the beautiful coastline of South Africa. We tasked our fixed-wing aircraft to track oil slicks in attempts to trace and photograph the offending tankers, but this was usually unsuccessfully. When the oil came ashore, helicopters deployed to assist in the rehabilitation of thousands of endangered penguins and seabirds. These poor creatures were gathered from the sea and flown to willing helpers who cleaned and fed them. Later, the choppers flew them back to suitable release points around the coast. An expensive operation, but necessary if the environment was to be preserved.

Air Force Base Hoedspruit was built on portions of three game farms that were purchased for the project. The environmental plan included retaining the game farms as a surround to the base security area. The reasoning was twofold; it would provide a security buffer around the perimeter of the base against any would be saboteur, and it would enhance the airfield as an environmentally friendly base. It was a delight to drive to work through a game reserve and see giraffe, kudu, and other animals in their natural surroundings.

However, there was one slight flaw in the Hoedspruit environmental plan—the plan did not consider the flying! We only discovered the flaw after we had started flying Mirages in and out of the airfield. It is the law of nature that predators kill other animals for food. However, the carcass attracts the scavengers. Hyenas and jackals were usually first on the scene, followed shortly by the vultures. These large birds would home in like magnets to enter a whirling orbit of hundreds of birds all waiting their turn to get at the carcass. Mirage pilots had to thread their way through and around these twirling towers on approach to land. It remains a problem to this day, and to my knowledge was the cause of one Mirage III crash, from which Major Leon Bath successfully ejected.

Lesotho (previously the British Protectorate of Basutoland) is a tiny, mountainous kingdom, landlocked by Kwazulu-Natal in the east and the Free State in the west. The SAAF had three ongoing operations that affected the pretty, little country. First, helicopters from 15 Squadron in Durban and from the Helicopter School at AFB Bloemspruit in Bloemfontein were on standby for mountain rescues. We regularly gathered up climbers, hikers, walkers, school parties, and elderly people from the Drakensberg Mountains in Natal and Lesotho.

Second, we used light aircraft to patrol the border between the Free State and Lesotho in an attempt to stop "Wild West" type cattle rustling. In these remote areas, it was fairly easy for people to sneak across the border and drive off cattle into Lesotho before the farmer became aware of the theft. The best we did was to curb this nefarious activity; we could not stop the crime on the ground. These affairs, like in the Texas of old, became quite heated. The cattle rustlers were not the least bit shy to use firearms to protect their stolen herds. Inevitably, an air force helicopter would have to fly in to collect the resulting Casevac.

Third, every winter we were called upon to fly food and blankets up to the rural Lesotho inhabitants trapped by the heavy snowfalls that occurred each year on these 10 000 foot high mountains.

One day I received an unusual request from the Natal Parks Board. They had had considerable success in saving the seriously endangered black rhinoceros from complete extinction in a protection and breeding programme initiated in the Umfolozi Game Reserve in Zululand. They proclaimed a large area of the park as a "wilderness" area, into which all vehicles were refused entry, including their own. The seclusion gave the rhino population the opportunity to breed and multiply. The increased numbers now threatened the sustainability of the wilderness area. They decided to remove a small breeding herd so the foliage and grazing could recover, and also as a further gene pool for further black rhino herd expansion.

They had no way of capturing these animals without vehicles, so they turned to the air force for help. I met up with Keith Meiklejohn, head of the game capture unit, and Peter Rogers, the veterinarian, and together we devised a suitable plan. The Parks Board would supply a light, fixed-wing spotter aircraft. An experienced pilot would pinpoint and select animals of the right age and sex for capture. He would then radio the light Parks Board chopper, carrying Peter Rogers armed with a darting rifle. After darting, the average rhino runs for about eight minutes before the drug takes effect. Throughout this time, the helicopter pilot and veterinarian closely follow the animal.

The moment the rhino stopped moving and fell over, the chopper landed and Peter, carrying his medicine chest, ran to the animal. He ascertained the state of the anaesthetic. Rhinos are extremely dangerous beasts when not properly sedated! He blindfolded the rhino, to protect the open eyes from the sun, and the horn was sawn off as protection against poachers. Peter took the opportunity to attend to any open wounds or tick infestation while keeping his eyes constantly on the rhino's ears. Twitching ears are the first sign that the rhino is coming round, which can apparently lead to some exciting moments.

In the meantime, the air force Oryx helicopter scrambled as soon as the animal was darted. A stout, wooden and steel-braced container slung underneath the belly of the chopper was lowered as close to the rhino as the thick bush would allow. The Oryx also brought in a team of men to assist with the loading of the rhino. While still sedated, one thick rope was tied around the animal's head and another to one of its back legs. The free end of the head-rope passed through the open door of the container and a hole at the far end. Team members gripped both ropes in preparation for the loading. After the first ear twitch, events followed in quick succession.

The bewildered animal was pushed into an erect position. They pulled the leading rope through the container and helping hands guided the drowsy animal into the box. The team hung onto the tail-rope as insurance, in case the animal recovered more rapidly than expected. With Keith managing the ground team and Peter monitoring the condition of the rhino, loading took a very short time—these were professional men. Peter sedated the creature in the crate once more to avoid the possibility of panic during the flight beneath the helicopter. At the destination, the crate was lowered so that the animals could be led directly into a holding pen, where they recovered quickly from their ordeal. In this manner, we captured 12 animals in a period of three days in what was probably a world's first type operation.

The Parks Board accommodated the entire team in one of their rest camps and the air force personnel had their wives with them for a most enjoyable few days. They allowed us into an enclosure where the Parks Board kept orphaned animals found in the park. Lion kills often account for mother animals so orphans are not uncommon. While we were there, two baby rhinos were being looked after. They answered to the names Pension and Paymaster, and they were adorable creatures. Like large, heavy dogs, they ran to each visitor in turn. They loved company and enjoyed being fussed over. By patting the inside of their rear legs, you could make the "little" fellows sit and roll over. Like most wild animals, this glorious period does not last long.

At this late stage in my career, I was beginning to think that I had "Been there, done that and got the T-shirt". I had been involved in insurgencies, emergencies, incursions, guerilla wars, conventional wars, and confrontations. I thought that was quite a full house, when Africa again produced the unexpected—a *coup d'état*!

Under the Nationalist government, South Africa was divided into unsustainable "homelands", some of them became, according to the label, "Independent Countries". This was a misnomer because, in practice, they all depended on the central government of South Africa for their existence. President Mangope ruled Bophuthatswana (sounds like a name in King Solomon's Mines). He was a nice old man who fully enjoyed all his privileges, and he maintained good relations with South Africa. Unfortunately, many of his politically indoctrinated subjects believed that this was an unacceptable state of affairs in a continent famous for confrontation.

Early one morning, I was informed, 'The people in Bophuthatswana are revolting'—an interesting word choice because he probably meant that there had been a revolt in Bophuthatswana. A quick joint planning session resulted in a mobile air and ground force team dispatching to Mafeking (now Mafikeng). I flew to the town as the air force representative in the Command Team led by General Jannie Geldenhuys. Our small group arrived before the ground troops so we were met by a slogan chanting, fist-shaking, weapon-waving mob, *toyi-toying* in front of the South African ambassador's house.

In the large, national stadium, a number of people were held hostage. It was really a fiasco—the rebel leaders could not have organized a piss up in a brewery! The arrival of the armoured cars and fire-force choppers saw the bravado vanish, resistance crumble, and within the same day the attempted *coup d'ètat* was over. I arrived back at work the following morning to find that some wag had pinned a notice to the door of the Command Post advertising, "Coups done here!" Not much of an event, but a first for us!

Within South Africa, political activity reached new heights. In 1989, President PW Botha paid a secret visit to Nelson Mandela in Pollsmoor Prison in Cape Town. Mandela had moved from his incarceration on Robben Island. In a historic speech, new President FW De Klerk lifted the state of emergency, and on 11 February 1990, Nelson Mandela was released after serving 27 years in jail. Expectations and aspirations reached new peaks when 27 April 1994 was selected as the day the first fully democratic elections in South Africa would be held.

Almost immediately, political activists began influencing the masses to ensure success for their particular party when voting finally took place. Propaganda usually sways unsophisticated populations easily. Political meetings were often very volatile; clever speakers fanned the embers of long-suppressed grievances. In the early 1990s, political turmoil and violence became the order of the day. Fortunately, the border war had ended, allowing the full potential of the country's security forces to control the internal situation.

We deployed light fixed-wing aircraft and helicopters to hastily set up Joint Operation Centres (JOCs) around the country. During particularly tense periods, we flew aerial patrols as top cover for school buses. A daily schedule of flights kept the townships under constant surveillance from the air. Fire-force operations flew policemen and soldiers in to trouble spots. Helicopters deposited ground teams at a system of mobile roadblocks to carry out gunrunning spot checks, which were rife throughout the country. Parties carried out these activities across the political spectrum. The security forces were the ham in the political sandwich!

As Election Day approached, the security situation reached unprecedented proportions and we were stretched to the limit trying to maintain law and order. The following is an extract of events covering just four days in April 1993:

April   14   Riotous crowds at Alexander Stadium
        14   700 plus in Daveyton, digging trenches and placing barricades across roads
        15   People breaking car and shop windows in Johannesburg
        15   5 000 in Vosloorus demanding transport and setting house alight
        15   4 000 gathered in Daveyton Stadium
        15   In Boksburg five buses loaded with people armed with traditional weapons
        16   500 blocking traffic in Orlando
        17   2 000 gathered near Sandton
        18   5 000 marching with ANC and SACP banners in Johannesburg.

By March 1994, the marching and protesting had turned more violent:

March 15   60 *toyi-toying* in Tembisa
       15   House on fire in Daveyton
       16   60 shooting and overturning cars in Kagiso
       17   450 in Kathlehong Stadium
       18   3 000 in Johannesburg CBD, 1 200 in Orlando, 200 moving to CBD from Soweto
       31   4 SA Police killed in an ambush.

The Independent Electoral Committee (IEC) was constituted, under the auspices of a member of the judiciary, to oversee the elections. In order to ensure a "free and fair" system, security force members were not invited onto the committee, thereby precluding people from the only apolitical organization in the country at that time. Instead, the team consisted of political-type people, who were excellent at talking but hopeless at getting anything done.

As March progressed into April, the IEC realized that without professional assistance all their efforts would be in vain. They invited me to sit in on IEC meetings to represent the SAAF. A first time nationwide election poses problems for most governments. In South Africa, the divergent populations, 12 different languages, and the vast distances exacerbated the problem. All the hopes and emotions of the population centred on the prospect of being able to vote. If for any reason the election failed, or was delayed, the pot of political tension would boil over with dire consequences for the entire nation.

Without doubt, the most important operational decision I have ever made in my entire career was at one of those IEC meetings. I told them that the SAAF would solve the outstanding problems encountered by the IEC. We temporarily closed down fighter squadrons and dispersed their personnel across the country to man additional Command Posts. For the only time in my career, I transgressed one of the golden "Rules of Warfare" by deploying our entire force of aircraft. We placed choppers and crews in remote centres to ensure that all corners of the country could be reached in the shortest possible time. Our transport force centred at AFB Waterkloof was ready to carry IEC personnel, ballot boxes, and voting papers to airfields around South Africa. Helicopters distributed bulk equipment and people even further a field. The air force utilized all their resources to ensure the success of the elections. The army's eventual task was to ensure safety and non-intimidation around the thousands of election booths—a necessary precaution in Africa. Nelson Mandela emerged as president of South Africa from a successful, "free and fair" democratic election.

Only someone with knowledge of Africa can understand how important the 1994 elections were to this country. Had they failed, it is probable that a bloodbath would have ensued. The success released pent-up emotions, allowing a peaceful transition of power, a process aided immensely by the charisma of the new president. My final thoughts on the subject were similar to those uttered by Winston Churchill after the Battle of Britain. Few people realize that, but for the actions of the South African Air Force, the 1994 election could not have succeeded. I am therefore convinced that the SAAF saved South Africa from inevitable anarchy, in her darkest hour.

To illustrate the immense danger the country faced, I want to mention an operation that took place through the night of 26/27 April just before the polling booths opened. Helicopter crews at AFB Swartkop informed me that a member of the security police had approached them for assistance. I arranged to attend the briefing late in the afternoon of 26 April. A plainclothes policeman explained that he had received "red-hot" information concerning an attempt to disrupt the elections. They required the air force's assistance in raiding a house near Pretoria.

Over the years, I have learnt the hard way—the police and the military differ substantially in their conduct of operations. The police normally react to a situation by storming in to solve the problem. Air operations cannot proceed in this manner. We must receive information and carry out an appreciation before we can approve a workable plan. Safety of air assets is a prerequisite of all operations.

I did not enjoy the policeman's request and insisted on more information before employing aircraft. Later that evening he came rushing back with additional intelligence. The house was nowhere near Pretoria and, in fact, the target was the clubhouse of a shooting range near Rustenburg. Satisfied that the information was valid, we formulated our plan. At first light the next morning, Election Day, ground forces would move in to cover both roads leading out of the target area. They would halt short of the target until a force of Puma helicopters descended into the area to deploy ground forces and stopper groups around the clubhouse.

Well before dawn the next morning, I clambered aboard one of the choppers, along with flak-jacketed, camouflaged members of the police reaction team. The plan went as advertised and we swooped down into the target area. We arrested 25 suspects; some did not even have time to climb out of their sleeping bags. The men lay face down and the police handcuffed them. Their equipment was searched. All the private cars, 4x4s, and *bakkies* contained ammunition, weapons, hand-grenades, and sticks of commercial dynamite used in the gold-mining industry. On the veranda of the clubhouse stood a crude, but effective, pipe bomb-manufacturing machine. These men were about to set off to various polling stations around the Transvaal (now Gauteng), to sow death, destruction and mayhem, in an attempt to derail the elections.

We had missed two men who had left the previous evening. They were the ones who had planted the well-publicized bomb that damaged Johannesburg International Airport. A further 25 incidents of that nature could have ignited the flames of anarchy. All these men were white supporters of the radical, right-wing, Afrikaner Weerstand Beweging (Afrikaner Resistance Movement). The fate of South Africa had balanced on a knife-edge!

All's well that ends well—a peaceful transition ended with the triumphant inauguration of Nelson Mandela as president on 10 May 1994. The auspicious occasion culminated fittingly in a flypast over the Union Buildings, the seat of government in Pretoria, by aircraft of the

South African Air Force. Every aircraft type in the inventory was represented, because each unit wanted to honour the new president. It was a wonderful flypast on a brilliant day, but behind the scenes, it had involved much blood, sweat and tears! For some unaccountable reason, people who arrange ceremonial programmes always place the flypast after completion of the political speeches. This is a very unsatisfactory situation! Despite promises to the contrary, no politician ever completes his speech on time! If he is enjoying the moment, or he has a captive audience, then guaranteed he overruns his time.

Nobody would blame Nelson Mandela for making the most of his special day—he had earned the privilege. The first three changes to flypast time occurred before any of our aircraft had taken-off. Five different air force bases accommodated the aircraft; so good communications were essential. Road traffic was so heavy in Pretoria that many guests could not arrive on time. Some delegations were so huge that they could not all be seated in the time or space allotted (for instance, the United States of America's representatives). Eventually, we made the decision to start the take-off programme. Formations climbed out and joined up into a huge holding pattern east of Pretoria.

Much to our consternation, a group of well-wishers went up to greet the new president on the podium; this was supposed to occur after the flypast. No self-respecting politician would dare to miss out on his turn of being seen with the charismatic president. A royal, ambassadorial and political forward surge occurred. Mr Mandela is a lovely man who could not refuse the rush. We had no option but to order the aircraft pilots to fly for endurance. Those that could topped up their fuel from orbiting tanker aircraft. Helicopters fluttered in and out of AFB Swartkop at regular intervals to refuel. Finally, 75 minutes after the planned flypast time, the first aircraft passed over the Union Buildings. To my amazement, every formation had the correct number of aircraft. The timing and formation keeping was superb, and it was a wonderful spectacle to end a magnificent day.

As it turned out, it was also the last operation I was involved in. Two months later, at the end of June, I retired from the air force.

During my final week of service, I was grateful for the many tokens of appreciation I received, none more so than that by the personnel at AFB Hoedspruit. My old pal, Mac van der Merwe, the commander of Hoedspruit, phoned to ask me to give a motivational talk to the new batch of training fighter pilots at his base. Of course, I agreed; my life had been based on fighter flying. A twin-engine Beechcraft flew me down to the base. Sitting at the back of the cabin, I enjoyed the luxury of being able to relax and read the morning paper.

The pilot turned on the VHF speaker and I could hear a ground-controlled interception taking place. With a start, I realized that we were the target. Dropping the paper, I crouched on my knees in the cabin to look for fighters behind us. At four o'clock low, I saw the shark-like shapes of Mirage F1AZs curving menacingly behind us. Shouting instructions to the transport pilot, I had him break into the pair of jets that were closing rapidly. After forcing an overshoot, I had the Beechcraft reverse into a hard port turn, hoping to embarrass the fighters by ending up astern of them. Because they were old hands, they just zoomed up out of harm's way and dropped in behind again. They then joined on either side of the Beechcraft for a nice tight vic-formation arrival at Hoedspruit. The fighters were from 1 Squadron, my old squadron, and they were according me an honour normally reserved for visiting Heads of State. Mac was there to meet me on landing, and then he sent me off to 85 Advanced Flying School, also a unit I had previously commanded. Naïve to the last, I could not understand why the present unit commander kept us waiting on the hardstanding instead of taking me straight to the lecture hall.

Suddenly, from below the level of the surrounding trees, an Impala jet screamed into view. It was painted in the colour scheme of the Malgas seabird, which adorns the unit crest. Jeronkie Venter, the pilot, gave a very polished low-level aerobatic display solely for me. After he landed, I had the opportunity to thank him before they finally led me off to the lecture hall—or so I thought! Instead of turning right, they steered me left into the aircrew changing room. Hanging on a hook was a flying suit, with bone dome and gloves on the bench alongside. They invited me to change, where after I returned to the hardstanding. They had pulled a Vampire T11 trainer, property of the SAAF museum, into position and told me to climb aboard.

I received my wings on a similar Vampire 36 years before at RAF Linton-on-Ouse, in the plains of Yorkshire. The instructor took-off and then gave me control for the rest of the flight. What a nostalgic flight! I had the opportunity to reflect on all the water that had passed under the bridge to bring me to that point. After a session of aerobatics, I remembered that Vampires were notoriously thirsty aircraft and a glance at the fuel gauge confirmed this. My landing was a greaser—but I have to admit that Vamps were always easy to land.

They had devoted the entire day to me—the address was the subterfuge used to get me there! The lecture room, laid out for a party, was filled to capacity with well-wishers. It was an incredible day, which had taken a lot of thought and preparation. I was overwhelmed. It is nice to know that I had made good friends throughout my life.

Chapter 23

Retirement

I took to retirement like a duck to water. At 46 years of age, I had successfully coped with my midlife crisis by flying "mahogany bombers". Compared to that, transferal from active duty to the reserves turned out to be a piece of cake. Had I known how good it was going to be, I would have done it straight from school!

For years, I had wanted to write and now I could indulge myself. Around a campfire, deep inside Angola, I remember asking General Jannie Geldenhuys for advice on how to go about it, because he had recently published a book of his own. His advice was brief and straight to the point, 'Take a pile of paper and a pencil, then start to write.' He added that editors could polish the finished product, but only the author could tell the story by putting it down on paper.

My first effort was to expand the diary I had kept in 1983 into book form. 1983 was my first year as the air boss in Oshakati, and I wanted to record in detail the events and operations required to combat a war of insurgency. It was a most enjoyable project and I was pleased with the result, but I never had it published. After South Africa's transition to full democracy in 1994, a Truth and Reconciliation Commission (TRC) was constituted, in an attempt to exorcise the evils of the past.

Let me state categorically that I, and to my knowledge all members of the SAAF, conducted operations according to the norms and standards expected of a civilized Western nation. Only air operations sanctioned and approved by the cabinet and the government of the day were carried out, including cross-border raids. It appeared at the time that the TRC was intent on seeking scapegoats for some of these activities. What they could not understand was that any defence force is a just a tool of the government of the day.

Many people involved in the democratic struggle in South Africa received training and indoctrination in Communist countries. It was therefore difficult for them to appreciate that the moment Nelson Mandela acceded to the presidency the self-same defence force remained totally committed to serving the country and the dictates of his government. It is a concept foreign to most African minds, which traditionally find it safest to follow the reigning "strong man". An excellent example is Zimbabwe, where Mugabe remains in power by people's fear of reprisal should they try to switch allegiance.

My diary contained the names of personnel who participated in cross-border operations, at the behest of the government. I did not think it would be fair to have the manuscript printed so that others, with political agendas, could attempt to belittle, deride, or in the worst case, accuse personnel mentioned in my book. The pile of paper, titled "Another year in another war", is gathering dust at the bottom of my cupboard.

General Geldenhuys told another story that evening at the campfire concerning military logistics, which I remember every day. If you do not want this recurring story to bother you, then I suggest you skip the following paragraph!

As chief of the army, General Geldenhuys visited and inspected many units, depots, and facilities. Walking through a store one day, accompanied by the unit RSM, he noticed rolls of toilet paper packed from floor to ceiling. Making small talk, he asked the RSM how logistics experts calculate the requirement for this commodity during operations. The conversation went something like this:

RSM   'Each man defecates twice a day, Sah! We multiply the number of men going on the operation, by two, Sah! We multiply that figure by the expected number of days the operation should last, Sah!'

General 'I see, but how do you know how much paper to send?'

RSM   'We multiply the answer by three, Sah!'

General 'Why three?'

RSM   'Each defecation requires three sheets, Sah! One up, one down and one to polish, Sah!'

After "hanging up my uniform", I was recalled to duty on a number of occasions to assist in a consultancy capacity. During one of these periods, in early 1997, I faced the opportunity of a lifetime. The South African Navy was sending one of its supply ships to Antarctica to bring back personnel from the ice-shelf and I was invited to join them.

South Africa maintains a permanent base in Antarctica for research purposes. Since 1959, the South African National Antarctic Expedition (SANAE) base stood on the ice shelf in Queen Maud Land. Unfortunately, the weight and heat of the structures caused the buildings to sink into the ice. Almost every decade, new buildings were required as the weight of ice threatened to crush the now subterranean structures. In order to solve the sinkage problem, they decided to move the site of the base off the ice-shelf. During the mid-1990s, SANAE IV was built 220 kilometres south of SANAE III, using a solid *nunatak* (rocky outcrop) as the foundation.

Because the Antarctic summer is very short, the new base was prefabricated in South Africa to expedite the erection process. Under normal conditions, SA *Agulhas*, a ship built specifically for Antarctic conditions, serviced SANAE annually. However, defence force's assistance was requested to aid the transportation of prefabricated materials and construction personnel to and from Antarctica. SAS *Outeniqua* was tasked to recover some of these people and scientists before the onset of winter, and I would journey south as an observer.

The day after we sailed from Cape Town, the ship's Daily Orders proclaimed the formation of a new party on board, and all crewmembers joined for a small subscription. Members of PASAS (People Against Shaving at Sea) had to present themselves before a panel of judges at the end of the voyage. Participants could win a certificate in the competition. The competition had five categories:

a.   Best beard
b.   Most colourful beard
c.   Longest beard
d.   Funniest beard
e.   Wasted effort

The proceeds, together with those from numerous other on-board competitions and events, went to Nazareth House, the society that cares for babies born with AIDS. This simple gesture reminded me of my service in the Royal Navy where acts of kindness were also commonplace. Seafarers are traditionally a very caring group of people.

Our route took us close to Bouvet Island on both legs to and from Antarctica. Huge glaciers, sliding inexorably into the sea, break the rugged coastline. A tremendously thick ice cap covers the island. Bouvet is home to millions of sea birds and seal colonies, and the seas abound with spouting and diving whales. In winter, a huge ice-shelf forms around the island. This is probably why navigational charts still carry the warning that the precise location of the island is unknown. Captain Cook plotted it first, and it is aptly described as "the remotest island on the globe!"

Passage to the ice is through the notorious "Roaring Forties", "Furious Fifties", and the "Screaming Sixties". Unlike the Northern Hemisphere, there is no landmass to interrupt, or reduce, the flow of the westerly winds in these high latitudes apart from the narrow spit of land reaching to Cape Horn in South America. The winds are free to pick up speed in a passage of thousands of miles across the open ocean. This long reach has the capacity of whipping the surface of the sea into mountainous swells. Passage through this region of sea and swell is not for the faint-hearted!

One morning I awoke at about 04h00; the reduction in the ship's motion probably disturbed me. Sounds Irish, but after a week of tossing and rolling, the change in motion was marked. Pulling on warm clothes, I made my way up to the bridge just as the sky was beginning to glow in the east, and the sea swell had reduced to a slow lift and fall. What a morning!

More and more icebergs appeared on the horizon. Bergy bits and growlers (remains of melting icebergs) became two a penny. The visibility was unlimited—there was absolutely no pollution in the atmosphere. The wind had dropped to a gentle breeze after the gales experienced on passage. At 04h20, the sun, a brilliant golden globe, came over the sea horizon. The reflections under the cloud layer continually changed colour from bright silvery yellow to dark red, almost maroon. Silhouetted against the silvery shimmer of the sunrays over the water was a large tabular iceberg, that looked black against the sun.

As the iceberg passed astern, the blackness changed through all the shades of blue, until the rising sun illuminated the pure white upper surface. No pack ice was present to reduce the ship speed, but the closer the ship came to the ice-shelf the greater the number of icebergs that started appearing. Apart from the predominately white colour, and the low temperature, the scenery was very reminiscent of the Karoo. Flat koppies interspersed the vast distances, only here they were made of ice! Each iceberg differed in shape, size, and colour, providing a continually changing panorama.

A variety of sea birds was present, including the pure white petrel. The ice-shelf came into view, stretching from horizon to horizon across our path. As the ship drew closer to this massive shelf, the detail was stunning. The 15 000 ton ship was unhindered by a layer of pack ice, slicing a path straight through. Minke whales in small pods spouted and swam close by. Seals were plentiful on the ice floes, some of them only waking up when the bow of the ship nosed their ice block aside. In the water, penguins made their presence known, while a large, lone Emperor played sentinel on an ice floe as the ship slid by. Pack ice changed into beautiful pancake ice; each piece had a noticeable lip, much like the huge Amazon Lily leaves I had seen in the hot house at Kew Gardens in London.

Flying operations began immediately in the superb weather conditions. Men and material flew ashore. A tractor-train driven by the men from SANAE met them. This snow-tractor pulled sleds for freight and men. The human compartments were sensibly enclosed and heated against the elements. Activity never ceased while the good weather lasted, except for an hour church service on Sunday.

The service, held in the open on the helicopter deck, was awe-inspiring. The ship moved slowly, within 200 metres of the vast Blaskiemin ice-shelf. Blue skies, calm seas, broken ice, and enormous icebergs completed the setting. Led by the Padres vigorous guitar, the Ship's Company sang a very spirited rendition of *How great thou art* and *The Lord is my Shepherd* to the tune of Crimond. I have never seen such a wonderful cathedral, albeit a little chilly!

The close proximity of the ice-shelf afforded everyone on board a close view. Like the annual rings on a tree trunk, stratified layers of yearly snow could easily be seen on the shelf above the waterline and, in places, we counted 25 layers. Great crevasses existed on nearby icebergs. Inside these crevasses, the colour changed from purest white, to aquamarine, and to ice blue. Ice blocks, resembling piled rubble on the edges of some icebergs, testified to the power of collision between these giants. Scanning eastwards towards the horizon, I remembered RAF airfields on the Plain of York in mid-winter. The level white-packed snow and the serried ranks of tabular icebergs looked remarkably like the icy covering over an airfield, with rectangular hangars spread around the perimeter track.

All activities halted with the sudden deterioration of the weather. Bitterly cold, katabatic winds sweep down from the Antarctic high ground, which in places reached 9 000 foot above sea level. Sudden gusts, which could exceed 90 miles per hour, raised blown snow into the atmosphere, causing the dreaded whiteout conditions. The whole world suddenly turned white, no horizon was visible, and all depth perception was lost. It was horrific for anyone walking or driving on the ice-shelf, and it was a nightmare for any pilot unable to land before the onset of the condition. These winds have wreaked havoc with many manned explorations of Antarctica and caused Scott to write in his diary, 'My God, this is an awful place!'

On a bad day one cannot disagree with Scott's statement, but in good conditions Antarctica is a place of spectacular beauty. In both cases, however, danger is always present and no chances should ever be taken. Sunglasses, the fashion accessory of beautiful people, are essential items on the ice. Without them, even for very short periods, snow blindness is guaranteed and the accompanying pain is excruciating. Without gloves, contact with metal tends to be of a rather permanent nature. Hands and fingers adhere instantly to frozen spars and hasty withdrawals often leave layers of skin behind. At the traditional South African braai, you learn new techniques. If for some reason you need to put your beer-can down, you must place it on the grill above the fire otherwise the contents freeze.

On the annual rotation of personnel, it was customary for the nations involved on the ice to offer each other assistance—only the climate is unfriendly on the polar cap! South Africa often helped the Germans by transporting their personnel and rations from Cape Town, and dropping them off at their base at Neumeyer en-route to SANAE.

The system did have a drawback—during the changeover, Neumeyer had to accommodate both new and old members. Consequently, the base was very crowded and control became difficult. Control is the key to safety on the ice so this period was fraught with danger. Filled with visions of Amundsen, Schackleton, and Scott, the new members were the most at risk, because they had not yet learnt the necessity for safety first on the ice.

During this period in 1986, a report from Neumeyer generated much excitement. Whales were visible in the *bukta* (Antarctic name for a bay). Unlike SANAE, which stood on the ice-shelf away from the sea, Neumeyer was virtually at the water's edge. Five of the newcomers, eager to witness all the sights of Antarctica, grabbed their cameras, jumped onto a skidoo ice transporter, and headed off to look at the whales.

Procedures at all ice bases are very strict. Before going anywhere, all safety factors have to be completed. One must write in a book the destination and expected time of return. Section heads must be informed. Warm clothing and radios must be taken along. To the experienced old hands, all of this is second nature, but on this occasion, the eager newcomers ignored all the precautions.

In the overcrowded base, no one missed the newcomers until the following morning, when someone noticed that they had not slept in their beds. An emergency was immediately declared. The Germans launched their fixed-wing Dornier aircraft on a search and the South Africa base at SANAE rendered help with a Puma helicopter. Taking off in squally, snowy conditions, the crew flew the 120 nautical miles along the ice-shelf to Neumeyer.

Base personnel traced the tracks of the skidoo down to the water's edge. They found the skidoo and protective jackets, but there was no sign of the men or their cameras. They had apparently ventured out onto the ice to get a closer look at the whales. As they approached the edge, the ice cracked and the men found themselves adrift on a piece the size of a football field. During the night, the ice drifted 14 kilometres out to sea. The circulatory pattern of the currents then drifted them back to within a kilometre of the shore, where the searching Dornier spotted them and passed their position to the approaching Puma crew.

On approaching the stranded men, the Puma crew noticed that the football-field-size piece of ice had melted to squash-court size, too small for the Puma to land. The Puma hoisted all five survivors to safety and took them back to Neumeyer. A few years earlier, in similar circumstances, a British expedition lost two full dog teams without a trace.

All polar bases erupted into a hive of activity during the short summer season and SANAE was no exception. Building and maintenance work continued around the clock in the permanent daytime on the polar cap. Geologists and scientists traversed the snow-clad landscapes in pursuit of the advancement of knowledge. By late January, the short working season was drawing rapidly to a close and all scientists on field trips returned to the protection of the SANAE base before the onset of winter. A Puma was dispatched to refuel at the mountain base of Grunehogna, 120 nautical miles south of SANAE, before uplifting two geologists out on the snow a further 120 miles to the east.

On landing at Grunehogna, they tied the helicopter down because of the imminent onset of a storm. This was a wise precaution because they were grounded for the next five days during the passage of this severe storm. Winds gusting up to 70 knots, visibility down to tens of metres in driving snow, and ambient temperatures of -12°C were the norm. The chill factor, for anyone unlucky enough to be outside, drove the temperatures into the -20°C region.

During the height of the storm, the constant movement of the helicopter rotor blades was sufficient to break the heavy-duty blade tip covers put in place by the crew. Because they were aerofoil sections, these blades were flapping in the gusts, at times bending until the tips were overhead the helicopter's cabin. To prevent major structural damage occurring to the machine, the crew ventured out into the blizzard to rectify the situation.

The safe accomplishment of even the simplest outdoor task in these conditions necessitated lifeline attachments. Severe winds and only 10 metres of visibility could easily result in a person getting lost. The crew manufactured new covers and then spent nearly an hour at the helicopter attempting to capture and secure the blades. Between gusts, the blades drooped and the men tried to grab the tip to replace the covers. On one occasion, all three men caught and clung onto a blade when another fierce gust struck the chopper. All three lifted with the blade and fell off as the blade passed eight feet above the ground. After completing the task, the exhausted, frozen men returned to the austere comforts of the temporary base camp.

Five days later the storm abated, leaving the men to prepare their frozen aircraft for flight. Easier said than done! The wind had blown snow into the cabin and cockpit through a tiny orifice, and they had to shovel it out.

Waiting to return, the geologists were down to their last rations, two days' supply of heating fuel. The weather forecast indicated the approach of the next storm within two days, so it became imperative that these men return as soon as possible. The crew started up as soon as they could and set off, heading east.

Forty miles and 20 minutes flying time from Grunehogna, they crossed a large glacier and then lost all electrical systems in the aircraft. The only remaining electrical power came from the emergency battery with an expected lifetime of 25 minutes. The flight-time to pick up the geologists and return to Grunehogna was one hour. Knowing about the ration situation and the approaching storm, the crew decided to press on with the flight. What began as a normal pick-up now developed into a full-blown rescue!

Switching the battery off to conserve its life, they flew onwards. Every five minutes they switched it back on to scan the instrumentation for any other problems, before switching it off again. They lost all the engine instrumentation—temperatures and pressures, and their Attitude Direction Indicator (ADI). They had to fly using the standby artificial horizon.

They kept the engines running after touchdown, because they had no way of starting them again. The geologists loaded themselves and their equipment into the cabin. On the flight back to Grunehogna, just as they crossed the glacier, they tried to reset the alternators for the umpteenth time. Lo and behold, the alternators and transformer rectifiers (TRUs) came back on line, restoring full electrical capabilities to the aircraft.

The snow that had blown into the aircraft was probably the cause of the problems. There was so much of it that some must have found its way into the electrical boxes. After 20 minutes of flight, the rising temperatures melted the snow and it is common knowledge that water and electrics do not mix. After a further 40 minutes, the heat build-up dried out the circuits and power was restored.

The landing at Grunehogna was uneventful. The meteorologist correctly forecasted the approach of the next storm, but he was out in his timing. Within hours, they battened down the hatches again and sat out another three days of blizzard before they could all safely withdraw to SANAE.

Fortunately, nothing untoward occurred during my trip to the ice. The task was successfully carried out and the visit was spectacular. As always, it was a thrill to see Table Mountain appear over the horizon and a pleasure to set foot again on *terra firma* after an unforgettable experience.

On reflection, this trip completed the full circle of my military career that had started and ended in the navy. My career began on a cold, grey, morning in Plymouth, England, in January 1958, and ended on a beautiful summer day in Cape Town, South Africa, in 1997. I was fortunate to travel, live, work, and fly, in countries around the world. I sailed all the major oceans and could now claim to have operated within both polar circles. The best part of all is that given the opportunity I would do it all again.

Appendix: US Navy Flight Classification System

NAVAL AIRCRAFT FLIGHT CLASSIFICATION SYSTEM

The character or kind of flight by Navy aircraft, as required to be entered on the various flight records and reports, will be described by a NUMBER-LETTER-NUMBER Code as follows:
   1st NUMBER- to denote CONDITION of flight
   LETTER- to denote GENERAL PURPOSE of flight
   2nd NUMBER- to denote SPECIFIC PURPOSE of flight

No variation from the classification is to be made without CNO approval; however, commands may expand, for more detail for local purposes, the code number denoting specific purpose of flight. Complete codes will be in such form as 2A7, K, 179. The pilot selects the classification best describing the flight and enters it on the flight record sheet for that flight; all subsequent flight record and report entries will reflect that selection.

1.   The Code for CONDITION OF FLIGHT *(first number)* shall be selected as appropriate from the following:
   1 – Day Visual   3 – Night Visual
   2 – Day Instrument   4 – Night Instrument

Use Code 2 if over 50% of flight duration was under actual Instrument conditions.

Use Code 3 if over 50% of flight duration was in darkness, unless classifiable as 4.

Use Code 4 if over 50% of flight duration was in darkness, and either (a) 50% of the flight was under actual instrument conditions or (b) final landing was in darkness and by actual Instrument approach.

Use Code 1 for all other cases.

2.   The Code for GENERAL PURPOSE of flight *(first letter)* shall be selected from the following:

General Training *(Navy, Marine and Reserve Pilots, active or inactive duty)*

A – Unit Training
B – Individual proficiency, CNO standards
C – Individual training *(Special local requirements)*

Student syllabus training *(NATRACOM students and instructors only)*
D – Student aviator training
E – Refresher training
F – Flight Instructor training
G – Other student training

Training – Pilots of other services
H – U.S. *(Air Force, Coast Guard, Army)*
I – Foreign

Service flights:
J – Ferry
K – Experiment development evaluation
L – Test Flight
M – Utility, aviation forces
N – Utility, non-aviation forces
P – Search and Rescue
Q – Miscellaneous training
R – Transport

Combat Flights:
S – Attack ASC targets
T – Attack, non-ASC targets
U – Counter-Air offensive
V – Reconnaissance
W – Air Defense own base
X – Air Defense of other forces
Y – Offensive anti-submarine
Z – Defensive anti-submarine

3.   The appropriate code for SPECIFIC PURPOSE of flight *(second number)* shall be selected from the following:

For GENERAL PURPOSE Code A thru I:
1 – Fundamentals   6 – Air Combat
2 – Instrument   7 – Attack

3 – Field carrier landing   8 – Anti-submarine
4 – Carrier Qualifications 9 – Special equipment
5 – Transition   10 – Special operations

For GENERAL PURPOSE Code J thru L:
    1 – Ferry or test flight funded from Lant fund *(Subhead 1911)*
    2 – Ferry or test flight funded from Unit Brave Account *(Subhead 1911)*
    3 – Ferry or test flight funded from Charlie Account *(Subhead 1916)*

For GENERAL PURPOSE Code Q:
    1 – Aerological
    2 – Non-combat patrol or search
    3 – Non-combat photo or radar mapping
    4 – Airshows, demonstrations
    5 - Non-combat, non-training, not elsewhere classified
    6 – AEW flights *(Carrier or Land based)* in support of *either* Fleet Tactical Exercises or Fleet Operations.

NOTE: These GENERAL PURPOSE Codes continue from R thru to Z covering all possible types of missions.

(Extract from: *Aviators Flight Log Book, US Navy*)

Glossary

AAA   Anti-aircraft artillery.

ACM   Air Combat Manoeuvring (old fashioned dogfighting).

Adhemar   French word meaning Angle-of-Attack Indicator (AAI), sometimes irreverently referred to as ADI (Angle-of-Dangle indicator).

AFB   Air Force Base.

AFCP   Air Force Command Post. The SAAF uses a system of Command Posts to efficiently command and control all of the resources available to the air force. This includes aircraft, personnel, radars, air defence systems, and ground security squadron specialists and their dogs. An AFCP controls the air force involvement in its designated area of responsibility, which includes ground and air battles.

AI   Air interception.

ATC   Air Traffic Control.

ATCO   Air Traffic Controller.

AWFS   All Weather Fighter School.

AWI   Air Warfare Instructor.

Back-end   The stern of a carrier.

Bakkie   South African word for a light truck.

Balbo   A large, usually mixed formation, named after the Italian general of aviation fame.

Banyan   Royal Naval term describing a picnic.

Blue   One of the four hydraulic systems used in a Sea Vixen. The "Blue" is used to power the aircraft's flying controls, which require unusually high demands the closer the pilot gets to the back-end.

Blue jobs   Anybody serving in the Royal Air Force.

BOAC   British Overseas Airways (the airline famous for its beautiful cabin staff).

Boat   An expression used by Fleet Air Arm pilots to describe the carrier, with the express purpose of annoying Fish heads who are only allowed to use the word ship.

BOQ   Bachelor Officers' Quarters.

Braai   Open-air barbecue, evolved from the Afrikaans *Braaivleis*, to grill meat.

Brown jobs   The common name for any soldier.

Bukta   The name given to a bay or inlet in Antarctica.

Bum-freezer   Short, formal, dinner jacket.

Caley Gear   The system of rollers that automatically centre aircraft on the catapult before launch.

CAP   Combat Air Patrol.
Casevac   Casualty Evacuation.
Casspir   Mine-protected, armoured, personnel carrier.
Cat   Abbreviated form of catapult; the steam powered aircraft launching system used on carriers.
CCA   Carrier Controlled Approach. Radar controlled, aircraft talk-down system used at night and in bad weather.
CFS   Central Flying School.
Charlie Time   The time the carrier staff specify for the next land-on to begin. (Pilots who miss this time are under threat of emasculation.)
CO   Commanding Officer. (*see* OC)
Coalhole   An adequate description of the observer's compartment in a Sea Vixen.
Crabs   RAF personnel.
CPO   Chief Petty Officer. (Second only in authority to the Admiral!)
DFC   Distinguished Flying Cross.
Dobies   Fighter pilot's dark glasses along with a large watch and "G" suit—essential for the image!
Dominee   Afrikaans Padre.
DR   Dead Reckoning. Navigation without electronic aids; the way Orville and Charles Lindbergh used to do it.
EW   Electronic Warfare.
FAA   Fleet Air Arm.
FAC   Forward Air Controller.
FDO   Flight Deck Officer.
Fireforce   A highly mobile offensive force comprising combinations of the following:
    Gunships
    Offensive fire power
    Troopers
    Command and Control
    Bosboks
    Recce or Telstar
    Pumas
    Insertion of stopper groups
    Troops
    Usually highly-trained and motivated Parabats; all inter-linked by communications and on rapid response standby for immediate deployment.

Fish head Dartmouth trained naval officer, in USN parlance a "Black-shoe".

Flossie C130 Hercules used as the air link between South Africa and South West Africa during the border war.

FLOT Forward Line Own Troops. A very necessary requirement during close air support operations, which ensures safety of own forces.

Foo-foo powder Any baby powder substance used to protect the skin and hair on wrists and neck in the rubberized immersion suits.

Front-end The sharp end, or bow, of a boat.

FTS Flying Training School.

"G" Gravity. Under normal circumstances, everything on earth is affected by the pull of gravity (1 "G"). In tight turns or loops, centrifugal force effectively increases the pull of gravity. A "G" meter in the cockpit registers this increase. Readings of -2 and +7 "G" are the usual range experienced during a typical fighter sortie. At +7 "G", the body's blood effectively becomes seven times heavier than normal and hastens the onset of blackout as blood drains towards the pilot's feet. At -"G" readings, blood is forced to the head, sometimes resulting in red-out because the capillary blood vessels in the eyes burst when pressure increases.

"G" suit The inflatable garment, zipped around abdomen and legs that inhibits blood flow to the pilot's feet as aircraft "G" loading is increased.

GCA Ground Controlled Approach. Radar talk-down used to guide pilots to a safe landing in bad weather or at night. The land equivalent of a CCA.

GCI Ground Controlled Interception.

GIB Guy in the back. The FAA observer or the USN RIO.

Glow-worm 3-inch rocket with an illuminating parachute flare carried in the warhead of the missile. Used for illuminating targets for night attacks.

Goofers The platform above the bridge from where people watch flying operations on a carrier; or the name given to these viewers.

HAA Helicopter Administration Area. A designated area, planned and secured by ground forces, from where helicopters could operate to expedite operations. Very often it was co-located with a forward headquarters where immediate tactical plans could be coordinated. Fuel in drums or bladders was available to refuel the helicopters, and gunship ammunition. The HAA could be stationary for two or three days depending on the area, but longer than that was considered dangerous, because SWAPO could locate the HAA in that time. In South Africa, the Afrikaans equivalent *HAG* was normally used because the sound came more easily to the tongue.

HF   High Frequency radio.

Hi-Lo   A British system that replaced the mirror-landing aid on carriers, so pilots could pick-up the glide path at greater visual range from the carrier. On HMS *Ark Royal* during the 1960s, it was a cause of great concern.

HMS   Her Majesty's Ship.

IAS   Indicated Air Speed.

IEC   Independent Electoral Committee.

ILH   Imperial Light Horse. Famous South African regiment of PBI, no longer using the prefix Imperial.

IMC   Instrument Meteorological Conditions. Used when it is mandatory to fly with sole reference to aircraft instrumentation.

IP   Initial Point. A well-defined navigational position, from where navigation or attack profiles can be commenced with accuracy.

IRT   Instrument Rating Test. An annual requirement for all pilots.

Jack   Sailor, seaman, matelot from the traditional Jack Tar.

Jolly Jack   *see* Jack, who by nature and tradition is usually of happy disposition.

JPT   Jet Pipe Temperature.

"Kill"   During simulated ACM, missile launch or gun firing is expressed as "a kill".

LABS   Low Altitude Bombing System. The system originally designed to "throw" tactical nuclear weapons in a toss type manoeuvre. The launch aircraft pulls up from low-level, at high speeds and releases the bomb as the nose passes 45° above the horizon. The aircraft continues in a looping manoeuvre to escape the detonation, while the bomb flies nearly five miles before exploding. Never a terribly accurate method of delivery but probably sufficient for a nuclear blast!

MADDLS   Mirror Assisted Dummy Deck Landings. Landing practice on shore-based runways used by carrier pilots before heading out to a carrier.

MAOT   The abbreviation stands for Mobile Air Operations Team. The air force team usually comprised an OC (pilot), an ops officer, an intelligence officer, a radio operator, and one or two clerks. The team plus their equipment could be airlifted into a tactical headquarters co-located with the army or police, or the team could move with the ground forces in mine-protected vehicles, as an integral part of the Command headquarters. The OC of the team was often called "The MAOT".

MAYDAY   International Distress Call.

MCAS   Marine Corp Air Station.

Meatball   The central ball of light seen by a pilot, hopefully, in the centre of a landing mirror during a carrier approach to land.

MiG   Common abbreviation for the Russian-designed family of jet fighters.

Milk the flaps   To adjust the flap setting of a Hunter during gunsight tracking, the pilot can "milk" the flaps, raise and lower them by notches, to keep his aiming pipper on the target.

MPLA   The Popular Movement for the Liberation of Angola.

MRG   Master Reference Gyro. The main gyro that controls all the flying instruments in a Sea Vixen or Buccaneer. Failure of the Master can, under certain circumstances, cause instant dyspepsia, hysteria and uncontrollable tears.

NA-39   Under-powered prototype of the Blackburn Buccaneer.

NAS   Naval Air Station.

NATO   North Atlantic Treaty Organization.

O   Observer (SOBS would be the senior observer in a squadron).

Obs   Observer.

OC   *see* CO (Officer Commanding or vice versa).

OCU   Operational Conversion Unit.

Oggie   Cornish pasty (Served with scrumpy in rural Cornish pubs.)

OHMS   On Her Majesty's Service.

OPS CO   Operations Coordinator.

ORBAT   Order of Battle. Force levels of protagonists.

Parabat   Parachute soldier, qualified to wear the famous red beret.

PBI   Poor Bloody Infantry; foot soldiers.

POMZ   Russian anti-personnel mine, commonly known as "the widow-maker".

Pongo   Another name for a Brown job.

QFI   Qualified Flying Instructor. (Like transport pilots, the QFI is normally an excellent knitter!)

R&R   Rest and Recreation. (Any time a pilot is away from the squadron.)

RAF   Royal Air Force.

RAT   Ram Air Turbine. Emergency spring-mounted propeller, released into the airstream to supplement hydraulic pressure or electrical power.

Red Flag   Famous series of operational flying exercises where every known enemy threat is simulated.

RIO   Radar Intercept Officer or GIB.

Round-down   The curved, back-end of a carrier's flight-deck, incorporated to reduce pilot terror as he approaches the back-end to land.

RN   Royal Navy (often referred to as The Andrew).

RNAS   Royal Navy Air Station.

SAAF   South African Air Force.

SAM   Surface-to-air missile. (When seen in flight, it is known to relieve constipation.)

SAMS   South African Medical Services.

SANAE   South African National Antarctic Expedition.

SAP   South African Police.

SAR   Search and Rescue.

SATCO   Senior Air Traffic Control Officer.

Scrumpy   Rough, but sweet, apple cider served in huge mugs in rural Cornish pubs. (One pint can produce a singsong or two fights, while two pints ensures divorce.)

Shona   An open area in the bush that fills with rain during the rainy season, and is invariably dry during the winter months.

Silly Season   The summer air show season in Britain, so called because of the almost inevitable event when one pilot exceeds his, or the aircraft's, limitations.

Sir Ponsonby   Name given to the very sophisticated automatic pilot fitted in the Mirage F1. Abbreviated to Sir Pons and used in preference to the more common "George".

SOOW   Second Officer of the Watch. Duties thought up by Fish heads to prevent the entire aircrew from going ashore at each port.

Souties   An abbreviation of *Soutpiel*. Used as a derogatory name for Englishmen. It originated from the Afrikaans idea that English immigrants to South Africa had one leg in Africa and the other in Britain. The piece between, known as a *piel* in Afrikaans, was said to dangle in the salty (*sout*) sea.

Sprog   A new, or trainee, pilot. Also known as studs, shirt-tails, second lieuts or bicycles.

SSO OPS   Senior Staff Officer Operations

SWAPO   South West African Peoples Organization. (A misnomer as the organization truly represented only the Owambo people.)

SWA   South West Africa. The old German Colony, now known as Namibia.

TACAN   Tactical Air Navigation facility.

Tail-dragger   Any propeller-driven aircraft that has two main wheels and the third under the tail. This aircraft requires different techniques when approaching and taking off than the more usual tricycle-configured aircraft.

Takkies   Originally the South African name for canvas sandshoes. Known as plimsolls (by expatriates of the Old Country) and tennis shoes (by us South African geriatrics unused to the modern, astronomically expensive, brand-name trainers/joggers). More commonly used to spice up expressions like:

"Piece of old takkie"   An easy or simple task.

"His takkies are dangling"   The aircraft's wheels are down.

Tallyho   The fighter pilot's call used when the enemy has been spotted. This call is usually the precursor to a few minutes of mayhem.

Telstar   An aircraft flown at medium altitude to relay VHF messages from aircraft on low-flying operational missions.

Terr   Short name for terrorist. (In some circles these people were known as Freedom Fighters, but in the heat of the battle they were known as Terrs to us.)

Top Gun   US Navy School for Advanced Operational Training. The name achieved prominence from the film starring Tom Cruise.

Toyi toyi   African protest dance.

TRU   Transformer Rectifier Units, used in electrical systems.

UNITA   National Union for the Total Independence of Angola. The breakaway party led by Jonas Savimbi that was eventually supported by the western powers, including South Africa, in the fight against the communist-backed MPLA in Angola.

USAF   United States Air Force.

USMC   United States Marine Corp.

USN   United States Navy.

USS   United States Ship.

VHF   Very High Frequency radio, limited to line-of-sight communication.

Vlammie   South African name for a fighter pilot. Taken from the Afrikaans word *Vlamgat* meaning literally, flaming hole—the afterburner flame produced by a fighter.

Vulture's Roost   *see* Goofers

WRNS   Women's Royal Naval Service, commonly known as the Wrens.

Index

A

Aberdeen 23, 93
Accident Summary 16-17
Active Citizen Force (ACF) 190
ACM (Air Combat Manoeuvring)
139, 141-143, 146, 148, 162-164,
167, 169, 171, 173, 175-177, 179,
181, 183, 197, 199-200, 205,
226-227
ACM department 141
ACM instruction 143
ACM instructor 146, 163, 176
ACM programme 163, 167, 197
ACM syllabus 162, 167
ACM theory instruction 142
ACM training 142, 199, 226-227
ACM training flight 227
Adams, Col Brian 242
adhemar 195-197
admiral 24-25, 50, 152, 159, 282
Admiralty 2, 6, 54, 76, 110
Advanced Combat Flying School,
85 199, 302
Advanced Fighter School 205
advanced training 20
Aegean 87
aerial combat 91, 93, 140, 160, 162,
221
aerobatics 52, 93, 99, 102, 141, 175,
204, 302
aeronautical beacon 28
AFCP (Air Force Command Post)
230-231, 233, 235, 237, 239, 241,
243, 245, 247, 249, 251, 253,
266-267, 269, 271, 273, 275, 277,
279, 281, 283, 285, 287, 289, 291,
293, 295, 297, 299, 301, 303
Afghanistan 255, 267
Africa 2, 4-5, 7, 10, 12, 19, 61-62, 72,

87, 95, 109, 115, 121, 127, 139,
161-162, 170, 182, 185-192,
196-198, 206, 208-210, 212, 216,
218-219, 227-228, 230, 235-236,
238-239, 241-245, 247-250, 252-253,
255-256, 258-260, 262-268, 270-275,
277, 280-283, 285, 288-290, 293,
296-301, 304-306, 309-310, 312
African National Congress 196
Afrikaans 5, 190-191, 196, 208-210,
213, 235, 252, 292
Afrikaans Party 5
Afrikaner Weerstand Beweging 300
after brow 79
afterburner 53, 100, 137, 143,
146-147, 151-152, 155, 158,
168-170, 175, 192, 200, 211, 217,
221, 224
Aircraft
Aermacchi
Bosbok 263-265
Impala 198-199, 205, 207,
234-235, 250-251, 302
Aérospatiale
Alouette 234-235, 238-249, 281,
283, 286, 292
Frelon 217
Puma 229, 231, 234, 246-247,
260, 263-265, 276, 278-280,
283-286, 300, 310
Antonov 272
Avro
Shackelton 75, 198, 205, 279
Vulcan 53-54
Beechcraft 302
Baron 286
Blackburn
Beverley 15, 18-19
Buccaneer 2, 19, 24-25, 38, 190,